Second Workshop on Insights from Negative Results in NLP 2021

Punta Cana, Dominican Republic and Online
10 November 2021

ISBN: 978-1-7138-9182-6

Printed from e-media with permission by:

Curran Associates, Inc.
57 Morehouse Lane
Red Hook, NY 12571

CURRAN ASSOCIATES INC. proceedings.com

Some format issues inherent in the e-media version may also appear in this print version.

Printed with permission by Curran Associates, Inc. (2024)

Association for Computational Linguistics
209 N. Eighth Street
Stroudsburg, Pennsylvania 18360

Phone: 1-570-476-8006
Fax: 1-570-476-0860

acl@aclweb.org

Additional copies of this publication are available from:

Curran Associates, Inc.
57 Morehouse Lane
Red Hook, NY 12571 USA
Phone: 845-758-0400
Fax: 845-758-2633
Email: curran@proceedings.com
Web: www.proceedings.com

ACL 2021

Second Workshop on Insights from Negative Results in NLP

Proceedings of the Workshop

November 10, 2021
Online and Punta Cana, Dominican Republic

Introduction

Publication of negative results is difficult in most fields, and the current focus on benchmark-driven performance improvement exacerbates this situation and implicitly discourages hypothesis-driven research. As a result, the development of NLP models often devolves into a product of tinkering and tweaking, rather than science. Furthermore, it increases the time, effort, and carbon emissions spent on developing and tuning models, as the researchers have little opportunity to learn from what has already been tried and failed.

Historically, this tendency is hard to combat. ACL 2010 invited negative results as a special type of research paper submissions[1], but received too few submissions and did not continue with it. *The Journal for Interesting Negative Results in NLP and ML*[2] has only produced one issue in 2008.

However, the tide may be turning. Despite the pandemic, the second iteration of the *Workshop on Insights from Negative Results* attracted 39 submissions and 14 presentation requests for papers accepted to "Findings of EMNLP". NeurIPS 2021 also accepted the second iteration of *"I (Still) Can't Believe It's Not Better"*[3].

The workshop maintained roughly the same focus, welcoming many kinds of negative results with the hope that they could yield useful insights and provide a much-needed reality check on the successes of deep learning models in NLP. In particular, we solicited the following types of contributions:

- broadly applicable recommendations for training/fine-tuning, especially if X that didn't work is something that many practitioners would think reasonable to try, and if the demonstration of X's failure is accompanied by some explanation/hypothesis;
- ablation studies of components in previously proposed models, showing that their contributions are different from what was initially reported;
- datasets or probing tasks showing that previous approaches do not generalize to other domains or language phenomena;
- trivial baselines that work suspiciously well for a given task/dataset;
- cross-lingual studies showing that a technique X is only successful for a certain language or language family;
- experiments on (in)stability of the previously published results due to hardware, random initializations, preprocessing pipeline components, etc;
- theoretical arguments and/or proofs for why X should not be expected to work.

In terms of topics, 19 papers from our submission pool discussed "great ideas that didn't work", 11 dealt with the issues of generalizability, 3 were on the topic of "right for the wrong reasons", 2 papers focused on reproducibility issues, and 4 papers in other relevant topics. Some submissions fit in more than one category. We accepted 20 short papers (51.2% acceptance rate) and granted 4 presentation requests for Findings papers.

We hope the workshop will continue to contribute to the many reality-check discussions on progress in NLP. If we do not talk about things that do not work, it is harder to see what the biggest problems are and where the community effort is the most needed.

[1] `https://mirror.aclweb.org/acl2010/papers.html`

[2] `http://jinr.site.uottawa.ca/`

[3] `https://i-cant-believe-its-not-better.github.io/neurips2021/`

Organizers:

João Sedoc, New York University (USA)
Anna Rogers, University of Copenhagen (Denmark)
Anna Rumshisky, University of Massachusetts Lowell (USA)
Shabnam Tafreshi, University of Maryland: ARLIS (USA)

Program Committee:

Abeer Aldayel, King Saud University (Saudi Arabia)
Amittai Axelrod, DiDi Labs (USA)
Mark Anderson, Cardiff University (UK)
Nada Almarwani, Taibah University (Saudi Arabia)
Sawsan Alqahtani, Amazon (USA)
Wazir Ali, University of Electronic Science and Technology (China)
Aditya Bhargava, Torento (Canada)
Federico Bianchi, Bocconi University Milano (Italy)
Jeremy Barnes, Forsiden IFI (Germany)
Vasudha Bhatnagar, University of Delhi (India)
Yash Butala, Indian Institute of Technology Kharagpur (India)
Meghana Moorthy Bhat, Ohio State University (USA)
Shubham Chandel, Microsoft (USA)
Shubham Chatterjee, University of New Hampshire (USA)
Somnath Basu Roy Chowdhury, University of North Carolina at Chapel Hill (USA)
Yulong Chen, Zhejiang University, Westlake University (China)
Aleksandr Drozd, Tokyo Institute of Technology (Japan)
Alexandra DeLucia, John Hopkins University (USA)
Daria Dzendzik, ADAPT Centre (Ireland)
Lingjia Deng, Bloomberg (USA)
Luis Fernando D'Haro, University of Pennsylvania (USA)
Darren Edmonds, Donald Bren School of ICS (USA)
Antske Fokkens, VU (Amsterdam)
Elisabetta Fersini, University of Milano (Italy)
Haley Fong, City University of Hong Kong (Hong Kong)
Jason Fries, Stanford University (USA)
Catherine Finegan-Dollak, IBM (USA)
Salvatore Giorgi, University of Pennsylvania (USA)
Pedram Hosseini, George Washington University (USA)
Sardar Hamidian, Comcast (USA)
Christopher Klamm, (UKP) Lab - TU Darmstadt (Germany)
Huda Khayrallah, John Hopkins University (USA)
Neha Nayak Kennard, University of Massachusetts Amherst (USA)
Alka Khurana, University of Delhi (India)
Olha Kaminska, Ghent University (Belgium)
Siddharth Karamcheti, Stanford University (USA)
Constantine Lignos, Brandeis University (USA)
Shayne Longpre, Apple (USA)
Sotiris Lamprinidis, Copenhagen Business School (Copenhagen)
Tal Linzen, New York University (USA)

Yiyuan Li, University of North Carolina, Chapel Hill (USA)
Andrei Mircea Romascanu, McGill University (Canada)
Ansel MacLaughlin, Amazon (USA)
Ashutosh Modi, CSE - IIT Kanpur (India)
Deepa Muralidhar, Georgia State University (USA)
Edison Marrese-Taylor, University of Tokyo (Japan)
Jay Mundra, IIT Kanpur (India)
Karo Moilanen, AIG (USA)
Kenton Murray, John Hopkins University (USA)
Enrico Meloni, Università degli Studi di Firenze (Italy)
Markus Müller, Amazon (USA)
Tristan Naumann, Microsoft Research (USA)
Anmol Nayak, Bosch (India)
Constantin Orăsan, University of Surrey (England)
Jessica Ouyang, The University of Texas at Dallas (USA)
John Ortega, JP Morgen (USA)
Adam Poliak, Barnard College (USA)
Ellie Pavlick, Brown University (USA)
Leibny Paola Garcia Perera, John Hopkins University (USA)
Michal Ptaszynski, Kitami Institute of Technology (Japan)
Jordan Rodu, University of Virginia (USA)
Neville Ryant, Linguistic Data Consortium (USA)
Ali Seyfi, George Washington University (USA)
Michael Saxon, UC Santa Barbara (USA)
Mihai Surdeanu, University of Arizona (USA)
Sashank Santhanam, UNC Charlotte (USA)
Vivek Srivastava, TCS Research (India)
Yow-Ting Shiue, University of Maryland (USA)
Silvia Terragni, University of Milano-Bicocca (Italy)
Jannis Vamvas, Zurich University (Switzerland)
Derry Tanti Wijaya, Boston University (USA)
Jin-Ge Yao, Microsoft Research (USA)
Mahsa Yarmohammadi, University of Pennsylvania (USA)
Xiang Zhou, University of North Carolina at Chapel Hill (USA)
Zhuosheng Zhang, Shanghai Jiao Tong University (China)

Invited Speakers:

Zachary Lipton, Carnegie Mellon University
Noah Smith, University of Washington / Allen Institute for AI
Rachael Tatman, Rasa
Bonnie Webber, University of Edinburgh

Table of Contents

Program

Wednesday, November 10, 2021

8:45–9:00	*Opening remarks*
9:00–10:00	*Invited talk: Noah Smith (University of Washington / Allen Institute for AI)* *What Makes a Result Negative?*
10:00–11:15	*Poster session 1*
11:15–11:30	*Social break / coffee time*
11:30–12:30	*Invited talk: Bonnie Webber (University of Edinburgh)* *The Reviewers and the Reviewed: Institutional Memory and Institutional Incentives*
12:30–13:00	*Oral presentation session 1*
13:00–14:00	*Lunch break*
14:00–15:00	*Invited talk: Zachary Lipton (Carnegie Mellon University)* *Some Results on Label Shift and Label Noise*
15:00–16:15	*Poster session 2*
16:15–16:30	*Social break / coffee time*
16:30–17:00	*Oral presentation session 2*
17:00–18:00	*Invited talk: Rachael Tatman (Rasa)* *Chatbots can be good: What we learn from unhappy users*
18:00–18:15	*Closing remarks*

The program is subject to change, please check the EMNLP 2021 conference website for the final program and schedule in different time zones. The program will also be available at `https://insights-workshop.github.io`. All times above are specified in Atlantic Standard Time (GMT-4).

Corrected CBOW Performs as well as Skip-gram

Ozan İrsoy **Adrian Benton**
Bloomberg
{oirsoy,abenton10}@bloomberg.net

Karl Stratos
Rutgers University
karl.stratos@rutgers.edu

Abstract

Mikolov et al. (2013a) observed that continuous bag-of-words (CBOW) word embeddings tend to underperform Skip-gram (SG) embeddings, and this finding has been reported in subsequent works. We find that these observations are driven not by fundamental differences in their training objectives, but more likely on faulty negative sampling CBOW implementations in popular libraries such as the official implementation, word2vec.c, and Gensim. We show that after correcting a bug in the CBOW gradient update, one can learn CBOW word embeddings that are fully competitive with SG on various intrinsic and extrinsic tasks, while being many times faster to train.

1 Introduction

Pre-trained word embeddings are a standard way to boost performance on many tasks of interest such as named-entity recognition (NER), where contextual word embeddings such as BERT (Devlin et al., 2019) are computationally expensive and may only yield marginal gains. Word2vec (Mikolov et al., 2013a) is a popular method for learning word embeddings because of its scalability and robust performance. There are two main Word2vec training objectives: (1) continuous bag-of-words (CBOW) that predicts the center word by averaging context embeddings, and (2) Skip-gram (SG) that predicts context words from the center word.[1]

It has been frequently observed that while CBOW is fast to train, it lags behind SG in performance.[2] This observation is made by the inventors of Word2vec themselves (Mikolov, 2013), and also independently in subsequent works (Pennington et al., 2014; Stratos et al., 2015). This result is surprising since the CBOW and SG objectives lead to very similar weight updates. This is also contrary to the enormous success of contextual word embeddings based on masked language modeling (MLM), as CBOW follows a rudimentary form of MLM (i.e., predicting a masked target word from a context window without any perturbation of the masked word).

In this work, we find that the performance discrepancy between CBOW and SG embeddings is founded less on theoretical differences in their training objectives but more on faulty CBOW implementations in standard libraries such as the official implementation `word2vec.c` (Mikolov et al., 2013b), Gensim (Řehůřek and Sojka, 2010) and fastText (Bojanowski et al., 2017). Specifically, we find that in these implementations, the gradient for source embeddings is incorrectly multiplied by the context window size, resulting in incorrect weight updates and inferior performance.

We make the following contributions. First, we show that our correct implementation of CBOW indeed yields word embeddings that are fully competitive with SG while being trained in less than a third of the time (e.g., with a single machine it takes less than 73 minutes to train CBOW embeddings on the entire Wikipedia corpus). We present experiments on intrinsic word similarity and analogy tasks, as well as extrinsic eval uations on the SST-2, QNLI, and MNLI tasks from the GLUE benchmark (Wang et al., 2018), and the CoNLL03 English named entity recognition task (Sang and De Meulder, 2003).

Second, we make our implementation, `kōan`,

[1]In this work, we always use the negative sampling formulations of Word2vec objectives which are consistently more efficient and effective than the hierarchical softmax formulations.

[2]SG requires sampling negative examples from every word in context, while CBOW requires sampling negative examples only for the target word.

Proceedings of the Second Workshop on Insights from Negative Results in NLP, pages 1–8
November 10, 2021.

publicly available.[3] With this implementation, it is possible to train 768-dimensional CBOW embeddings on one epoch of English C4 (Raffel et al., 2020) in 1.61 days on a single 16 CPU machine.[4]

2 CBOW Implementation

The parameters of CBOW are two sets of word embeddings: "source-side" and "target-side" vectors $v_w, v'_w \in \mathbb{R}^d$ for every word type $w \in V$ in the vocabulary. A window of text in a corpus consists of a center word w_O and context words $w_1 \ldots w_C$. For instance, in the window `the dog laughed`, we have $w_O =$ `dog` and $w_1 =$ `the` and $w_2 =$ `laughed`. Given a window of text, the CBOW loss is defined as:

$$v_c = \frac{1}{C}\sum_{j=1}^{C} v_{w_j}$$

$$\mathcal{L} = -\log \sigma({v'_{w_O}}^\top v_c) - \sum_{i=1}^{k} \log \sigma(-{v'_{n_i}}^\top v_c)$$

where $n_1 \ldots n_k \in V$ are negative examples drawn iid from some noise distribution P_n over V. The gradients of $\mathcal{L}$ with respect to the target (v'_{w_O}), negative target (v'_{n_i}), and average context source (v_c) embeddings are:

$$\begin{aligned}
\frac{\partial \mathcal{L}}{\partial v'_{w_O}} &= (\sigma({v'_{w_O}}^\top v_c) - 1)v_c \\
\frac{\partial \mathcal{L}}{\partial v'_{n_i}} &= \sigma({v'_{n_i}}^\top v_c)v_c \\
\frac{\partial \mathcal{L}}{\partial v_c} &= (\sigma({v'_{w_O}}^\top v_c) - 1)v'_{w_O} + \\
&\sum_{i=1}^{k} \sigma({v'_{n_i}}^\top v_c)v'_{n_i} \qquad (1)
\end{aligned}$$

and by the chain rule with respect to a source context embedding:

$$\begin{aligned}
\frac{\partial \mathcal{L}}{\partial v_{w_j}} = &\frac{1}{C}[(\sigma({v'_{w_O}}^\top v_c) - 1)v'_{w_O} + \\
&\sum_{i=1}^{k} \sigma({v'_{n_i}}^\top v_c)v'_{n_i}] \qquad (2)
\end{aligned}$$

However, the CBOW negative sampling implementations in `word2vec.c`[5], Gensim[6], and fastText[7] incorrectly update each context vector, v_{w_j}, by Eq. (1), without normalizing by the number of context words, given in Eq. (2). In fact, this error has been pointed out in several Gensim issues as well as a fastText issue.[8]

Why This Error Matters Aside from being incorrect, this update matters for two reasons. First, in both Gensim and `word2vec.c`, the width of the context window is randomly sampled from $1, \ldots, C_{\max}$ for every target word. This means that source embeddings which were averaged over wider context windows will experience a larger update than their contribution, relative to source embeddings averaged over narrower windows. Second, in the incorrect gradient, $\frac{\partial \mathcal{L}}{\partial v}$ is incorrectly scaled by C, while $\frac{\partial \mathcal{L}}{\partial v'}$ is not; the correct stochastic gradient with respect to all embeddings actually points in a different direction than what was implemented in `word2vec.c`. Section 5 touches on both of these issues in more detail.

3 Experiments

We evaluated CBOW and SG embeddings under Gensim and our implementations (both corrected and original CBOW). Unless otherwise noted, we learn word embeddings on the entire Wikipedia corpus PTB sentence split and tokenized with default settings, where words occurring fewer than ten times were dropped. Training hyperparameters were held fixed for each set of embeddings: negative sampling rate 5, maximum context window of 5 words, number of training epochs 5, and embedding dimensionality 300 unless otherwise noted.

[3] `https://github.com/bloomberg/koan`

[4] See Appendix B for training time benchmarks of popular Word2vec implementations against kōan.

[5] `https://github.com/tmikolov/word2vec/blob/20c129af10659f7c50e86e3be406df663beff438/word2vec.c#L483`

[6] `https://github.com/RaRe-Technologies/gensim/blob/a93067d2ea78916cb587552ba0fd22727c4b40ab/gensim/models/word2vec_inner.pyx#L455-L456.`

[7] `https://github.com/facebookresearch/fastText/blob/a20c0d27cd0ee88a25ea0433b7f03038cd728459/src/model.cc#L85` In fastText, the normalization option is guarded by a boolean flag, but it defaults to `false` for CBOW.

[8] `https://github.com/RaRe-Technologies/gensim/issues/1873`, `https://github.com/RaRe-Technologies/gensim/issues/697`, `https://github.com/facebookresearch/fastText/issues/910.`

We found that the default initial learning rate in Gensim, 0.025, learned strong SG embeddings. However, we swept separately for CBOW initial learning rate for Gensim and our implementation. We swept over initial learning rate in $\{0.025, 0.05, 0.075, 0.1\}$ selecting 0.025 to learn Gensim CBOW embeddings and 0.075 for corrected CBOW, to maximize average performance on the development fold (random partition of 50% of examples) of intrinsic evaluation tasks described in 3.1. We selected learning rate as this was a critical hyperparameter, and we found that CBOW embeddings learned with 0.075 learning rate with Gensim suffered compared to learning with a low learning rate.

3.1 Evaluation

We evaluated each set of embeddings intrinsically on the `MEN`, `WS353`, `MIXED`, and `SYNT` word similarity and analogy tasks, as described in Levy and Goldberg (2014). We also evaluate on the Stanford rare words analogy task, `RW` (Luong et al., 2013). Analogy tasks were evaluated by top-1 accuracy and similarity tasks using Spearman's rank correlation coefficient.

We also evaluated embeddings extrinsically on the SST-2, QNLI, and MNLI GLUE tasks, following the methodology in Wang et al. (2018) and use the frozen pre-trained word embeddings in a BiLSTM classifier. In addition, we also evaluated word embeddings in a CoNLL03 English named entity recognition (NER) sequence tagger (Sang and De Meulder, 2003). For NER, we use a single-layer BiLSTM with 256-dimensional hidden layer as the sequence tagger, and evaluate under frozen and finetuned word embedding settings. See Appendix C for model selection details in extrinsic evaluation.

4 Results

Intrinsic Evaluation CBOW embeddings trained with our implementation achieve similar intrinsic performance to SG embeddings, surpassing SG embeddings for the `RW` and `SYNT` tasks (Table 1). On the other hand, CBOW embeddings trained by Gensim or our incorrect implementation achieve much worse performance than SG. We also report performance of CBOW embeddings, with and without the corrected update, trained for one epoch on the entirety of the English C4 dataset (768 dimensions and 5 million word vocabulary). These embeddings took 1.61 days per epoch to train on a single 16-core machine.

Extrinsic Evaluation Development and test set performance on GLUE tasks for each set of embeddings is reported in Table 2. We also compare performance against 300-dimensional GloVe embeddings (Pennington et al., 2014) pre-trained on Wikipedia and Gigaword 5 and random embeddings drawn from a standard normal distribution as baselines.

Table 3 contains CoNLL 2003 NER performance for each set of word embeddings. We used the same set of hyperparameters sampled in the GLUE evaluation for model selection (dev F1 as computed by the CoNLL evaluation script). NER test performance of corrected CBOW embeddings is within 1% F1 to SG embeddings, whereas Gensim CBOW embeddings suffer up to 4% F1 test performance relative to SG.

5 Discussion

The Gensim-trained CBOW embeddings achieve better test accuracy on SST-2 despite achieving similar performance on the development set as corrected CBOW embeddings. Gensim CBOW embeddings also outperform on QNLI. However, performance on MultiNLI is slightly different. In this case, corrected CBOW embeddings are almost 2% more accurate than Gensim embeddings when evaluated on the out of domain test set. For these GLUE tasks, it is unclear whether CBOW embeddings learned with our implementation are universally more performant than those learned by Gensim. We hypothesize this may be due to the susceptibility of models overfitting to the development set (especially since our classifier has 1024 dimensional hidden layers).

5.1 Problems with Faulty CBOW

Aside from being incorrect, the faulty update leads to two major issues during training: (1) the norm of the source side vectors grows as a function of context width, and (2) despite being a descent direction, the faulty update diverges from the SGD direction as the number of negative samples increases.

Embedding Norm Grows with Context Because the effective learning rate for source embeddings is greater than that for the source

Package	Objective	ws353	men	rw	syn	mixed	AVG
Gensim	SG	72.2/61.9	72.1/72.5	46.8/44.9	72.8/72.4	82.5/81.3	69.3/66.6
	CBOW	61.5/62.6	69.2/70.0	43.2/38.1	69.9/71.1	79.1/78.0	64.6/64.0
kōan	SG	72.8/62.0	72.7/72.0	44.9/43.8	73.6/71.8	83.0/80.2	69.4/66.0
	CBOW [s]	61.2/62.6	68.8/69.4	48.6/39.9	73.4/74.7	78.3/76.8	66.1/64.7
	CBOW [f]	70.6/65.8	74.0/74.6	49.0/45.5	76.7/76.5	**83.8/82.1**	70.8/68.9
	CBOW [s]; C4	72.9/68.0	81.0/79.9	51.1/50.3	80.5/79.9	81.5/81.1	73.4/71.8
	CBOW [f]; C4	**74.1/68.1**	**79.8/80.2**	**53.1/54.8**	**82.9/81.6**	82.2/81.9	**74.4/73.3**

Table 1: Intrinsic evaluation of Wikipedia-trained Word2vec embeddings on `dev/test` folds. Spearman's rank correlation coefficient is reported for: `wordsim353`, `men`, and `rw`, and accuracy for: `syn` and `mixed`. `AVG` is the average across all five tasks. The best test performance for each task is bolded. *CBOW [s]* refers to the standard, incorrect implementation of CBOW, and *CBOW [f]* is the fixed version.

Package	Objective	SST-2	QNLI	MNLI-m	MNLI-mm
Baselines	Random	83.49/81.4	63.88/63.9	61.41/60.3	61.41/59.6
	GloVe	85.09/83.6	66.37/67.7	66.93/66.7	66.93/66.1
Gensim	SG	86.93/85.6	69.39/67.9	68.02/67.3	68.02/67.9
	CBOW	**88.07/86.7**	**69.06/70.7**	68.15/68.2	68.15/66.9
kōan	SG	86.24/84.5	69.06/68.2	68.20/67.4	68.20/67.7
	CBOW	88.42/85.3	68.17/68.6	**69.22/68.4**	**69.22/68.6**

Table 2: Percent accuracy of word embeddings on the dev/test sets of the SST, QNLI, and MNLI GLUE tasks. In the case of MNLI, development accuracy is averaged over the matched and mismatched development sets, which is also used for model selection. Test performance is reported separately for matched and mismatched domains. The best test performance for each task is in bold.

		Frozen		Finetuned	
Package	Objective	Dev	Test	Dev	Test
Gensim	Random	83.6	75.4	83.0	74.3
	SG	92.5	**88.4**	92.9	**88.2**
	CBOW	90.1	84.4	90.0	85.3
kōan	SG	92.5	88.2	92.9	88.0
	CBOW	92.3	87.8	92.3	87.4

Table 3: Percent F1 on the CoNLL 2003 English NER heldout sets for each set of word embeddings.

embeddings, one would expect the magnitude of the source embeddings to also grow larger. Growing source norms can be a problem during learning, as larger embedding norms can easily lead to saturated sigmoid activations, effectively halting learning. See Appendix D for an empirical analysis of embedding magnitude.

Update Worsens with More Negatives The faulty CBOW update for source embeddings is a stochastic[9] multiple of the correct update. However, CBOW learns both source and target embeddings, which means that the update direction no longer follows the SGD update direction.

Even though the faulty update is still a descent direction, we can analyze how the angle between it and the true SGD direction changes as a function of context width. If we make the simplifying assumption that the norm of the source and target gradients are equal, then one can derive the cosine similarity between $\delta\theta$ (true gradient) and $\widetilde{\delta\theta}$ (faulty gradient) with respect to CBOW parameters θ as:

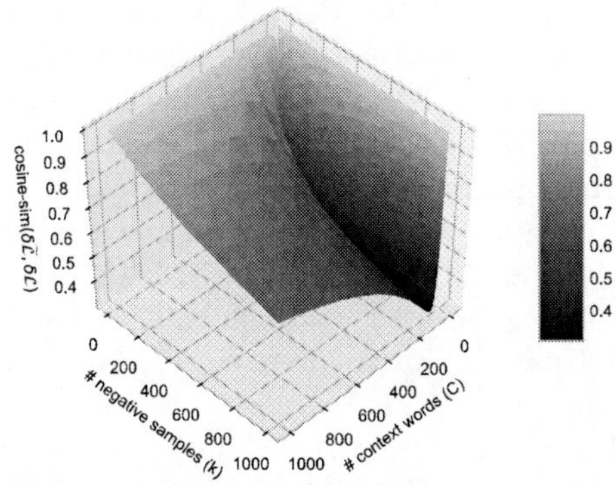

Figure 1: Cosine similarity of incorrect to correct stochastic gradient as a function of C and k assuming that the norm of the gradient with respect to each embedding is fixed to a shared constant. The minimum cosine similarity displayed in this plot is 0.303.

$$\cos(\widetilde{\delta\theta}, \delta\theta) = \frac{C^2 + k + 1}{\sqrt{(C^3 + k + 1)(C + k + 1)}} \quad (3)$$

Where C is the number of context tokens and k is the number of negative samples. For a moderate context width, as the number of negative examples increases, the faulty update points further away from the true gradient (Figure 1). See Appendix E for the full derivation.

[9]Context width is sampled uniformly at random between 1 and maximum context width in standard word2vec implementations.

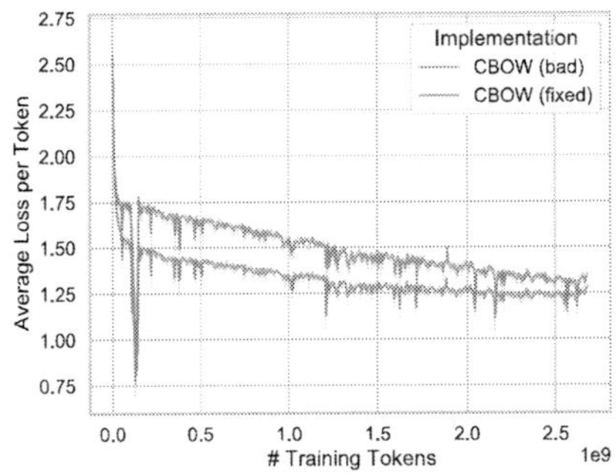

Figure 2: Average negative sampling loss per token for every batch of 5 million tokens for a single epoch of CBOW training on Wikipedia. The shaded region corresponds to the 95% bootstrapped confidence interval over average token loss on 100K token batches.

In practice, we found performance of CBOW embeddings to only decay moderately as a function of number of negatives, regardless of correction to the update, consistent with that reported in Pennington et al. (2014). Nevertheless, we find that our correct CBOW implementation decreases training loss more quickly than the incorrect update, even in the typical setting of 5 negative samples and context width of 5 (Figure 2). Ultimately, increased sensitivity to hyperparameters is not a concern under typical training regimes.

FastText Although we do not investigate fastText specifically in this work, we do note in Section 2 that fastText CBOW defaults to using the same incorrect source embedding gradient. Sent2vec (Gupta et al., 2019) is also exposed to this bug, since it builds on fastText. In spite of this, fastText embeddings trained with the CBOW objective were found to outperform SG across multiple languages (Grave et al., 2018). To achieve better performance of CBOW, Grave et al. (2018) tuned hyperparameters and trained on a web-scale corpus (enabled by the faster CBOW training).

FastText also represents each word vector as the sum of vectors of its constituent character n-grams, and includes positional embeddings as part of the training procedure. In this work, we only consider the original CBOW and SG models described in Mikolov et al. (2013a) and hold hyperparameters and training set fixed between models whenever possible. We leave investigation of whether correcting this gradient bug could further improve fastText embeddings as future work.

6 Conclusion

Before the widespread adoption of automatic differentiation libraries, it was the modeler's responsibility to derive the correct gradient for updating model weights. This `word2vec.c` gradient bug could have been avoided if a finite difference check was run to ensure the derivation of the stochastic gradient was correct. These checks are standard practice (Bengio, 2012; Bottou, 2012), and we strongly encourage other researchers to use finite difference gradient checks to verify the correctness of manually derived gradients. According to Bottou (2012): "*When the computation of the gradients is slightly incorrect, stochastic gradient descent often works slowly and erratically... It is not uncommon to discover such bugs in SGD code that has been quietly used for years.*"

We find that CBOW can learn embeddings that are as performant as SG, when trained with the correct update, allowing efficient training of strong word embeddings on web-scale datasets on an academic budget. We release our implementation, `kōan`, along with trained C4 CBOW embeddings at `https://github.com/bloomberg/koan`.

References

Yoshua Bengio. 2012. Practical recommendations for gradient-based training of deep architectures. In *Neural networks: Tricks of the trade*, pages 437–478. Springer.

Piotr Bojanowski, Edouard Grave, Armand Joulin, and Tomas Mikolov. 2017. Enriching word vectors with subword information. *Transactions of the Association for Computational Linguistics*, 5:135–146.

Léon Bottou. 2012. Stochastic gradient descent tricks. In *Neural networks: Tricks of the trade*, pages 421–436. Springer.

Stephen P Boyd and Lieven Vandenberghe. 2004. *Convex optimization.* Cambridge university press.

Jacob Devlin, Ming-Wei Chang, Kenton Lee, and Kristina Toutanova. 2019. Bert: Pre-training of deep bidirectional transformers for language understanding. In *Proceedings of the 2019 Conference of the North American Chapter of the Association for Computational Linguistics: Human Language Technologies, Volume 1 (Long and Short Papers)*, pages 4171–4186.

Édouard Grave, Piotr Bojanowski, Prakhar Gupta, Armand Joulin, and Tomáš Mikolov. 2018. Learning word vectors for 157 languages. In *Proceedings of the Eleventh International Conference on Language Resources and Evaluation (LREC 2018)*.

Prakhar Gupta, Matteo Pagliardini, and Martin Jaggi. 2019. Better word embeddings by disentangling contextual n-gram information. In *Proceedings of the 2019 Conference of the North American Chapter of the Association for Computational Linguistics: Human Language Technologies, Volume 1 (Long and Short Papers)*, pages 933–939, Minneapolis, Minnesota. Association for Computational Linguistics.

Omer Levy and Yoav Goldberg. 2014. Neural word embedding as implicit matrix factorization. In *Advances in neural information processing systems*, pages 2177–2185.

Minh-Thang Luong, Richard Socher, and Christopher D Manning. 2013. Better word representations with recursive neural networks for morphology. In *Proceedings of the Seventeenth Conference on Computational Natural Language Learning*, pages 104–113.

Mikolov. 2013. *Google Code Archive: word2vec*. `https://code.google.com/archive/p/word2vec/`.

Tomas Mikolov, Kai Chen, Greg Corrado, and Jeffrey Dean. 2013a. Efficient estimation of word representations in vector space. *arXiv preprint arXiv:1301.3781*.

Tomas Mikolov, Ilya Sutskever, Kai Chen, Greg S Corrado, and Jeff Dean. 2013b. Distributed representations of words and phrases and their compositionality. In *Advances in neural information processing systems*, pages 3111–3119.

Jeffrey Pennington, Richard Socher, and Christopher D Manning. 2014. Glove: Global vectors for word representation. In *Proceedings of the 2014 conference on empirical methods in natural language processing (EMNLP)*, pages 1532–1543.

Colin Raffel, Noam Shazeer, Adam Roberts, Katherine Lee, Sharan Narang, Michael Matena, Yanqi Zhou, Wei Li, and Peter J Liu. 2020. Exploring the limits of transfer learning with a unified text-to-text transformer. *Journal of Machine Learning Research*, 21:1–67.

Radim Řehůřek and Petr Sojka. 2010. Software Framework for Topic Modelling with Large Corpora. In *Proceedings of the LREC 2010 Workshop on New Challenges for NLP Frameworks*, pages 45–50, Valletta, Malta. ELRA. `http://is.muni.cz/publication/884893/en`.

Erik F Sang and Fien De Meulder. 2003. Introduction to the conll-2003 shared task: Language-independent named entity recognition. *arXiv preprint cs/0306050*.

Karl Stratos, Michael Collins, and Daniel Hsu. 2015. Model-based word embeddings from decompositions of count matrices. In *Proceedings of the 53rd Annual Meeting of the Association for Computational Linguistics and the 7th International Joint Conference on Natural Language Processing (Volume 1: Long Papers)*, pages 1282–1291.

Alex Wang, Amanpreet Singh, Julian Michael, Felix Hill, Omer Levy, and Samuel Bowman. 2018. Glue: A multi-task benchmark and analysis platform for natural language understanding. In *Proceedings of the 2018 EMNLP Workshop BlackboxNLP: Analyzing and Interpreting Neural Networks for NLP*, pages 353–355.

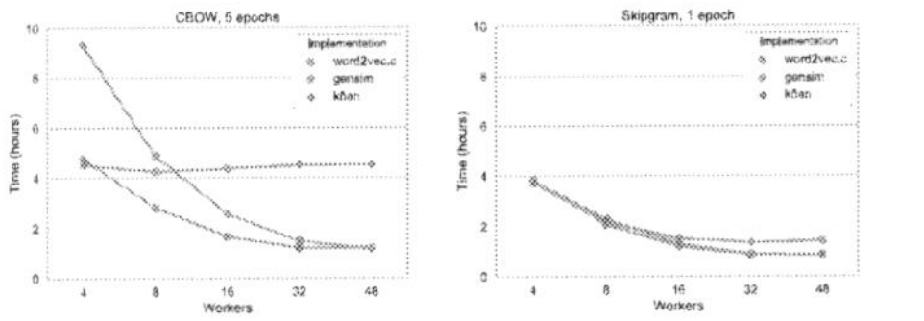

Figure 3: Hours to train CBOW (left) and SG (right) embeddings as a function of number of worker threads for different Word2vec implementations.

A Versions of Gensim and `word2vec.c`

We compare against the Gensim implementation[10] at commit

`a93067d2ea78916cb587552ba0fd22727c4b40ab`

and the `word2vec.c` implementation[11] at commit

`e092540633572b883e25b367938b0cca2cf3c0e7`

which are the most recent commits at the time of writing.

B Training time

Figure 3 shows the time to train each set of embeddings as a function of number of worker threads on the tokenized Wikipedia corpus. All implementations were benchmarked on an Amazon EC2 c5.metal instance (96 logical processors, 196GB memory) using `time`, and embeddings were trained with a minimum token frequency of 10 and downsampling frequency threshold of 10^{-3}. We benchmark our implementation with a buffer of 100,000 sentences. We trained CBOW for five epochs and SG for a single epoch, as it is much slower. Gensim seems to have trouble exploiting more worker threads when training CBOW, and both `word2vec.c` and our implementation learn embeddings faster. `word2vec.c` achieves slightly better scaling than our implementation during CBOW training (68m46s vs. 72m57s for 48 threads), although ours is faster with fewer workers (e.g., 559m0s vs. 284m58s for 4 threads and 88m28s vs. 72m29s for 32 threads). Although we did not comprehensively benchmark SG training for 5 epochs, we found that training SG embeddings for 5 epochs with 48 threads took us 3.31 times as long as training CBOW.

[10] `https://github.com/RaRe-Technologies/gensim/blob/develop/gensim/models/word2vec.py`

[11] `https://github.com/tmikolov/word2vec/`

C Extrinsic Evaluation Hyperparameters

We evaluate a given set of embeddings on GLUE tasks by using the frozen pre-trained word embeddings in a neural classifier. Words that were out of vocabulary are represented with a zero embedding vector. We use a two layer BiLSTM with 1024 hidden layer width, and a final projection layer. For the NLI tasks, we encode each sequence with an independent BiLSTM encoder. If the embeddings of sequence 1 and 2 are v and w, respectively, then a prediction is made using a multilayer perceptron over $[v; w; v - w; v \odot w]$ with a single 512 unit hidden layer. This is identical to the NLI classifier described in Wang et al. (2018). We performed a random search over dropout rate $\in [0.0, 0.7]$ and learning rate $\in [10^{-6}, 10^{-2}]$ with a budget of ten runs. All models are trained for up to 100 epochs with a patience of 2 epochs for early stopping. The same set of sampled hyperparameters was used for model selection for each set of word embeddings.

D CBOW Embedding Norm

If we train embeddings using the correct implementation of CBOW, the l_2 norms of target and source vectors are unaffected by the width of the context window (Figure 4). With the faulty implementation Equation (1), the source vector norms increase as a function of the maximum context window width. Growing source norms can be a problem during learning, as larger embedding norms can easily lead to saturated sigmoid activations, effectively halting learning. This problem is further exacerbated by fast implementations of CBOW and SG that approximate the sigmoid activation function by a piecewise linear function. In these approximations, when the logit is above or below some threshold (e.g., 6 and -6 for `word2vec.c`) and the prediction agrees with ground truth, the gradient for this example is not back-propagated at all.

E Analysis of the Incorrect CBOW Gradient

Relationship to correct CBOW update Although the incorrect CBOW update for source and target embeddings points in a different direction than the SGD update, this is still a descent direction for the CBOW loss. In other words, taking a sufficiently small step in

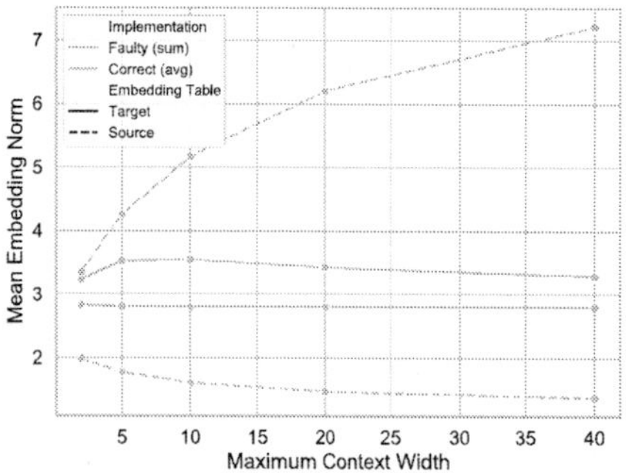

Figure 4: Average target and source vector norms as a function of context width for the correct and incorrect implementations of CBOW. All embeddings were trained for five epochs over a one million sentence sample of the Wikipedia corpus.

this direction will reduce the stochastic loss. This can be easily seen by:

$$
\begin{aligned}
D =& \left(\begin{array}{c|c} C I_{dC} & 0 \\ \hline 0 & I_{d(k+1)} \end{array} \right) \\
\delta v =& [\frac{\partial \mathcal{L}}{\partial v_{w_1}}; \ldots; \frac{\partial \mathcal{L}}{\partial v_{w_C}}] \\
\delta v' =& [\frac{\partial \mathcal{L}}{\partial v'_{n_1}}; \ldots; \frac{\partial \mathcal{L}}{\partial v'_{n_k}}; \frac{\partial \mathcal{L}}{\partial v'_{w_O}}] \\
\delta \theta =& [\frac{\partial \mathcal{L}}{\partial v}; \frac{\partial \mathcal{L}}{\partial v'}] \\
\widetilde{\delta \theta} =& D\,(\delta \theta)
\end{aligned} \tag{4}
$$

where d is the word embedding dimensionality, D is a diagonal matrix that scales the gradient with respect to each context word by C, and leaves the gradient with respect to the negative sampled target words and true target word unchanged. $\delta\theta$ and $\widetilde{\delta\theta}$ denote the correct and incorrect gradients of the loss, respectively, with respect to source and target embeddings. Since all diagonal entries on D are strictly positive, D is positive definite. Therefore, if $\|\delta\theta\| > 0$ then $(-\widetilde{\delta\theta})^T \delta\theta < 0$ and $-\widetilde{\delta\theta}$ is a descent direction for the stochastic loss (Boyd and Vandenberghe, 2004).

Even though the incorrect negative gradient is guaranteed to be a descent direction, the angle between this descent direction and the negative gradient can be influenced by the number of negative samples and the number of context words to average over. For the sake of simplicity, suppose that the gradient of the loss with respect to each source and target embedding has the same norm: $\forall j \in \{1, \ldots, C\}, i \in \{1, \ldots, k\} : \|\frac{\partial L}{\partial v_{w_j}}\|_2^2 = \|\frac{\partial L}{\partial v'_{n_i}}\|_2^2 = \alpha$. Then the cosine similarity between the incorrect and correct gradient can be written as:

$$
\begin{aligned}
\cos(\widetilde{\delta\theta}, \delta\theta) &= \frac{(\widetilde{\delta\theta})^T \delta\theta}{\|\widetilde{\delta\theta}\|_2 \|\delta\theta\|_2} \\
&= \frac{(C^2 + k + 1)\alpha}{\sqrt{(C^3 + k + 1)\alpha}\sqrt{(C + k + 1)\alpha}} \\
&= \frac{(C^2 + k + 1)}{\sqrt{(C^3 + k + 1)(C + k + 1)}}
\end{aligned}
$$

We can better understand how the angle between the incorrect and correct gradient varies as a function of number of context words and negative samples by looking at a plot of this function (Figure 1). What this plot makes clear is that for a moderate number of context words (around 10, which corresponds to a maximum context window of 5), the incorrect stochastic gradient can differ significantly from the true gradient as the number of negative samples increases. However, for sensible settings of $C, k \leq 20$, the minimum cosine similarity is 0.68, achieved by $C = 9$ and $k = 20$, with 0.82 cosine similarity with $C = 5$ and $k = 5$ (typical for Word2vec training). Because of this, the CBOW update bug may have gone unnoticed. If one were to sample a large number of negatives, then the bug may have been more apparent.

Does Commonsense help in detecting Sarcasm?

Somnath Basu Roy Chowdhury **Snigdha Chaturvedi**
{somnath, snigdha}@cs.unc.edu
UNC Chapel Hill

Abstract

Sarcasm detection is important for several NLP tasks such as sentiment identification in product reviews, user feedback, and online forums. It is a challenging task requiring a deep understanding of language, context, and world knowledge. In this paper, we investigate whether incorporating commonsense knowledge helps in sarcasm detection. For this, we incorporate commonsense knowledge into the prediction process using a graph convolution network with pre-trained language model embeddings as input. Our experiments with three sarcasm detection datasets indicate that the approach does not outperform the baseline model. We perform an exhaustive set of experiments to analyze where commonsense support adds value and where it hurts classification. Our implementation is publicly available at: https://github.com/brcsomnath/commonsense-sarcasm.

1 Introduction & Related Work

The topic of sarcasm has received attention in various research fields like linguistics (Utsumi, 2000), psychology (Gibbs, 1986; Kreuz and Glucksberg, 1989) and the cognitive sciences (Gibbs Jr et al., 2007). Identifying sarcasm is essential to understanding the opinion and intent of a user in downstream tasks like opinion mining, sentiment classification, etc. Initial approaches for this task (Kreuz and Glucksberg, 1989) mostly relied on handcrafted features to capture the lexical and contextual information. On similar lines, the efficacy of special characters, emojis and n-gram features in the discrimination task have also been studied (Carvalho et al., 2009; Lukin and Walker, 2013).

In recent years, this task has gained traction in the machine learning and computational linguistic community (Davidov et al., 2010; González-Ibáñez et al., 2011; Riloff et al., 2013; Maynard and Greenwood, 2014; Wallace et al., 2014; Ghosh et al., 2015; Joshi et al., 2015; Muresan et al., 2016; Amir et al., 2016; Mishra et al., 2016; Ghosh and Veale, 2017; Chakrabarty et al., 2020). Several approaches have studied the role of context in this sarcasm detection task (Ghosh et al., 2020). However, none of the previous works have explored the idea of incorporating commonsense knowledge in sarcasm detection. Common sense has been used in several natural-language based tasks like controllable story generation (Zhang et al., 2020; Brahman and Chaturvedi, 2020), sentence classification (Chen et al., 2019), question answering (Dzendzik et al., 2020), natural language inference (K M et al., 2018; Wang et al., 2019) and other related tasks but not for sarcasm detection. We hypothesize that commonsense knowledge, capturing general beliefs and world knowledge, can prove instrumental in understanding sarcasm. For example in Figure 1, for the event "I loved the movie so much that I left during the interval" (an example of sarcasm with polarity contrast), we show how commonsense is able to capture the contrast between the intentions of the subject before and during the event. Incorporating such commonsense knowledge ideally should make it easier for the learning model to detect sarcasm where it is not apparent from the input.

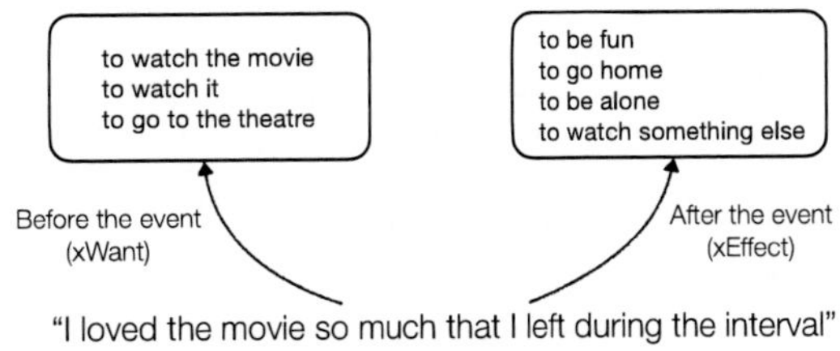

Figure 1: COMET output for the sentence "I loved the movie so much that I left during the interval". The commonsense sequences capture the contrast between intent and action of the subject.

With this motivation, we study the utility of common sense information for sarcasm detection. For

Proceedings of the Second Workshop on Insights from Negative Results in NLP, pages 9–15
November 10, 2021.

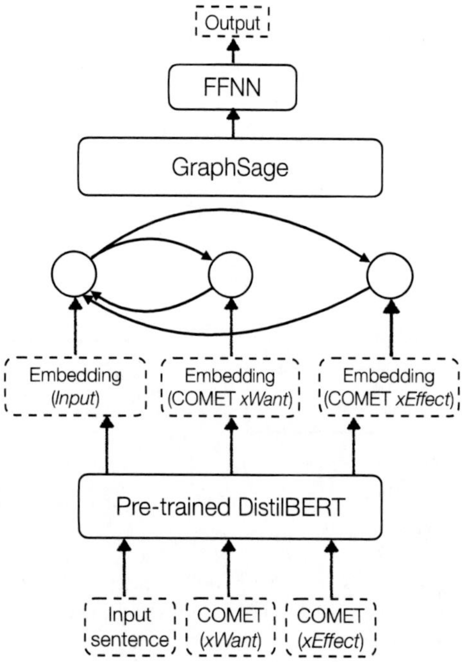

Figure 2: Proposed model architecture. Representations of the input sentence along with two COMET sequences are retrieved from pre-trained DistilBERT that are used to initialize a GCN. Post training, node representations of the graph is passed through a fully-connected neural network to generate the output.

this, we leverage COMET (Bosselut et al., 2019) to extract the relevant social commonsense information for a sentence. Given an event, COMET provides likely scenarios relating to various attributes like intent of the subject, effect on the object etc.

We use a GCN (Kipf and Welling, 2017) based model for infusing commonsense knowledge in the sarcasm detection task. Our experiments reveal that the commonsense augmented model performs at par with the baseline model. We perform an array of analysis experiments to identify where the commonsense infused model outperforms the baseline and where it fails.

2 Model

We use a graph convolution-based model to enable incorporation of COMET sequences given an input sentence. The sentence representations are retrieved from the pre-trained encoder of our baseline model. Our **baseline model** consists of a Transformer (Vaswani et al., 2017) based DistilBERT (Sanh et al., 2019) encoder followed by a feed-forward neural network (FFNN). DistilBERT is a light-weight encoder, which enables faster training, while achieving similar performance as other Transformer based encoders.

DATASET	TRAINING	TEST
SemEval Irony	3833	958
News Headline	27691	27691
FigLang 2020 Reddit	3520	880

Table 1: Number of training samples in train/test split for each dataset.

The model is shown in Figure 2. For every input instance, a graph is formed with edges between the input sentence and COMET sequences. No edges are present between individual COMET sequences. Sentence embeddings retrieved from the baseline DistilBERT form the initial graph embeddings. The intuition behind leveraging a graph-based architecture was to enable information flow between the representations of the input sentence and COMET sequences, thereby reducing the domain discrepancy between them.

The graph is then fed into a GraphSage (Hamilton et al., 2017) network which produces the node embedding vector $V \in \mathbb{R}^{(M+1)\times N}$, where M is the number of COMET sequences and N is the output dimension of the GCN. The node embedding vector V is then forwarded to a fully connected neural network layer to produce the final output. In section 4, we experiment with different edge configurations and observe how each edge configuration affects the downstream performance.

We experimented with another model that incorporated COMET sequences with an attention-mechanism. In that model, the representation of the input sentence was concatenated with an aggregate representation of the COMET sequences, formed in an attentive fashion. Its performance was not better than the GCN-based model, so we do not describe it here.

3 Experimental Setup

We evaluate the models on three datasets (a) **Irony detection SemEval task**: Van Hee et al. (2018) conducted a SemEval task for irony detection considering an utterance in isolation. They also released a secondary task where the sarcastic samples were classified into *three* broad categories: verbal irony with polarity contrast, situational irony, and others. (b) **News Headlines dataset** (Misra and

APPROACH	News Headlines	SemEval Irony	FigLang 2020 (Reddit)
Baseline	96.13%	69.09%	67.95%
GCN (*bidirectional* edges)	96.16%	67.88%	67.50%
GCN (input → COMET edges)	96.14%	68.66%	67.35%
GCN (COMET → input edges)	96.18%	68.40%	67.54%

Table 2: Accuracy of the baseline DistilBERT and GCN model (in various edge configurations). We do not observe any significant change in sarcasm detection performance with the incorporation of commonsense sequences.

Edge configuration	Performance
GCN (*bidirectional*)	67.27%
GCN (COMET → input)	55.00%
GCN (input → COMET)	67.36%

Table 3: Performance of the proposed model for different edge configurations. We observe a sharp performance drop in (COMET → input) configuration.

Dataset	Overlap
News Headline	99.5%
SemEval Irony	91.6%
FigLang 2020 (Reddit)	92.7%

Table 4: Test set overlap where the output label from the GCN and DistilBERT model is the same.

Arora, 2019): contains sarcastic news headlines from *TheOnion* and non-sarcastic ones from *HuffPost*. (c) **FigLang 2020 Sarcasm detection task**: We experiment on the Reddit dataset of the shared task introduced by Ghosh et al. (2020). The statistics of the datasets are specified in Table 1.

All the aforementioned datasets are balanced. We report our results by randomly splitting into training and test set, and averaging the accuracy over 5 iterations. In our experiments, we incorporate a subset of COMET predicates (*xWant* and *xEffect*) related to the subject in a sentence.

4 Results

We report the classification accuracy of the models for all datasets in Table 2. The baseline denotes the DistilBERT performance. We see a high performance in the *News headline* dataset where the sentences are self-contained and language is not noisy. We see relatively lower performance of the baseline in FigLang 2020 Reddit, where we ignored the available context. Performance in SemEval dataset is low due to noisy tweets.

We conduct an ablation study with three configurations of the graph edges (a) *bidirectional* edges (b) edges from *input → COMET* sequences and (c) edges from *COMET sequences → input*. The results of the GCN-based model in different settings are shown in Table 2. The performance of the GCN model is at par with the baseline and varying edge configurations doesn't have any effect on the downstream performance. COMET produces sequences for an input event in the following format.
Input: "they should have put $125 million termination payout in each of their contract"
xWant : *to save money*
We wish to have more complete COMET sentences like: *they wanted to save money*. In order to improve the setup, we replace COMET sequences with complete sentences of the form: `[subject] [MASK] [raw COMET sequence]`. We replace the `[subject]` placeholder with the SUBJECT POS tag in the input sentence. We leverage a pre-trained BERT model to predict the unknown `[MASK]` word. All reported results use this setup.

We examine whether the COMET representations leverage information from the input in the GCN setup by **removing the input sentence representation** before the FFNN module (shown in Figure 2) and experimenting with different edge-configurations. In Table 3, we observe a significant performance dip with COMET→input setup. This illustrates that the information flowing from input sentence to COMET sequences is more relevant.

We also measure the share of instances in the test set having the same predicted label from the baseline and the model. We observe a significant overlap (>90%) between the predictions of the baseline and the proposed model across all datasets in Table 4, illustrating that the model isn't able to tackle new instances.

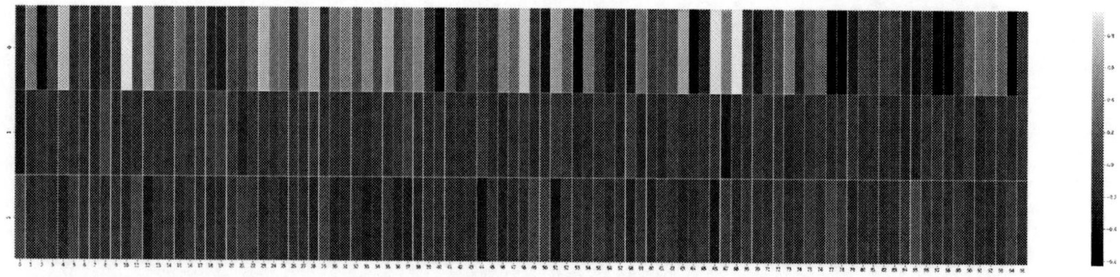

Figure 3: Visualization of gradient-based saliency tests. Darker shade denotes lower absolute values. The first row shows the features corresponding to the input sentence, and the other two rows are features from COMET sequences *xWant* and *xEffect*. We observe that features from input sentence (first row) receive high saliency values.

Occluded Element	Δ
Input sentence	27.99%
COMET sequences	1.38%

Table 5: Confidence change when different segments of the input are occluded. Δ denotes the change in confidence when different parts of the input is occluded.

DATASET	$\mathcal{C}_{\text{GCN}}^{NS}$
News Headline	83.8%
SemEval Irony	64.6%
FigLang 2020 Reddit	96.8%

Table 6: $\mathcal{C}_{\text{GCN}}^{NS}$ statistic across different datasets.

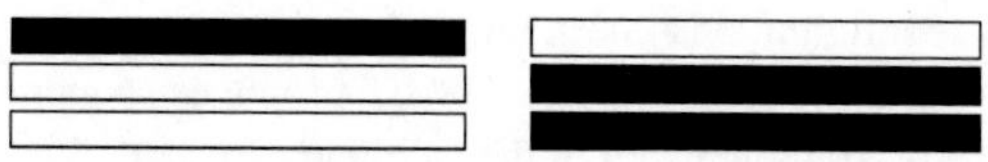

Figure 4: Occlusion setup. First setup shows that the input sentence representation (first row) is occluded. Second setup commonsense sequence representations are occluded (second and third rows).

5 Saliency Test

We perform saliency tests to investigate whether the model is reliant on commonsense sequences while taking decisions.

(a) **Gradient-based saliency** (Bastings and Filippova, 2020) measure for a feature x_i given an output class c is computed as $\nabla_{x_i}\mathcal{L}(y, f(x)) \cdot x_i$, where $\mathcal{L}(\cdot,\cdot)$ is the loss function. The saliency map is shown in Figure 3. The saliency map vector has a dimension of 3×768, where the first row showcases the saliency values of the features corresponding to the input sentence while the remaining two rows correspond to the saliency of COMET sequences. For better visualization, all values are normalized between 0-1 and average pooling is performed on adjacent blocks of 8 to form a vector of dimension 3×192. From Figure 3, it is evident that the model learns to identify important input features but assigns similar saliency values to all COMET features.

(b) **Occlusion-based saliency** test involves occluding a part of the input and observing the change in the output probability vector. We occlude the input representation and COMET representations respectively as shown in Figure 4. The occlusion metric (Bastings and Filippova, 2020) is defined as $\mathrm{E}_{x\sim\mathcal{D}}[|f_c(\mathbf{x}) - f_c(\mathbf{x}|x_i = 0)|]$. Table 5 reports the results of this test. We observe that occluding the input sentence leads to a significant change in the output confidence while occluding the COMET sequences has little impact.

These tests demonstrate that the model is more reliant on the input sentence and less on the COMET sequences for making the prediction.

6 Efficacy of Commonsense

In this section, we try to uncover why COMET sequences don't help in the sarcasm detection task. In order to identify instances where commonsense incorporation hurts the performance, we focus on samples where the model's prediction is wrong but the baseline is correct. Among these samples, we measure how many were non-sarcastic by defining a new measure **non-sarcastic class coverage**,

$$\mathcal{C}_{\text{GCN}}^{NS} = \frac{|\{x|x \in \mathcal{S}_{\text{GCN}}^{B}, l(x) = \mathcal{NS}\}|}{|\mathcal{S}_{\text{GCN}}^{B}|}$$

where $\mathcal{S}_{\text{GCN}}^{B}$ is the set of samples in which the model predicted incorrectly while the baseline was correct, $l(\cdot)$ is the oracle function which returns the true label of an input instance x, and $\mathcal{NS}$ denotes the non-sarcastic class label. Results in Ta-

Ground Truth	Input Sentence	COMET Support *(xWant and xEffect)*	Explanations
Non-sarcastic	*@usertag* i wonder if they have that in an audio book	• He gets to learns something new • He wants to be entertained	COMET sequences don't add value for classifying the non-sarcastic sample.
Sarcastic	Going to watch a movie about murder. merry christmas ;)	• The person wants to have fun • The person gets tired as a result	COMET sequences fail to explain the satire.
Sarcastic	final at 7am, I'm ready	• The person wants to go to bed • The person has to go to work	COMET captures the contrast between the intentions and results.
Sarcastic	As a girl my reason not to put on makeup is I'm satisfied with my face	• She wanted to look pretty • As a result she got complements	COMET doesn't provide relevant commonsense for capturing polarity contrast.

Table 7: Example input instances along with their ground truth label and corresponding commonsense sentences retrieved from COMET. We analyze the utility of COMET sequences described as explanations.

ble 6 demonstrate a high value of C_{GCN}^{NS} across all datasets, this indicates that the large fraction of the instances where the model was incorrect but the baseline was correct were non-sarcastic. After surveying non-sarcastic instances we infer that commonsense knowledge fails to explain non-sarcastic samples and is present as irrelevant context hurting downstream performance (Petroni et al., 2020).

There are cases where the prediction failed either due to noisy input (prevalent in the Twitter based SemEval dataset) or subtle play of words which COMET sequences fail to explain.

In order to investigate the utility of commonsense for specific type of sarcasm, we form a subset of the SemEval Irony dataset with samples only from irony with polarity contrast and non-sarcastic class by leveraging labels from the secondary SemEval task (mentioned in Section 3). C_{GCN}^{NS} for the new dataset is 57.1%, a significant reduction from the 64.6% in SemEval dataset in Table 6. We infer that commonsense is only useful in detecting sarcasm with polarity contrast but struggles with other types of sarcasm.

7 Qualitative Analysis

In this section, we analyze a few examples shown in Table 7 and observe whether the COMET sequences are helpful in detecting sarcasm. We have anonymized any twitter handle with "*@usertag*" to prevent any leak of private information.

- In the first example of Table 7, the input sentence is non-sarcastic. Retrieved commonsense sequences don't capture any information that may help in prediction.

- In several instances, a sentence is sarcastic due to a subtle play of words or use of language. The commonsense based model struggles in such scenarios as COMET sequences cannot explain such events as shown in the second instance of Table 7.

- In the third example of Table 7, we show that COMET sequences are able to perfectly capture the contrast between the intention and effect on the person.

- In rare cases like the fourth instance of Table 7, which is an example of irony with polarity contrast. It is still difficult for the commonsense model to explain the satire.

8 Conclusion and Future work

In this paper, we proposed the idea of integrating commonsense knowledge in the task of sarcasm detection. We observe that COMET infused model performs at par with the baseline. Through saliency tests, we observe that the model is less reliant on the commonsense representations in many cases. From our analysis, we infer that commonsense is most effective in identifying sarcasm with polarity contrast but fails to explain non-sarcastic samples or other types of sarcasm effectively, which hurts the overall performance. In the future, we will explore the utility of other forms of external knowledge such as factual world knowledge for sarcasm detection. We will also try to leverage commonsense to *explain* why a certain remark is sarcastic.

References

Silvio Amir, Byron C. Wallace, Hao Lyu, Paula Carvalho, and Mário J. Silva. 2016. Modelling context with user embeddings for sarcasm detection in social media. In *Proceedings of The 20th SIGNLL Conference on Computational Natural Language Learning*, pages 167–177, Berlin, Germany. Association for Computational Linguistics.

Jasmijn Bastings and Katja Filippova. 2020. The elephant in the interpretability room: Why use attention as explanation when we have saliency methods? In *Proceedings of the Third BlackboxNLP Workshop on Analyzing and Interpreting Neural Networks for NLP*, pages 149–155, Online. Association for Computational Linguistics.

Antoine Bosselut, Hannah Rashkin, Maarten Sap, Chaitanya Malaviya, Asli Celikyilmaz, and Yejin Choi. 2019. COMET: Commonsense transformers for automatic knowledge graph construction. In *Proceedings of the 57th Annual Meeting of the Association for Computational Linguistics*, pages 4762–4779, Florence, Italy. Association for Computational Linguistics.

Faeze Brahman and Snigdha Chaturvedi. 2020. Modeling protagonist emotions for emotion-aware storytelling. In *Proceedings of the 2020 Conference on Empirical Methods in Natural Language Processing (EMNLP)*, pages 5277–5294.

Paula Carvalho, Luís Sarmento, Mário J Silva, and Eugénio De Oliveira. 2009. Clues for detecting irony in user-generated contents: oh...!! it's" so easy";-. In *Proceedings of the 1st international CIKM workshop on Topic-sentiment analysis for mass opinion*, pages 53–56.

Tuhin Chakrabarty, Debanjan Ghosh, Smaranda Muresan, and Nanyun Peng. 2020. r^3: Reverse, retrieve, and rank for sarcasm generation with commonsense knowledge. *arXiv preprint arXiv:2004.13248*.

Jindong Chen, Yizhou Hu, Jingping Liu, Yanghua Xiao, and Haiyun Jiang. 2019. Deep short text classification with knowledge powered attention. In *The Thirty-Third AAAI Conference on Artificial Intelligence, AAAI 2019, The Thirty-First Innovative Applications of Artificial Intelligence Conference, IAAI 2019, The Ninth AAAI Symposium on Educational Advances in Artificial Intelligence, EAAI 2019, Honolulu, Hawaii, USA, January 27 - February 1, 2019*, pages 6252–6259. AAAI Press.

Dmitry Davidov, Oren Tsur, and Ari Rappoport. 2010. Semi-supervised recognition of sarcasm in Twitter and Amazon. In *Proceedings of the Fourteenth Conference on Computational Natural Language Learning*, pages 107–116, Uppsala, Sweden. Association for Computational Linguistics.

Daria Dzendzik, Carl Vogel, and Jennifer Foster. 2020. Q. can knowledge graphs be used to answer boolean questions? a. it's complicated! Association for Computational Linguistics (ACL).

Aniruddha Ghosh and Tony Veale. 2017. Magnets for sarcasm: Making sarcasm detection timely, contextual and very personal. In *Proceedings of the 2017 Conference on Empirical Methods in Natural Language Processing*, pages 482–491, Copenhagen, Denmark. Association for Computational Linguistics.

Debanjan Ghosh, Weiwei Guo, and Smaranda Muresan. 2015. Sarcastic or not: Word embeddings to predict the literal or sarcastic meaning of words. In *Proceedings of the 2015 Conference on Empirical Methods in Natural Language Processing*, pages 1003–1012, Lisbon, Portugal. Association for Computational Linguistics.

Debanjan Ghosh, Avijit Vajpayee, and Smaranda Muresan. 2020. A report on the 2020 sarcasm detection shared task. In *Proceedings of the Second Workshop on Figurative Language Processing*, pages 1–11, Online. Association for Computational Linguistics.

Raymond W Gibbs. 1986. On the psycholinguistics of sarcasm. *Journal of experimental psychology: general*, 115(1):3.

Raymond W Gibbs Jr, Raymond W Gibbs, and Herbert L Colston. 2007. *Irony in language and thought: A cognitive science reader*. Psychology Press.

Roberto González-Ibáñez, Smaranda Muresan, and Nina Wacholder. 2011. Identifying sarcasm in Twitter: A closer look. In *Proceedings of the 49th Annual Meeting of the Association for Computational Linguistics: Human Language Technologies*, pages 581–586, Portland, Oregon, USA. Association for Computational Linguistics.

William L. Hamilton, Zhitao Ying, and Jure Leskovec. 2017. Inductive representation learning on large graphs. In *Advances in Neural Information Processing Systems 30: Annual Conference on Neural Information Processing Systems 2017, December 4-9, 2017, Long Beach, CA, USA*, pages 1024–1034.

Aditya Joshi, Vinita Sharma, and Pushpak Bhattacharyya. 2015. Harnessing context incongruity for sarcasm detection. In *Proceedings of the 53rd Annual Meeting of the Association for Computational Linguistics and the 7th International Joint Conference on Natural Language Processing (Volume 2: Short Papers)*, pages 757–762, Beijing, China. Association for Computational Linguistics.

Annervaz K M, Somnath Basu Roy Chowdhury, and Ambedkar Dukkipati. 2018. Learning beyond datasets: Knowledge graph augmented neural networks for natural language processing. In *Proceedings of the 2018 Conference of the North American Chapter of the Association for Computational Linguistics: Human Language Technologies, Volume 1 (Long Papers)*, pages 313–322, New Orleans, Louisiana. Association for Computational Linguistics.

Thomas N. Kipf and Max Welling. 2017. Semi-supervised classification with graph convolutional networks. In *5th International Conference on Learning Representations, ICLR 2017, Toulon, France, April 24-26, 2017, Conference Track Proceedings*. OpenReview.net.

Roger J Kreuz and Sam Glucksberg. 1989. How to be sarcastic: The echoic reminder theory of verbal irony. *Journal of experimental psychology: General*, 118(4):374.

Stephanie Lukin and Marilyn Walker. 2013. Really? well. apparently bootstrapping improves the performance of sarcasm and nastiness classifiers for online dialogue. In *Proceedings of the Workshop on Language Analysis in Social Media*, pages 30–40, Atlanta, Georgia. Association for Computational Linguistics.

Diana Maynard and Mark Greenwood. 2014. Who cares about sarcastic tweets? investigating the impact of sarcasm on sentiment analysis. In *Proceedings of the Ninth International Conference on Language Resources and Evaluation (LREC'14)*, pages 4238–4243, Reykjavik, Iceland. European Language Resources Association (ELRA).

Abhijit Mishra, Diptesh Kanojia, Seema Nagar, Kuntal Dey, and Pushpak Bhattacharyya. 2016. Harnessing cognitive features for sarcasm detection. In *Proceedings of the 54th Annual Meeting of the Association for Computational Linguistics (Volume 1: Long Papers)*, pages 1095–1104, Berlin, Germany. Association for Computational Linguistics.

Rishabh Misra and Prahal Arora. 2019. Sarcasm detection using hybrid neural network. *arXiv preprint arXiv:1908.07414*.

Smaranda Muresan, Roberto Gonzalez-Ibanez, Debanjan Ghosh, and Nina Wacholder. 2016. Identification of nonliteral language in social media: A case study on sarcasm. *Journal of the Association for Information Science and Technology*, 67(11):2725–2737.

Fabio Petroni, Patrick Lewis, Aleksandra Piktus, Tim Rocktäschel, Yuxiang Wu, Alexander H Miller, and Sebastian Riedel. 2020. How context affects language models' factual predictions. *arXiv preprint arXiv:2005.04611*.

Ellen Riloff, Ashequl Qadir, Prafulla Surve, Lalindra De Silva, Nathan Gilbert, and Ruihong Huang. 2013. Sarcasm as contrast between a positive sentiment and negative situation. In *Proceedings of the 2013 Conference on Empirical Methods in Natural Language Processing*, pages 704–714, Seattle, Washington, USA. Association for Computational Linguistics.

Victor Sanh, Lysandre Debut, Julien Chaumond, and Thomas Wolf. 2019. Distilbert, a distilled version of bert: smaller, faster, cheaper and lighter. *arXiv preprint arXiv:1910.01108*.

Akira Utsumi. 2000. Verbal irony as implicit display of ironic environment: Distinguishing ironic utterances from nonirony. *Journal of Pragmatics*, 32(12):1777–1806.

Cynthia Van Hee, Els Lefever, and Véronique Hoste. 2018. SemEval-2018 task 3: Irony detection in English tweets. In *Proceedings of The 12th International Workshop on Semantic Evaluation*, pages 39–50, New Orleans, Louisiana. Association for Computational Linguistics.

Ashish Vaswani, Noam Shazeer, Niki Parmar, Jakob Uszkoreit, Llion Jones, Aidan N. Gomez, Lukasz Kaiser, and Illia Polosukhin. 2017. Attention is all you need. In *Advances in Neural Information Processing Systems 30: Annual Conference on Neural Information Processing Systems 2017, December 4-9, 2017, Long Beach, CA, USA*, pages 5998–6008.

Byron C. Wallace, Do Kook Choe, Laura Kertz, and Eugene Charniak. 2014. Humans require context to infer ironic intent (so computers probably do, too). In *Proceedings of the 52nd Annual Meeting of the Association for Computational Linguistics (Volume 2: Short Papers)*, pages 512–516, Baltimore, Maryland. Association for Computational Linguistics.

Xiaoyan Wang, Pavan Kapanipathi, Ryan Musa, Mo Yu, Kartik Talamadupula, Ibrahim Abdelaziz, Maria Chang, Achille Fokoue, Bassem Makni, Nicholas Mattei, et al. 2019. Improving natural language inference using external knowledge in the science questions domain. In *Proceedings of the AAAI Conference on Artificial Intelligence*, volume 33, pages 7208–7215.

Mingda Zhang, Keren Ye, Rebecca Hwa, and Adriana Kovashka. 2020. Story completion with explicit modeling of commonsense knowledge. In *Proceedings of the IEEE/CVF Conference on Computer Vision and Pattern Recognition Workshops*, pages 376–377.

BERT Cannot Align Characters

Antonis Maronikolakis and **Philipp Dufter** and **Hinrich Schütze**
Center for Information and Language Processing (CIS), LMU Munich, Germany
antmarakis,philipp@cis.lmu.de

Abstract

In previous work, it has been shown that BERT can adequately align cross-lingual sentences on the word level. Here we investigate whether BERT can also operate as a char-level aligner. The languages examined are English, Fake-English, German and Greek. We show that the closer two languages are, the better BERT can align them on the character level. BERT indeed works well in English to Fake-English alignment, but this does not generalize to natural languages to the same extent. Nevertheless, the proximity of two languages does seem to be a factor. English is more related to German than to Greek and this is reflected in how well BERT aligns them; English to German is better than English to Greek. We examine multiple setups and show that the similarity matrices for natural languages show weaker relations the further apart two languages are.

a	**a**	0.96
b	z	0.94
c	l	0.95
d	x	0.92
e	h	0.96
f	**f**	0.94
g	**g**	0.97
h	x	0.93
i	**i**	0.97
j	z	0.97
k	c	0.95
l	z	0.96
m	**m**	0.96
n	**n**	0.98
o	**o**	0.98
p	**p**	0.97
q	c	0.96
r	**r**	0.98
s	x	0.94
t	k	0.93
u	z	0.93
v	h	0.94
w	**w**	0.96
x	**x**	0.98
y	c	0.97
z	c	0.94

(a) $EngDeu$

a	ρ	0.98
b	ξ	0.98
c	ι	0.96
d	σ	0.96
e	o	0.98
f	ι	0.98
g	λ	0.98
h	τ	0.98
i	τ	0.98
j	η	0.96
k	ν	0.97
l	ν	0.98
m	ψ	0.96
n	η	0.95
o	α	0.97
p	$\boldsymbol{\pi}$	0.97
q	ρ	0.97
r	λ	0.99
s	ν	0.99
t	$\boldsymbol{\tau}$	0.98
u	ϕ	0.97
v	π	0.99
w	τ	0.98
x	ν	0.99
y	ν	0.98
z	τ	0.98

(b) $EngEll$

Table 1: Max alignments for English → German and English → Greek, as extracted from a cosine similarity matrix between the two alphabets for each experiment. Correct alignments are in bold. We see low accuracy for both setups, but especially low for English → Greek.

1 Introduction

For the many sweeping successes BERT has had in the field of Natural Language Processing, the model's alignment capabilities have been lacking and under-explored. Work in this area is picking up and it has been shown that BERT can operate with adequate efficiency in word alignment tasks (Zenkel et al., 2019; Jalili Sabet et al., 2020). The question whether or not BERT can perform character-level alignment, though, has not been answered yet.

Even though characters on their own do not necessarily hold much semantic meaning, we investigate whether BERT is able to generate useful representation spaces for characters. Character-level alignment would be useful in tasks like transliteration (Li et al., 2009; Sajjad et al., 2017) or word-level alignment (Legrand et al., 2016). In a lot of occurrences of transliterations, grammatical inflections are added or dropped, which causes difficulties in an array of tasks (Czarnowska et al., 2019; Vania and Lopez, 2017). With character-level awareness, we can have better models for transliteration detection and extraction tasks. Word alignment could also benefit from character-level information in instances where words get split up within a sentence (eg., separable verbs in German or phrasal verbs in English).

With our work we show that even though BERT is not able to align languages on the character level, the closer these languages are the better the alignment. In the trivial case of English to Fake-English alignment, the model successfully learns to align characters. For English to German performance drops substantially and it drops even more for English to Greek. Languages seem to be put on an intuitive scale by BERT, with more similar languages having better alignment than highly dissimilar ones.

Proceedings of the Second Workshop on Insights from Negative Results in NLP, pages 16–22
November 10, 2021.

2 Related Work

Research has been conducted to uncover elements of multilinguality in mBERT. In Pires et al. (2019), an analysis of mBERT is presented, while in Conneau and Lample (2019); Wu and Dredze (2019); Artetxe et al. (2020) zero-shot cross-lingual transfer is analyzed. Dufter and Schütze (2020) further analyzes mBERT's capabilities with BERT's architecture and the structure of languages examined. The authors performed their experiments on a pairing of English with Fake-English, as proposed by K et al. (2020) in their rigorous empirical study of mBERT where linguistic properties of languages, architecture and learning objectives are investigated.

In Wu et al. (2021); Garg et al. (2019), it is shown that transformers (Vaswani et al., 2017) can achieve similar performance with sequence-to-sequence approaches based on Recurrent Neural Networks (Luong et al., 2015) for character-level tasks such as transliteration and grapheme-to-phoneme conversion. Further work to develop character-level BERT-based models is conducted in El Boukkouri et al. (2020); Ma et al. (2020).

Och and Ney (2003); Legrand et al. (2016) worked towards representation-based word alignment, with implementations of aligners proposed in Dyer et al. (2013); Östling and Tiedemann (2016).

We also note recent efforts towards unsupervised word alignment. In Zenkel et al. (2019), an extension to the usual Machine Translation encoder-decoder is proposed to jointly learn language translation and word alignment in an unsupervised manner. BERT has also been shown to be able to perform word alignment (Jalili Sabet et al., 2020) through embedding matrix similarities.

3 Experimental Setup

3.1 Data Setup

The EuroParl Corpus (Koehn, 2005) is a parallel corpus containing recorded proceedings of the European Parliament. Originally 21 languages were included, although here we examined three: English (ENG), German (DEU) and Greek (ELL).[1] Each set is split by words and each word is further split in characters. Finally, special start and end tokens are added around each (split) word. This process results in a data file where each line contains a word split in characters. Finally, these language sets are merged together, alternating between lines. For example, in the English → German setup, the first line contains an English word (split in characters), the second line a German word (split in characters), and so on. For the conversion of English to Fake-English, we employ a mapping of characters to integers. The integers are in the range $[100, 151]$. The same mapping takes place for the English → German setup, since the two languages share the same script. Data is given as input line-by-line to the model.

3.2 Model Setup

We experimented with different BERT (Devlin et al., 2019) model sizes and parameters. In our hyperparameter search, we mainly examined the effect of hidden layer size, layer numbers, embedding space size and attention heads number. We found that when models have fewer than 3 layers or more than 9 layers, we see underfitting and overfitting respectively. In the end, we settled for a 6-layer model with a quarter of the original BERT-base parameters, trained for 50 epochs. An analysis of model size effect on performance is omitted. We are training from scratch on the usual Masked Language Modeling task as described in (Devlin et al., 2019), with the difference that we are masking individual characters instead of subword tokens.

3.3 Experiments

For our control experiment, we tried to align English and Fake-English. This setup serves as aid to hyperparameter tuning. Because of the nature of English and Fake-English, if a model cannot align these two then it would not work for natural languages. English data was split in two sets, with the second converted to Fake-English. In our setup, Fake-English is a simple mapping from English characters to numbers ranging from 100 to 151. That is, 'a' is converted to '100', 'b' to '101', 'A' to '126' etc. All other numbers were removed from both sets. We call this setup $EngFake_{base}$.

Apart from the base setup, we tried minor alterations. Namely, we tried to break the one-to-one mapping from English to Fake-English. The letter 'f' was mapped not to a single, unique integer, but instead two new indices (denoted by f_1 and f_2). So, 'f' was mapped to '200 201', which are the unique tokens for f_1 and f_2 respectively. In the same way, capital 'F' was replaced by the tokens for F_1 and F_2. We call this setup $EngFake_{f_1 f_2}$.

[1]We follow the ISO 639-3 standard for language codes: https://iso639-3.sil.org/

After the successful $EngFake$ experiments, we experiment with English to Greek ($EngEll$) and English to German ($EngDeu$). For English to German, since the languages share the same script, we converted German to Fake-German in an analogous method to the Fake-English conversion. Finally, German to Greek ($DeuEll$) experiments were also conducted for completion.

Firstly, we examine the uncontextualized embeddings of characters. To retrieve the representation of a character, we give it as input to the model and extract the embedding layer activations. We also investigate contextualized embeddings by feeding entire words into the model and extracting the activations for a particular character at the 5th layer.

For all the setups, a separate development set was used for evaluation by holding out 30% of examples (ie., the lines in the dataset). After training the respective models, we compute the cosine similarity matrix between the two alphabets.

4 Results

4.1 Similarity Matrix Comparisons

The cosine similarity matrices are shown for our different setups. First, we give as input the characters of the two alphabets separately and extract their first-layer representations. We examined all layer representations, but since the characters are given without context, we decided to go with the first layer, which has been shown to contain context-independent information (Jawahar et al., 2019).

In Figure 1 (a) the cosine similarity matrix for $EngFake_{base}$ is presented. The diagonal shows that the model correctly aligns English with the base Fake-English language. In Figure 1 (b) we see the similarity matrix of $EngFake_{f_1 f_2}$. The strong diagonal indicates that BERT indeed manages to align English with its Fake-English equivalent. The added perturbation ($f_1 f_2$ instead of 'f') is correctly captured by the model as well. The English 'f' has high similarity scores with both f_1 and f_2, with f_1 having a slightly higher score. We also compare against the combined $f_1 f_2$ bigram, by computing its joint representation. We denote this new, combined token simply with 'f' in the matrix.

For $EngDeu$, in Table 2 (a), we see lower performance. The diagonal is still observed, but less prominently than before. The two languages are relatively similar and belong to the same language family, so some similarity on the character level is to be expected. Nevertheless, the similarity matrix shows quite significant noise that obscures the diagonal. Note that even though the diagonal is not the best indicator of performance, the model was overall less efficient than expected.

One of the patterns that emerged is the high compatibility of the matrix's right hand side (German 'w', 'x', 'y' and 'z') with most of the English characters. High similarities can be found between these characters and most English characters across the board. This could be because of the low frequency of these letters in German.[2] Apart from that, there are few other clusters around the matrix, for example 'w', 'x' and 'y' for English and the 'h'-'o' range in German.

When compared against a language further away from English than German, in this case Greek, similarities become even fainter. In Table 2 (b) the similarity matrix for $EngEll$ is presented. We see weaker similarity scores across the board with results mostly random. As we show in Section 4.2, only a few characters were correctly aligned. In English, 'e', 'j', 't' and 'z' have high similarity scores overall, with 'ρ', 'σ' and 'τ' in Greek scoring highly across the board as well.

Finally, in Table 2 (c), $DeuEll$ is shown. There is very little that can be inferred from this matrix, since performance seems to be random.

4.2 Max Alignment Accuracy

Here we take a closer look at the similarity matrices and quantify how well our model aligns characters compared to a ground truth value. Even though ground truth alignment between characters is not always clear (for example, the English 'a' has multiple pronunciations: 'allure', 'ball', 'make', which would arguably map to three distinct characters in Greek), there are some obviously incorrect alignments we can observe (for example, the English 'a' should never be aligned with any of the Greek consonants). Thus, this max alignment method is an adequate indicator of model performance.

In Table 1 we examine alignments for $EngDeu$ and $EngEll$. When choosing a target character, we search in the similarity matrix for the given pair of languages and choose the character with the maximum cosine similarity. In the natural language setups, the model fares fairly badly. In $EngDeu$ the model correctly aligns 11 characters (this is of course a mere simplification, since alignments such

[2] https://www.sttmedia.com/characterfrequency-german

m	μ	0.63
o	ο	0.50
n	ν	0.37
a	α	0.49
s	η	0.23
t	τ	0.43
e	η	0.34
r	ρ	0.31
y	ι	0.22

(a) monastery

t	τ	0.29
e	ε	0.21
s	τ	0.13
t	σ	0.34

(b) test

c	χ	0.77
a	α	0.63
r	ρ	0.55
d	ρ	0.19
i	ι	0.24
a	α	0.49
c	χ	0.52

(c) cardiac

Table 2: Max alignments for 'monastery', 'test' and 'cardiac' as computed by our model.

as 'k' → 'c' could also be considered correct; here we consider only the most basic of alignments: the ones on the diagonal). The situation is worse in $EngEll$, where only 3 characters were correctly aligned. $EngFake$ results are omitted, since the model correctly aligned all characters in all setups.

4.3 Contextualized Embeddings

We also perform a qualitative study on contextualized character-level representations. We choose three pairs of words, feed them separately to the model and extract their 5th-layer representations (averages of all layers were also examined with similar results, as well as other individual layers; the best performing layer was chosen). After computing the contextual representations for all characters in the English word, we align them with the contextual representations of the characters in the Greek word. In Table 2 these alignments are shown.

Results are seemingly random with a strong bias towards the diagonal[3]. The model, thus, has not learned any contextual representations either.

5 Ablation Studies

We also performed some minor experiments with static embeddings and adjustments to the MLM task, as well as a variation to our $EngFake$ setup.

Apart from the BERT embeddings, we also examined static embeddings, to introduce another baseline. Specifically, we used the FastText algorithm (Bojanowski et al., 2017). Data was the same as the previous experiments. Results were seemingly random, with FastText unable to capture any meaningful representations. Cosine similarities were generally very low and alignments incoherent.

For the MLM task, we experimented with different probabilities for token masking. In the original BERT paper, the chosen token is replaced by [MASK] 80% of the time, while it remains the same 10% of the time and gets replaced by a random token the rest 10%. We experimented with the following distributions: 80/20/0, 60/20/20 and 50/50/0 with no noticeable change in performance.

We also experimented with overlapping Fake-English mappings in the form 'a' → '100 101 102'. That is, each character is mapped to the tokens corresponding to itself and its next two characters (eg. 'a' is mapped to the tokens for 'a', 'b' and 'c'). This is an extreme case of the $EngFake_{f_1 f_2}$ setup, where each character is mapped to three (instead of 'f' getting mapped to 'f1' and 'f2'). Results deteriorated to random performance.

Finally, we conducted another $EngFake$ experiment. Namely, we restricted the context where we present each character. For the previous experiments each word was split in characters. Now, we further split each word into trigrams. So, instead of 'e x a m p l e' we end up with multiple overlapping trigram entries: 'e x a', 'x a m', 'a m p', etc. The motivation for this experiment is that since the transliteration of a character in a word doesn't need the entire word but instead only its direct neighbors, we should examine a setup with more restricted context[4]. In this case, results deteriorated heavily and are seemingly random with no meaningful representation captured.

6 Conclusion

In our work BERT is shown to be unable to create consistently good cross-lingual spaces on the character level. We train models on English, German, Greek and Fake-English and we compare character-level alignments between them. Cosine similarity matrices between the target and source alphabets were examined and we found that the closer two languages are, the better BERT does in aligning them. Fake-English is the easiest to align with English, whereas German is worse, with Greek trailing far behind. We conclude that BERT is not able to perform adequate character alignment.

Acknowledgments

This work was supported by ERCAdG #740516. We want to thank the anonymous reviewers for their insightful comments and suggestions.

[3]To control for character positions, we also aligned characters without positional embeddings and results got worse.

[4]While this is a more nuanced subject, for the purposes of this ablation experiment we assumed this statement stood.

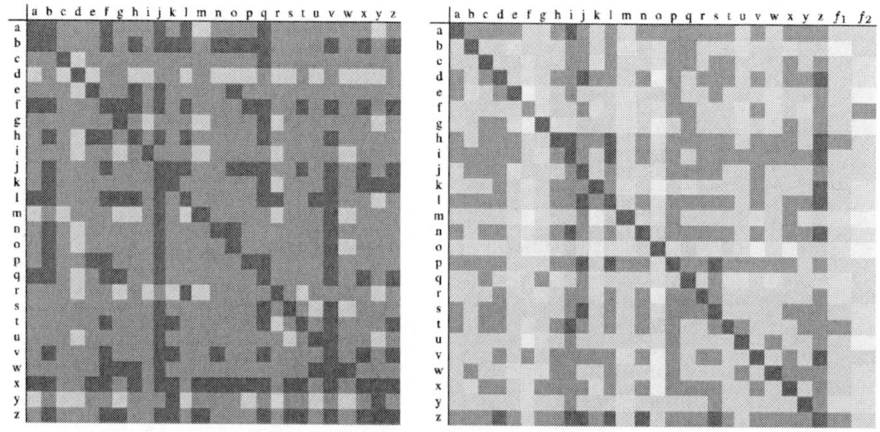

(a) $EngFake$ (b) $EngFake_{f_1 f_2}$

Figure 1: Showing heatmaps for (a) $EngFake$ and (b) $EngFake_{f_1 f_2}$. The lighter green cells show lower cosine similarity, the darker green cells show higher cosine similarity.

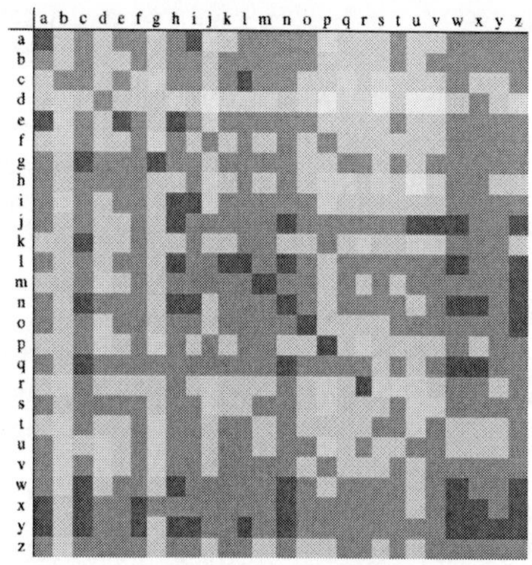

(a) $EngDeu$

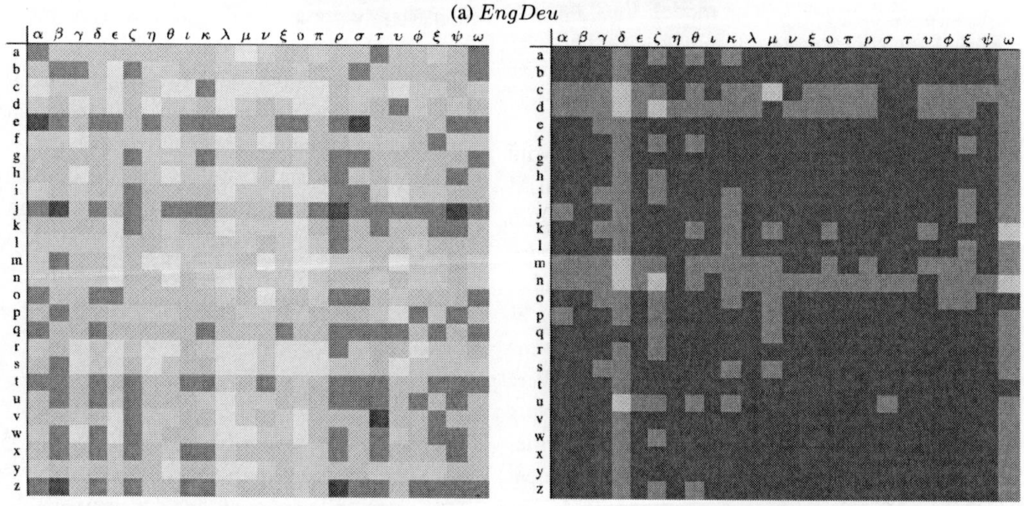

(b) $EngEll$ (c) $DeuEll$

Figure 2: Showing heatmaps for (a) $EngDeu$, (b) $EngEll$ and (c) $DeuEll$. The lighter green cells show lower cosine similarity, the darker green cells show higher cosine similarity.

References

Mikel Artetxe, Sebastian Ruder, and Dani Yogatama. 2020. On the cross-lingual transferability of monolingual representations. In *Proceedings of the 58th Annual Meeting of the Association for Computational Linguistics*, pages 4623–4637, Online. Association for Computational Linguistics.

Piotr Bojanowski, Edouard Grave, Armand Joulin, and Tomas Mikolov. 2017. Enriching word vectors with subword information. *Transactions of the Association for Computational Linguistics*, 5:135–146.

Alexis Conneau and Guillaume Lample. 2019. Cross-lingual language model pretraining. In *Advances in Neural Information Processing Systems*, volume 32, pages 7059–7069. Curran Associates, Inc.

Paula Czarnowska, Sebastian Ruder, Edouard Grave, Ryan Cotterell, and Ann Copestake. 2019. Don't forget the long tail! a comprehensive analysis of morphological generalization in bilingual lexicon induction. In *Proceedings of the 2019 Conference on Empirical Methods in Natural Language Processing and the 9th International Joint Conference on Natural Language Processing (EMNLP-IJCNLP)*, pages 974–983, Hong Kong, China. Association for Computational Linguistics.

Jacob Devlin, Ming-Wei Chang, Kenton Lee, and Kristina Toutanova. 2019. BERT: Pre-training of deep bidirectional transformers for language understanding. In *Proceedings of the 2019 Conference of the North American Chapter of the Association for Computational Linguistics: Human Language Technologies, Volume 1 (Long and Short Papers)*, pages 4171–4186, Minneapolis, Minnesota. Association for Computational Linguistics.

Philipp Dufter and Hinrich Schütze. 2020. Identifying elements essential for BERT's multilinguality. In *Proceedings of the 2020 Conference on Empirical Methods in Natural Language Processing (EMNLP)*, pages 4423–4437, Online. Association for Computational Linguistics.

Chris Dyer, Victor Chahuneau, and Noah A. Smith. 2013. A simple, fast, and effective reparameterization of IBM model 2. In *Proceedings of the 2013 Conference of the North American Chapter of the Association for Computational Linguistics: Human Language Technologies*, pages 644–648, Atlanta, Georgia. Association for Computational Linguistics.

Hicham El Boukkouri, Olivier Ferret, Thomas Lavergne, Hiroshi Noji, Pierre Zweigenbaum, and Jun'ichi Tsujii. 2020. CharacterBERT: Reconciling ELMo and BERT for word-level open-vocabulary representations from characters. In *Proceedings of the 28th International Conference on Computational Linguistics*, pages 6903–6915, Barcelona, Spain (Online). International Committee on Computational Linguistics.

Sarthak Garg, Stephan Peitz, Udhyakumar Nallasamy, and Matthias Paulik. 2019. Jointly learning to align and translate with transformer models. In *Proceedings of the 2019 Conference on Empirical Methods in Natural Language Processing and the 9th International Joint Conference on Natural Language Processing (EMNLP-IJCNLP)*, pages 4453–4462, Hong Kong, China. Association for Computational Linguistics.

Masoud Jalili Sabet, Philipp Dufter, François Yvon, and Hinrich Schütze. 2020. SimAlign: High quality word alignments without parallel training data using static and contextualized embeddings. In *Proceedings of the 2020 Conference on Empirical Methods in Natural Language Processing: Findings*, pages 1627–1643, Online. Association for Computational Linguistics.

Ganesh Jawahar, Benoît Sagot, and Djamé Seddah. 2019. What does BERT learn about the structure of language? In *Proceedings of the 57th Annual Meeting of the Association for Computational Linguistics*, pages 3651–3657, Florence, Italy. Association for Computational Linguistics.

Karthikeyan K, Zihan Wang, Stephen Mayhew, and Dan Roth. 2020. Cross-lingual ability of multilingual bert: An empirical study. In *International Conference on Learning Representations*.

Philipp Koehn. 2005. Europarl: A Parallel Corpus for Statistical Machine Translation. In *Conference Proceedings: the tenth Machine Translation Summit*, pages 79–86, Phuket, Thailand. AAMT, AAMT.

Joël Legrand, Michael Auli, and Ronan Collobert. 2016. Neural network-based word alignment through score aggregation. In *Proceedings of the First Conference on Machine Translation: Volume 1, Research Papers*, pages 66–73, Berlin, Germany. Association for Computational Linguistics.

Haizhou Li, A Kumaran, Vladimir Pervouchine, and Min Zhang. 2009. Report of NEWS 2009 machine transliteration shared task. In *Proceedings of the 2009 Named Entities Workshop: Shared Task on Transliteration (NEWS 2009)*, pages 1–18, Suntec, Singapore. Association for Computational Linguistics.

Thang Luong, Hieu Pham, and Christopher D. Manning. 2015. Effective approaches to attention-based neural machine translation. In *Proceedings of the 2015 Conference on Empirical Methods in Natural Language Processing*, pages 1412–1421, Lisbon, Portugal. Association for Computational Linguistics.

Wentao Ma, Yiming Cui, Chenglei Si, Ting Liu, Shijin Wang, and Guoping Hu. 2020. CharBERT: Character-aware pre-trained language model. In *Proceedings of the 28th International Conference on Computational Linguistics*, pages 39–50, Barcelona, Spain (Online). International Committee on Computational Linguistics.

Franz Josef Och and Hermann Ney. 2003. A Systematic Comparison of Various Statistical Alignment Models. *Computational Linguistics*, 29(1):19–51.

Telmo Pires, Eva Schlinger, and Dan Garrette. 2019. How multilingual is multilingual BERT? In *Proceedings of the 57th Annual Meeting of the Association for Computational Linguistics*, pages 4996–5001, Florence, Italy. Association for Computational Linguistics.

Hassan Sajjad, Helmut Schmid, Alexander Fraser, and Hinrich Schütze. 2017. Statistical models for unsupervised, semi-supervised supervised transliteration mining. *Computational Linguistics*, 43(2):349–375.

Robert Östling and Jörg Tiedemann. 2016. Efficient word alignment with markov chain monte carlo. *The Prague Bulletin of Mathematical Linguistics*, 106.

Clara Vania and Adam Lopez. 2017. From characters to words to in between: Do we capture morphology? In *Proceedings of the 55th Annual Meeting of the Association for Computational Linguistics (Volume 1: Long Papers)*, pages 2016–2027, Vancouver, Canada. Association for Computational Linguistics.

Ashish Vaswani, Noam Shazeer, Niki Parmar, Jakob Uszkoreit, Llion Jones, Aidan N. Gomez, Łukasz Kaiser, and Illia Polosukhin. 2017. Attention is all you need. In *Proceedings of the 31st International Conference on Neural Information Processing Systems*, NIPS'17, page 6000–6010, Red Hook, NY, USA. Curran Associates Inc.

Shijie Wu, Ryan Cotterell, and Mans Hulden. 2021. Applying the transformer to character-level transduction. In *Proceedings of the 16th Conference of the European Chapter of the Association for Computational Linguistics: Main Volume*, pages 1901–1907, Online. Association for Computational Linguistics.

Shijie Wu and Mark Dredze. 2019. Beto, bentz, becas: The surprising cross-lingual effectiveness of BERT. In *Proceedings of the 2019 Conference on Empirical Methods in Natural Language Processing and the 9th International Joint Conference on Natural Language Processing (EMNLP-IJCNLP)*, pages 833–844, Hong Kong, China. Association for Computational Linguistics.

Thomas Zenkel, Joern Wuebker, and John DeNero. 2019. Adding interpretable attention to neural translation models improves word alignment.

Two Heads are Better than One? Verification of Ensemble Effect in Neural Machine Translation

Chanjun Park[1], **Sungjin Park**[2], **Seolhwa Lee**[3], **Taesun Whang**[4], **Heuiseok Lim**[1†]
[1]Korea University, [2]NAVER Corp., [3]University of Copenhagen, [4]Wisenut Inc.
{bcj1210, whiteldark, limhseok}@korea.ac.kr
sungjin.park@navercorp.com
taesunwhang@wisenut.co.kr

Abstract

In the field of natural language processing, ensembles are broadly known to be effective in improving performance. This paper analyzes how ensemble of neural machine translation (NMT) models affect performance improvement by designing various experimental setups (i.e., intra-, inter-ensemble, and non-convergence ensemble). To an in-depth examination, we analyze each ensemble method with respect to several aspects such as different attention models and vocab strategies. Experimental results show that ensembling is not always resulting in performance increases and give noteworthy negative findings.

1 Introduction

Ensemble is a technique for obtaining accurate predictions by combining the predictions of several models. In neural machine translation (NMT), ensembles are most closely related to vocabulary (vocab). In particular, by aggregating the prediction results of multiple models, the ensemble averages the probability values over the vocab of the softmax layer (Garmash and Monz, 2016; Tan et al., 2020).

Most existing studies on ensembling for NMT focus on improving the performance of shared tasks. For example, in WMT's shared task, almost every participating team applied the ensemble technique to improve performance (Fonseca et al., 2019; Chatterjee et al., 2019; Specia et al., 2020). However, in most cases, only experimental results that improved performance by applying the ensemble technique are introduced; in-depth comparative analysis is rarely conducted (Wei et al., 2020; Park et al., 2020a; Lee et al., 2020). In this study, we attempt to investigate three main aspects regarding ensembles for machine translation.

First, we investigate the ensemble effect when using various vocab strategies and different attention models. For the vocab that plays the most important role in the machine translation ensemble, three different experimental conditions—independent vocab, share vocab, and share embedding—are applied to two different attention networks (Bahdanau et al., 2014; Vaswani et al., 2017).

Second, we investigate which among intra-ensemble and inter-ensemble is more effective for performance improvement. Notably, intra-ensemble is an ensemble of identical models, while inter-ensemble represents an ensemble between models that follow different network structures.

Third, we analyze the effect of the non-converging model on ensemble performance. Most existing studies create an ensemble using only those models that have been fitted. However, we perform in-depth comparative analysis experiments, raising the question of whether the non-converging model has only negative effects.

2 Ensemble Design

2.1 Ensemble in NMT

Ensemble prediction is a representative method for improving the translation performance of NMT systems. A commonly reported method involves aggregating predictions by training different models of the same architecture in parallel. Then, during decoding, we average the probabilities over the output layers of the target vocab at each time step.

In this study, we follow the above method for ensembles using the same model architecture (*i.e.,* intra-ensemble). Because the target vocabs are the same, ensembles of components with different model structures (*i.e.,* inter-ensemble) also follow the same method. We conduct experiments on intra- and inter-ensemble effects on LSTM-Attention (Bahdanau et al., 2014) and Transformer (Vaswani et al., 2017) networks, combined with various vocab strategies. A detailed description of the vocab strategies is provided in the next section.

Proceedings of the Second Workshop on Insights from Negative Results in NLP, pages 23–28
November 10, 2021. ©2021 Association for Computational Linguistics

2.2 Vocab Strategies

Independent vocab means learning separate weights from each encoder and decoder without any connection or communication between the source and target languages. Most NMT research follows this methodology (Cho et al., 2014; Vaswani et al., 2017; Park et al., 2021b).

Share vocab means that the model uses a common vocab for a combination of the source and target languages (Lakew et al., 2018). That is, the encoder and decoder interact within the same vocab, and can refer to each other's vocabs, thus making the model more robust.

Share embedding goes a step beyond sharing the source–target vocabs, and shares the vocab embedding matrix of the encoder and decoder (Liu et al., 2019). It enables the sharing of vocab from various languages through one integrated embedding space. Consequently, it has been widely used in recent multilingual NMT (Aharoni et al., 2019).

2.3 Experimental Design

2.3.1 Design of Intra- and Inter-ensemble

Intra-ensemble is an ensemble of identical models. We use the LSTM-Attention and Transformer networks with three different weights for the combinations to average the probabilities of ensemble. Inter-ensemble represents an ensemble of models that follow different network structures. We experiment with different combinations of the two attention-based models and vocab strategies. In this experiment, we aim to suggest directions for creating a better ensemble technique by analyzing the effect of intra- and inter-ensemble combined with the vocab strategy and size of vocabs. Moreover, all experiments compare vocab size (*i.e.,* 32k and 64k) by considering performance difference with respect to vocab capacity.

2.3.2 Design of Non-convergence Ensemble

In general, ensembles comprise well-fitted models; however, we conduct experiments to examine how models with less convergence affect the ensemble. Non-converging models are trained using ¼ of the iterations needed for convergent models. Consequently, we can determine whether non-converging models will cause only negative effects on the ensemble.

Vocab size	Cases	Baseline	Intra-ensembles			
			$\{w_1,w_2\}$	$\{w_1,w_3\}$	$\{w_2,w_3\}$	$\{w_1,w_2,w_3\}$
32,000	LSTM_{ind}	24.51	24.44 ▼	24.45 ▼	24.40 ▼	**24.47** ▼
	LSTM_{sv}	21.36	21.34 ▼	21.33 ▼	**21.49** ▲	21.36 -
	LSTM_{se}	21.49	21.40 ▼	21.47 ▼	**21.50** ▲	21.41 ▼
	Transformer_{ind}	33.40	33.71 ▲	**34.13** ▲	33.82 ▲	33.92 ▲
	Transformer_{sv}	29.23	29.48 ▲	29.80 ▲	29.70 ▲	**29.88** ▲
	Transformer_{se}	29.54	29.89 ▲	29.92 ▲	29.96 ▲	**30.19** ▲
64,000	LSTM_{ind}	25.02	24.86 ▼	24.98 ▼	24.96 ▼	**25.03** ▲
	LSTM_{sv}	22.89	22.83 ▼	22.79 ▼	**22.92** ▲	22.79 ▼
	LSTM_{se}	22.94	22.92 ▼	22.91 ▼	22.95 ▲	**22.98** ▲
	Transformer_{ind}	32.45	33.75 ▲	33.82 ▲	33.91 ▲	**33.97** ▲
	Transformer_{sv}	30.37	30.60 ▲	30.80 ▲	**31.02** ▲	30.97 ▲
	Transformer_{se}	30.82	30.96 ▲	31.22 ▲	31.14 ▲	**31.28** ▲

Table 1: Performance of intra-ensembles (combinations of vocab sizes and attention networks). The baseline score is the average of the three models that have different weights. Note that the bold numbers indicate the best score in each case.

3 Experimental Settings and Results

3.1 Experimental Setup

In this study, we use the Korean–English parallel corpus released on AI Hub [1] as the training data (Park and Lim, 2020). Several studies (Park et al., 2020b, 2021a) have adopted this corpus for Korean language NMT research. The total amount of sentence pairs is 1.6M. We randomly extract 5k sentence pairs twice from the training data, and use these data for the validation and test sets.

We employ sentencepiece (Kudo and Richardson, 2018) for subword tokenization. The performance evaluation of all the translation results are proceeds with BLEU score by leveraging multi-bleu.perl script given by Moses.

3.2 Results

Our negative findings and their insights are illustrated by **NF** and **Insight**, respectively. The performance results of the baseline models (seen as recipes of an ensemble) are shown in Tables 1 to 4.

3.2.1 Comparison of Intra-ensemble Effect

We show the results of applying the vocab strategies to two different models, namely LSTM-Attention and Transformer with three different weights (*i.e.,* w_1, w_2, and w_3) for intra-ensemble in Table 1. Additionally, we compare the combinations of those weights to investigate the apparent intra-ensemble effect.

Table 1 shows the significant variation in ensemble effect, according to the vocab strategies. The Transformer and LSTM-Attention models exhibit the highest performance in the order of independent vocab (ind), share embedding (se), and share

[1] `https://aihub.or.kr/aidata/87`

vocab (sv) in both vocab sizes (32k and 64k, respectively).

NF1: *Although Lakew et al. (2018); Park et al. (2021a) found that share vocab (sv) is effective when subword tokenization is applied as a pre-tokenize step during training, it has a negative effect in model training.* However, we find that sharing the vocab improves performance; nevertheless, sharing the embedding space is more helpful. However, training with independent vocab strategy shows the highest performance without interference.

To an in-depth examination, we analyze the intra-ensemble performance with respect to four aspects: i) different attention models, ii) vocab strategy, iii) vocab size, and iv) the number of models in the ensemble.

i) Different attention models We investigate the influence of the different attention networks on an ensemble. Self-attention-based networks refine (▲) all vocab strategies; however, there are more cases without performance improvement than those with performance improvement using the Bahdanau attention-based networks. That is, **NF2:** *specifically, with the Bahdanau attention network, there is a case in which a negative result (▼) occurred in an ensemble.* This result is interpreted as a difference in the robustness (*i.e.,* with minimum performance degradation) and capacity (*i.e.,* parallelism) of the model, as the following interpretations show. The Bahdanau attention network is exposed to problems with long-term dependencies (Bengio et al., 1993), resulting in the weak processing of long-sequences and requiring more data than self-attention. Furthermore, the Bahdanau attention network is well-known for not being context-aware, leading to variance in model prediction (Gao et al., 2021). Thus, **Insight:** *it can be seen that there is a lack of capacity and robustness in the Bahdanau attention network. Owing to this, it can be inferred that this network has a negative influence on the ensemble effect.*

ii) Vocab strategy We observe that there is performance variation among the vocab strategies. Our finding is in line with the aforementioned result in terms of the ensemble effect being the same as the ordering in LSTM-Attention, which is *ind, se* and *sv*. This is reasonable because of the previous result; however, **NF3:** *mixing the vocab (i.e., sv) has a negative effect on the ensemble performance.*

Vocab size	Cases	Intra (Baseline)	Inter
32,000	LSTM_{ind} + Transformer_{ind}	34.13	31.70 (-2.43)
	LSTM_{sv} + Transformer_{sv}	29.88	27.46 (-2.42)
	LSTM_{se} + Transformer_{se}	30.19	27.25 (-2.94)
64,000	LSTM_{ind} + Transformer_{ind}	33.97	31.95 (-2.02)
	LSTM_{sv} + Transformer_{sv}	31.02	28.98 (-2.04)
	LSTM_{se} + Transformer_{se}	31.28	28.97 (-2.31)

Table 2: Performance of inter-ensembles (combinations of vocab sizes and attention networks). Here, the column "Intra" records the highest score among the two different models, according to each vocabulary strategy in Table 1.

iii) Vocab size As illustrated in Table 1, the performance of intra-ensemble models shows vast differences owing to vocab sizes. We confirm that a vocab size of 64k is more effective than that of 32k; consequently, we theorize that vocab size is closely related to the effect of ensemble. In the Transformer ensemble with independent vocab (*i.e.,* Transformer_{ind}), the BLEU score is improved by 0.73 in the baseline model at 32k; in contrast, the BLEU score is improved by 1.52 at 64k, which is an improvement of more than two times. In other words, **NF4:** *even a slight alteration of vocab size significantly affects the ensemble performance*, and we know that a broader capacity leads to better performance when conducting vocab prediction using softmax.

iv) Number of ensemble models We explore the number of ensembles, and further validate the performance using the model combinations. **NF5:** *Contrary to the expectation that the number and performance of the ensemble models would show a positive correlation, this was not the case.* As shown in Table 1, only six cases, i.e., 50% of the 12 cases, demonstrate a good score in the three models ($\{w_1, w_2, w_3\}$) of the ensemble. The remaining six cases demonstrate a good score in two models ($\{w_1, w_3\}$, $\{w_2, w_3\}$). This result proves the statement of NF5.

3.2.2 Intra-ensemble or Inter-ensemble?

Inter-ensemble is feasible if the same vocab is used across the two models. Therefore, an ensemble of Transformer and LSTM-Attention model with the corresponding vocab strategy can be created; a comparison of the performance results with intra-ensembles is presented in Table 1. The results for inter-ensembles are shown in Table 2.

This result shows that the baseline (*i.e.,* Intra) exhibits better performance than inter-ensembles. Notably, inter-ensembles show a negative effect.

Vocab size	Cases	Baseline		Intra-ensembles with non-convergence							
		Best Intra	w_{nc}	$\{w_{nc}, w_1\}$	$\{w_{nc}, w_2\}$	$\{w_{nc}, w_3\}$	$\{w_{nc}, w_1, w_2\}$	$\{w_{nc}, w_1, w_3\}$	$\{w_{nc}, w_2, w_3\}$	$\{w_{nc}, w_1, w_2, w_3\}$	$\Delta\%$
32,000	LSTM_{ind}	**24.47**	19.06	22.84	22.79	22.84	23.54	23.53	23.56	23.75	-4.93
	LSTM_{sv}	**21.49**	16.11	19.25	19.32	19.31	20.14	20.11	20.28	21.42	-7.05
	LSTM_{se}	**21.50**	17.20	19.94	20.13	20.12	20.71	20.65	20.77	20.92	-4.82
	Transformer_{ind}	**34.13**	31.87	33.37	33.87	33.70	33.83	34.03	34.12	34.04	-0.82
	Transformer_{sv}	**29.88**	27.81	28.94	28.94	29.38	29.53	29.42	29.51	29.59	-1.84
	Transformer_{se}	**30.19**	27.72	29.01	29.23	29.56	29.67	29.96	29.83	29.93	-1.96
64,000	LSTM_{ind}	**25.03**	19.54	23.57	23.74	23.64	24.55	24.53	24.37	24.56	-3.57
	LSTM_{sv}	**22.92**	18.87	21.76	21.76	21.77	22.35	22.36	22.39	22.54	-3.43
	LSTM_{se}	**22.98**	17.64	21.07	21.21	21.22	22.09	22.11	22.15	22.43	-5.33
	Transformer_{ind}	33.97	31.22	33.23	33.68	33.71	33.79	33.85	34.14 ▲	**34.29** ▲	-0.46
	Transformer_{sv}	31.02	28.73	29.90	30.50	30.64	30.52	30.80	**31.03** ▲	30.90	-1.31
	Transformer_{se}	**31.28**	28.41	30.16	30.48	30.62	30.79	31.05	31.05	31.18	-1.66

Table 3: Performance of combinations of intra-ensembles using non-convergence models (w_{nc}) with vocab sizes and attention networks. $\Delta\%$ represents the average relative rate (i.e., the difference) $\{w_{nc}, w_1\}$ to $\{w_{nc}, w_1, w_2, w_3\}$ over "Best Intra." Note that the bold numbers represent the best score in each case.

Vocab size	Cases	Baseline	Inter-Ensembles			$\Delta\%$
		Best Inter	C(LSTM) & NC(Transformer)	NC(LSTM) & C(Transformer)	NC(LSTM) & NC(Transformer)	
32,000	LSTM_{ind} + Transformer_{ind}	**31.70**	30.40	29.74	28.09	-7.22
	LSTM_{sv} + Transformer_{sv}	**27.46**	26.22	25.32	23.64	-8.74
	LSTM_{se} + Transformer_{se}	**27.25**	26.12	25.66	24.30	-6.94
64,000	LSTM_{ind} + Transformer_{ind}	**31.95**	30.87	30.26	28.96	-6.01
	LSTM_{sv} + Transformer_{sv}	**28.98**	27.41	27.56	26.15	-6.70
	LSTM_{se} + Transformer_{se}	**28.97**	27.21	27.16	24.99	-8.69

Table 4: Performance of combinations of inter-ensembles with non-convergence (NC) and convergence (C) conditions along with vocab sizes and attention networks. $\Delta\%$ represents the average relative rate (i.e., the differences), from first to third columns, of inter-ensembles over "Best Inter." Note that the bold numbers indicate the best score in each case.

That is, **NF6:** *inter-ensemble exhibits a negative effect on performance, resulting in performance degradation in all cases.* It seems that the heterogeneous model architecture from the two different models acted as a hindrance to performance improvement.

3.2.3 Does Non-convergence Ensemble Cause Negative Results?

In this section, we investigate the effect of non-convergence on intra- and inter-ensembles. We choose the model with the best score (intra- and inter-ensembles) from Table 1 and Table 2, respectively, as target models for comparison.

The performance results of intra- and inter-ensemble with non-convergence models are illustrated in Table 3 and Table 4, respectively.

Intra-ensemble In Table 3, intra-ensemble with a non-convergence model leads to negative results compared to the baseline model (*i.e.,* Best Intra) in LSTM-Attention. Using the Transformer model as a baseline generally lead to performance degradation; however, the decrease is relatively small. There are a few exceptions (▲) that show that non-converging models with Transformer sometimes perform better when ensembled together.

These results revealed that **NF7:** *the Transformer model is more robust than the LSTM-Attention model and stronger under adverse conditions.* Additionally, it is inferred that the underfitted model plays a role in noise injection, boosting performance. **Insight:** *This result is a meaningful in that even a non-convergence model, which many researchers neglect, can help improve performance.*

Inter-ensemble As detailed in Table 4, the performance decreased in all cases, and **NF8:** *non-converging model causes a highly negative result in inter-ensembles compared to intra-ensembles.* In conclusion, inter-ensemble provide negative results in all cases for the experiments conducted in this study.

4 Conclusion

Most researchers consider it common sense that ensembles are better; however, few studies have conducted any type of close verification. In this study, we perform various tests based on three experimental designs related to the ensemble technique, and demonstrate its negative aspects. Thus, we provide insights into the positives and negatives of ensembling for machine translation. In the future, we plan to conduct expanded experiments based on different language pairs.

Acknowledgments

This work was supported by Institute for Information communications Technology Planning & Evaluation(IITP) grant funded by the Korea government(MSIT) (No. 2020-0-00368, A Neural-Symbolic Model for Knowledge Acquisition and Inference Techniques) and MSIT(Ministry of Science and ICT), Korea, under the ICT Creative Consilience program(IITP-2021-2020-0-01819) supervised by the IITP(Institute for Information & communications Technology Planning Evaluation)

References

Roee Aharoni, Melvin Johnson, and Orhan Firat. 2019. Massively multilingual neural machine translation. *arXiv preprint arXiv:1903.00089*.

Dzmitry Bahdanau, Kyunghyun Cho, and Yoshua Bengio. 2014. Neural machine translation by jointly learning to align and translate. *arXiv preprint arXiv:1409.0473*.

Yoshua Bengio, Paolo Frasconi, and Patrice Simard. 1993. The problem of learning long-term dependencies in recurrent networks. In *IEEE international conference on neural networks*, pages 1183–1188. IEEE.

Rajen Chatterjee, Christian Federmann, Matteo Negri, and Marco Turchi. 2019. Findings of the wmt 2019 shared task on automatic post-editing. In *Proceedings of the Fourth Conference on Machine Translation (Volume 3: Shared Task Papers, Day 2)*, pages 11–28.

Kyunghyun Cho, Bart Van Merriënboer, Caglar Gulcehre, Dzmitry Bahdanau, Fethi Bougares, Holger Schwenk, and Yoshua Bengio. 2014. Learning phrase representations using rnn encoder-decoder for statistical machine translation. *arXiv preprint arXiv:1406.1078*.

Erick Fonseca, Lisa Yankovskaya, André FT Martins, Mark Fishel, and Christian Federmann. 2019. Findings of the wmt 2019 shared tasks on quality estimation. In *Proceedings of the Fourth Conference on Machine Translation (Volume 3: Shared Task Papers, Day 2)*, pages 1–10.

Peng Gao, Shijie Geng, Xiaogang Wang, Jifeng Dai, and Hongsheng Li. 2021. Scalable transformers for neural machine translation. *arXiv preprint arXiv:2106.02242*.

Ekaterina Garmash and Christof Monz. 2016. Ensemble learning for multi-source neural machine translation. In *Proceedings of COLING 2016, the 26th International Conference on Computational Linguistics: Technical Papers*, pages 1409–1418.

Taku Kudo and John Richardson. 2018. Sentencepiece: A simple and language independent subword tokenizer and detokenizer for neural text processing. *arXiv preprint arXiv:1808.06226*.

Surafel M Lakew, Aliia Erofeeva, Matteo Negri, Marcello Federico, and Marco Turchi. 2018. Transfer learning in multilingual neural machine translation with dynamic vocabulary. *arXiv preprint arXiv:1811.01137*.

Jihyung Lee, WonKee Lee, Jaehun Shin, Baikjin Jung, Young-Gil Kim, and Jong-Hyeok Lee. 2020. Postech-etri's submission to the wmt2020 ape shared task: Automatic post-editing with cross-lingual language model. In *Proceedings of the Fifth Conference on Machine Translation*, pages 777–782.

Xuebo Liu, Derek F Wong, Yang Liu, Lidia S Chao, Tong Xiao, and Jingbo Zhu. 2019. Shared-private bilingual word embeddings for neural machine translation. *arXiv preprint arXiv:1906.03100*.

Chanjun Park, Sugyeong Eo, Hyeonseok Moon, and Heui-Seok Lim. 2021a. Should we find another model?: Improving neural machine translation performance with one-piece tokenization method without model modification. In *Proceedings of the 2021 Conference of the North American Chapter of the Association for Computational Linguistics: Human Language Technologies: Industry Papers*, pages 97–104.

Chanjun Park, Chanhee Lee, Yeongwook Yang, and Heuiseok Lim. 2020a. Ancient korean neural machine translation. *IEEE Access*, 8:116617–116625.

Chanjun Park and Heuiseok Lim. 2020. A study on the performance improvement of machine translation using public korean-english parallel corpus. *Journal of Digital Convergence*, 18(6):271–277.

Chanjun Park, Kinam Park, Hyeonseok Moon, Sugyeong Eo, and Heuiseok Lim. 2021b. A study on performance improvement considering the balance between corpus in neural machine translation. *Journal of the Korea Convergence Society*, 12(5):23–29.

Chanjun Park, Yeongwook Yang, Kinam Park, and Heuiseok Lim. 2020b. Decoding strategies for improving low-resource machine translation. *Electronics*, 9(10):1562.

Lucia Specia, Zhenhao Li, Juan Pino, Vishrav Chaudhary, Francisco Guzmán, Graham Neubig, Nadir Durrani, Yonatan Belinkov, Philipp Koehn, Hassan Sajjad, et al. 2020. Findings of the wmt 2020 shared task on machine translation robustness. In *Proceedings of the Fifth Conference on Machine Translation*, pages 76–91.

Liang Tan, Lin Li, Yifeng Han, Dong Li, Kaixi Hu, Dong Zhou, and Peipei Wang. 2020. An empirical study on ensemble learning of multimodal machine translation. In *2020 IEEE Sixth International Conference on Multimedia Big Data (BigMM)*, pages 63–69. IEEE.

Ashish Vaswani, Noam Shazeer, Niki Parmar, Jakob Uszkoreit, Llion Jones, Aidan N Gomez, Łukasz Kaiser, and Illia Polosukhin. 2017. Attention is all you need. In *Advances in neural information processing systems*, pages 5998–6008.

Daimeng Wei, Hengchao Shang, Zhanglin Wu, Zhengzhe Yu, Liangyou Li, Jiaxin Guo, Minghan Wang, Hao Yang, Lizhi Lei, Ying Qin, et al. 2020. Hw-tsc's participation in the wmt 2020 news translation shared task. In *Proceedings of the Fifth Conference on Machine Translation*, pages 293–299.

Finetuning Pretrained Transformers into Variational Autoencoders

Seongmin Park **Jihwa Lee**
ActionPower
Seoul, Republic of Korea
{seongmin.park, jihwa.lee}@actionpower.kr

Abstract

Text variational autoencoders (VAEs) are notorious for *posterior collapse*, a phenomenon where the model's decoder learns to ignore signals from the encoder. Because posterior collapse is known to be exacerbated by expressive decoders, Transformers have seen limited adoption as components of text VAEs. Existing studies that incorporate Transformers into text VAEs (Li et al., 2020; Fang et al., 2021) mitigate posterior collapse using massive pretraining, a technique unavailable to most of the research community without extensive computing resources. We present a simple two-phase training scheme to convert a sequence-to-sequence Transformer into a VAE with just *finetuning*. The resulting language model is competitive with massively pretrained Transformer-based VAEs in some internal metrics while falling short on others. To facilitate training we comprehensively explore the impact of common posterior collapse alleviation techniques in the literature. We release our code for reproducability[1].

1 Introduction

Properly tamed latent models offer explainable and interpolatable representations of observed data. Recent works have shown such models to be especially useful in unsupervised learning settings. He et al. (2019) adapt a generative latent text model for successful unsupervised text style transfer and machine translation. Li et al. (2020) achieve superior language modeling performance against common conditional counterparts.

A popular variant of deep latent models is the variational autoencoder (VAE) (Kingma and Welling, 2014). For each observed **x**, the model assumes the existence of a corresponding multi-dimensional latent vector **z**. Since the log evidence $\log p(x)$ is intractable for most interesting problems, the training process for VAEs opts instead to minimize the log evidence lower bound (ELBO):

$$E_{z\sim q(z|x)}[log(p(x|z))] - D_{KL}(q(z|x)||p(z)) \quad (1)$$

$q(z|x)$ is a tractable, assumed posterior commonly modeled with a parametrized encoder $q_\phi(z|x)$, while $p(x|z)$ is the likelihood parametrized with a decoder $p_\theta(x|z)$ that optimizes against reconstruction loss. While effective in theory, a common empirical challenge VAEs present during training is posterior collapse – a phenomenon where the decoder ignores the latent signal from **z** (and thus the originating input) during reconstruction. Posterior collapse can be diagnosed by checking if $D_{KL}(q(z|x)||p(z))$ tends to zero during training.

After Bowman et al. (2016) adopted VAE for text, subsequent studies have been introduced with attempts to mitigate posterior collapse in VAE language models (LMs). However, the brittle training process of VAE LMs remains an unsolved problem.

Li et al. (2020) present a method to utilize deep Transformer (Vaswani et al., 2017) models as components of VAE LMs. Transformer-based VAEs tap into the state-of-the-art capabilities of Transformers while retaining representational advantages of VAE LMs. The paper mitigates posterior collapse by massive pretraining and a cyclical annealing schedule (Fu et al., 2019).

While the study presents a promising outlook for Transformer VAEs, the suggested method is not accessible to researchers who lack access to large, target-domain-specific corpora or the computing power for massive LM pretraining. Therefore, a demand arises for a way to finetune an existing Transformer model into a VAE LM with limited resources. Our research attempts to fill this gap in the literature, and makes the following contributions:

- We present a simple but reliable (as replicated across several datasets) scheme to teach latent

[1] https://github.com/seongminp/transformers-into-vaes

Proceedings of the Second Workshop on Insights from Negative Results in NLP, pages 29–35
November 10, 2021.

structure to a pretrained Transformer model by just finetuning.

- We convert a pretrained sequence-to-sequence Transformer into a VAE, instead of using two separate encoder-only (Devlin et al., 2019) and decoder-only (Radford et al., 2019) Transformers as in previous literature. This eliminates the need to maintain separate tokenizers and configurations for encoder and decoder.

- We conduct ablation studies and extensive experiments to gauge the effectiveness of commonly used posterior collapse mitigation methods in taming Transformer VAEs.

The resulting model extends existing Transformer architectures and can be initialized from pretrained non-latent model checkpoints.

2 Background

2.1 Transformer Text VAEs

Most VAE LMs employ recurrent neural networks (RNNs) as encoders and decoders. This is in part because enforcing a latent bottleneck layer undermines the effectiveness of encoder-decoder cross-attention in Transformers, and in significant part due to the co-occurrence of posterior collapse and powerful and deep decoder layers. Li et al. (2020) overcome such training difficulties by massively increasing the number of training samples (104,213,036 sentences) for LM pretraining.

Liu and Liu (2019) and Fang et al. (2021) also finds success with Transformer VAEs for text generation. To avoid posterior collapse, Fang et al. (2021) follow the exact cyclic KL mitigation approach as that of Li et al. (2020), while Liu and Liu (2019) introduce noise to network input.

2.2 Techniques to mitigate posterior collapse

This study identifies and explores the effect of popular posterior collapse mitigation methods in low-resource Transformer VAE training. We do not examine importance-weighted autoencoders (Burda et al., 2016) and semi-amortized autoencoders (Kim et al., 2018) to limit the scope of our experiments to unsophisticated prior distributions.

2.2.1 KL Weighting / Annealing

Bowman et al. (2016) increases the KL term of the ELBO from zero to its full value during early stages of training, where the decoder learns to simply treat latent signal **z** as noise. Fu et al. (2019) extend this technique by cyclically manipulating the weight of the KL term. β-VAE (Higgins et al., 2017) and Yan et al. (2020) adopt a similar approach.

2.2.2 Encoder warm-up (Li et al., 2019)

We train the network without the KL term of the ELBO and retain encoder weights before jointly training the whole network.

2.2.3 Input text denoising (Shen et al., 2020)

Denoising text inputs by deleting random tokens motivate autoencoders (AEs) to learn better latent representations. Our study compares 0%, 15%, and 40% deletion noising schemes.

2.2.4 KL thresholding (Kingma et al., 2016)

KL-thresholding enforces a minimum λ for each dimension of the KL term in the ELBO:

$$\mathcal{L}_{D_{KL}} = \sum_i max[\lambda, D_{kl}(q_\phi(z_i|x)||p(z_i))] \quad (2)$$

where z_i is a single dimension of **z**.

2.2.5 Encoder pooling (Long et al., 2019)

Instead of using the last hidden state as encoder output, averaging or taking the maximum of all encoder hidden states results in a more diverse latent representation. We experiment with both mean- and max-pooling schemes from the encoder.

3 Model architecture

We extend the T5 architecture (Raffel et al., 2020) into a VAE. We modify a popular pretrained T5 model (Wolf et al., 2020) that deviates minimally from the original Transformer (Figure 1).

Hidden states from all layers of T5's encoder $q_\phi(z|x)$ are mean- or max-pooled into a vector $h_{pooled} \in R^H$, where H is the encoder's hidden dimension.

Assumed prior $q(z)$'s mean μ and log variance σ vectors of dimension L is obtained from h_{pooled}:

$$\mu = h_{pooled}W_\mu,\ log\sigma = h_{pooled}W_\sigma \quad (3)$$

where $W_\mu, W_\sigma \in R^L$.

As in a standard VAE, a stochastic latent vector **z** is sampled using the reparameterization trick to enable back-propagation through sampling:

$$z = \mu + \sigma \odot \epsilon,\ \epsilon \sim \mathcal{N}(0,1) \quad (4)$$

We pass **z** into the decoder $p_\theta(x|z)$ as the only component of decoder's cross attention. Our

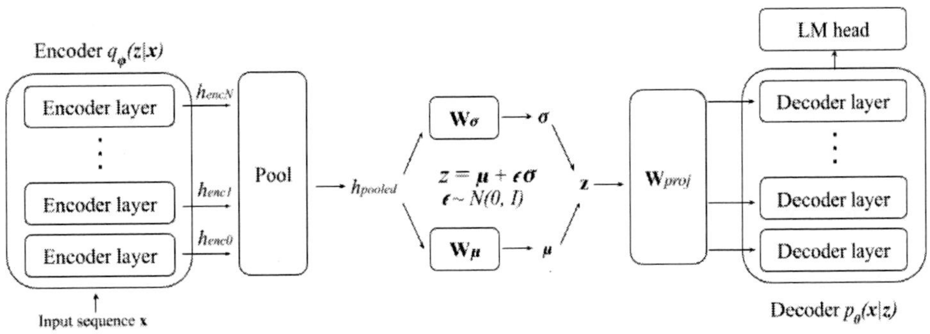

Figure 1: Transformer VAE architecture. A "bottleneck" step (W_σ and W_μ) is placed between the encoder and the decoder of T5. Latent information from pooled encoder hidden states is captured in the bottleneck layer before being passed to the decoder. The network is optimized against regularization loss in the bottleneck and reconstruction loss at the decoder.

method injects **z** into every layer of the decoder as in previous literature (Li et al., 2020; Fang et al., 2021), but deviates in two important ways: first, we pass **z** as the sole key and value of encoder-decoder cross attention, instead of self-attention; second, we project z into the correct dimension ($L \times A \times S$, where L is the decoder layer count, A is the number of attention heads, and S is the embedding dimension per head) with a feed-forward network, instead of taking a copy of **z** to inject to each decoder layer.

$$(K_{ca}, V_{ca}) = (zW_{proj}, zW_{proj}) \tag{5}$$

where $W_{proj} \in R^{L \times A \times S}$ and K_{ca} and V_{ca} are key and value in decoder cross-attention.

4 Experiments

During preliminary experiments, posterior collapse was observed in all training schemes without encoder warmup training. The decoder learns to ignore the initially noisy input signal from the encoder. Thus, we compose our finetuning method in two separate phases.

Phase 1 - Encoder warmup: Weight of KL loss is set to zero, making our model's objective function similar to that of an AE. Different input denoising percentages, encoder pooling strategies, latent dimension sizes, and decoder freezing configurations are compared.

Phase 2 - Full finetuning: KL loss is reinstated and full VAE training are conducted. We compare different input denoising percentages, encoder pooling strategies, KL annealing schedules, and KL thresholds.

We run our proposed two-phase finetuning training scheme on four standard VAE LM benchmark datasets: PTB (Marcus et al., 1993), SNLI (Bowman et al., 2016), Yahoo (Yang et al., 2017), and Yelp (Shen et al., 2017).

Following Li et al. (2020) and Li et al. (2019), we perform intrinsic evaluation of our proposed Transformer VAE architecture. We report perplexity (PPL), KL-divergence between model posterior and assumed posterior (KL), and negative ELBO on the test set. To assess the quality of learned latent codes, we also report mutual information (MI) (Hoffman and Johnson, 2016) and the number of active units (AU) (Burda et al., 2016). MI measures the dependence of latent codes to encoder input. AU measures the covariance between encoder input and latent codes.

Experimental hyperparameters such as specific annealing schedules and training epochs per phase are detailed in the appendix.

5 Results

5.1 Phase 1

We find that freezing the decoder and the memory projection layer W_{proj} while training with an AE objective is crucial in learning meaningful encoder outputs. Denoising is important for datasets with longer inputs (Yahoo, Yelp), but not critical in datasets with shorter input lengths (PTB, SNLI). Mean-pooling encoder hidden states presents a trade-off between MI and AU. Max-pooling consistently learns more informative encoder representations. Changes in MI and AU during training is illustrated in Figure 2.

Latent dimensions of 64 and 128 were also tested. Increasing the latent dimension did not necessarily boost representational quality in terms

Model	PPL↓	KL	-ELBO↓	MI↑	AU↑
Optimus ($\lambda = 0.5$) (Li et al., 2020)	23.11	17.45	301.21	8.85	32
GPT-2 (Radford et al., 2019)	22.00	-	-	-	-
Encoder pretraining ($\lambda = 3$) (Li et al., 2019)	59.24	7.44	328.73	6.41	32
Ours (Max pool)	20.90	0.21	343.02	0.04	0
Ours (Max pool + Denoise)	30.13	41.49	301.86	1.32	24
Ours (Max pool + Denoise + KLT)	60.44	119.89	223.69	4.73	29
Ours (Max pool + Denoise + KLT + Deep)	54.40	155.50	140.57	5.43	28

Table 1: Phase 2 results on Yahoo. Due to space constraints, we report experimental results on other datasets in the appendix. Results on baselines are quoted from Li et al. (2020) and (Li et al., 2019). KLT denotes KL thresholding with $\lambda = 3$. Our models are finetuned from a pretrained 6-layer T5, except the deep variant with 12 layers.

of AU percentage. For latent dimensions of 32 and 64, 90% of latent dimension units were activated in best-performing models. For latent dimension of 128, around 60% of latent units were active.

Another interesting observation is that KL divergence on the validation set, although not part of the AE training objective, plateaus after repeated training. We regard this phenomenon as the signal of convergence in terms of representation quality.

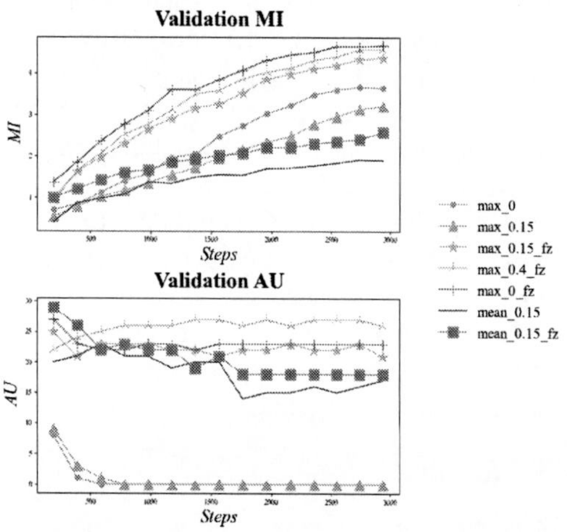

Figure 2: Phase 1 training on Yahoo. Labels are in the form *{pooling strategy}_{denoise percentage}_{decoder frozen}*.

5.2 Phase 2

We observe, as in previous literature, a trade-off between language modeling PPL and representation quality metrics (MI and AU). This trade-off is exacerbated when using KL thresholding. While KL thresholding does significantly increase latent representation capabilities, it is not in itself sufficient in preventing posterior collapse.

Denoising and encoder pooling configurations display the same characteristics as in Phase 1. No version of the experiment existed where cyclical annealing schedule was able to prevent posterior collapse, a result not in accordance with Li et al. (2020). Figure 3 illustrates the training progression of Phase 2.

We also experimented with increasing model depth from 6 layers to 12 layers. Our proposed two-phase training scheme prevents posterior collapse for deeper models as well, resulting in higher performance in most metrics compared to 6-layer models. Results are reported in Table 1. Note that lower PPL does not necessarily indicate better language modeling capabilities, since models with collapsed posterior display better PPL.

Rows with KL above zero indicate successful aversion of posterior collapse.

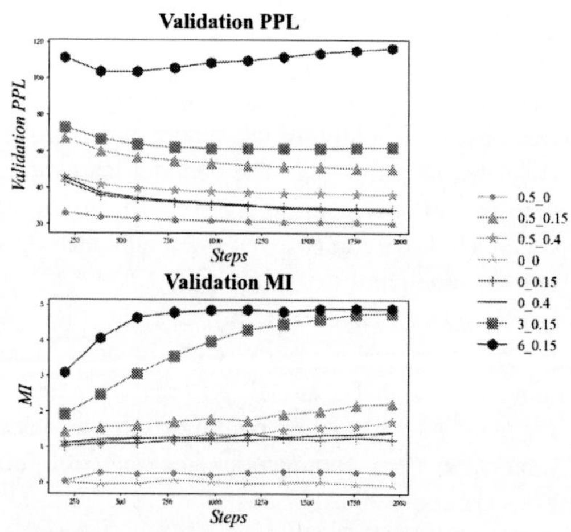

Figure 3: Phase 2 training on Yahoo. Labels are in the form *{KL threshold}_{denoise percentage}*. Encoder hidden states in plotted experiments were max-pooled.

In the literature, no consensus yet exists on the optimal value of KL in training VAEs. Overall, we find that a denoising scheme between 0.15 and 0.4 in both phases, coupled with a low (0.5) KL threshold strikes a good balance between reconstruction and latent representation quality.

6 Conclusions and Future Work

This paper explores common methods in the literature for combatting posterior collapse, and the extent to which they help in teaching latent information to pretrained Transformer models.

Comprehensive experiments show that commonly employed posterior collapse mitigation techniques provide meaningful benefits in transforming existing language models into latent-aware architectures. Among the tested procedures, we find that Li et al. (2019)'s two-step training, coupled with Shen et al. (2020)'s denoising through token deletion, was the most impactful in mitigating posterior collapse. However, language models obtained via only finetuning exhibit consistent trade-offs between their latent representation metrics (MI, AU) and language model metrics (PPL). Optimizing our model to be competitive with massively pretrained baselines in one of the two metrics results in the model falling behind in the other.

We also find that increasing training epochs further improves the impact of tested techniques, a result consistent with previous literature on large-scale text VAE pretraining.

From our experiments, we identify several questions to be answered by future research. The impact of homogenizing finetuning (as suggested in this paper) and original pretraining objectives on language model metrics has to be further explored. While the original T5 architecture was also pretrained with a self-supervised denoising scheme, the model employs mask tokens for denoising, contrary to simple token deletions suggested by this paper.

Our findings also highlight the need for an established heuristic to interpret the quality of latent representations learned by language models. The research community has yet to decide on the optimal value of KL-divergence between the assumed prior and the model posterior to target during text VAE training. Empirical guidelines to dictate even a vague threshold for the KL-divergence, below which we declare the occurrence of posterior collapse, will help both training and evaluation of latent-aware language models.

References

Samuel Bowman, Luke Vilnis, Oriol Vinyals, Andrew Dai, Rafal Jozefowicz, and Samy Bengio. 2016. Generating sentences from a continuous space. In *Proceedings of The 20th SIGNLL Conference on Computational Natural Language Learning*, pages 10–21.

Yuri Burda, Roger B Grosse, and Ruslan Salakhutdinov. 2016. Importance weighted autoencoders. In *ICLR (Poster)*.

Jacob Devlin, Ming-Wei Chang, Kenton Lee, and Kristina Toutanova. 2019. BERT: Pre-training of deep bidirectional transformers for language understanding. In *Proceedings of the 2019 Conference of the North American Chapter of the Association for Computational Linguistics: Human Language Technologies, Volume 1 (Long and Short Papers)*, pages 4171–4186, Minneapolis, Minnesota. Association for Computational Linguistics.

Le Fang, Tao Zeng, Chaochun Liu, Liefeng Bo, Wen Dong, and Changyou Chen. 2021. Transformer-based conditional variational autoencoder for controllable story generation. *arXiv preprint arXiv:2101.00828*.

Hao Fu, Chunyuan Li, Xiaodong Liu, Jianfeng Gao, Asli Celikyilmaz, and Lawrence Carin. 2019. Cyclical annealing schedule: A simple approach to mitigating kl vanishing. In *Proceedings of the 2019 Conference of the North American Chapter of the Association for Computational Linguistics: Human Language Technologies, Volume 1 (Long and Short Papers)*, pages 240–250.

Junxian He, Xinyi Wang, Graham Neubig, and Taylor Berg-Kirkpatrick. 2019. A probabilistic formulation of unsupervised text style transfer. In *International Conference on Learning Representations*.

Irina Higgins, Loïc Matthey, Arka Pal, Christopher Burgess, Xavier Glorot, Matthew Botvinick, Shakir Mohamed, and Alexander Lerchner. 2017. beta-vae: Learning basic visual concepts with a constrained variational framework. In *5th International Conference on Learning Representations, ICLR 2017, Toulon, France, April 24-26, 2017, Conference Track Proceedings*. OpenReview.net.

Matthew D Hoffman and Matthew J Johnson. 2016. Elbo surgery: yet another way to carve up the variational evidence lower bound. In *Workshop in Advances in Approximate Bayesian Inference, NIPS*, volume 1.

Yoon Kim, Sam Wiseman, Andrew Miller, David Sontag, and Alexander Rush. 2018. Semi-amortized variational autoencoders. In *Proceedings of the 35th International Conference on Machine Learning*, volume 80 of *Proceedings of Machine Learning Research*, pages 2678–2687. PMLR.

Diederik P. Kingma and Max Welling. 2014. Auto-Encoding Variational Bayes. In *2nd International Conference on Learning Representations, ICLR 2014, Banff, AB, Canada, April 14-16, 2014, Conference Track Proceedings*.

Durk P Kingma, Tim Salimans, Rafal Jozefowicz, Xi Chen, Ilya Sutskever, and Max Welling. 2016. Improved variational inference with inverse autoregressive flow. In *Advances in Neural Information Processing Systems*, volume 29. Curran Associates, Inc.

Bohan Li, Junxian He, Graham Neubig, Taylor Berg-Kirkpatrick, and Yiming Yang. 2019. A surprisingly effective fix for deep latent variable modeling of text. In *Proceedings of the 2019 Conference on Empirical Methods in Natural Language Processing and the 9th International Joint Conference on Natural Language Processing (EMNLP-IJCNLP)*, pages 3603–3614, Hong Kong, China. Association for Computational Linguistics.

Chunyuan Li, Xiang Gao, Yuan Li, Baolin Peng, Xiujun Li, Yizhe Zhang, and Jianfeng Gao. 2020. Optimus: Organizing sentences via pre-trained modeling of a latent space. In *Proceedings of the 2020 Conference on Empirical Methods in Natural Language Processing (EMNLP)*, pages 4678–4699.

Danyang Liu and Gongshen Liu. 2019. A transformer-based variational autoencoder for sentence generation. In *2019 International Joint Conference on Neural Networks (IJCNN)*, pages 1–7. IEEE.

Teng Long, Yanshuai Cao, and Jackie Chi Kit Cheung. 2019. Preventing posterior collapse in sequence vaes with pooling. *arXiv e-prints*, pages arXiv–1911.

Ilya Loshchilov and Frank Hutter. 2019. Decoupled weight decay regularization. In *International Conference on Learning Representations*.

Mitchell P. Marcus, Beatrice Santorini, and Mary Ann Marcinkiewicz. 1993. Building a large annotated corpus of English: The Penn Treebank. *Computational Linguistics*, 19(2):313–330.

Alec Radford, Jeff Wu, Rewon Child, David Luan, Dario Amodei, and Ilya Sutskever. 2019. Language models are unsupervised multitask learners.

Colin Raffel, Noam Shazeer, Adam Roberts, Katherine Lee, Sharan Narang, Michael Matena, Yanqi Zhou, Wei Li, and Peter J. Liu. 2020. Exploring the limits of transfer learning with a unified text-to-text transformer. *Journal of Machine Learning Research*, 21(140):1–67.

Tianxiao Shen, Tao Lei, Regina Barzilay, and Tommi Jaakkola. 2017. Style transfer from non-parallel text by cross-alignment. In *Proceedings of the 31st International Conference on Neural Information Processing Systems*, NIPS'17, page 6833–6844, Red Hook, NY, USA. Curran Associates Inc.

Tianxiao Shen, Jonas Mueller, Regina Barzilay, and Tommi Jaakkola. 2020. Educating text autoencoders: Latent representation guidance via denoising. In *International Conference on Machine Learning*, pages 8719–8729. PMLR.

Ashish Vaswani, Noam Shazeer, Niki Parmar, Jakob Uszkoreit, Llion Jones, Aidan N Gomez, Ł ukasz Kaiser, and Illia Polosukhin. 2017. Attention is all you need. In *Advances in Neural Information Processing Systems*, volume 30. Curran Associates, Inc.

Thomas Wolf, Lysandre Debut, Victor Sanh, Julien Chaumond, Clement Delangue, Anthony Moi, Pierric Cistac, Tim Rault, Remi Louf, Morgan Funtowicz, Joe Davison, Sam Shleifer, Patrick von Platen, Clara Ma, Yacine Jernite, Julien Plu, Canwen Xu, Teven Le Scao, Sylvain Gugger, Mariama Drame, Quentin Lhoest, and Alexander Rush. 2020. Transformers: State-of-the-art natural language processing. In *Proceedings of the 2020 Conference on Empirical Methods in Natural Language Processing: System Demonstrations*, pages 38–45, Online. Association for Computational Linguistics.

Chaochao Yan, Sheng Wang, Jinyu Yang, Tingyang Xu, and Junzhou Huang. 2020. Re-balancing variational autoencoder loss for molecule sequence generation. In *Proceedings of the 11th ACM International Conference on Bioinformatics, Computational Biology and Health Informatics*, BCB '20, New York, NY, USA. Association for Computing Machinery.

Zichao Yang, Zhiting Hu, Ruslan Salakhutdinov, and Taylor Berg-Kirkpatrick. 2017. Improved variational autoencoders for text modeling using dilated convolutions. In *Proceedings of the 34th International Conference on Machine Learning - Volume 70*, ICML'17, page 3881–3890. JMLR.org.

A Phase 2 results on PTB, Yelp, and SNLI

Model	PPL↓	KL	-ELBO↓	MI↑	AU↑
Optimus ($\lambda = 0.5$) (Li et al., 2020)	26.69	15.72	96.82	7.64	32
GPT-2 (Radford et al., 2019)	24.23	-	-	-	-
Encoder pretraining ($\lambda = 3$) (Li et al., 2019)	96.75	3.85	101.56	3.19	32
Ours (Max pool)	51.60	0.09	104.14	0	0
Ours (Max pool + Denoise)	57.69	3.05	101.17	11	
Ours (Max pool + Denoise + KLT)	250.44	41.93	62.25	2.17	24
Ours (Max pool + Denoise + KLT + Deep)	705.73	84.28	4.95	13	

Table 2: Phase 2 results on PTB

Model	PPL↓	KL	-ELBO↓	MI↑	AU↑
Optimus ($\lambda = 0.5$) (Li et al., 2020)	22.79	15.09	344.10	9.13	32
GPT-2 (Radford et al., 2019)	23.40	-	-	-	-
Encoder pretraining ($\lambda = 3$) (Li et al., 2019)	-	-	-	-	-
Ours (Max pool)	21.65	0.25	404.54	0	0
Ours (Max pool + Denoise)	39.09	77.85	327.17	1.06	26
Ours (Max pool + Denoise + KLT)	86.71	182.24	223.34	5.46	27
Ours (Max pool + Denoise + KLT + Deep)	53.05	178.48	166.15	5.55	10

Table 3: Phase 2 results on Yelp.

Model	PPL↓	KL	-ELBO↓	MI↑	AU↑
Optimus ($\lambda = 0.5$) (Li et al., 2020)	16.67	16.35	38.50	8.89	32
GPT-2 (Radford et al., 2019)	20.24	-	-	-	-
Encoder pretraining ($\lambda = 3$) (Li et al., 2019)	21.23	5.86	33.87	5.25	32
Ours (Max pool)	12.79	0.11	34.61	0.06	0
Ours (Max pool + Denoise)	15.16	2.41	32.32	0.194	7
Ours (Max pool + Denoise + KLT)	85.88	26.12	8.62	0.88	13
Ours (Max pool + Denoise + KLT + Deep)	2358.31	74.95	43.77	5.27	17

Table 4: Phase 2 results on SNLI.

B Experimental details

For all experiments we used a AdamW optimizer (Loshchilov and Hutter, 2019) with a starting learning rate of 1×10^{-3}, $\beta_1 = 0.9$, $\beta_2 = 0.999$, and $\epsilon = 1 \times 10^{-3}$. The linear KL annealing schedule we used was as follows:

$$KL\ weight = \frac{current\ global\ step}{steps\ per\ epoch * 50} \tag{6}$$

Our slower, linear KL annealing schedule of 0 to 1 over 50 epochs yielded better empirical results than the linear schdule used in Li et al. (2019) (0 to 1 over 10 epochs). We attribute this result to the small number of training samples in our experiments.

We train for 5 epochs on Phase 1, and 3 epochs on Phase 2. While further training leads to increased MI and AU, we limit the number of epochs to confer to the spirit of this study, which is to learn latent representations with minimal training. The 5 epoch limit on Phase 1 was empirically determined as the point where encoder MI begins to plateau. Most experiments were conducted with **z** dimension of 32 for comparison with previous literature.

Are BERTs Sensitive to Native Interference in L2 Production?

Zixin Tang
The Pennsylvania State University
zqt5035@psu.edu

Prasenjit Mitra
The Pennsylvania State University
pmitra@psu.edu

David Reitter
Google Research
reitter@google.com

Abstract

With the essays part from The International Corpus Network of Asian Learners of English (ICNALE) and the TOEFL11 corpus, we fine-tuned neural language models based on BERT to predict English learners' native languages. Results showed neural models can learn to represent and detect such native language impacts, but multilingually trained models have no advantage in doing so.

1 Introduction

With globalization progress, more and more people start acquiring more than one language. Therefore, computational models and theories to better understand multilingualism among machines and humans start receiving more and more attention. Even though language models (LMs) succeeded in a wide range of tasks in natural language understanding and processing (i.e. Enguehard et al., 2017; Linzen and Leonard, 2018; Mueller et al., 2020), how to do such models process and represent languages and knowledge remain unclear. We also have few ideas about these models' abilities when facing various types of language input, such as input from non-native speakers or speakers with lower proficiency. In this study, we implemented state-of-the-art neural LMs to predict non-native (L2) speakers with different language backgrounds through native language identification tasks. Furthermore, we investigated whether cross-lingual training can help identify a language learner's writing patterns, which his native languages (L1s) can cause interference. This study wants to expand current knowledge on representations and cross-lingual components in transformer-based LMs.

2 Related Work

With developments in computer science, data sciences, and cognitive and language sciences, artificial language models (LMs) based on language representations and embeddings have received attention in multiple areas. Current deep neural LMs based on various architectures can capture syntactic information through natural language input and utilize language knowledge to complete different tasks, such as identifying specific sentence structures (Enguehard et al., 2017; Kelly et al., 2020; Marvin and Linzen, 2018) and predicting grammar acceptability (Warstadt et al., 2019). Beyond training on a single language, multilingual neural language models could process cross-lingual tasks such as language identification and translation. Studies found that language representations in these types of models are transferable or overlapped across languages to create universal representations of grammatical structures (Chi et al., 2020). Models can also develop language-neutral components for better word alignment and improve performance on several cross-linguistic tasks (Libovický et al., 2019). However, studies indicated that these LMs have lower performance in cross-linguistic tasks such as machine translations (Libovický et al., 2019). Comparing to monolingual models, multilingual LMs have relatively lower performance and unbalanced performance in syntactic-related tasks between English and other languages (Mueller et al., 2020).

Even though transformer-based LMs showed impressive abilities in multiple tasks, few studies tried to analyze whether and how multilingual LMs identify and distinguish writers' native interference in their L2 production caused by their L1s. One task for detecting such interference across speakers is the native language identification task, which predicts a speaker's L1 using his language production in L2. By sharing representations and transferring knowledge across languages (Putnam et al., 2018; Hartsuiker et al., 2004), multilingual speakers can have different structures, preferences, and variations for language comprehension and production than monolingual speakers, result in cross-

Proceedings of the Second Workshop on Insights from Negative Results in NLP, pages 36–41
November 10, 2021.

linguistic behaviors such as cross-lingual priming effects (Bernolet et al., 2007; Hartsuiker et al., 2016, 2004; Gries and Kootstra, 2017) and syntactic preferences in language processing (Hsiao and Gibson, 2003). Previously, statistical-based language models (N-gram models) dominated the tasks (Malmasi et al., 2017), as statistical models are more sensitive in detecting syntactic and morpho-syntactic patterns. Embedding models, on the other hand, are more sensitive in capturing semantic and lexical information and less sensitive in classifying syntactic patterns and differences (Vajjala and Banerjee, 2017).

Given the high performance in syntactic-related tasks (Devlin et al., 2018; Mueller et al., 2020), comparing to previous embedding-based models, transformer-based models may perform better in detecting native language interference. Such advantages can help models better identify specific patterns in L2 learners. Furthermore, LMs with multilingual pre-training may be benefited in identifying different non-native speakers using additional knowledge across languages. However, existed results contradicted such assumptions, indicating that multilingual LMs generally performed worse than monolingual models in the same tasks (Mueller et al., 2020). To better understand transformer-based LMs, multilingual pre-training experiences, and language representations in LMs, our study aims to use native language identification task to answer the following research questions:

1. Can transformer-based LMs detect native interference among L2 learners with different L1s?
2. Can multilingual-LMs transfer knowledge from other languages to gain advantages in such native language prediction tasks?

3 Methods

3.1 Corpora and data pre-processing

We used two different corpora in this study: the TOEFL11 corpus (Blanchard et al., 2013) used in previous native language identification shared task (Malmasi et al., 2017), and the written essays from The International Corpus Network of Asian Learners of English (ICNALE)[1] (Ishikawa, 2013). The TOEFL11 corpus contains TOEFL essays written by English learners with 11 native languages, while ICNALE corpus contains short essays written by English learners from 10 regions and English native speakers. We used document-level input to capture general writing patterns and styles among writers. We excluded essays with less than 50 words for future processes. Both corpora have held-out testing data sets: for TOEFL11, the development set serves as the held-out testing set; for ICNALE, we randomly selected 20% essays to serve as the testing set. Table 1 is the detailed description for each corpus.

Two potential factors could interfere with the final result: speakers' proficiency in the target language (English) and the semantic/lexical information inside essays. To minimize effects from the proficiency, we further developed two types of subsets to examine whether and how proficiency influences transformer-based LMs in native language identification tasks during the fine-tuning process:

- Proficiency subsets (**B1 and Mid set**): serve as proficiency control during the fine-tuning process. These subsets included essays written by intermediate level (B1) English learners in ICNALE and speakers with median TOEFL scores (Mid) from TOEFL11.
- Balanced subset (**BA set**): serve as data input control during the fine-tuning process to provide better comparisons to proficiency subsets. These subsets had the same number of essays as the proficiency subsets, formed by randomly selected essays from the original fine-tuning set.

We also developed another version of testing sets by randomly shuffling the original texts in the essays. Through the shuffling process, we minimized the impact of syntactic information, leaving most of the lexical and semantic information available inside the testing sets. This shuffling test set can examine whether LMs rely on lexical and semantic information to process native language identification tasks.

3.2 Baseline and models for comparison

For models fine-tuned on ICNALE data, essays were converted into measures of syntax complexity using syntax complexity analyzer developed by Lu (2010). The baseline model is a multiple logistic regression model developed with outcome measures. Since there is no previous identification task involves ICNALE, we did not include any other models for comparison.

For models fine-tuned on TOEFL11 data, we

[1] The ICNALE corpus: http://language.sakura.ne.jp/icnale/

Corpus	# of documents	# of prompts	Length	# of L1 background
ICNALE	5600 (**1200**)	2	173 - 479	11
TOEFL11	9892 (**1100**)	6	100 - 795	11

Table 1: Corpus Description. Bold numbers are the size of testing sets.

used the baseline unigram model mentioned in Malmasi et al. (2017). We also included some models mentioned in Malmasi et al. (2017) with the best performance in statistic-based models and embedding-based models. The best statistic-based model (stacked SVM, Cimino and Dell'Orletta, 2017) is an SVM-based model stacked with lexical, morpho-syntactic, and syntactic features. Examples of features include word-level and character-level N-grams, part-of-speech N-grams, and dependency N-grams. The embedding-based model (Doc2Vec, Vajjala and Banerjee, 2017) is a document-level embedding model with concatenated representations from 11 individual trained models representing 11 categories in the original data set.

3.3 Model fine-tuning

For this study, we fine-tuned pre-trained BERT models to predict a speaker's L1 background through different sets of corpora mentioned above. Introduced in 2018, the BERT model is still considered a top pre-trained model in current natural language processing studies. One advantage of using BERT comparing to other non-pre-trained models is its rich knowledge in lexical information, syntactic representations, and semantic networks, which comes from the large scale of training data (Devlin et al., 2018). For this study, two different BERT models will be fine-tuned with multiple datasets: the 12-layer English BERT_base model (BERT-base) and the 12-layer multilingual BERT_base model (mBERT-base).

We fine-tuned all models with an additional linear classification layer through the Transformer package. The classification layer is directly fine-tuned on the final [CLS] embedding with the default Adams optimizer, a learning rate of 2e-5, and an early-stop of 8 epoch. The performance of each model was reported with F-scores using the held-out testing set.

4 Results

Overall, all models with different architectures and fine-tuning data sets captured some features among speakers with different L1 backgrounds, as accuracy is better than random guessing and baseline models. Table 2 and Table 3 showed the results of models trained on ICNALE and TOEFL11 corpus.

	Full	B1	BA
BERT-base	0.86	**0.84**	**0.85**
mBERT-base	**0.87**	0.83	0.83
Random	0.15	0.18	0.15
Baseline	0.43	0.41	0.43

Table 2: Models weighted F-scores for Native Language Identification: ICNALE

	Full	Mid
BERT-base	0.72	0.64
mBERT-base	0.68	0.62
Doc2Vec	0.71	-
Stacked SVM	**0.88**	-
Random	0.09	0.09
Baseline	0.71	-

Table 3: Models weighted F-scores for Native Language Identification: TOEFL11. Results of Doc2Vec (Vajjala and Banerjee, 2017) and Stacked SVM (Cimino and Dell'Orletta, 2017) come from Malmasi et al. (2017).

Performance. The models fine-tuned with TOEFL11 data did not beat the state-of-the-art native language identifier using statistical models. For models fine-tuned with ICNALE data, controlling learners' proficiency did not critically impact models in identification. This showed that speaker proficiency did not strongly interfere with language background identification, indicating the robustness of native language interference across learners' L2 written production. Shuffling word orders did impact all models severely in prediction (Table 4), which showed that BERT models cannot identify and detect native language interference solely with lexical information in the essays. In summary, transformer-based LMs can capture and involve representations of word orders, general writing patterns, and sentence structures to detect English learners' native languages, and rely less on lexical or semantic information.

Multilingual pre-training. When using the

Corpus	Full	Shuffled
ICNALE	0.86 (**0.87**)	0.24 (**0.29**)
TOEFL11	0.72 (**0.68**)	0.46 (**0.26**)

Table 4: Performance of BERT (**mBERT**) models on original and shuffle text. All models were fine-tuned without proficiency control.

same data sets, models fine-tuned on mBERT had slightly lower or similar results comparing to models fine-tuned on BERT. Additional knowledge across multiple languages did not help in predicting speakers' syntax background in their L1s.

5 General Discussion

While transformer-based LMs reached impressive results in language processing and generation, we still know little about how LMs acquire, process, and store language representations. Our study used native language identification task to investigate 1) whether transformer-based models (BERT & mBERT) can detect native interference in written production; 2) whether multilingual pre-training help in identifying native interference. Overall, the results were negative, indicating 1) compared to statistical models, transformer-based models are less capable of capturing native impacts and interference, and 2) additional knowledge across multiple languages in mBERT did not help predict such impacts across multilingual speakers.

5.1 Statistical vs. embedding models

Compared to state-of-the-art native language identifiers relying on statistical methods (such as N-grams) with F-scores above 0.85, the performance of embedding models is still worse. Previous studies (Vajjala and Banerjee, 2017; Jing et al., 2020) argued that such worse predictions from embedding models indicate embedding models might have a stronger ability in capturing semantic information; while statistical-based language models might have better performance in capturing morphosyntactic and syntactic information.

Another explanation for the current lower performance for our embedding models relates to the knowledge structures in BERTs. Previously, studies indicated that for BERTs, the mid-layers have the best performance in syntactic-related tasks (Kelly et al., 2020). Such results may indicate that, unlike previous statistical models that reach the highest performance in output layers, embedding-based models like BERTs may store different types of knowledge across different layers: the deeper the layers are, the more abstract concepts they will store. Therefore, mid-layer embeddings may contain and utilize more syntactic and morpho-syntactic information than final-layer embeddings, leading to a better performance in language interference identification. The simplicity of our classification layer may also lead to lower performance across our BERT-based models. Future studies can further investigate how embeddings from different layers of BERTs respond to these similar tasks, and how different classification algorithms change the overall performance.

5.2 Multilingualism

Another key result from this study, as mentioned previously, is that cross-lingual pre-training did not help in predicting English learner's L1 background. Based on previous findings of language-neutral components within the models (Libovickỳ et al., 2019) and existences of universal linguistics (Chi et al., 2020), we expected that models trained with multiple languages should be more sensitive to syntactic preferences or specific patterns in English interfered with by L2 syntactic knowledge. Unfortunately, similar to the study by Mueller et al. (2020), we did not find advantages of cross-lingual pre-training for native language identification tasks. We had two potential explanations for such results: the training data size and the representation structures in mBERT.

Through the pre-training process, mBERT uses a smaller training English corpus for the mBERT compared to the English BERT: English BERT has an addition Book corpus as training data (Devlin et al., 2018)[2]. The smaller English training set may lead to less knowledge and representations for English in mBERT, making it a less proficient "speaker" than English BERT. Previous research also found similar deficits related to language resources and training data size. Mueller et al. (2020) found that mBERT models perform best in English-related tasks; Wu and Dredze (2020) found that lower-resource languages had significantly lower performance than higher-resource languages when handling the same tasks.

The second explanation for mBERT's lower performance belongs to the structures of knowledge within the models. Even though existing evidence

[2]https://github.com/google-research/bert/blob/master/multilingual.md

showed the possibilities of forming components and representations across languages within embedding models (Chi et al., 2020; Libovický et al., 2019; Artetxe et al., 2019). However, Libovický et al. (2019) pointed out, these cross-lingual components are still not sufficient enough for higher-level tasks such as automatic machine translation. Our study provided further evidence on such insufficiency, indicating that while identifying native languages across English learners, knowledge from other languages and the language-general component may not involve, even when interference might appear in writers' original writing.

5.3 Future studies

To build a better multilingual model, we need further investigations on the multilingual pre-training processes, the cross-linguistic components, and how they interact across languages within multilingual LMs. Even though our models did not reach our expectations, future studies can help better understand why it happened. Specifically, we can focus on three areas: layer-wise embeddings within embedding models, size for pre-training data and models, and cross-lingual representations. For embeddings within models, future studies can use probing tasks for layer-wise embeddings to help us better understand how contextual embedding models process, represent, and utilize syntactic information and knowledge. Second, future studies can compare mBERT with smaller monolingual BERT models to balance out the impact on BERT's richer knowledge in high-resource languages. Lastly, we need more studies and methods to measure the cross-lingual components in multilingual models, which help us better understand multilingualism and cross-lingual knowledge in state-of-the-art LMs. In short, more studies, models, and theories are needed to develop LMs with better abilities in multilingual and cross-linguistic tasks to serve multilingual communities better in practical applications.

6 Summary

While transformer-based language models and multilingual language models start dominating the natural language process area, little is known about the knowledge structures within such models. In this study, we explored Bert-like models' performance in identifying a speaker's native language. Our models did not outperform the state-of-the-art native language identifier based on statistical-based models. Multilingual pre-training did not improve the performance in predicting native language, indicating the insufficiencies for detecting writing styles and structural patterns among different multilingual speakers in current LMs. Further explorations are needed to investigate how multilingual LMs store, process, communicate, and transfer representations and knowledge across languages.

Acknowledgements

This study was supported by the National Science Foundation (PAC 1734304). We thank Dr. Michael T. Putnam, Dr. M. Alex Kelly, and Saranya Venkatraman for their comments and suggestions on the original manuscript. We also thank the anonymous reviewers for providing helpful comments on the earlier draft.

References

Mikel Artetxe, Sebastian Ruder, and Dani Yogatama. 2019. On the cross-lingual transferability of monolingual representations. *arXiv preprint arXiv:1910.11856*.

Sarah Bernolet, Robert J Hartsuiker, and Martin J Pickering. 2007. Shared syntactic representations in bilinguals: Evidence for the role of word-order repetition. *Journal of Experimental Psychology: Learning, Memory, and Cognition*, 33(5):931.

Daniel Blanchard, Joel Tetreault, Derrick Higgins, Aoife Cahill, and Martin Chodorow. 2013. Toefl11: A corpus of non-native english. *ETS Research Report Series*, 2013(2):i–15.

Ethan A Chi, John Hewitt, and Christopher D Manning. 2020. Finding universal grammatical relations in multilingual bert. *arXiv preprint arXiv:2005.04511*.

Andrea Cimino and Felice Dell'Orletta. 2017. Stacked sentence-document classifier approach for improving native language identification. In *Proceedings of the 12th Workshop on Innovative Use of NLP for Building Educational Applications*, pages 430–437.

Jacob Devlin, Ming-Wei Chang, Kenton Lee, and Kristina Toutanova. 2018. Bert: Pre-training of deep bidirectional transformers for language understanding. *arXiv preprint arXiv:1810.04805*.

Emile Enguehard, Yoav Goldberg, and Tal Linzen. 2017. Exploring the syntactic abilities of rnns with multi-task learning. *arXiv preprint arXiv:1706.03542*.

Stefan Th Gries and Gerrit Jan Kootstra. 2017. Structural priming within and across languages: A corpus-based perspective. *Bilingualism: Language and Cognition*, 20(2):235–250.

Robert J Hartsuiker, Saskia Beerts, Maaike Loncke, Timothy Desmet, and Sarah Bernolet. 2016. Cross-linguistic structural priming in multilinguals: Further evidence for shared syntax. *Journal of Memory and Language*, 90:14–30.

Robert J Hartsuiker, Martin J Pickering, and Eline Veltkamp. 2004. Is syntax separate or shared between languages? cross-linguistic syntactic priming in spanish-english bilinguals. *Psychological science*, 15(6):409–414.

Franny Hsiao and Edward Gibson. 2003. Processing relative clauses in chinese. *Cognition*, 90(1):3–27.

Shin'ichiro Ishikawa. 2013. The icnale and sophisticated contrastive interlanguage analysis of asian learners of english. *Learner corpus studies in Asia and the world*, 1:91–118.

Wang Jing, Matthew A Kelly, and David Reitter. 2020. Do we need neural models to explain human judgments of acceptability? In *Proceedings of the 42nd Annual Conference of the Cognitive Science Society*, pages 1289–1295.

M Alex Kelly, Yang Xu, Jesús Calvillo, and David Reitter. 2020. Which sentence embeddings and which layers encode syntactic structure? In *Proceedings of the 42nd Annual Conference of the Cognitive Science Society*, pages 2375–2381.

Jindřich Libovický, Rudolf Rosa, and Alexander Fraser. 2019. How language-neutral is multilingual bert? *arXiv preprint arXiv:1911.03310*.

Tal Linzen and Brian Leonard. 2018. Distinct patterns of syntactic agreement errors in recurrent networks and humans. *arXiv preprint arXiv:1807.06882*.

Xiaofei Lu. 2010. Automatic analysis of syntactic complexity in second language writing. *International journal of corpus linguistics*, 15(4):474–496.

Shervin Malmasi, Keelan Evanini, Aoife Cahill, Joel Tetreault, Robert Pugh, Christopher Hamill, Diane Napolitano, and Yao Qian. 2017. A report on the 2017 native language identification shared task. In *Proceedings of the 12th Workshop on Innovative Use of NLP for Building Educational Applications*, pages 62–75.

Rebecca Marvin and Tal Linzen. 2018. Targeted syntactic evaluation of language models. *arXiv preprint arXiv:1808.09031*.

Aaron Mueller, Garrett Nicolai, Panayiota Petrou-Zeniou, Natalia Talmina, and Tal Linzen. 2020. Cross-linguistic syntactic evaluation of word prediction models. *arXiv preprint arXiv:2005.00187*.

Michael T Putnam, Matthew Carlson, and David Reitter. 2018. Integrated, not isolated: Defining typological proximity in an integrated multilingual architecture. *Frontiers in psychology*, 8:2212.

Sowmya Vajjala and Sagnik Banerjee. 2017. A study of n-gram and embedding representations for native language identification. In *Proceedings of the 12th Workshop on Innovative Use of NLP for Building Educational Applications*, pages 240–248.

Alex Warstadt, Yu Cao, Ioana Grosu, Wei Peng, Hagen Blix, Yining Nie, Anna Alsop, Shikha Bordia, Haokun Liu, Alicia Parrish, et al. 2019. Investigating bert's knowledge of language: Five analysis methods with npis. *arXiv preprint arXiv:1909.02597*.

Shijie Wu and Mark Dredze. 2020. Are all languages created equal in multilingual bert? In *Proceedings of the 5th Workshop on Representation Learning for NLP*, pages 120–130.

Zero-Shot Cross-Lingual Transfer is a Hard Baseline to Beat in German Fine-Grained Entity Typing

Sabine Weber
School of Informatics
University of Edinburgh, UK
s.weber@sms.ed.ac.uk

Mark Steedman
School of Informatics
University of Edinburgh, UK
steedman@inf.ed.ac.uk

Abstract

The training of NLP models often requires large amounts of labelled training data, which makes it difficult to expand existing models to new languages. While zero-shot cross-lingual transfer relies on multilingual word embeddings to apply a model trained on one language to another, Yarowsky and Ngai (2001) propose the method of annotation projection to generate training data without manual annotation. This method was successfully used for the tasks of named entity recognition and coarse-grained entity typing, but we show that it is outperformed by zero-shot cross-lingual transfer when applied to the similar task of fine-grained entity typing. In our study of fine-grained entity typing with the FIGER type ontology for German, we show that annotation projection amplifies the English model's tendency to underpredict level 2 labels and is beaten by zero-shot cross-lingual transfer on three novel test sets.

1 Introduction

The task of fine-grained entity typing (FET) is to assign a semantic label to a span in a text. The task is distinct from coarse-grained entity typing as done by named entity recognition systems because these systems are restricted to a small set of labels like 'person', 'organization' and 'location' which are not helpful for tasks that require more precise information about the entities. For example, FET assigns the label '/location/city' to the named entity '*Berlin*' in the sentence *'From 1997 to 2000, it had a permanent exhibition in Berlin.'*

Fine-grained entity typing uses a high number of types in a multilevel hierarchy, which can be seen in the level 2 label '/location/city' (see Figure 1). In this work we use the FIGER type hierarchy which consists of two levels with 112 types in total (37 level 1, 75 level 2). FIGER types are derived from the knowledge graph Freebase (Bollacker et al., 2008). They are both interpretable

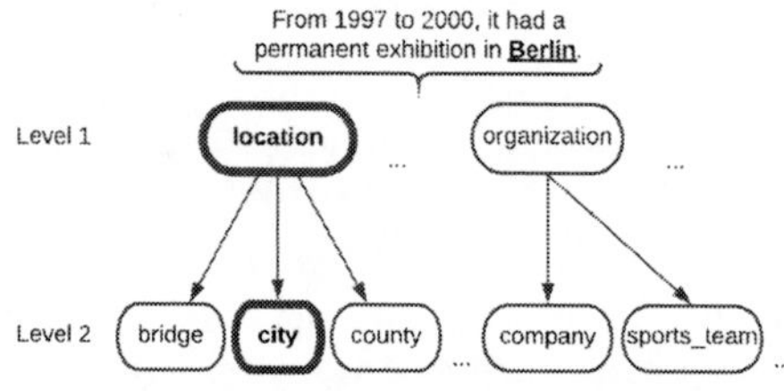

Figure 1: An example of fine-grained entity typing with the FIGER ontology. Correct types are highlighted.

by humans and useful in NLP applications such as relation extraction (Kuang et al., 2020).

There are systems for named entity recognition and coarse-grained entity typing in languages other than English (e.g. Stanza (Qi et al., 2020)), but systems for FET with FIGER types are only available in English, due to the lack of FIGER annotated data in other languages. Because manual annotation is time consuming and expensive, various methods have been proposed to expand NLP models to other languages without additional manual annotation. The method of **annotation projection** (Yarowsky and Ngai, 2001) uses parallel text to automatically create annotated corpora. Annotations from the resource-rich language are transferred to the resource-poor language using word alignment between translated sentences.

Annotation projection has been used successfully for the task of coarse-grained named entity typing in conjunction with named entity recognition (Agerri et al., 2018; Li et al., 2021; Ni et al., 2017). We follow these examples by using a parallel English-German corpus, automatic named entity recognition and a state of the art English FET model (Chen et al., 2020) to assign FIGER type labels on the English side for transfer. We then project the labels onto the German half of the corpus. The output of this process is a German corpus annotated with FIGER types, which we use to train a German FET model.

Proceedings of the Second Workshop on Insights from Negative Results in NLP, pages 42–48
November 10, 2021.

Another approach to the same problem is **zero-shot cross-lingual transfer**, in which a model built on multilingual word embeddings and trained on high-resource language data is applied to test data in a different language. Because the English FET model used in this work (Chen et al., 2020) relies on contextualised multilingual word embeddings (XLM-RoBERTa) (Conneau et al., 2019) it is possible to train it on English data and to test it on German.

We compare the two approaches and show that the annotation projection approach amplifies the model's tendency to underpredict level 2 types, which lowers model performance. We also introduce three new test sets for German FET[1] on which zero-shot cross-lingual transfer performs better than models trained with German or a mix of German and English data.

2 Related Work

To the best of our knowledge there is no work that compares annotation projection directly against zero-shot cross-lingual transfer. While annotation projection has been used in a variety of tasks, there has not been a study of a case where this approach fails. Authors admit that the quality of the annotating system plays role (e.g. Ehrmann et al. (2011); Ni et al. (2017)), but they don't specify model properties that are necessary for the approach to work, instead focusing on ways to mitigate noise.

Pires et al. (2019); Hsu et al. (2019) and Artetxe and Schwenk (2019) show the strengths of zero-shot cross-lingual transfer on a variety of different NLP tasks, but they do not address fine-grained entity typing. Zhao et al. (2020) conclude that zero-shot performance can be improved by choosing a small amount of high quality training data from the target language. We test their approach for the FET scenario, but arrive at unclear results.

3 Method

In this work we use the **hierarchical typing model** of Chen et al. (2020) trained on English gold data for the zero-shot approach and also to annotate the English side of the parallel text for annotation projection. We train the model with English silver data to show the amount of noise added by automatic annotation and finally we train it with German data which was produced by annotation projection.

In the hierarchical typing model the entity and its context are encoded using multilingual XLM-RoBERTa (Conneau et al., 2019). For each type in the FIGER ontology the model learns a type embedding. It passes the concatenated entity and context vector through a 2-layer feed-forward network that maps into the same space as the type embedding. The score is the inner product between the transformed entity and context vector and the type embedding. For further model details refer to Chen et al. (2020).

4 Experimental Setup

Training Data To contrast the zero-shot cross-lingual transfer approach with models trained on automatically annotated and projected data we use three sources of training data. We use the 2M sentences English FIGER corpus as described by (Ling and Weld, 2012) as a source of **English human annotated data**, which we will refer to as *EN gold*. The data set consists of English Wikipedia articles and we use it to train the *zero-shot gold* model.

Second, we use **English machine annotated data** (*EN automatic*). Annotating English data using a model is the first step of the annotation projection. We use this data to train the *zero-shot automatic* model to examine the amount of noise added by automatic annotation. We generate *EN automatic* from English sentences from the WikiMatrix corpus Schwenk et al. (2019) [2], using the hierarchical typing model trained on 2 M sentences *EN gold*. Lastly, we use **German annotation projected data** (*DE projected*) that was generated by projecting the labels from the *EN automatic* onto German. For the details of our annotation projection pipeline please refer to appendix A. We use this data to train the *annotation projected* model.

We portion each training corpus into slices of 100, 200, 300 and 400 K sentences to compare the influence of data size. For *DE projected* only 300 K sentences are available, because only part of the parallel sentences in the WikiMatrix corpus are of high enough quality for annotation projection. For details of the selection process refer to appendix A.

An important point for our experiments is the **label distribution** in the training corpora (see table 1). The hierarchical typing model has the tendency

[1]all test data sets and relevant code are available under https://github.com/webersab/german_FET

[2]While higher quality parallel data sets are available, this is the only one in the domain of Wikipedia articles. Preliminary experiments have shown that domain is an important factor for the quality of automatic FET, which is why we chose domain consistency over data quality for our experiments.

	EN gold	EN aut.	DE proj.
Lvl1 labels	60%	78%	77%
Lvl2 labels	40%	22%	23%
Lvl1 labels	155679	148571	150166
Lvl2 labels	104807	42008	43604

Table 1: Percentage and total numbers of level 1 and level 2 labels in 100 K sentences of the training corpora. Data created by annotation with the hierarchical-typing model contains fewer level 2 labels than human annotated gold data.

	size	unique lab.	t. lab.
EN-FIGER	563 sent.	42	624
DE-FIGER	563 sent.	42	624
DE-Wiki	500 sent.	57	771
DE-GermEnt	135 sent.	34	213

Table 2: Statistics of the different test sets listing size, number of unique labels and total number of labels. While DE-FIGER is parallel to the commonly used English FIGER test set, DE-Wiki contains more unique labels and more labels in total.

to underpredict the finer-grained level 2 labels (e.g. /person/actor, as opposed to level 1 label /person), which leads to a different distribution of labels in *EN gold* and the other corpora. Compared to approximately 100 K level 2 labels per 100 K sentences in the gold data, we only see about 50 K level 2 labels in the silver data. This tendency does not depend on the different input data: If we use a model trained on 100 K *EN gold* to predict labels on an unseen portion of *EN gold*, only 25% of the resulting annotations are level 2 labels.

Metrics Following previous FET literature we evaluate the results of our model using strict accuracy (Acc). The strict accuracy is the ratio of instances where the predicted type set is exactly the same as the gold type set. We also evaluate per hierarchy level.

Test sets We compare performance using the following test corpora: **1)** a German machine translation of the test split of the English FIGER corpus (Ling and Weld, 2012) using DeepL, which was manually corrected to eliminate translation and labelling errors (*DE-FIGER*); **2)** 500 manually annotated German sentences from the WikiMatrix corpus (*DE-Wiki*), which we consider to be more challenging than DE-FIGER, because it contains a wider range of type labels; **3)** a small challenge set of 135 sentences taken from DE-Wiki, in which we replaced entities with close string matches to English (e.g. 'Präsident Nixon') with specifically German entities of the same type (e.g. 'Bundeskanzler Kohl'), which we call *DE-GermEnt*; and **4)** for experiments where we mix German and English data, we also compare against test split of the English FIGER corpus (Ling and Weld, 2012) (*EN-FIGER*). Data set statistics can be seen in table 2.

5 Results

Monolingual training Figure 2 compares the performance of the models *zero-shot gold*, *zero-shot automatic* and *annotation projected* at different training data sizes on the *DE-FIGER* and the *DE-Wiki* test sets. *Zero-shot gold* outperforms *zero-shot automatic* and *annotation projected* on both test sets and in all training data sizes. *Zero-shot gold* trained on the full *EN gold* data set of 2 M sentences performs only 1% better on level 1 labels and 3% better on level 2 labels than a model trained with 400 K sentences, which shows that smaller data slices are sufficient to reach most of the possible performance with this data set.

While for level 1 type labels *annotation projected* gets close to the performance of *zero-shot gold* on both test sets, on level 2 type labels the system falls behind *zero-shot gold*, with a wider gap on *DE-Wiki*. The comparison between *zero-shot automatic* and *annotation projected* is less clear. On the *DE-Wiki* test set *annotation projected* consistently outperforms *zero-shot automatic*, while on *DE-FIGER* both systems perform very similarly.

The high performance of *zero-shot gold* and the noisier *zero-shot automatic* might be due to the quality of English and German embeddings in XLM-RoBERTa, as both are high resource languages from the same language family. This confirms Lauscher et al. (2020) who show that this method works especially well for close high resource language pairs and low level semantic tasks. The noise introduced by annotation projection affects level 2 label performance the most (see appendix B and table 1). But the amount of level 2 labels in the training data can not be the only reason for this. The total number of labels in the silver corpora (see table 1) shows that 200 K of silver training data contain approximately the same amount of level 2 labels as 100 K of gold data. Nevertheless, the level 2 performance of systems trained on 200 K of silver data lies behind the model trained on 100 K of *EN gold*. This points towards the possibility, that not only the amount of level 2 labels in the training data, but also their quality and their

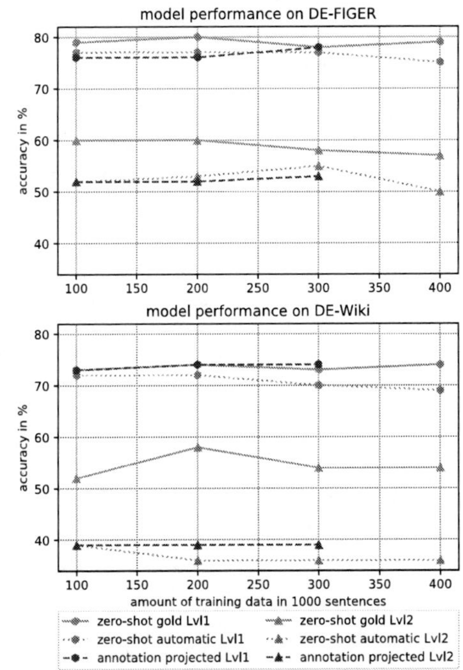

Figure 2: Zero-shot cross-lingual transfer performs best on both German data sets. *EN automatic* and *DE projected* perform similar on both data sets, with a wider gap in level 2 performance on *DE-Wiki*

	DE-FIGER		EN-FIGER	
name, size	Lvl1	Lvl2	Lvl1	Lvl2
DE proj., 200K	75	52	79	54
DE+EN, 200K	**77**	**54**	78	54
EN aut., 200K	76	53	**79**	**55**

Table 3: Performance of a model trained with both English and German data, in comparison with monolingual data tested on parallel test sets. While performance in German is best with mixed data, performance in English is best with only English training data.

proportion with level 1 labels play a role here.

Multilingual training The underlying XLM-RoBERTa embeddings allow to train a model with both German and English data. For this we combine slices from *DE projected* with *EN automatic*, because these data sets have the same distribution of labels. Table 3 shows the performance of a model trained with evenly mixed data (*EN+DE*) in comparison with monolingually trained models of the same size tested on *DE-FIGER* and *EN-FIGER*. German performance benefits from using both German and English training data, while performance in English is best with only English data. The mixed model does not outperform *zero-shot gold* on these test sets.

The low performance in the data mixing scenario compared to *zero-shot gold* can be explained with the distribution of labels in the silver corpora. Due to the noise added when labels are projected from English to German, the mixed model tested in German profits from the addition of higher quality English data, but not vice versa.

Few-shot training Zhao et al. (2020) suggest that few-shot learning improves zero-shot performance. To test this we take a model trained on 100 K sentences *EN gold* and fine-tune it by training on the 135 sentence manually annotated *DE-GermEnt* data set. We evaluate the resulting model's performance on *DE-FIGER*. In comparison with the model trained on 100 K *EN gold* only, the performance of the resulting model is 10% lower in accuracy of level 1 labels and 12% lower on level 2 labels. We did not specifically select which sentences to use like Zhao et al. (2020), which is an avenue for future work. The low performance of the few-shot model could be due to the high number of different labels, only a few of which can be observed during few-shot training, but further work is needed to confirm this.

German entities To challenge *zero-shot gold*, we test a model trained 2 M sentences *EN gold* on the test set *DE-GermEnt*. Surprisingly, we find that the model performs better on *DE-GermEnt* than on its English entity counter part, with 1% higher performance on level 1 labels and 3% higher performance on level 2 labels. It is unclear why *zero-shot gold* behaves this way, and examining this with larger challenge data sets it an avenue for future work.

6 Discussion and Conclusions

Our results show that zero-shot cross-lingual transfer building upon XLM-RoBERTa is a strong baseline for the task of FET and the language pair of English and German. It outperforms annotation projection on three new test sets. We also show that in our specific scenario annotation projection using the hierarchical typing model amplifies the models tendency to underpredict level 2 types.

One way to mitigate these shortcomings would be to sample level 1 and level 2 labels in a training corpus so that they have the same distribution as in the gold data, although this would not control for data quality. Another way could be to machine translate the manually annotated English corpus into German and then use annotation projection, as suggested by Ehrmann et al. (2011). This way the label distribution of the human annotated data could be preserved as well. Lastly, improving the few-shot approach and designing more challenging test sets are other avenues to explore.

7 Acknowledgements

This work was funded by the ERC H2020 Advanced Fellowship GA 742137 SEMANTAX.

References

Rodrigo Agerri, Yiling Chung, Itziar Aldabe, Nora Aranberri, Gorka Labaka, and German Rigau. 2018. Building named entity recognition taggers via parallel corpora. In *Proceedings of the Eleventh International Conference on Language Resources and Evaluation (LREC 2018)*.

Mikel Artetxe and Holger Schwenk. 2019. Massively Multilingual Sentence Embeddings for Zero-Shot Cross-Lingual Transfer and Beyond. *Transactions of the Association for Computational Linguistics*, 7:597–610.

Kurt Bollacker, Colin Evans, Praveen Paritosh, Tim Sturge, and Jamie Taylor. 2008. Freebase: a collaboratively created graph database for structuring human knowledge. In *Proceedings of the 2008 ACM SIGMOD international conference on Management of data*, pages 1247–1250.

Tongfei Chen, Yunmo Chen, and Benjamin Van Durme. 2020. Hierarchical entity typing via multi-level learning to rank. In *Proceedings of the 58th Annual Meeting of the Association for Computational Linguistics, ACL 2020, Online, July 5-10, 2020*, pages 8465–8475.

Alexis Conneau, Kartikay Khandelwal, Naman Goyal, Vishrav Chaudhary, Guillaume Wenzek, Francisco Guzmán, Edouard Grave, Myle Ott, Luke Zettlemoyer, and Veselin Stoyanov. 2019. Unsupervised cross-lingual representation learning at scale. *arXiv preprint arXiv:1911.02116*.

Chris Dyer, Victor Chahuneau, and Noah A Smith. 2013. A simple, fast, and effective reparameterization of ibm model 2. In *Proceedings of the 2013 Conference of the North American Chapter of the Association for Computational Linguistics: Human Language Technologies*, pages 644–648.

Maud Ehrmann, Marco Turchi, and Ralf Steinberger. 2011. Building a multilingual named entity-annotated corpus using annotation projection. In *Proceedings of the International Conference Recent Advances in Natural Language Processing 2011*, pages 118–124.

Tsung-Yuan Hsu, Chi-Liang Liu, and Hung-yi Lee. 2019. Zero-shot reading comprehension by cross-lingual transfer learning with multi-lingual language representation model. In *Proceedings of the 2019 Conference on Empirical Methods in Natural Language Processing and the 9th International Joint Conference on Natural Language Processing (EMNLP-IJCNLP)*, pages 5933–5940, Hong Kong, China. Association for Computational Linguistics.

Jun Kuang, Yixin Cao, Jianbing Zheng, Xiangnan He, Ming Gao, and Aoying Zhou. 2020. Improving neural relation extraction with implicit mutual relations. In *2020 IEEE 36th International Conference on Data Engineering (ICDE)*, pages 1021–1032. IEEE.

Anne Lauscher, Vinit Ravishankar, Ivan Vulić, and Goran Glavaš. 2020. From zero to hero: On the limitations of zero-shot language transfer with multilingual transformers. In *Proceedings of the 2020 Conference on Empirical Methods in Natural Language Processing (EMNLP)*, pages 4483–4499.

Bing Li, Yujie He, and Wenjin Xu. 2021. Cross-lingual named entity recognition using parallel corpus: A new approach using xlm-roberta alignment. *arXiv preprint arXiv:2101.11112*.

Xiao Ling and Daniel S Weld. 2012. Fine-grained entity recognition. In *AAAI*, volume 12, pages 94–100.

Jian Ni, Georgiana Dinu, and Radu Florian. 2017. Weakly supervised cross-lingual named entity recognition via effective annotation and representation projection. In *Proceedings of the 55th Annual Meeting of the Association for Computational Linguistics (Volume 1: Long Papers)*, pages 1470–1480.

Franz Josef Och and Hermann Ney. 2003. A systematic comparison of various statistical alignment models. *Computational Linguistics*, 29(1):19–51.

Telmo Pires, Eva Schlinger, and Dan Garrette. 2019. How multilingual is multilingual BERT? In *Proceedings of the 57th Annual Meeting of the Association for Computational Linguistics*, pages 4996–5001, Florence, Italy. Association for Computational Linguistics.

Peng Qi, Yuhao Zhang, Yuhui Zhang, Jason Bolton, and Christopher D. Manning. 2020. Stanza: A Python natural language processing toolkit for many human languages. In *Proceedings of the 58th Annual Meeting of the Association for Computational Linguistics: System Demonstrations*.

Holger Schwenk, Vishrav Chaudhary, Shuo Sun, Hongyu Gong, and Francisco Guzmán. 2019. Wikimatrix: Mining 135m parallel sentences in 1620 language pairs from wikipedia. *arXiv preprint arXiv:1907.05791*.

David Yarowsky and Grace Ngai. 2001. Inducing multilingual pos taggers and NP bracketers via robust projection across aligned corpora. In *Proceedings*

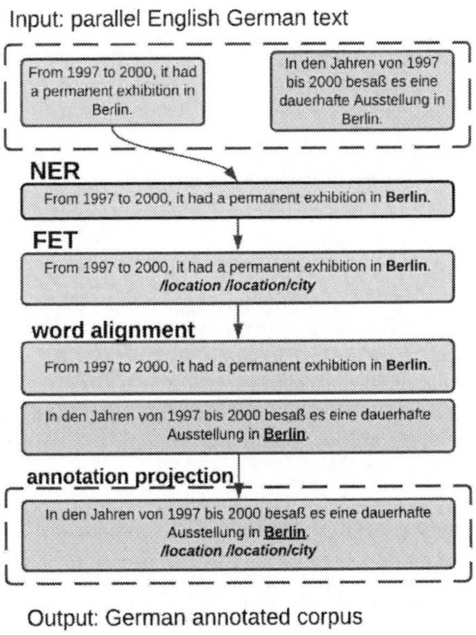

Figure 3: Our annotation projection setup uses parallel text and an automatic named entity recognition component to generate an annotated corpus in German.

of the 2nd Meeting of the North American Chapter of the Association for Computational Linguistics, pages XXX–XXX. ACL.

Mengjie Zhao, Yi Zhu, Ehsan Shareghi, Roi Reichart, Anna Korhonen, and Hinrich Schütze. 2020. A closer look at few-shot crosslingual transfer: Variance, benchmarks and baselines. *arXiv preprint arXiv:2012.15682*.

A German Data Creation

A.1 Preprocessing

A diagram of our pipeline can be seen in figure 3. To annotate the English halves of our parallel corpora with FIGER types preprocessing is necessary. Due to its automatic creation the WikiMatrix corpus contains a small amount of German sentences in its English half and English sentences in its German half, the translations of which are assigned very high confidence. We remove these by discarding the 5000 highest-confidence sentences.

To enable annotation by the English FET system, we run a named entity recognition system over the English input sentences (see the second box of Figure 3). We used the NER component of Stanza (Qi et al., 2020) for this task. We then use the English FET model to assign FIGER types to the named entities (see the third box of Figure 3). The FET model only annotates one entity per sentence.

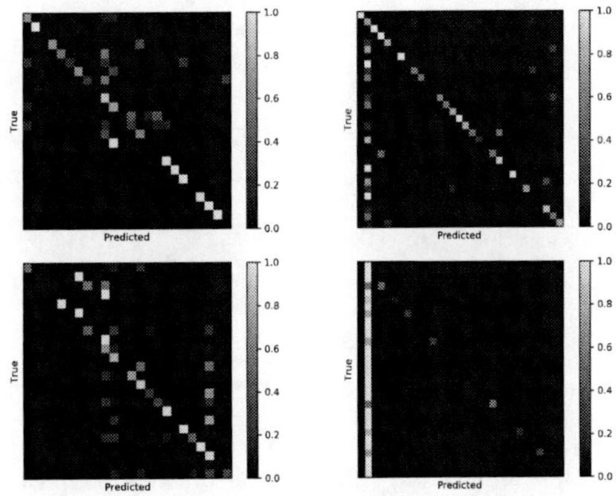

Figure 4: The upper two matrices show level 1 and level 2 performance of EN gold 2 M, the lower two matrices show the same for DE silver 200K. While the English model has a slight tendency to predict no label for level 2 label, this tendency is stronger in the German model. The yellow vertical line shows this effect.

Sentences that contain more than one named entity occur multiple times in the English input, so that each entity receives an annotation.

A.2 Annotation projection and training with noise mitigation

We use ZAP to obtain a word alignment between the English and German halves of our parallel corpora (see the fourth box of Figure 3). While the similar tools fast_align (Dyer et al., 2013) and Giza++ (Och and Ney, 2003) are language agnostic, ZAP's model for English-German word alignment uses probabilities computed from large-scale parallel corpora. We then use our own code to project the fine grained entity type labels from the annotated English text to its German translation. We use static rules to filter out misalignments, e.g. discarding all cases where not all words of an entity were aligned.

We then use the resulting German FET annotated corpus to train our FET model. Because of the ordering by alignment quality in the machine-aligned WikiMatrix corpus, we introduce a preprocessing epoch to the training to mitigate noisy input. During training the model receives the sentences in exactly the order that they occur in the corpus. In the WikiMatrix corpus the sentences are sorted by the confidence of the alignment algorithm. This means that the sentences towards the bottom of the corpus are more likely to be incorrectly aligned. Incorrectly aligned sentences are more likely to have incorrectly projected labels. Therefor the quality of FIGER type annotations in the resulting German

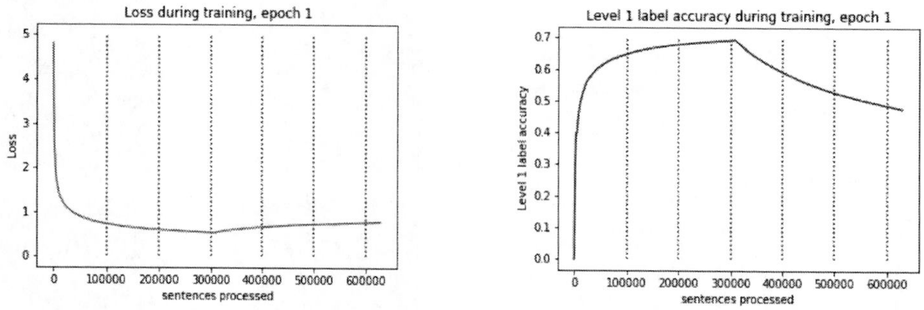

Figure 5: Loss rises and level 1 label accuracy deteriorates as the quality of samples gets worse towards the end of the automatically aligned and sorted corpus. The graphs show a cut-off point at approximately 300 thousand sentences. We use this information to select a high-quality slice of the corpus to train our system.

data is higher towards the beginning of the corpus and lower towards its end.

During the first epoch of training this drop in quality can be observed in the change of learning rate and the accuracy of predictions after approximately 300,000 sentences (see Figure 5). These curves give us important information about what portion of the data is clean enough to be used in the following epochs of training. It gives us a possible cut off point for our data set at 300,000 sentences, so that in the next epochs we only train on a slice of the corpus before this point.

To show the effect of increasing training data size we select for our experiments 3 slices of data that were processed before the cut off point: the first 100K, 200K and 300K sentences of the corpus.

B Confusion matrices

The hierarchical typing model of Chen et al. (2020)'s model tends to under-predict level 2 labels. This property of the model is exacerbated by our annotation projection approach, because we use data generated by this model in English to train the same model in German. Figure 4 shows the confusion matrices for level 1 and level 2 labels for EN gold 2 Mil and DE silver 200K. While for level 1 labels in EN gold there is no dominant class that labels are misclassified to, the most common misprediction for level 2 labels is to assign no label at all, which can be seen as the dotted vertical line in the second upper confusion matrix. When comparing the upper confusion matrices to the lower ones, it becomes clear that this trend to under-predict level 2 labels is even stronger in the German model.

This makes sense because the German model is trained on output from the English model, which contains fewer level 2 labels than the human annotated data used to train the English model in he first place. The German model sees less level 2 labels in its training data and therefore doesn't learn to predict them.

C System and model specifications

In keeping with the EMNLP reproducibility guidelines we report the specifications of the systems that our models where trained on. We trained all models using a single GeForce RTX 2080 Ti GPU. Running the largest model (EN zero-shot trained on 2 million sentences) took approximately 8 hours. Training the other models took under an hour per model. The number of model parameters is 50484362. All hyperparameters of the model were taken from the implementation of Chen et al. (2020). For the few-shot experiment we increased the training epoch number to stop if there was no more improvement on the development set.

Comparing Euclidean and Hyperbolic Embeddings on the WordNet Nouns Hypernymy Graph

Sameer Bansal, Adrian Benton
Bloomberg
731 Lexington Ave
New York, NY 10022 USA
{sbansal70,abenton10}@bloomberg.net

Abstract

Nickel and Kiela (2017) present a new method for embedding tree nodes in the Poincaré ball, and suggest that these hyperbolic embeddings are far more effective than Euclidean embeddings at embedding nodes in large, hierarchically structured graphs like the WordNet nouns hypernymy tree. This is especially true in low dimensions (Nickel and Kiela, 2017, Table 1). In this work, we seek to reproduce their experiments on embedding and reconstructing the WordNet nouns hypernymy graph. Counter to what they report, we find that Euclidean embeddings are able to represent this tree at least as well as Poincaré embeddings, when allowed at least 50 dimensions. We note that this does not diminish the significance of their work given the impressive performance of hyperbolic embeddings in very low-dimensional settings. However, given the wide influence of their work, our aim here is to present an updated and more accurate comparison between the Euclidean and hyperbolic embeddings.

1 Introduction

Nickel and Kiela (2017) introduced a method for learning embeddings in hyperbolic space for large, hierarchically structured objects like the WordNet nouns hypernymy graph. This work convincingly shows that across a range of embedding dimensions, from as low as 5 to as high as 200, hyperbolic embeddings consistently outperformed their Euclidean counterparts (Nickel and Kiela, 2017, Table 1). Illustrating the difference in performance at the highest experimental setting of 200 dimensions, the mean average precision (MAP) score for hyperbolic embeddings was shown to be around 5 times that of Euclidean for embedding nouns in the WordNet hypernymy graph.[1] These experiments have been extremely influential, with the results on embedding the WordNet nouns hypernymy graph baselines often cited in later works on enhanced hyperbolic embeddings (De Sa et al., 2018; Ganea et al., 2018; Dhingra et al., 2018; López et al., 2019; Balazevic et al., 2019; Feyisetan et al., 2019; Chami et al., 2020).[2]

In this work, we reproduce the reconstruction error experiments on the WordNet noun hypernymy graph from Nickel and Kiela (2017). Counter to what they report, we find that Euclidean word embeddings are as effective at encoding the WordNet nouns graph as hyperbolic embeddings when given at least 50 dimensions. In fact, Euclidean embeddings with $\geq$ 100 dimensions achieve lower reconstruction error over embeddings in the Lorentz model, an improved hyperbolic embedding method, which was published the following year (Nickel and Kiela, 2018).

The inability to reproduce the reported Euclidean experiments has been raised in several issues in the associated GitHub repository.[3] This has also been acknowledged by the authors of the original study, who suggest that the original Euclidean embeddings were regularized in a way that may have hurt performance.[4] However, the published manuscript has not been updated to reflect these problems with reproducing the Euclidean embedding baselines. As such, we hope that our reproduction will serve as a useful reference for those who are interested in exploring hyperbolic embeddings.

2 Experimental Setup

We use the source code released by the authors to carry out all experiments in this study, reusing the data processing, model training, and evaluation pipelines.

Dataset. Following Nickel and Kiela (2017), we embed the WordNet noun hierarchy (Fellbaum, 1998, *WordNet-Nouns)* in both Euclidean and hyperbolic space. Though the original study also published results on additional datasets, we restrict our focus to *WordNet-Nouns*, which exhibited a considerable gap in performance between embeddings.

Model training. Other than learning rate, we retain the default hyperparameters specified in the released source code, and train embeddings for 1,500 epochs.

[1] The embeddings were evaluated on a reconstruction task where a MAP score closer to 1 indicates better performance.

[2] Nickel and Kiela (2017) has been cited over 500 times (source: www.semanticscholar.org).

[3] https://github.com/facebookresearch/poincare-embeddings/issues/35 ; 68 ; 72

[4] Author response on GitHub github.com/facebookresearch/poincare-embeddings/issues/35#issuecomment-685174866

Proceedings of the Second Workshop on Insights from Negative Results in NLP, pages 49–53
November 10, 2021.

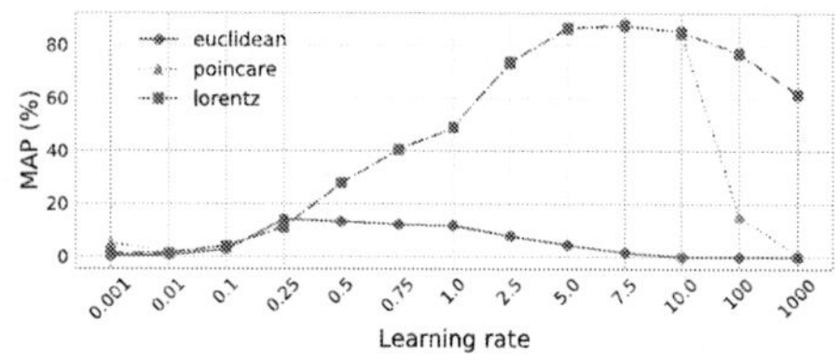

Figure 1: MAP of Euclidean, Poincaré, and Lorentz 20-dimensional embeddings as a function of learning rate. MAP scores for Poincaré and Lorentz embeddings are very similar up to a learning rate of 10.0.

The learning rate is tuned in the range $10^{[-2,3]}$ independently for each class of embeddings (Figure 1) with dimensionality fixed to 20, and selection based on loss after 200 epochs. We selected a learning rate of 0.5 for Euclidean and 5.0 for both Poincaré and Lorentz embeddings. In our initial experiments, we found that other hyperparameters, such as number of negative samples, also affected embeddings performance, but were less influential than learning rate. See Appendix A for details on the exact version of the codebase used in our experiments and how it was called. See the original study (Nickel and Kiela, 2017) for additional details on model training and evaluation.

Evaluation. Embeddings are evaluated under the original reconstruction error setting. For each hypernym pair $< u, v >$ in the tree, rank all non-hypernyms along with v by distance from u in the embedded space. The fidelity to which a set of embeddings represents the tree is evaluated according to mean average precision (MAP) and mean rank (MR) of the positive example, v, averaged across rankings.

We focus on reconstruction error experiments as they are meant to highlight the capacity of each embedding space. The ability to generalize out of sample is an orthogonal question, however which we don't address in this work. This is mostly since the source code to reproduce these results from Nickel and Kiela (2017) has not yet been released, and the particular folds of heldout edges are also not provided. As such, we leave reproduction of the link prediction evaluation of Euclidean vs. hyperbolic embeddings to future work.[5]

3 Results

Table 1 shows the MAP and MR results for the *WordNet-Nouns* hierarchy reconstruction task. There are clear differences between the reproduced and reported performance for Euclidean embeddings. In the 50 dimensions setting, the reproduced Euclidean embeddings achieve a MAP score of 88.9 compared to 14 in the original study, and an MR score of 1.8 compared to 1,281. In fact, this MR score for Euclidean embed-

[5]At the time of writing, there is an open GitHub issue to provide more details on the out of sample, link prediction evaluation `https://github.com/facebookresearch/poincare-embeddings/issues/10`.

dims	5	10	20	50	100	200
Mean Average Precision % (higher is better):						
Euclidean						
N&K	2.4	5.9	8.7	14	16.2	16.8
ours	2.7	4.5	11.2	88.9	91.7	92.2
Poincaré						
N&K	82.8	86.5	85.5	86	85.7	87
ours	85.6	88.7	89.1	89.3	89.2	89.3
Lorentz						
N&K	92.3	92.8	—	—	—	—
ours	87.4	88.6	89.5	89.3	89.4	89.4
Mean Rank (lower is better):						
Euclidean						
N&K	3542	2286	1685	1281	1187	1157
ours	3646	1455	244	1.8	1.5	1.5
Poincaré						
N&K	4.9	4.0	3.8	3.9	3.9	3.8
ours	6.8	5.6	5.2	4.9	4.9	4.9
Lorentz						
N&K	3.1	2.9	—	—	—	—
ours	6.6	5.5	5	4.9	4.8	4.8

Table 1: Mean average precision and mean rank for reconstructing the *WordNet-Nouns* hypernymy graph. *N&K* refers to best published results from Nickel and Kiela (2017, 2018).

Embedding	MAP	MR
Euclidean	89.2 ± 0.33	1.8 ± 0.00
Poincaré	89.4 ± 0.09	4.9 ± 0.01
Lorentz	89.4 ± 0.26	4.9 ± 0.10

Table 2: Mean and standard deviation of MAP and MR for 50-dimensional embeddings across three different random restarts.

dings at 50 dimensions is better than that achieved by Poincaré and Lorentz embeddings even with 200 dimensions. With greater than 50 dimensions, Euclidean embeddings outperform both Lorentz and Poincaré embeddings according to MR and MAP.

In contrast, the performance of hyperbolic embeddings remain stable across dimensionality and are similar between reproduced and reported results. The improved reconstruction error of Lorentz embeddings in prior work is likely due to a more comprehensive hyperparameter search.

We also found that performance is robust to random seed for all methods, with a standard deviation of less than a point for both MAP and MR score when training 50-dimensional Euclidean, Poincaré, or Lorentz embeddings (Table 2).

4 Analysis

In Section 3, we show it is possible to learn Euclidean embeddings that can reconstruct *WordNet-Nouns* more

dims	5	10	20	50	100	200
Mean Average Precision % (higher is better):						
N&K	2.4	5.9	8.7	14.0	16.2	16.8
ours: unit norm	2.4	5.0	7.6	10.6	12.0	12.5
ours: no norm	2.7	4.5	11.2	88.9	91.7	92.2
Mean Rank (lower is better):						
N&K	3542	2286	1685	1281	1187	1157
ours: unit norm	3807	2275	1697	1276	1184	1159
ours: no norm	3646	1455	244	1.8	1.5	1.5

Table 3: MAP and MR for reconstructing the *WordNet-Nouns* hypernymy graph. Results from *N&K* (Nickel and Kiela, 2017, 2018) and our reproduction with Euclidean embeddings constrained to unit norm are similar.

faithfully than similarly trained hyperbolic embeddings with at least 50 dimensions. In this section, we discuss possible reasons for the discrepancy between reported and reproduced Euclidean embeddings performance. We first posed this question to the authors themselves (Nickel and Kiela, 2017) who clarified on GitHub that the difference in performance for Euclidean embeddings in their published manuscript was due to a regularization method used at the time. They further added that in the released code they *"disabled this regularization by default and it turned out to work better"*.[6] Follow-up questions regarding the details of this regularization method have yet to be addressed, at the time of writing.[7]

Constraining Euclidean Embedding Norm We speculate that the authors may have normalized the Euclidean embeddings to constrain them to lie within a unit 2-norm ball, similar to how Poincaré embeddings are trained (Nickel and Kiela, 2017, Section 3.1). Note that while projection into the unit ball is necessary to learn valid Poincaré embeddings, Euclidean embeddings require no such constraint.

The released source code actually supports projecting Euclidean embeddings into the unit ball after each iteration, but this is disabled by default, with the argument *max_norm* set to *None*.[8] To test whether this constraint has an effect on embedding quality, we train Euclidean embeddings constrained to the unit ball by setting *max_norm* to 1. Table 3 shows that reconstruction scores for Euclidean embeddings constrained to the unit ball are much closer to those published in Nickel and Kiela (2017, 2018) than unconstrained Euclidean embeddings.

Varying Norm Constraints To explore the impact of norm constraints, we conduct further experiments on training 100 dimensional Euclidean embeddings. We vary the *max_norm* setting between 1 and 10, allowing the Euclidean embeddings to grow larger during training. As an alternative method for controlling the norm of the embeddings, we also vary the strength of an L2 penalty as an additional term in the loss. MAP and MR scores improve as the *max_norm* setting is increased, the norm constraint is relaxed (Table 4). In fact, setting *max_norm* to 5 yields Euclidean embeddings that achieve similar reconstruction performance as unconstrained embeddings.

We found that including an L2 regularization penalty in the loss has little effect on the final reconstruction scores. Thus, although we suspect unnecessary renormalization of the Euclidean embeddings may have caused the poor reconstruction performance reported in prior work, we defer to the authors of the original study for confirmation.

Constraint	MAP	MR
None (default)	91.7	1.5
L2 regularization = 0.01	92.3	1.5
L2 regularization = 1.0	92.3	1.5
L2 regularization = 100.0	92.2	1.5
max norm = 1	11.2	1150.0
max norm = 2	38.3	40.3
max norm = 5	92.3	1.5
max norm = 10	92.3	1.5
N&K	16.2	1187.3

Table 4: MAP and MR for 100 dimensional embeddings. We include results with no regularization or constraints (row 1) and with L2 regularization of varying degree. *max norm* = k means that embeddings are projected back into a radius k 2-norm ball after each iteration. *N&K* refers to best published results from Nickel and Kiela (2017, 2018).

[6]Author response regarding difference in Euclidean performance `https://github.com/facebookresearch/poincare-embeddings/issues/35#issuecomment-685261354`

[7]Question seeking further information regarding regularization `https://github.com/facebookresearch/poincare-embeddings/issues/35#issuecomment-685261354` and a relevant comment in `issuecomment-735209781`.

[8]L2 normalization disabled by default: `https://github.com/facebookresearch/poincare-embeddings/blob/4c7316b/hype/manifolds/euclidean.py#L16`.

5 Conclusion

In our reproduction of the experiments in Table 1 of Nickel and Kiela (2017), we find that Euclidean actually outperform Poincaré embeddings when allowed a moderate number of dimensions. This is a realistic number of dimensions for typical non-contextual word embeddings, and a far lower dimensionality than subword token embeddings used in pretrained transformer language models. For example, released GloVe embeddings range from 50 to 300 dimensions (Pennington et al., 2014) and BERT base uses 768-dimensional subword embeddings (Devlin et al., 2019).

Nevertheless, the strong performance of hyperbolic embeddings in very low dimensions (less than 20) highlights their main strength: succinctly embedding nodes in hierarchically structured graphs with tight limitations on embedding size.

However, part of Nickel and Kiela (2017)'s impact came from the astounding gains from hyperbolic embeddings over Euclidean across a wide range of embedding widths. Subsequent application of Poincaré embeddings often report mixed results when using non-Euclidean vs. Euclidean embeddings in downstream tasks (Dhingra et al., 2018; López et al., 2019). We hope that this reproduction will serve as a valuable reference for others who are just beginning to explore hyperbolic embeddings.

Acknowledgments

We thank Maximilian Nickel and Douwe Kiela for their helpful feedback while carrying out this study and for making the source code available. We also thank the workshop organizers for providing an avenue for such work to be published and the anonymous reviewers whose feedback helped us improve this work. Thanks also to the GitHub users who reported similar issues in the source code repository, which motivated us to publish this study.

References

Ivana Balazevic, Carl Allen, and Timothy Hospedales. 2019. Multi-relational poincaré graph embeddings. In *Proc. NeurIPS*.

Ines Chami, Adva Wolf, Da-Cheng Juan, Frederic Sala, Sujith Ravi, and Christopher Ré. 2020. Low-dimensional hyperbolic knowledge graph embeddings. In *Proc. ACL*.

Christopher De Sa, Albert Gu, Christopher Ré, and Frederic Sala. 2018. Representation tradeoffs for hyperbolic embeddings. *Proc. MLR*, 80:4460.

Jacob Devlin, Ming-Wei Chang, Kenton Lee, and Kristina Toutanova. 2019. Bert: Pre-training of deep bidirectional transformers for language understanding. In *Proc. NAACL*, pages 4171–4186.

Bhuwan Dhingra, Christopher Shallue, Mohammad Norouzi, Andrew Dai, and George Dahl. 2018. Embedding text in hyperbolic spaces. In *Proc. (TextGraphs-12)*.

Christiane Fellbaum. 1998. *WordNet: An Electronic Lexical Database*.

Oluwaseyi Feyisetan, Tom Diethe, and Thomas Drake. 2019. Leveraging hierarchical representations for preserving privacy and utility in text. In *Proc. ICDM*.

Octavian Ganea, Gary Bécigneul, and Thomas Hofmann. 2018. Hyperbolic neural networks. In *Proc. NeurIPS*.

Federico López, Benjamin Heinzerling, and Michael Strube. 2019. Fine-grained entity typing in hyperbolic space. In *Proc. (RepL4NLP-2019)*.

Maximillian Nickel and Douwe Kiela. 2017. Poincaré embeddings for learning hierarchical representations. In *Proc. NeurIPS*.

Maximillian Nickel and Douwe Kiela. 2018. Learning continuous hierarchies in the lorentz model of hyperbolic geometry. In *Proc. ICML*.

Jeffrey Pennington, Richard Socher, and Christopher D Manning. 2014. Glove: Global vectors for word representation. In *Proc. EMNLP*, pages 1532–1543.

A Call to Poincaré Embedding Trainer

Sample call to train embeddings and run reconstruction evaluation:

```
### Parameters
LR=0.5
DIM=20
MANIFOLD="euclidean"

# Train model
python -m hype.embed \
  -checkpoint model.bin
  -dset wordnet/noun_closure.csv
  -epochs 1500
  -negs 50
  -burnin 20
  -dampening 0.75
  -ndproc 4
  -eval_each 100 \
  -fresh
  -sparse
  -burnin_multiplier 0.01
  -neg_multiplier 0.1
  -lr_type constant
  -train_threads 1
  -dampening 1.0
  -batchsize 50
  -manifold ${MANIFOLD}
  -dim ${DIM}
  -lr ${LR}

python reconstruction.py model.bin.1499
```

We use the `poincare-embeddings` implementation `https://github.com/facebookresearch/poincare-embeddings` at commit `4c7316b14dce3b89e6a2d0c7994d418dffb42c94`.

When does Further Pre-training MLM Help? An Empirical Study on Task-Oriented Dialog Pre-training

Qi Zhu[1], **Yuxian Gu**[1], **Lingxiao Luo**[1], **Bing Li**[1],
Cheng Li[2], **Wei Peng**[2], **Xiaoyan Zhu**[1], **Minlie Huang**[1]*
[1]CoAI Group, DCST, IAI, BNRIST, Tsinghua University, Beijing, China
[2]Artificial Intelligence Application Research Center, Huawei Technologies, Shenzhen, China
zhu-q18@mails.tsinghua.edu.cn, aihuang@tsinghua.edu.cn

Abstract

Further pre-training language models on in-domain data (domain-adaptive pre-training, DAPT) or task-relevant data (task-adaptive pre-training, TAPT) before fine-tuning has been shown to improve downstream tasks' performances. However, in task-oriented dialog modeling, we observe that further pre-training MLM does not always boost the performance on a downstream task. We find that DAPT is beneficial in the low-resource setting, but as the fine-tuning data size grows, DAPT becomes less beneficial or even useless, and scaling the size of DAPT data does not help. Through Representational Similarity Analysis, we conclude that more data for fine-tuning yields greater change of the model's representations and thus reduces the influence of initialization.[1]

1 Introduction

Pre-trained models such as BERT (Devlin et al., 2019) and GPT2 (Radford et al., 2019) have been used in a wide range of NLP tasks and achieved superior performance. These models usually follow the *pre-train* and *fine-tune* paradigm, which adopts unsupervised pre-training on large-scale corpora and supervised fine-tuning for downstream task adaption. However, the pre-training corpora are in the general domain, while the data of downstream tasks fall in more task-specific domains.

To bridge the data distribution gap, further pre-training has been applied and shows consistent improvements (Sun et al., 2019). According to the training data used in this process, Gururangan et al. (2020) termed *domain-adaptive pre-training* (DAPT), which uses the data in the same domain of the target task and *task-adaptive pre-training* (TAPT), which uses much less unlabeled training data from the target task than DAPT. They found that DAPT masked LM leads to performance gains under both high- and low-resource settings and TAPT is beneficial with or without DAPT.

DAPT has shown effectiveness for task-oriented dialog modeling. Wu et al. (2020) further pre-trained BERT on 9 task-oriented dialog corpora and outperformed BERT on four downstream tasks, especially in the few-shot setting. Gu et al. (2020) further pre-trained GPT-2 on 13 dialog corpora ranging from chitchats to task-oriented dialogs, leading to better results on three task-oriented datasets.

However, does further pre-training always help? Mehri et al. (2020) performed DAPT on 700M open-domain dialogs and TAPT, but the resulting model only outperforms BERT in 4 out of 7 task-oriented dialog datasets. We also observe that replacing BERT with TOD-BERT-mlm (Wu et al., 2020) that is further pre-trained MLM on 101K task-oriented dialogs does not always bring a significant difference on downstream tasks. So far, however, there has been little discussion about when and why further pre-training on in-domain data can boost the performance on a downstream task and how the DAPT data size can affect this.

In this paper, we conduct an empirical study on the effect of further pre-training $\text{BERT}_{\text{BASE}}$ on task-oriented dialogs. Our experiments are organized around the following research questions:

- **RQ1** When can DAPT improve the performance on a downstream task?
- **RQ2** How does the amount of data for DAPT affect the performance on a downstream task?

We evaluate further pre-trained models on five downstream tasks involving seven task-oriented dialog datasets. Our main findings are summarized as follows: (1) DAPT and TAPT do not always improve fine-tuning performance: the effect varies for different tasks, models, and fine-tuning data sizes. (2) DAPT is more beneficial in the low-resource setting. As the fine-tuning data size grows, the model's representations change more, implying that the in-

*Corresponding author.

[1]Codes are available at https://github.com/zqwerty/ToDDAPT.

Proceedings of the Second Workshop on Insights from Negative Results in NLP, pages 54–61
November 10, 2021. ©2021 Association for Computational Linguistics

fluence of pre-training decays, thus the benefit of DAPT decreases or even vanishes. (3) Increasing the amount of data for DAPT mostly improves the performance in the relative low-resource setting.

2 Experimental Setup

2.1 Further Pre-training

We further pre-train $\text{BERT}_{\text{BASE}}$ uncased model using masked language modeling loss with 15% tokens masked. Our DAPT dataset consists of several multi-turn task-oriented dialog datasets, including Schema (Rastogi et al., 2020), Taskmaster-1&2 (Byrne et al., 2019), MetaLWOZ (Li et al., 2020), MSR-E2E (Li et al., 2018), SMD (Eric et al., 2017), Frames (El Asri et al., 2017), WOZ (Mrkšić et al., 2017), and Camrest (Wen et al., 2017), which has 103K dialogs (13M words) in total. To investigate **RQ2**, we also use 25%, 5% and 1% dialogs to perform DAPT. For TAPT, we use the training set of each downstream task. We use 95% dialogs for training and select the best checkpoint with the lowest MLM loss on the other 5% dialogs. To obtain a training sample $D_{1:t} = \{U_1, S_1, ..., U_t\}$ where U_i, S_i are user's utterance and system's utterance respectively, we randomly pick a dialog D and sample a turn $t \in [1, T]$ uniformly, where T is the length of D. Then all the utterances are concatenated into a sequence as the model input: "`[CLS]` `[USR]` U_1 `[SEP]` `[SYS]` S_1 `[SEP]` ... `[USR]` U_t `[SEP]`", where `[USR]` and `[SYS]` are two special tokens prepended to user's and system's utterances respectively. See Appendix A for the hyper-parameter setting.

2.2 Evaluation

We conduct comprehensive evaluations on 5 downstream tasks. Models on these tasks are adapted from TOD-BERT (Wu et al., 2020), DialoGLUE (Mehri et al., 2020), or ConvLab-2 (Zhu et al., 2020). See Appendix B for fine-tuning details.

Intent Classification (IC) is a sequence classification problem, where models take an utterance as input and predict its intent. We use three datasets: **HWU** (Liu et al., 2019) that has 64 intents and 26K utterances, **BANKING** (Casanueva et al., 2020) that has 77 intents and 13K utterances, and **OOS** (Larson et al., 2019) that has 151 intents and 24K utterances. We pass the representation of `[CLS]` token to a linear layer for prediction.

Slot Filling (SF) requires models to extract slots' values in an utterance, which is often formulated as a sequence tagging problem. We use **REST8K** dataset (Coope et al., 2020) that has 5 slots and 8K utterances. We add a linear layer on the top of the tokens' representations to predict BIO format tags.

Semantic Parsing (SP) aims at identifying both intents and slots' values in an utterance. We use **TOP** dataset (Gupta et al., 2018) that has 45K utterances spanning 25 intents and 36 slots and **MultiWOZ** 2.3 dataset (Han et al., 2020) that has 10K dialogs and 143K utterances spanning 7 domains, 13 intents, and 25 slots. We use two linear layers to predict intent and tokens' tags respectively.

Dialog State Tracking (DST) is the task of recognizing user constraints throughout the conversation. We use MultiWOZ dataset version 2.1 (Eric et al., 2020) that has 30 domain-slot pairs to track. We adopt two BERT-based models: **TripPy** (Heck et al., 2020) and **TOD-DST** (Wu et al., 2020). Both models use BERT to encode dialog history.

Dialog Act Prediction (DAP) is a multi-label sequence classification problem, where models predict the intents of the system response given the dialog history. We use two datasets: **MultiWOZ** and **GSIM** (Shah et al., 2018) that contains 6 intents and 3K dialogs. For each intent, we feed the representation of `[CLS]` token to a linear layer and predict whether the intent is in the response.

As for evaluation metrics, we use accuracy for intent prediction, macro-F1 for slot filling and dialog act prediction, exact-match for semantic parsing, and joint goal accuracy for dialog state tracking.

2.3 Representational Similarity Analysis

Representational similarity analysis (RSA) is a technique to measure the similarity between models' representations (Laakso and Cottrell, 2000). Following Merchant et al. (2020), we encode samples from a test dataset and randomly select the same $n = 5000$ tokens as stimuli, whose contextual representations at each layer are used to compute an $n \times n$ pairwise cosine similarity matrix. The final similarity score between two models' representations at a certain layer is computed as the Pearson correlation between the flattened upper triangular of the two similarity matrices.

3 Empirical Analysis

3.1 Full Data Experiments

We fine-tune BERT, TOD-BERT-mlm (Wu et al., 2020) that is further pre-trained on 9 task-oriented

	IC			SF	SP		DST (MultiWOZ)		DAP	
	HWU	BANKING	OOS	REST8K	TOP	MultiWOZ	TripPy	TOD-DST	MultiWOZ	GSIM
BERT	91.14	92.61	84.76	95.32	81.49	76.94	58.39	44.63	79.67	45.46
- Std of 3 runs	0.48	0.23	1.21	0.25	0.21	0.14	0.24	0.28	0.44	0.02
TOD-BERT-mlm	91.17	92.82	84.35	95.50	80.86	78.20	58.59	47.66	81.47	45.78
DAPT (all data)	90.80	92.89	84.64	**96.21**	80.96	77.59	58.45	45.71	79.92	45.42
25% data	91.26	91.88	85.55	95.77	80.98	77.71	58.00	**46.32**	**81.80**	45.70
5% data	91.26	**93.08**	84.91	96.03	81.35	77.66	58.06	45.48	80.28	**45.72**
1% data	90.33	91.72	85.64	95.83	**81.81**	**77.93**	58.75	46.08	79.72	45.37
TAPT	**91.91**	92.24	**87.45**	95.76	81.57	77.66	58.49	45.85	80.57	45.56
DAPT+TAPT	91.17	92.89	85.02	96.03	81.17	77.73	**59.12**	45.85	78.92	45.70
$\overline{\Delta}_{\text{DAPT}}$	-0.22	-0.21	0.42	0.63	-0.21	0.79	-0.08	1.27	0.76	0.10
Δ_{TAPT}	0.77	-0.37	2.69	0.43	-0.26	0.72	0.10	1.22	0.90	0.10

Table 1: Performance on downstream tasks. We report the means and standard deviations across three random seeds for BERT. Note that TOD-BERT-mlm has pre-trained on MultiWOZ dataset. A task is in red if further pre-training all outperform BERT by at least one standard deviation. The best task performances are boldfaced.

datasets including MultiWOZ, and our further pre-trained models on downstream tasks using the same hyper-parameters. The results are shown in Table 1. To measure the performance variance, we fine-tune BERT three times using different random seeds and report means and standard deviations. We evaluate the effect of DAPT, denoted by $\overline{\Delta}_{\text{DAPT}}$, through averaging the improvements of the models with different DAPT data sizes (100%, 25%, 5%, 1%) compared with BERT. Similarly, Δ_{TAPT} is the benefit of TAPT.

We find that $\overline{\Delta}_{\text{DAPT}}$ and Δ_{TAPT} sometimes are small or even negative, indicating that **DAPT and TAPT does not always improve performances on downstream tasks.** Consistently, TOD-BERT-mlm does not always outperform BERT significantly. Only on tasks in red in Table 1, the benefits of further pre-training are larger than the standard deviations of BERT. In some cases, interestingly, further pre-training can lead to inferior performance. Even on the same MultiWOZ dataset, further pre-training effects vary according to the model architectures used (TripPy, TOD-DST) and the downstream tasks (SP, DST, DAP). Compared with DAPT and DAPT+TAPT, TAPT obtains similar results but requires much lower training cost, which is worth trying before DAPT.

3.2 RQ1: When can DAPT improve the performance on a downstream task?

Since further pre-training does not help in some cases, we want to explore when DAPT can improve the performance on a downstream task. We first show that DAPT does improve the model's LM ability on downstream datasets (Figure 1), and TAPT can more efficiently improve this ability. This

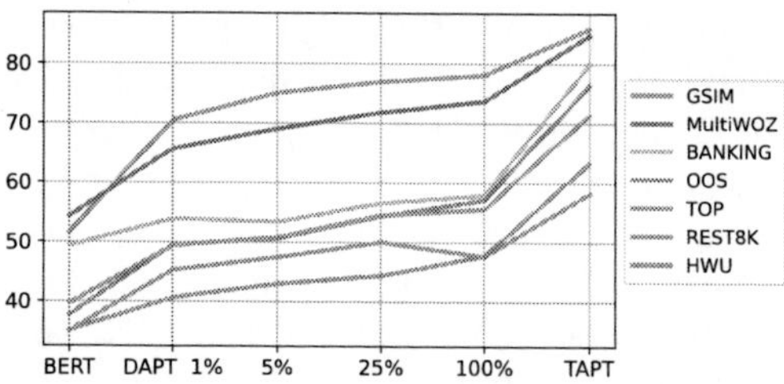

Figure 1: Masked LM prediction accuracy of BERT, DAPT with different data sizes, and TAPT models.

means that further pre-training does reduce the data distribution gap (for LM) between pre-training and fine-tuning but does not guarantee task performance improvement.

A possible hypothesis is that **further pre-training encodes shallow domain knowledge that has obvious influence only when there are insufficient labeled data providing task-specific knowledge for fine-tuning.** By further pre-training, a model learns the co-occurrence of words and their context, which can be viewed as a kind of statistics feature of the target domain. When the fine-tuning data are deficient, this general domain knowledge can alleviate the lack of task-specific knowledge. However, models can learn to encode task-specific knowledge directly through fine-tuning when there are sufficient labeled data and thus rely less on further pre-training.

To verify the hypothesis, we use RSA to assess the representation similarity between fine-tuned models and their initializations for different fine-tuning data sizes. As illustrated in Figure 2, for both BERT and the full data DAPT model, the RSA similarity decreases as the fine-tuning data size grows, especially on the top layers. We ob-

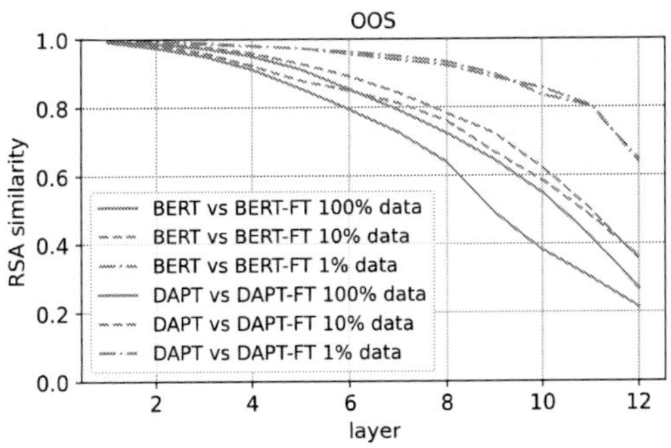

Figure 2: RSA on OOS test set for BERT and DAPT model with 1%, 10%, and 100% fine-tuning data sizes.

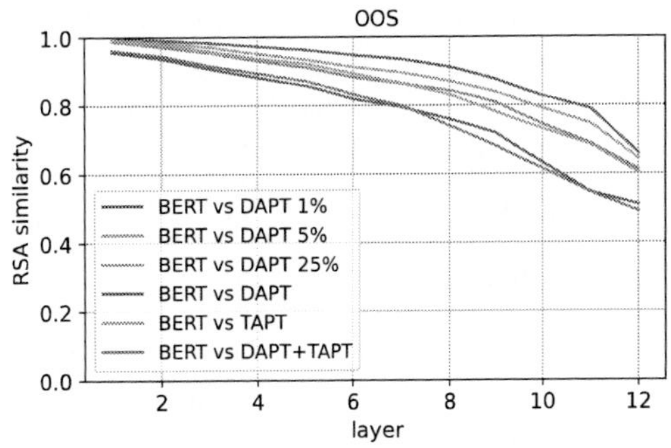

Figure 3: RSA on OOS test set between BERT and further pre-training: 1%, 5%, 25%, and 100% data DAPT, TAPT, and TAPT after full data DAPT.

		$\overline{\Delta}_{\text{DAPT}}$		RSA avg.		best DAPT	
Fine-tune data		100%	10%	100%	10%	100%	10%
IC	HWU	-0.22	0.46	0.73	0.83	5%	5%
	BANKING	-0.21	-0.53	0.74	0.82	5%	25%
	OOS	0.42	1.02	0.69	0.77	1%	25%
SF	REST8K	0.63	0.63	0.73	0.79	100%	25%
SP	TOP	-0.21	0.35	0.71	0.72	1%	5%
	MultiWOZ	0.79	2.44	0.57	0.70	1%	100%
DST	TripPy	-0.08	1.44	0.52	0.56	1%	5%
	TOD-DST	1.27	3.67	0.39	0.49	25%	100%
DAP	MultiWOZ	0.76	0.35	0.26	0.45	25%	100%
	GSIM	0.10	0.28	0.66	0.69	5%	25%

Table 2: Comparison of full and 10% data fine-tuning. We use the same 10% data and average the performance of 3 runs using different random seeds. The RSA similarity averaged across layers is between full data DAPT model and its fine-tuned counterpart. We also report which DAPT data size performs best as "best DAPT".

serve similar trends for all tasks, supporting that less fine-tuning data highlights the importance of pre-training. We also fine-tune the models with and without DAPT in the low-resource setting. Table 2 compares the average performance gain of DAPT ($\overline{\Delta}_{\text{DAPT}}$) and RSA similarity of full data DAPT model and its fine-tuned counterpart (averaged across layers) with full data and low-resource fine-tuning. In the low-resource setting, RSA similarity increases, and DAPT is more beneficial in most cases, which means the knowledge learned through DAPT is more useful when the fine-tuning data are deficient.

3.3 RQ2: How does the amount of data for DAPT affect the performance on a downstream task?

We have shown that models can encode general domain knowledge after DAPT and improve the performance on a downstream task in the low-resource setting. However, how much gain can we obtain by enlarging the DAPT data? To investigate this question, we perform DAPT with 1%, 5%, 25%, and 100% data, ranging from 1020 dialogs to 102K dialogs. From Figure 1, we can see that the more data used in DAPT, the stronger language model on downstream datasets we can get. We also show the change of the model's representation caused by further pre-training in Figure 3. Like fine-tuning, using more data for DAPT brings greater change, and the trend is similar for all tasks. It is also worth noting that compared with DAPT, TAPT changes the model more efficiently in the target dataset.

However, change brought by enlarging DAPT data does not guarantee performance improvement. We compare how much data the best DAPT model used in both full data and low-resource fine-tuning. **As shown in Table 2, including more data for DAPT may not always improve downstream task performance. Nevertheless, when there are less fine-tuning data, the best model needs more data for DAPT.**

4 Conclusion

In this work, we conduct an empirical study to investigate the effect of further pre-training MLM on task-oriented dialogs. Different from earlier findings (Sun et al., 2019; Gururangan et al., 2020), neither DAPT nor TAPT always improves performances on downstream tasks in our experiments. In the low-resource setting, however, DAPT is more helpful, and the size of DAPT data needed to perform best increases. Through RSA, we find that as the fine-tuning data grows, the impact of model initialization fades away, which could be the explanation. We also show that although further pre-training can improve the model's LM ability on downstream datasets, this may not contribute much to downstream tasks under *pre-train* and *fine-tune* paradigm, calling for novel pre-training objectives and effective ways to use pre-trained models.

Acknowledgments

This work was supported by the National Science Foundation for Distinguished Young Scholars (with No. 62125604) and the NSFC projects (Key project with No. 61936010 and regular project with No. 61876096). This work was also supported by the Guoqiang Institute of Tsinghua University, with Grant No. 2019GQG1 and 2020GQG0005. We would like to thank colleagues from HUAWEI for their constant support and valuable discussion.

References

Bill Byrne, Karthik Krishnamoorthi, Chinnadhurai Sankar, Arvind Neelakantan, Ben Goodrich, Daniel Duckworth, Semih Yavuz, Amit Dubey, Kyu-Young Kim, and Andy Cedilnik. 2019. Taskmaster-1: Toward a realistic and diverse dialog dataset. In *Proceedings of the 2019 Conference on Empirical Methods in Natural Language Processing and the 9th International Joint Conference on Natural Language Processing (EMNLP-IJCNLP)*, pages 4516–4525, Hong Kong, China. Association for Computational Linguistics.

Iñigo Casanueva, Tadas Temčinas, Daniela Gerz, Matthew Henderson, and Ivan Vulić. 2020. Efficient intent detection with dual sentence encoders. *ArXiv*, abs/2003.04807.

Samuel Coope, Tyler Farghly, Daniela Gerz, Ivan Vulić, and Matthew Henderson. 2020. Span-ConveRT: Few-shot span extraction for dialog with pretrained conversational representations. In *Proceedings of the 58th Annual Meeting of the Association for Computational Linguistics*, pages 107–121, Online. Association for Computational Linguistics.

Jacob Devlin, Ming-Wei Chang, Kenton Lee, and Kristina Toutanova. 2019. BERT: Pre-training of deep bidirectional transformers for language understanding. In *Proceedings of the 2019 Conference of the North American Chapter of the Association for Computational Linguistics: Human Language Technologies, Volume 1 (Long and Short Papers)*, pages 4171–4186, Minneapolis, Minnesota. Association for Computational Linguistics.

Layla El Asri, Hannes Schulz, Shikhar Sharma, Jeremie Zumer, Justin Harris, Emery Fine, Rahul Mehrotra, and Kaheer Suleman. 2017. Frames: a corpus for adding memory to goal-oriented dialogue systems. In *Proceedings of the 18th Annual SIGdial Meeting on Discourse and Dialogue*, pages 207–219, Saarbrücken, Germany. Association for Computational Linguistics.

Mihail Eric, Rahul Goel, Shachi Paul, Abhishek Sethi, Sanchit Agarwal, Shuyag Gao, and Dilek Hakkani-Tur. 2019. Multiwoz 2.1: Multi-domain dialogue state corrections and state tracking baselines. *ArXiv*, abs/1907.01669.

Mihail Eric, Rahul Goel, Shachi Paul, Abhishek Sethi, Sanchit Agarwal, Shuyang Gao, Adarsh Kumar, Anuj Goyal, Peter Ku, and Dilek Hakkani-Tur. 2020. MultiWOZ 2.1: A consolidated multi-domain dialogue dataset with state corrections and state tracking baselines. In *Proceedings of the 12th Language Resources and Evaluation Conference*, pages 422–428, Marseille, France. European Language Resources Association.

Mihail Eric, Lakshmi Krishnan, Francois Charette, and Christopher D. Manning. 2017. Key-value retrieval networks for task-oriented dialogue. In *Proceedings of the 18th Annual SIGdial Meeting on Discourse and Dialogue*, pages 37–49, Saarbrücken, Germany. Association for Computational Linguistics.

Jing Gu, Qingyang Wu, Chongruo Wu, Weiyan Shi, and Zhou Yu. 2020. A tailored pre-training model for task-oriented dialog generation. *ArXiv*, abs/2004.13835.

Abhirut Gupta, Anupama Ray, Gargi Dasgupta, Gautam Singh, Pooja Aggarwal, and Prateeti Mohapatra. 2018. Semantic parsing for technical support questions. In *Proceedings of the 27th International Conference on Computational Linguistics*, pages 3251–3259, Santa Fe, New Mexico, USA. Association for Computational Linguistics.

Suchin Gururangan, Ana Marasović, Swabha Swayamdipta, Kyle Lo, Iz Beltagy, Doug Downey, and Noah A. Smith. 2020. Don't stop pretraining: Adapt language models to domains and tasks. In *Proceedings of the 58th Annual Meeting of the Association for Computational Linguistics*, pages 8342–8360, Online. Association for Computational Linguistics.

Ting Han, Ximing Liu, Ryuichi Takanobu, Yixin Lian, Chongxuan Huang, Wei Peng, and Minlie Huang. 2020. Multiwoz 2.3: A multi-domain task-oriented dataset enhanced with annotation corrections and co-reference annotation. *ArXiv*, abs/2010.05594.

Michael Heck, Carel van Niekerk, Nurul Lubis, Christian Geishauser, Hsien-Chin Lin, Marco Moresi, and Milica Gasic. 2020. TripPy: A triple copy strategy for value independent neural dialog state tracking. In *Proceedings of the 21th Annual Meeting of the Special Interest Group on Discourse and Dialogue*, pages 35–44, 1st virtual meeting. Association for Computational Linguistics.

Aarre Laakso and Garrison Cottrell. 2000. Content and cluster analysis: assessing representational similarity in neural systems. *Philosophical psychology*, 13(1):47–76.

Stefan Larson, Anish Mahendran, Joseph J. Peper, Christopher Clarke, Andrew Lee, Parker Hill, Jonathan K. Kummerfeld, Kevin Leach, Michael A. Laurenzano, Lingjia Tang, and Jason Mars. 2019. An evaluation dataset for intent classification and out-of-scope prediction. In *Proceedings of the 2019 Conference on Empirical Methods in Natural Language Processing and the 9th International Joint Conference on Natural Language Processing (EMNLP-IJCNLP)*, pages 1311–1316, Hong Kong, China. Association for Computational Linguistics.

Jinchao Li, Baolin Peng, Sungjin Lee, Jianfeng Gao, Ryuichi Takanobu, Qi Zhu, Minlie Huang, Hannes Schulz, Adam Atkinson, and Mahmoud Adada. 2020. Results of the multi-domain task-completion dialog challenge. In *Proceedings of the 34th AAAI Conference on Artificial Intelligence, Eighth Dialog System Technology Challenge Workshop*.

Xiujun Li, Yu Wang, Siqi Sun, Sarah Panda, Jingjing Liu, and Jianfeng Gao. 2018. Microsoft dialogue challenge: Building end-to-end task-completion dialogue systems. *ArXiv*, abs/1807.11125.

Xingkun Liu, Arash Eshghi, Pawel Swietojanski, and Verena Rieser. 2019. Benchmarking natural language understanding services for building conversational agents. In *Proceedings of the Tenth International Workshop on Spoken Dialogue Systems Technology (IWSDS)*, Ortigia, Siracusa (SR), Italy. Springer.

Shikib Mehri, Mihail Eric, and Dilek Hakkani-Tur. 2020. Dialoglue: A natural language understanding benchmark for task-oriented dialogue. *ArXiv*, abs/2009.13570.

Amil Merchant, Elahe Rahimtoroghi, Ellie Pavlick, and Ian Tenney. 2020. What happens to BERT embeddings during fine-tuning? In *Proceedings of the Third BlackboxNLP Workshop on Analyzing and Interpreting Neural Networks for NLP*, pages 33–44, Online. Association for Computational Linguistics.

Nikola Mrkšić, Diarmuid Ó Séaghdha, Tsung-Hsien Wen, Blaise Thomson, and Steve Young. 2017. Neural belief tracker: Data-driven dialogue state tracking. In *Proceedings of the 55th Annual Meeting of the Association for Computational Linguistics (Volume 1: Long Papers)*, pages 1777–1788, Vancouver, Canada. Association for Computational Linguistics.

Alec Radford, Jeff Wu, Rewon Child, David Luan, Dario Amodei, and Ilya Sutskever. 2019. Language models are unsupervised multitask learners. *Technical report, OpenAi*.

Abhinav Rastogi, Xiaoxue Zang, Srinivas Sunkara, Raghav Gupta, and Pranav Khaitan. 2020. Towards scalable multi-domain conversational agents: The schema-guided dialogue dataset. *Proceedings of the AAAI Conference on Artificial Intelligence*, 34(05):8689–8696.

Pararth Shah, Dilek Hakkani-Tür, Gokhan Tür, Abhinav Rastogi, Ankur Bapna, Neha Nayak, and Larry Heck. 2018. Building a conversational agent overnight with dialogue self-play. *ArXiv*, abs/1801.04871.

Chi Sun, Xipeng Qiu, Yige Xu, and Xuanjing Huang. 2019. How to fine-tune bert for text classification? In *China National Conference on Chinese Computational Linguistics*, pages 194–206. Springer.

Tsung-Hsien Wen, David Vandyke, Nikola Mrkšić, Milica Gašić, Lina M. Rojas-Barahona, Pei-Hao Su, Stefan Ultes, and Steve Young. 2017. A network-based end-to-end trainable task-oriented dialogue system. In *Proceedings of the 15th Conference of the European Chapter of the Association for Computational Linguistics: Volume 1, Long Papers*, pages 438–449, Valencia, Spain. Association for Computational Linguistics.

Chien-Sheng Wu, Steven C.H. Hoi, Richard Socher, and Caiming Xiong. 2020. TOD-BERT: Pre-trained natural language understanding for task-oriented dialogue. In *Proceedings of the 2020 Conference on Empirical Methods in Natural Language Processing (EMNLP)*, pages 917–929, Online. Association for Computational Linguistics.

Qi Zhu, Zheng Zhang, Yan Fang, Xiang Li, Ryuichi Takanobu, Jinchao Li, Baolin Peng, Jianfeng Gao, Xiaoyan Zhu, and Minlie Huang. 2020. ConvLab-2: An open-source toolkit for building, evaluating, and diagnosing dialogue systems. In *Proceedings of the 58th Annual Meeting of the Association for Computational Linguistics: System Demonstrations*, pages 142–149, Online. Association for Computational Linguistics.

A Pre-Training Details

A.1 Dataset Description

In this section, we present a detailed description of the data we use for further pre-training.

Domain Adaptive Pre-Training (DAPT): We use the pure text of several multi-turn task-oriented dialog datasets for DAPT, including Schema[2] (Rastogi et al., 2020), Taskmaster-1&2[3] (Byrne et al., 2019), MetaLWOZ[4] (Li et al., 2020), MSR-E2E[5] (Li et al., 2018), Frames[6] (El Asri et al., 2017), SMD[7] (Eric et al., 2017), WOZ[8] (Mrkšić et al., 2017), and Camrest[9] (Wen et al., 2017). Table 3 shows the corpus statistics of each dataset. Note that for Schema, we only use its train set as the corpus, and for other datasets, we combine their train, dev, and test sets. For validation, to evaluate the pre-training performance on each corpus separately, we split 5% of the dialogs from each corpus and compute masked language modeling losses on them respectively. For DAPT, we merge the other 95% of each corpus. To reduce the gap between pre-training and fine-tuning, we remove system side utterances at the beginning and the end in each dialog to ensure that the first sentence and the last sentence of each dialog are both from the user side.

Task Adaptive Pre-Training (TAPT): We use the pure text of each downstream task dataset for TAPT and delete the system side utterances at the beginning and the end of each dialog. Similar to DAPT, we use 95% dialogs for training and 5% for validation.

A.2 Hyper-Parameters

In this section, we describe the hyper-parameters we use for further pre-training and how we choose them in our experiments.

	Dialogs	Utterances	Tokens
Schema*	16,142	313,822	3.14M
Taskmaster	30,483	540,311	4.96M
MetalWOZ	40,201	384,381	2.96M
MSR-E2E	10,087	65,451	0.744M
SMD	3,030	13,044	0.116M
Frames	1,369	19,445	0.247M
WOZ	1,200	8,824	1.00M
Camrest	676	4,812	0.0557M
SUM	103,188	1,350,090	13.2M

Table 3: Statistics of pre-training corpus from datasets. The Schema corpus (marked with *) is obtained from the train set and others are obtained by merging train, dev, and test set.

Domain Adaptive Pre-Training (DAPT): In DAPT, we further pre-train the $\text{BERT}_{\text{BASE}}$ uncased model from the official checkpoint in (Devlin et al., 2019) with masked language modeling loss. We use 100%, 25%, 5% and 1% dialogs to perform DAPT respectively. For each setting, we search the hyper-parameters and select the best model according to MLM loss on valid set. We use Adam optimizer with $\beta_1 = 0.9, \beta_2 = 0.999, \epsilon = 1e-6$, L2 weight decay of 0.01, and linear decay of the learning rate. We search maximum learning rate in {5e-5, 1e-4, 3e-4}, warmup proportion in {0, 0.06, 0.1}, batch size in {64, 256}, max sequence length in {256, 512}, training steps in {5K, 10K, 20K, 40K}. For other hyper-parameters, we keep them the same as (Devlin et al., 2019). We further pre-train our model on a single Quadro RTX 6000 GPU. It takes 0.3 hours to finish 1K steps pre-training.

Task Adaptive Pre-Training (TAPT): In TAPT, we search the hyper-parameters as in DAPT except that we search training steps in {500, 1K, 2K, 5K, 10K}.

B Fine-Tuning Details

B.1 Dataset Description

In our experiments, we use seven downstream datasets across five tasks, including HWU[10] (Liu et al., 2019), BANKING[11] (Casanueva et al., 2020),

[2] https://github.com/google-research-datasets/dstc8-schema-guided-dialogue

[3] https://github.com/google-research-datasets/Taskmaster

[4] https://www.microsoft.com/en-us/research/project/metalwoz/

[5] https://github.com/xiul-msr/e2e_dialog_challenge

[6] https://www.microsoft.com/en-us/research/project/frames-dataset/#!download

[7] https://nlp.stanford.edu/blog/a-new-multi-turn-multi-domain-task-oriented-dialogue-dataset/

[8] https://github.com/nmrksic/neural-belief-tracker/tree/master/data/woz

[9] https://github.com/zhangzthu/ConvLab2-Pretraining/tree/pretraining/data/camrest

[10] https://github.com/xliuhw/NLU-Evaluation-Data

[11] https://github.com/PolyAI-LDN/task-specific-datasets

Corpus	|Train|	|Dev|	|Test|	Input Format	Labels	Metrics
			Intent Classification			
HWU†	8,954	1,076	1,076	Single-Turn	Intent	Accuracy
BANKING†	8,622	1,540	3,080	Single-Turn	Intent	Accuracy
OOS‡	15,100	3,100	5,500	Single-Turn	Intent	Accuracy
			Slot Filling			
REST8K†	7,244	1,000	3,731	Single-Turn	Intent, Slot	Macro F1
			Semantic Parsing			
TOP†	31,279	4,462	9,042	Single-Turn	Intent, Slot	Exact Match
MultiWOZ 2.3◇	8,434	999	1,000	Multi-Turn	Intent, Slot	Exact Match
			Dialog State Tracking			
MultiWOZ 2.1†‡	8,434	999	1,000	Multi-Turn	Dialog State	Joint Goal Accuracy
			Dialog Act Prediction			
MultiWOZ 2.1‡	8,434	999	1,000	Multi-Turn	Dialog Act	Macro F1
GSIM‡	1,500	469	1,039	Multi-Turn	Dialog Act	Macro F1

Table 4: Downstream datasets information and the model architecture we used for each dataset. The sizes of train/dev/test sets are the number of dialogs. Note that we mark MultiWOZ 2.1 in dialog state tracking with two symbols, † and ‡, because we adopt two model architectures on this dataset: TripPy (Heck et al., 2020) from DialoGLUE (Mehri et al., 2020) (†) and the DST model from TOD-BERT (Wu et al., 2020) (‡).

OOS[12] (Larson et al., 2019), REST8K[13] (Larson et al., 2019), TOP[14] (Gupta et al., 2018), MultiWOZ 2.1[15] (Eric et al., 2019), MultiWOZ 2.3[16] (Han et al., 2020) and GSIM[17] (Shah et al., 2018). All these datasets are publicly available and can be downloaded directly from the Internet. The datasets information is shown in Table 4.

B.2 Model Architectures for Downstream Tasks

For different downstream tasks, we adopt task-specific model architectures from the three works as listed below and replaced the pre-trained $\text{BERT}_{\text{BASE}}$ with our model. Note that for multi-turn dialog inputs, we reverse the utterances as described in Section 2.1. We keep the original hyper-parameters in each work unchanged when fine-tuning the model.

DialoGLUE DialoGLUE (Mehri et al., 2020) is a benchmark for the language understanding of task-oriented dialogs. Apart from the datasets, DialoGLUE also provides the model architectures built on the pre-trained BERT model for different tasks. The datasets on which we adopt model architectures from DialoGLUE is marked as † in Table 4.

TOD-BERT TOD-BERT (Wu et al., 2020) is a recent model for task-oriented dialogs understanding. We use their models for dialog state tracking and dialog act prediction, marked as ‡ in Table 4.

Convlab-2 Convlab-2 (Zhu et al., 2020) is an open-source toolkit that helps researchers build, evaluate and diagnose task-oriented dialog systems. We mark the dataset on which we use the model architecture from Convlab-2 as ◇ in Table 4.

[12] https://github.com/clinc/oos-eval

[13] https://github.com/PolyAI-LDN/task-specific-datasets

[14] http://fb.me/semanticparsingdialog

[15] https://github.com/budzianowski/multiwoz

[16] https://github.com/budzianowski/multiwoz

[17] https://github.com/google-research-datasets/simulated-dialogue

Recurrent Attention for the Transformer

Jan Rosendahl **Christian Herold** **Frithjof Petrick** **Hermann Ney**
Human Language Technology and Pattern Recognition Group
Computer Science Department
RWTH Aachen University
D-52056 Aachen, Germany
{surname}@i6.informatik.rwth-aachen.de

Abstract

In this work, we conduct a comprehensive investigation on one of the centerpieces of modern machine translation systems: the encoder-decoder attention mechanism. Motivated by the concept of first-order alignments, we extend the (cross-)attention mechanism by a recurrent connection, allowing direct access to previous attention/alignment decisions. We propose several ways to include such a recurrency into the attention mechanism. Verifying their performance across different translation tasks we conclude that these extensions and dependencies are not beneficial for the translation performance of the Transformer architecture.

1 Introduction

Since its introduction by Vaswani et al. (2017), the Transformer architecture has enabled state of the art results on nearly all machine translation (MT) tasks (Bojar et al., 2018; Barrault et al., 2019; Ott et al., 2018). Compared to previous neural machine translation (NMT) approaches (Sutskever et al., 2014; Bahdanau et al., 2015), it introduces many new concepts like self-attention, positional encoding and multi-head attention. However, the Transformer still relies on the encoder-decoder attention mechanism introduced by Bahdanau et al. (2015) to translate a source sentence into the target language. While for earlier NMT models, this attention mechanism was thoroughly investigated and many different variants were proposed (Feng et al., 2016; Cohn et al., 2016; Sankaran et al., 2016; Tu et al., 2016), the same can not be said for the Transformer. In the present work, we discuss the Transformer encoder-decoder attention mechanism, propose different ways to enhance its capabilities and analyze the resulting systems.

One particular design decision in the Transformer attention mechanism catches the eye: When calculating the context vector in the current decoding step, there is no direct information flow coming from the previous steps. While earlier neural architectures explicitly incorporated the hidden state from the previous decoding step in the attention calculation (Bahdanau et al., 2015) and traditional count-based alignment models used higher order Markov assumptions, the Transformer relies on the self-attention mechanism and layer stacking to learn context dependencies. Therefore we ask the questions *if* and *how* an explicit dependency on the previous attention decisions should be included in the Transformer encoder-decoder attention mechanism. In order to provide an answer we propose numerous approaches towards modeling such an explicit dependency and report our findings across three language pairs.

2 Related Work

In recurrent network architectures (Bahdanau et al., 2015) the decoder state recurrently depends on the previous decoding step. Many works have extended this by additionally adding an explicit recurrent dependency within the attention mechanism itself.

Feng et al. (2016) concatenate the attention context produced in the previous decoding step to the input of the attention mechanism. Other approaches approximate a coverage value for every source position by accumulating the attention weights over all previous time steps, which is then included in the attention calculation (Cohn et al., 2016). Tu et al. (2016) extend this idea by renormalizing the coverage using a fertility model that predicts how much attention a specific source word should receive. In a similar spirit Sankaran et al. (2016) explicitly bias the attention weights to be more focused on source positions that did not receive much attention yet.

In contrast to network architectures with a recurrent decoder, the Transformer (Vaswani et al., 2017) is trained completely parallel and uses multi-head, additive cross-attention. This work tries to answer whether introducing a recurrent dependency can

Proceedings of the Second Workshop on Insights from Negative Results in NLP, pages 62–66
November 10, 2021.

also benefit the Transformer cross-attention.

3 Recurrent Cross-Attention

3.1 Encoder-Decoder Attention

The 'vanilla' Transformer is an intricate encoder-decoder architecture that uses an attention mechanism to map a sequence of input tokens f_1^J onto a sequence of output tokens e_1^I. In this framework, a *context vector* $c_i^{\ell,n}$ for the ℓ-th decoder layer and the n-th attention head is calculated in the i-th decoding step by

$$c_i^{\ell,n} = \sum_j \alpha_{i,j}^{\ell,n}(W_v^{\ell,n} h_j).$$

Here, h_j denotes the j-th output of the encoder which is transformed by a trainable weight matrix $W_v^{\ell,n}$ into the *value*. $\alpha_{i,j}^{\ell,n}$ is calculated using h_j as well as the output of the previous decoder layer (after self-attention) s_i^ℓ. More specifically, we calculate the *energy*

$$\hat{\alpha}_{i,j}^{\ell,n} = \frac{1}{\sqrt{d_k}}(W_k^{\ell,n} h_j)^\intercal (W_q^{\ell,n} s_i^\ell)$$

where d_k is the feature dimension, $W_k^{\ell,n}$ and $W_q^{\ell,n}$ are trainable weight matrices, transforming h_j and s_i^ℓ into the *key* and *query* respectively. This naming stems from the intuition that we use a query $W_q^{\ell,n} s_i^\ell$ to perform a lookup on a series of key-value pairs:

$$\left(W_k^{\ell,n} h_1, W_v^{\ell,n} h_1\right), \ldots, \left(W_k^{\ell,n} h_J, W_v^{\ell,n} h_J\right).$$

The energy $\hat{\alpha}_{i,j}^{\ell,n}$ is then normalized using the softmax operation to get the so called attention 'weights'

$$\alpha_{i,j}^{\ell,n} = \text{softmax}(\hat{\alpha}_{i,j}^{\ell,n}) = \frac{\exp(\hat{\alpha}_{i,j}^{\ell,n})}{\sum_{j'} \exp(\hat{\alpha}_{i,j'}^{\ell,n})}. \quad (1)$$

Once the $c_i^{\ell,n}$ are calculated, the *full context vector* c_i^ℓ is formed by concatenating the outputs of all attention heads followed by a linear transformation. A combination of residual connections, feedforward and self attention layers is used to transform c_i^ℓ into $s_i^{\ell+1} = f(c_i^\ell)$, the decoder state before the next cross-attention layer. In this work we focus on the cross-attention and refere the reader to Vaswani et al. (2017) for the details on the self-attention concept.

One thing that becomes obvious in the above description is the lack of information flow along the decoder 'time-axis' i. The only way the system can make use of such information is through the aforementioned self-attention concept. In this work we raise the question whether such an indirect way of information flow is sufficient or if the system can profit from a more direct integration of its 'past attention decisions'.

3.2 Modifying the Query

A straight forward way to use information from the previous decoder time step $i-1$ in the current attention calculation is by modifying the query vector. We do this by simple concatenation, resulting in

$$\hat{\alpha}_{i,j}^{\ell,n} = \frac{1}{\sqrt{d_k}}(W_k^{\ell,n} h_j)^\intercal \left(W_{q'}^{\ell,n} \begin{pmatrix} s_i^\ell \\ f_{i-1} \end{pmatrix}\right)$$

where f_{i-1} is some function holding information from the previous time step. One apparent way to define this function is the **concatenate previous context** variant,

$$f_{i-1} = c_{i-1}^{\ell,n} \quad (2)$$

where we simply use the context vector of the previous time step. One can argue that the previous attention weight of the j-th source position, $\alpha_{i-1,j}^{\ell,n}$, is more useful than the already condensed context vector. Therefore we consider the **concatenate previous weight** approach:

$$f_{i-1} = \alpha_{i-1,j}^{\ell,n}. \quad (3)$$

However, here we only take into account the time step directly preceding the current one. In order to investigate if additional information from earlier decisions might be helpful, we define the **concatenate previous accumulated weight** approach:

$$f_{i-1} = \sum_{i'=1}^{i-1} \alpha_{i',j}^{\ell,n} \quad (4)$$

specifying how much the encoder output from the j-th position has been attended to so far.

For all of the variants described in this section, the resulting energies $\hat{\alpha}_{i,j}^{\ell,n}$ are normalized using a softmax operation (see Equation 1).

3.3 Expanding the Key-Value List

Staying in the 'query-key-value' framework, the pendant to modifying the query vector (as in Section 3.2) would be to modify the key-value list in order to incorporate information from the previous time step. We expand this list by inserting one additional vector pair (g_k, g_v) along the time axis and name this approach **expand key-value list**.

For choosing the vectors g_k and g_v, we test four different variants. In **variant 1** we use the (linearly transformed) full context vector c_{i-1}^ℓ from the previous time step as both additional key and value vector

$$g_k = W_k^{\ell,n} c_{i-1}^{\ell}, \quad g_v = W_v^{\ell,n} c_{i-1}^{\ell}. \tag{5}$$

The context vector is transformed using the same matrices $W_k^{\ell,n}$ and $W_v^{\ell,n}$ which we also use for transforming the other keys and values respectively. One can argue that a separate transformation is needed for the context vector, which leads us to **variant 2**,

$$g_k = W_{g_k}^{\ell,n} c_{i-1}^{\ell}, \quad g_v = W_{g_v}^{\ell,n} c_{i-1}^{\ell} \tag{6}$$

where $W_{g_k}^{\ell,n}$ and $W_{g_v}^{\ell,n}$ are used specifically for transforming c_{i-1}^{ℓ}. Furthermore, we speculate that a specific attention head should mostly just benefit from incorporating its own previous output. Therefore we define **variant 3** as:

$$g_k = W_{g_k}^{\ell,n} c_{i-1}^{\ell,n}, \quad g_v = W_{g_v}^{\ell,n} c_{i-1}^{\ell,n}. \tag{7}$$

where just the context vector $c_{i-1}^{\ell,n}$, produced by the same head, is considered in the calculation. Finally we test **variant 4** in which only the key is transformed but the value is not:

$$g_k = W_{g_k}^{\ell,n} c_{i-1}^{\ell,n}, \quad g_v = c_{i-1}^{\ell,n}. \tag{8}$$

The rationale here is that $c_{i-1}^{\ell,n}$ already 'belongs' in the context vector embedding space (not the encoder output space like h_j) and therefore no transformation should be necessary. On a side note, while all of these changes might make sense from an architectural point of view, they certainly raise questions regarding the interpretability of the attention weights as a target to source alignment.

3.4 Re-scaling the Attention Weights

Finally, the most direct way to use information from the previous time step $i-1$ in the current attention calculation is by directly modifying the attention weights. We test two ways of doing this:

- **Encouraging continuous attention** patterns where the attention weights from the previous decoding step are similar to the weights of the current one

$$\mathring{\alpha}_{i,j}^{\ell,n} = \lambda \hat{\alpha}_{i,j}^{\ell,n} + \frac{1-\lambda}{2k+1} \sum_{j'=j-k}^{j+k} \mathring{\alpha}_{i-1,j'}^{\ell,n}. \tag{9}$$

- **Encouraging coverage** by reducing the attention weight by an amount proportional to the extend in which the source position j already has been attended to in all preceding time steps combined

$$\mathring{\alpha}_{i,j}^{\ell,n} = \hat{\alpha}_{i,j}^{\ell,n} - \frac{\lambda}{\sqrt{d_k}} \sum_{i'=1}^{i-1} \alpha_{i',j}^{\ell,n}. \tag{10}$$

For both variants we apply normalization

$$\alpha_{i,j}^{\ell,n} = \text{softmax}(\mathring{\alpha}_{i,j}^{\ell,n}) \tag{11}$$

and tune the hyperparameters: the scaling factor λ (both approaches) and the window size k (only first).

4 Experimental Setup

We evaluate our approaches on three tasks: The WMT 2016 news translation Romanian→English task, the WMT 2018 news translation Turkish→English task, as well as the IWSLT 2017 English→Italian translation task on TED data. Our training data consists of 612k (Ro→En: SE Times, Europarl v8), 208k (Tr→En: SE Times) and 227k (En→It: TED talk) parallel sentences, which we preprocess using 20k byte-pair-encoding operations (8k for En→It) learned jointly on source and target data.

We train a 6-layer Transformer for each task, similar to the 'base'-configuration of Vaswani et al. (2017). All models are implemented in RETURNN (Zeyer et al., 2018). We tie the weights of all embedding/projection matrices and apply a dropout of 20% for Ro→En and 30% for Tr→En and En→It. The baseline models use a batch size of 9600, however GPU memory limitations allow a batch size of maximum 7600 for some experiments that add a recurrency to the decoder. We select the best checkpoint according to BLEU on the development set and report case-sensitive BLEU calculated with SacreBLEU (Post, 2018) and TER with TERCom (Snover et al., 2006) on a holdout test set.

System Architecture	Variant	BLEU	TER
Baseline	-	35.7	51.4
Expand key-value list	1 (Eq. 5)	**35.9**	**51.1**
	2 (Eq. 6)	**35.9**	**51.1**
	3 (Eq. 7)	35.7	51.5
	4 (Eq. 8)	33.8	53.2

Table 1: Performance of the different variants of the **expand key-value lists** approach (Section 3.3) on the development set of the Ro→En task.

5 Experimental Results

5.1 Tuning of the Methods

We tune and select all presented hyperparameters of specific model variants on the development set of the Ro→En task.

The different variants of the **expand key-value list** approach introduced in Section 3.3 differ solely

System Architecture	Ro→En newstest2016		Tr→En newstest2018		En→It TED tst2010		Train Time
	BLEU	TER	BLEU	TER	BLEU	TER	
current state-of-the-art	34.5[1]	-	20.2[2]	-	28.5[3]	-	-
Baseline	34.2	53.5	19.6	**70.2**	28.9	58.5	**1.0x**
Concat prev context (Eq. 2)	33.8	53.8	19.5	70.3	28.9	58.3	5.6x
Concat prev weight (Eq. 3)	**34.3**	53.4	**19.8**	**70.2**	**29.1**	**58.0**	6.0x
Concat prev accum weight (Eq. 4)	34.2	53.4	19.7	70.3	**29.1**	58.3	6.1x
Expand key-value list (Eq. 5)	34.0	53.6	**19.8**	70.5	28.9	58.5	7.5x
Accumulation of the energies (Eq. 9)	34.2	**53.2**	19.6	**70.2**	28.7	58.7	5.4x
Subtract the weights (Eq. 10)	**34.3**	**53.2**	19.5	71.2	28.7	58.8	7.9x

Table 2: Performance comparison of the approaches using additional context information from the previous time steps as described in Section 3.1. Train time refers to the average GPU time per training checkpoint measured on Ro→En. We show the best results reported in literature for each task: [1] Kasai et al. (2020), [2] Marie et al. (2018) and [3] Lakew et al. (2017)

in the way in which the context vector is transformed before being used as an additional key-value pair. The performance of each variant in terms of BLEU and TER is shown in Table 1. The **variants 1** (Equation 5) and **2** (Equation 6) perform the strongest, being both slightly better than our baseline system. Re-using the transformation matrices from the other key-value pairs does not seem to hurt the system. Limiting the additional context information to the same attention head (**variant 3**, Equation 7) results in a slight performance loss. Additionally, omitting the transformation of $c_{i-1}^{\ell,n}$ for the value-list (**variant 4**, Equation 8) results in a significant performance loss, indicating that this vector is not directly compatible with the other vectors in the list after all. Since it exhibits the best balance between performance and complexity, we choose **variant 1** (Equation 5) for the complete system comparison.

Furthermore, we have to look at the different ways for re-scaling the attention weights as introduced in Section 3.4. We tune the hyperparameters k and λ for each method applicable. For the window size, we find $k = 5$ to work best and for the scaling factor we choose $\lambda = 0.5$ for all variants.

5.2 Main Comparison

The comparison of all the approaches defined in Section 3.1 and tuned/selected in Section 5.1 are shown in Table 2. Note that all the approach-specific hyperparameter tuning was done on the Ro→En task, distinguishing it from the other two.

For the most part there is very little variation in system performance across all proposed methods, none of which can outperform the Transformer baseline by a significant amount. While there were still some (although small) improvements visible when evaluating on the development set, e.g. for the methods discussed in Section 3.4, these mostly vanish when evaluating on unseen test sets and on different tasks. This might be a testament to overfitting on the development set when tuning the hyperparameters.

While one can argue that the proposed methods exhibit the same level of performance as the Transformer baseline, there is a significant downside: training speed. In the last column of Table 2 the average computation time per checkpoint relative to the Transformer baseline is shown. All proposed methods slow down the training by at least a factor of 5. This is due to a combination of breaking the parallelization inside the decoder (we have to wait for timestep $i-1$ to finish in order to do the computations for timestep i) and having to use a smaller batch size in training.

6 Conclusion

In this work we provide a detailed analysis on the encoder-decoder attention mechanism in the Transformer architecture. We argue that – compared to previous attention formulations – there does not exist a direct link to the context produced in the earlier decoding steps. We propose different approaches to explicitly model this link and test the resulting systems on three machine translation tasks. The results show no significant improvements for any of the tested approaches. This leads us to the conclusion that the context information which is incorporated through self-attention is already sufficient for the given task of machine translation.

References

Dzmitry Bahdanau, Kyunghyun Cho, and Yoshua Bengio. 2015. Neural machine translation by jointly learning to align and translate. In *3rd International Conference on Learning Representations, ICLR 2015, San Diego, CA, USA, May 7-9, 2015, Conference Track Proceedings*.

Loïc Barrault, Ondrej Bojar, Marta R. Costa-jussà, Christian Federmann, Mark Fishel, Yvette Graham, Barry Haddow, Matthias Huck, Philipp Koehn, Shervin Malmasi, Christof Monz, Mathias Müller, Santanu Pal, Matt Post, and Marcos Zampieri. 2019. Findings of the 2019 conference on machine translation (WMT19). In *Proceedings of the Fourth Conference on Machine Translation, WMT 2019, Florence, Italy, August 1-2, 2019 - Volume 2: Shared Task Papers, Day 1*, pages 1–61. Association for Computational Linguistics.

Ondrej Bojar, Christian Federmann, Mark Fishel, Yvette Graham, Barry Haddow, Philipp Koehn, and Christof Monz. 2018. Findings of the 2018 conference on machine translation (WMT18). In *Proceedings of the Third Conference on Machine Translation: Shared Task Papers, WMT 2018, Belgium, Brussels, October 31 - November 1, 2018*, pages 272–303. Association for Computational Linguistics.

Trevor Cohn, Cong Duy Vu Hoang, Ekaterina Vymolova, Kaisheng Yao, Chris Dyer, and Gholamreza Haffari. 2016. Incorporating structural alignment biases into an attentional neural translation model. *CoRR*, abs/1601.01085.

Shi Feng, Shujie Liu, Nan Yang, Mu Li, Ming Zhou, and Kenny Q. Zhu. 2016. Improving attention modeling with implicit distortion and fertility for machine translation. In *COLING 2016, 26th International Conference on Computational Linguistics, Proceedings of the Conference: Technical Papers, December 11-16, 2016, Osaka, Japan*, pages 3082–3092. ACL.

Jungo Kasai, James Cross, Marjan Ghazvininejad, and Jiatao Gu. 2020. Non-autoregressive machine translation with disentangled context transformer. In *International Conference on Machine Learning*, pages 5144–5155. PMLR.

Surafel M Lakew, Quintino F Lotito, Matteo Negri, Marco Turchi, and Marcello Federico. 2017. Improving zero-shot translation of low-resource languages. In *14th International Workshop on Spoken Language Translation*.

Benjamin Marie, Rui Wang, Atsushi Fujita, Masao Utiyama, and Eiichiro Sumita. 2018. Nict's neural and statistical machine translation systems for the wmt18 news translation task. In *Proceedings of the Third Conference on Machine Translation: Shared Task Papers*, pages 449–455.

Myle Ott, Sergey Edunov, David Grangier, and Michael Auli. 2018. Scaling neural machine translation. In *Proceedings of the Third Conference on Machine Translation: Research Papers, WMT 2018, Belgium, Brussels, October 31 - November 1, 2018*, pages 1–9. Association for Computational Linguistics.

Matt Post. 2018. A call for clarity in reporting BLEU scores. In *Proceedings of the Third Conference on Machine Translation: Research Papers, WMT 2018, Belgium, Brussels, October 31 - November 1, 2018*, pages 186–191. Association for Computational Linguistics.

Baskaran Sankaran, Haitao Mi, Yaser Al-Onaizan, and Abe Ittycheriah. 2016. Temporal attention model for neural machine translation. *CoRR*, abs/1608.02927.

Matthew Snover, Bonnie Dorr, Richard Schwartz, Linnea Micciulla, and John Makhoul. 2006. A study of translation edit rate with targeted human annotation. In *In Proceedings of Association for Machine Translation in the Americas*, pages 223–231.

Ilya Sutskever, Oriol Vinyals, and Quoc V. Le. 2014. Sequence to sequence learning with neural networks. In *Advances in Neural Information Processing Systems 27: Annual Conference on Neural Information Processing Systems 2014, December 8-13 2014, Montreal, Quebec, Canada*, pages 3104–3112.

Zhaopeng Tu, Zhengdong Lu, Yang Liu, Xiaohua Liu, and Hang Li. 2016. Modeling coverage for neural machine translation. In *Proceedings of the 54th Annual Meeting of the Association for Computational Linguistics, ACL 2016, August 7-12, 2016, Berlin, Germany, Volume 1: Long Papers*. The Association for Computer Linguistics.

Ashish Vaswani, Noam Shazeer, Niki Parmar, Jakob Uszkoreit, Llion Jones, Aidan N. Gomez, Lukasz Kaiser, and Illia Polosukhin. 2017. Attention is all you need. In *Advances in Neural Information Processing Systems 30: Annual Conference on Neural Information Processing Systems 2017, 4-9 December 2017, Long Beach, CA, USA*, pages 5998–6008.

Albert Zeyer, Tamer Alkhouli, and Hermann Ney. 2018. RETURNN as a generic flexible neural toolkit with application to translation and speech recognition. In *Proceedings of ACL 2018, Melbourne, Australia, July 15-20, 2018, System Demonstrations*, pages 128–133. Association for Computational Linguistics.

On the Difficulty of Segmenting Words with Attention

Ramon Sanabria Hao Tang Sharon Goldwater
School of Informatics
The University of Edinburgh
{r.sanabria, hao.tang}@ed.ac.uk, sgwater@inf.ed.ac.uk

Abstract

Word segmentation, the problem of finding word boundaries in speech, is of interest for a range of tasks. Previous papers have suggested that for sequence-to-sequence models trained on tasks such as speech translation or speech recognition, *attention* can be used to locate and segment the words. We show, however, that even on monolingual data this approach is brittle. In our experiments with different input types, data sizes, and segmentation algorithms, only models trained to predict phones from words succeed in the task. Models trained to predict words from either phones or speech (*i.e.*, the opposite direction needed to generalize to new data), yield much worse results, suggesting that attention-based segmentation is only useful in limited scenarios.[1]

1 Introduction

Word segmentation is the task of finding word boundaries in speech. The task has a wide range of applications, including documenting under-resourced languages (Dunbar et al., 2017) and bootstrapping speech recognizers (Juang and Rabiner, 1990). It is often the first step to a variety of unsupervised speech tasks (Chung and Glass, 2018; Chung et al., 2018; Baevski et al., 2021) and to the NLP pipeline for languages with no whitespace between words.

While unsupervised speech segmentation has been studied (Kamper et al., 2017; Räsänen et al., 2015), in many cases a parallel data source may be available, such as transcriptions, translations, or images. Previous researchers have suggested that it is possible to extract word segments from the attention map created by training an end-to-end sequence-to-sequence model on such parallel data (Palaskar and Metze, 2018; Boito et al., 2017, 2019, 2020; Godard et al., 2018). However, Palaskar and Metze's evaluation was non-standard[2] and the others (which we refer to collectively henceforth as BOITOEA) used models with text translations on the *input* side—decoding to phones or phone-like units—which means the trained models cannot be applied to segment novel (untranslated) sequences. In addition, the interpretation of attention as alignments in other areas of NLP has been questioned (Jain and Wallace, 2019; Wiegreffe and Pinter, 2019).

Prompted by the prior work, we set out to study word segmentation with attention in sequence-to-sequence models, aiming to better understand when and how attention can be interpreted as alignments and in what settings it can be used to segment words. Our main experiments follow BOITOEA in performing and evaluating word segmentation on the same data used to train the sequence-to-sequence model. However, instead of training translation models as in BOITOEA, we train models to perform speech recognition: a well-studied task with a simpler (monotonic) alignment structure. This setting is similar to forced alignment, where both the speech and the transcription are given, and the goal is to discover the hidden alignments. Aside from this potential use case, this setting is useful for analysis because it abstracts away from the need to generalize to a novel test set. If the attention is not able to provide acceptable word boundaries in this setting, then the approach is unlikely to succeed in other, more difficult, settings.

We perform experiments on both the low-resource Mboshi dataset from BOITOEA and a much larger English dataset, MuST-C (Di Gangi et al., 2019). We study models trained in both directions with a variety of input-output types (*e.g.*, phones, speech frames) and different postprocessing strategies to extract alignments from the atten-

[1] code available in the following link https://github.com/ramonsanabria/insights_2021

[2] For their ASR model, they reported mean frame error relative to a forced alignment. Positive and negative errors cancel, so a small mean error does not imply correct boundaries.

Proceedings of the Second Workshop on Insights from Negative Results in NLP, pages 67–73
November 10, 2021.

tion weights. We find that although the particular configuration used by BOITOEA works well, in most configurations the word segments extracted from the attention map are poor, even when using a larger dataset or model size. In particular, we did not get good results from any of the configurations that can be applied to a novel test set or to speech frames (rather than phone-like units). We conclude that even in the simple monotonic case studied here, attention typically does not provide clear word-level alignments.

2 Problem Setting

We consider an n-sample dataset $S = \{(\mathbf{x}_1, \mathbf{y}_1, \mathbf{z}_1), \dots, (\mathbf{x}_n, \mathbf{y}_n, \mathbf{z}_n)\}$, each of which is a triplet $(\mathbf{x}, \mathbf{y}, \mathbf{z}) \in \mathcal{X} \times \mathcal{Y} \times \mathcal{Z}$. As an example, $\mathcal{X}$ is the set of sequences of speech frames, $\mathcal{Y}$ is the set of sequences of words, and $\mathcal{Z}$ is the set of sequences of segments, where a segment is a triplet (s, t, w) that indicates the start time s, the end time t, and the word w.

The goal is to learn a function $f : \mathcal{X} \times \mathcal{Y} \to \mathcal{Z}$ given *only* $S|_{xy} = \{(\mathbf{x}_1, \mathbf{y}_1), \dots, (\mathbf{x}_n, \mathbf{y}_n)\}$, i.e., discovering the alignments without observing them. Formally, we aim to find f that minimizes $\sum_{i=1}^{n} \ell(f(\mathbf{x}_i, \mathbf{y}_i), \mathbf{z}_i)$ using only $S|_{xy}$, for some loss function ℓ that evaluates the quality of the segmentation. Note that the evaluation of f is on the set S. We could evaluate f on a test set, but, in general, generalization is *not* involved in this setting.[3]

The setting is general, subsuming many tasks. When $\mathcal{X}$ is the set of speech utterances and $\mathcal{Y}$ is the empty set, this is the usual unsupervised word segmentation. The set $\mathcal{Y}$ can be images or translations, grounding words from other modalities (Harwath et al., 2018). In this work, we focus on $\mathcal{Y}$ being transcriptions, *i.e.*, we have a forced alignment task.

3 Word Segmentation with Attention

Our pipeline, due to BOITOEA, consists of two steps: generating an attention map from a sequence-to-sequence model, followed by postprocessing to convert the map into an alignment.

3.1 Sequence-to-Sequence Models

Below is a review of sequence-to-sequence models. Readers should refer to, for example, Luong et al. (2015) for a detailed exposition.

[3]We do report generalization results in the Appendix, for completeness, though these do not change our main story.

(a) speech

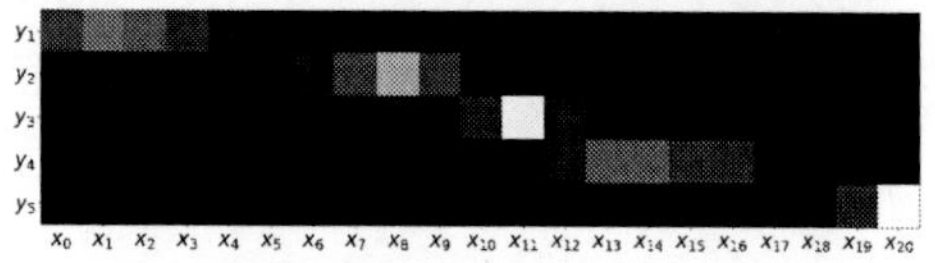

(b) phones

Figure 1: Example attention maps for sequences using (a) speech or (b) phones as input. Note that for space reasons, the maps are shown transposed: each row shows the attention for a single output timestep.

Given a speech utterance $\mathbf{x} = x_1 x_2 \cdots x_T$ or simply $x_{1:T}$ and its transcription $\mathbf{y} = y_{1:K}$, a sequence-to-sequence model learns a function of $\mathcal{X} \to \mathcal{Y}$. An encoder Enc and a decoder Dec take $\mathbf{x}$ and $\mathbf{y}$ as input and produce their respective hidden vectors $h_{1:T} = \text{Enc}(x_{1:T})$ and $q_{2:K} = \text{Dec}(y_{1:K-1})$.

The attention map

$$\alpha_{t,k} = \frac{\exp\left(W_a \begin{bmatrix} h_t \\ q_k \end{bmatrix}\right)}{\sum_{i=1}^{T} \exp\left(W_a \begin{bmatrix} h_i \\ q_k \end{bmatrix}\right)} \quad (1)$$

is computed with a weight matrix W_a. Examples are illustrated in Figure 1. In the early stages of the project, we experimented with dot product attention and the results were similar. Finally, the probability of the label is computed as

$$p(y_k | y_{1:k-1}, x_{1:T}) = \text{softmax}\left(W \begin{bmatrix} c_k \\ q_k \end{bmatrix}\right) \quad (2)$$

where $c_k = \sum_{t=1}^{T} \alpha_{t,k} h_t$. The model is trained to maximize the probability

$$p(y_{1:K} | x_{1:T}) = p(y_1 | x_{1:T}) \prod_{k=2}^{K} p(y_k | y_{1:k-1}, x_{1:T}).$$

We emphasize that, in our setting, $\mathbf{x}$ and $\mathbf{y}$ are always given, also known as teacher forcing (Lamb et al., 2016), and we are interested in the attention map α, not how well the model maps $\mathbf{x}$ to $\mathbf{y}$. Note that the assignments to $\mathbf{x}$ and $\mathbf{y}$ can be swapped since both are given. For example, we can align word transcriptions to phonetic transcriptions, or vice versa. However, the choice of directionality has two implications. First, for each output y_k, some parts of $\mathbf{x}$ will have high attention weights, whereas for parts of $\mathbf{x}$, there may be no y_k with high weights. This asymmetry affects the choice of postprocessing method, as described below. Second, typically only one direction will be feasible if we want to apply the trained model to new (unannotated) data. While our experiments here focus on segmenting the training set, we would ideally like to find a method that can also work on new data.

3.2 Postprocessing

We explore three types of postprocessing to obtain the alignments from the attention map α. The first of these was introduced by Boito et al. (2017); the others are novel.

Hard Assignment This approach aligns each output symbol y_k to the input that has the highest attention weight, i.e., to x_{t_k}, where $t_k = \arg\max_t \alpha_{t,k}$. Due to the attention map asymmetry noted above, this approach is only applied when the transcribed words are on the input side; otherwise some phones (or speech frames) may not be aligned to any word. This method hypothesizes a word boundary between two output symbols if they are aligned to different words; otherwise they are considered part of the same word.

BOITOEA mainly use this method to train *translation* models (French input words; Mboshi output phones), but Boito et al. (2020) also present monolingual results (Mboshi input words; Mboshi output phones), which we compare to below.

Thresholding When the attention weight is higher than a threshold τ_{onset}, then we hypothesize a start of a word segment. When the attention weight is lower than a threshold τ_{offset}, then we hypothesize an end of a word segment. Thresholds are set by exhaustive search using F-score on the development set as the search metric. Thresholding can generate multiple segments for a given output, which is not desirable for our setting. However, in an automatic speech translation setup, such behavior can be helpful in some language pairs.

Segmental Assignment Since we know that word segments are contiguous chunks of speech, this constraint should be baked into the postprocessing. In particular, we find a sequence $(s_1, t_1), \ldots, (s_K, t_K)$ such that the sum of attention weights that each segment covers, *i.e.*, $\sum_{t=s_k}^{t_k} \alpha_{t,k}$, is maximized, while respecting the connectedness constraint, *i.e.*, $s_{k+1} = t_k + 1$. This can be achieved by finding the maximum weighted path in a graph with edges as word segments and weights of the edges as the attention weights a segment covers. See a detailed description in Appendix A.1 and (Tang et al., 2017).

4 Experiments

Most of our experiments are conducted on the Mboshi dataset. It contains 4616 short read-speech utterances for training (3 seconds/6 words on average; 4.5h in total), with a vocabulary of 6638 words, and 514 utterances for development. Mboshi is a Bantu Language with no orthography, and the speech is transcribed at the word level using a phonetic orthography designed by linguists. We regard the basic units in the transcriptions as phones.[4] We do not use the French translations of the utterances.

For experiments with speech, we use Kaldi to extract speech features, with a 25 ms window shifted by 10 ms. Each acoustic frame consists of 40-dimensional log mel features and 3-dimensional pitch features. The acoustic feature vectors are used directly, we do no clustering or acoustic unit discovery.

We use a 1-layer bidirectional LSTM encoder and a 1-layer unidirectional LSTM decoder,[5] with 0.5 dropout on the encoder and a 256-dimensional hidden layer.[6] Further hyperparameter details are in Appendix A.2.

As noted above, our main questions do not require testing generalization, so except where otherwise noted (to compare to previous work), we evaluate all models on the training set. Results on the development set, which do not change the story, are reported in Appendix A.3. We report precision, recall, and F-score of the hypothesized word boundaries. When transcribing phones to words, a

[4]We use the term *phone* rather than *phoneme* both here and with reference to the MUST-C data set (below), to avoid making any commitments about the underlying cognitive/linguistic form, which the term *phoneme* implies. For the Mboshi data especially, we are not sure if these commitments hold. However, like phonemic transcriptions, the transcriptions we work with assume a single pronunciation for each word type (effectively, dictionary lookup of pronunciations).

[5]Boito et al. (2020) showed that LSTMs worked better than Transformer or CNN models with their framework.

[6]The number of layers, dropout, and dimensions were tuned on the development set. The values we found best are the same ones Boito et al. (2020) reported, except their hidden layer size is 64. It is unclear why dropout helps in this setting, since without generalization, there is no concern of overfitting, but we did find a small benefit.

Table 1: Word boundary scores on Mboshi for models predicting phones from words (w $\rightarrow$ p), as in Boito et al. (2020), using Hard or Segmental assignment. †Models trained on Train+Dev. *Results from Boito et al. (2020), averaging five attention maps.

		P	R	F	OS
w $\rightarrow$ p	Hard	92.3	83.2	87.5	-9.8
w $\rightarrow$ p	Seg	93.5	93.5	93.5	0.0
w $\rightarrow$ p†	Hard	95.5	85.7	90.4	-10.2
w $\rightarrow$ p†*	Hard	92.9	92.1	92.5	-

word boundary must be hypothesized at the exact place to be counted as correct. In later experiments, particularly for speech, we follow the The Zero Resource Speech Challenge (Dunbar et al., 2017) evaluation and use a 30ms tolerance window, *i.e.*, the hypothesized boundary is counted as correct if it falls withing 30 ms of the correct boundary. Similar to BOITOEA, we use force alignments extracted with a Kaldi (Povey et al., 2011) GMM-HMM model as ground truth word boundaries. We also report the amount of over-segmentation, defined as $(N_h - N_{\text{ref}})/N_{\text{ref}}$. If the quantity is positive, the model hypothesizes too many boundaries; if the quantity is negative, the model hypothesizes too few boundaries.

4.1 Predicting Phones From Words

We begin by confirming the positive results from previous work, following BOITOEA in training a model to predict phones given words.

Results for both Hard Assignment (Hard) and Segmental Assignment (Seg) are shown in Table 1. We transpose the attention matrix to run Seg so that a segment (word) can consist of multiple phones. As expected, both methods work well, with the more principled Seg performing slightly better—though it has a slight advantage, since (due to teacher forcing) it always generates the right number of word segments (yielding OS = 0).

However, these methods can only be applied to the annotated data, which is a significant weakness.

4.2 Words as Targets

Next, we consider the more typical direction of decoding, predicting words given phones. We do not use hard assignment in this setting for the reasons described in Section 3.2.

Results (Table 2) show that, when using phones, flipping the model direction from w $\rightarrow$ p to p $\rightarrow$ w makes the results much worse. The Thresholding method is especially bad, so we focus on Seg for the rest of the paper. The deterioration by simply flipping the model is unsatisfying, because the setting is simple enough that the model should be able to achieve near-perfect results by acting like a lexicon, mapping canonical pronunciations to words.

Table 2: Word boundary scores on Mboshi for models with words as targets, using phones, phone frames, or acoustic feature frames as input (p $\rightarrow$ w, f $\rightarrow$ w, and a $\rightarrow$ w, respectively), with Thresholding or Segmental assignment. The first row is copied from Table 1. Unsupervised baselines (acoustic input only) are also shown: R15 (Räsänen et al., 2015); K17 (Kamper et al., 2017).

		P	R	F	OS
w $\rightarrow$ p	Seg	93.5	93.5	93.5	0.0
p $\rightarrow$ w	Thr	19.2	20.4	19.8	6.3
p $\rightarrow$ w	Seg	58.0	58.0	58.0	0.0
f $\rightarrow$ w	Seg	57.6	57.6	57.6	0.0
a $\rightarrow$ w	Seg	13.4	13.4	13.4	0.0
a	R15	21.5	19.8	20.6	-8.1
a	K17	32.4	7.4	12.0	-77.1

This decoding direction allows us to build models that take acoustic features as input and produce words.

However, once we replace phone transcriptions as input with acoustic features, the result (denoted a $\rightarrow$ w in Table 2) is drastically worse—even underperforming one of the unsupervised baselines (note the change on attention structure between Figure 1b and Figure 1a) .

To understand what causes the dramatic drop in performance, we explore an intermediate input representation where we replace each acoustic frame with its phone label. This input format, which we refer to as phone frames, has the same length as the acoustic input sequence and reflects the duration of each phone, while abstracting away from acoustic variability. Results of this experiment (f $\rightarrow$ w in Table 2) show that most of the performance gap is recovered. This suggests that the model learns little about the phonetic variability in this experiment. This prompts us to work on a larger dataset, with the hope that the model is able to capture the phonetic variability given more data.

4.3 Scaling to Larger Data

We investigate if by exposing a model to more speech data it would learn to normalize phonetic variance and close the gap between f $\rightarrow$ w and a $\rightarrow$ w. For this experiment we use English data (speech, lexicon phone sequences, and word transcriptions) from the MuST-C dataset (Di Gangi

Table 3: Word boundary scores on MuST-C using Segmental assignment with a variety of models. The first three models have 1 hidden layer, while Lg has 5. Unsupervised baselines are also shown: R15 (Räsänen et al., 2015); K17 (Kamper et al., 2017)

		P	R	F	OS
p → w	Seg	44.0	44.0	44.0	0.0
f → w	Seg	42.6	42.6	42.6	0.0
a → w	Seg	21.2	21.2	21.2	0.0
a → w (Lg)	Seg	19.9	19.9	19.9	0.0
a	R15	20.0	28.6	23.5	43.7
a	K17	23.7	26.1	24.8	10.2

et al., 2019). MuST-C provides translations to other languages; we don't use these here but we do limit our data to the 145k English utterances (257h of speech) for which translations are available in all the languages[7]. Utterances have an average length of 6.5 seconds/18 words. We use the same speech feature extraction configuration as in the Mboshi experiments. Because we are using a larger dataset, we also try a deeper (5-layer) model for the speech input. Results are shown in Table 3. The results on p → w are lower than for Mboshi, suggesting that the longer utterances in MuST-C make the task more challenging. The speech in MuST-C is probably also harder than in Mboshi (TED talks vs. read speech); nevertheless, the performance on a → w is better on MuST-C than Mboshi, closer to the MuST-C f → w results. This suggests that adding more data does allow the model to learn more about acoustic variability. However, given the large size of this data set, all the results are underwhelming, and the results with speech still do not beat the unsupervised models.

5 Conclusion

Previous researchers had suggested a connection between attention weights and word alignments in both speech recognition and speech translation. However, we have experimented with several attention-based segmentation methods and demonstrated that these only succeed in the scenario where words are used as the input to the model—a scenario with limited application. Performance drops considerably for models with phones as input, and is no better than unsupervised segmentation for models using speech as input, even when the amount of training data is increased by two orders of magnitude. Although in principle the transcriptions provide an additional source of information, using this to help segment words from speech will likely require a completely different approach.

[7]Find the list of files in Kaldi format in the following link https://homepages.inf.ed.ac.uk/s1945848/must_c_insights.zip.

References

Alexei Baevski, Wei-Ning Hsu, Alexis Conneau, and Michael Auli. 2021. Unsupervised speech recognition. *arXiv preprint arXiv:2105.11084*.

Marcely Zanon Boito, Alexandre Bérard, Aline Villavicencio, and Laurent Besacier. 2017. Unwritten languages demand attention too! Word discovery with encoder-decoder models. In *Automatic Speech Recognition and Understanding Workshop (ASRU)*.

Marcely Zanon Boito, Aline Villavicencio, and Laurent Besacier. 2019. Empirical evaluation of sequence-to-sequence models for word discovery in low-resource settings. In *Interspeech*.

Marcely Zanon Boito, Aline Villavicencio, and Laurent Besacier. 2020. Investigating alignment interpretability for low-resource nmt. In *Machine Translation*. Springer.

Ozan Caglayan, Mercedes García-Martínez, Adrien Bardet, Walid Aransa, Fethi Bougares, and Loïc Barrault. 2017. NMTPY: a flexible toolkit for advanced neural machine translation systems. *Prague Bull. Math. Linguistics*.

Yu-An Chung and James Glass. 2018. Speech2vec: A sequence-to-sequence framework for learning word embeddings from speech. In *Interspeech*.

Yu-An Chung, Wei-Hung Weng, Schrasing Tong, and James Glass. 2018. Unsupervised cross-modal alignment of speech and text embedding spaces. In *Advances in Neural Information Processing Systems (NIPS)*.

Mattia A Di Gangi, Roldano Cattoni, Luisa Bentivogli, Matteo Negri, and Marco Turchi. 2019. MuST-C: a multilingual speech translation corpus. In *North American Chapter of the Association for Computational Linguistics (NAACL)*.

Ewan Dunbar, Xuan Nga Cao, Juan Benjumea, Julien Karadayi, Mathieu Bernard, Laurent Besacier, Xavier Anguera, and Emmanuel Dupoux. 2017. The zero resource speech challenge 2017. In *Automatic Speech Recognition and Understanding Workshop (ASRU)*.

Pierre Godard, Marcely Zanon-Boito, Lucas Ondel, Alexandre Berard, François Yvon, Aline Villavicencio, and Laurent Besacier. 2018. Unsupervised word segmentation from speech with attention. In *Interspeech*.

David Harwath, Adria Recasens, Dídac Surís, Galen Chuang, Antonio Torralba, and James Glass. 2018. Jointly discovering visual objects and spoken words from raw sensory input. In *European Conference on Computer Vision (ECCV)*.

Sarthak Jain and Byron C Wallace. 2019. Attention is not explanation. In *Empirical Methods in Natural Language Processing (EMNLP)*.

B-H Juang and Lawrence R Rabiner. 1990. The segmental K-means algorithm for estimating parameters of hidden markov models. *Transactions on Acoustics, Speech, and Signal Processing*.

Herman Kamper, Aren Jansen, and Sharon Goldwater. 2017. A segmental framework for fully-unsupervised large-vocabulary speech recognition. *Computer Speech & Language*.

Alex M Lamb, Anirudh Goyal Alias Parth Goyal, Ying Zhang, Saizheng Zhang, Aaron C Courville, and Yoshua Bengio. 2016. Professor forcing: A new algorithm for training recurrent networks. In *Advances in Neural Information Processing Systems (NIPS)*.

Thang Luong, Hieu Pham, and Christopher D Manning. 2015. Effective approaches to attention-based neural machine translation. In *Empirical Methods in Natural Language Processing (EMNLP)*.

Shruti Palaskar and Florian Metze. 2018. Acoustic-to-word recognition with sequence-to-sequence models. In *Spoken Language Technology Workshop (SLT)*.

Daniel Povey, Arnab Ghoshal, Gilles Boulianne, Lukas Burget, Ondrej Glembek, Nagendra Goel, Mirko Hannemann, Petr Motlicek, Yanmin Qian, Petr Schwarz, Jan Silovsky, Georg Stemmer, and Karel Vesely. 2011. The kaldi speech recognition toolkit. In *Workshop on Automatic Speech Recognition and Understanding*. IEEE.

Okko Räsänen, Gabriel Doyle, and Michael C Frank. 2015. Unsupervised Word discovery from speech using automatic segmentation into syllable-like units. In *Interspeech*.

Hao Tang, Liang Lu, Lingpeng Kong, Kevin Gimpel, Karen Livescu, Chris Dyer, Noah A Smith, and Steve Renals. 2017. End-to-end neural segmental models for speech recognition. *Journal of Selected Topics in Signal Processing*.

Sarah Wiegreffe and Yuval Pinter. 2019. Attention is not not explanation. In *Empirical Methods in Natural Language Processing (EMNLP)*.

A Appendix

A.1 Segmental Assignment

Given an attention map, the goal of segmental assignment is to find a segmentation that maximizes the amount of attention weights each word covers while making sure that the word segments are connected. To achieve this, we turn this into a problem of finding a maximum weighted path on a graph, where the edges of the graph are segments, the weights on the edges correspond to the amount attention weights covered, and the graph encodes the connectedness constraints.

Suppose the attention map is of dimension $T \times K$. Recall that T is the number of input tokens (such as speech frames) and K is the number of output tokens (such as words). We first create a vertex set $V = \{(t,k) :$ for $t = 0, \dots, T$ and $k = 0, \dots, K\}$, a grid marking every element in the attention map. An edge is a pair of vertices (t_1, k_1) and (t_2, k_2) while satisfying $t_1 < t_2$ and $k_2 = k_1 + 1$. That edge represents a segment of the k_2-th output token that aligns to t_1 to t_2 on the input side. This can be realized by defining the incoming edges

$$\text{in}((t_2, k_2)) = \Big\{ \Big((t_1, k_2 - 1), (t_2, k_2) \Big) : \text{for } t_1 = 0, \dots, t_2 \text{ if } k_2 > 1 \Big\}. \quad (3)$$

We assign the sum of attention weights from t_1 to t_2, *i.e.*, $\sum_{t=t_1+1}^{t_2} \alpha_{t,k_2}$ to the edge $((t_1, k_2 - 1), (t_2, k_2))$.

Once the graph is constructed, we find the maximum weighted path that starts at $(0,0)$ and ends at (T, K). An example is shown in Figure 2. Note that due to the imposed constraints and in turn due to how the graph is constructed, segmental assignment only considers monotonic alignments.

A.2 Hyperparameters and Implementation

We use the sequence-to-sequence implementation of nmtpytorch (Caglayan et al., 2017)[8]. The model comprises one-layer encoder and one-layer decoder with 0.5 dropout, except in the experiment of Section 4.3 where we use a five-layer encoder in the Large (Lg) model. We set a size of 256 to all hidden dimensions (*i.e.*, source and target embedding, encoder, and decoder). We use the Adam optimizer,

[8]https://github.com/lium-lst/nmtpytorch

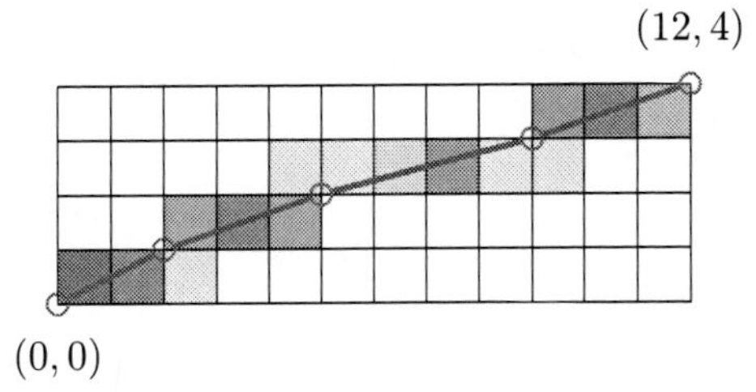

Figure 2: An example segmental assignment with 12 input tokens and 4 output tokens. Each box represents an element in the attention map. The darker the shade, the higher the attention weight. Edges of the maximum scoring path and the corresponding vertices are shown in blue. The shade being crossed by an edge is the amount of attention weights covered by the edge. The goal is of segmental assignment is to find the maximum weighted path from the bottom-left corner to the top-right corner.

and the scheduler applies a decay factor of 0.5 after two consecutive epochs where loss does not decrease. All models are trained until cross-entropy loss on training reaches 0. The implementation of each model has around 3M and 19M of learnable parameters for the 1 and 5 layers encoder model, respectively. They are trained with one Nvidia GEFORCE GTX 1080 Ti. To reduce computation on Segmental Assignment, we set the maximum duration of a word to 4 seconds (400 frames for speech or phone frames representation) for Mboshi and 10 seconds for MuST-C. We set them by analyzing their performance on the development set.

Regarding the unsupervised speech baseline models, we use the unigram public implementation of Kamper et al. (2017)[9] with a minimum word segment duration of 250 ms. Because its performance is linked to the syllable segmentation method, we select the best configuration by fine-tuning Räsänen et al. (2015)'s[10] hyperparameter values on the development set.

A.3 Results without Transcriptions

Finally, we consider a more traditional scenario where the model is exposed to unseen data. For this setting our model does not have access to transcriptions and therefore we do not use Teacher-Forcing. We evaluate the development set from Mboshi (used in Section 4.1), which has 1147 token types (where only 710 are observed during training). In terms of absolute tokens, it has 2993, and only 516 out-of-vocabulary. We experiment with the MuST-C by using 1162 utterances from MuST-C's superset unseen during training. In this case, the set has 3273 token types.

Table 4: Results from 1 layer, and 5 layers (Lg) models for word segmentation of the development (unseen) set of the Mboshi and MuST-C dataset.

DS	Model	P	R	F	OS (%)
Mb	p → w	51.9	54.2	53.0	4.4
Mb	f → w	48.5	47.3	47.9	-2.3
Mb	a → w	16.2	14.7	15.4	-8.9
Mb	a → w (Lg)	14.1	14.9	14.5	6.0
MC	p → w	43.8	44.0	43.9	0.5
MC	f → w	30.1	30.1	30.1	0.2
MC	a → w (Lg)	17.9	20.7	19.2	15.8

Surprisingly, for p and f → w, attention still produces meaningful segments although the model has not seen or early stopped with a development set. In that case, we observe a degradation in performance but not dramatic. The small number of unobserved absolute tokens do not have a critical effect on the segmentation performance of the model.

Finally, the small difference in performance between the train and development sets on a → w shows an already present weak segmentation signal not correlated with word in speech models.

[9] link to Kamper et al., 2017 Github implementation

[10] link to Rasanen et al., 2015 Github implementation

The Highs and Lows of Simple Lexical Domain Adaptation Approaches for Neural Machine Translation

Nikolay Bogoychev* **Pinzhen Chen***
School of Informatics, University of Edinburgh
{n.bogoych, pinzhen.chen}@ed.ac.uk

Abstract

Machine translation systems are vulnerable to domain mismatch, especially in a low-resource scenario. Out-of-domain translations are often of poor quality and prone to hallucinations, due to exposure bias and the decoder acting as a language model. We adopt two approaches to alleviate this problem: lexical shortlisting restricted by IBM statistical alignments, and hypothesis re-ranking based on similarity. The methods are computationally cheap, widely known, but not extensively experimented on domain adaptation. We demonstrate success on low-resource out-of-domain test sets, however, the methods are ineffective when there is sufficient data or too great domain mismatch. This is due to both the IBM model losing its advantage over the implicitly learned neural alignment, and issues with subword segmentation of out-of-domain words.

1 Introduction

Neural Machine translation (NMT) has achieved state-of-the-art performance in a variety of language pairs and settings (Bahdanau et al., 2015; Vaswani et al., 2017), but it is vulnerable to domain mismatch, where the test set differs significantly from the training data in terms of vocabulary, genre, length, etc. This issue is exacerbated in a low-resource condition (Koehn and Knowles, 2017).

Teacher forcing is used during traditional maximum likelihood neural network training, leading to a strong exposure bias, and model confusion when presented with unexpected sequences. This typically results in hallucinations in the output (Müller et al., 2020), because the overly zealous language model component prefers a fluent translation, as opposed to an adequate one. A number of methods have been proposed in order to tackle the issue: exposing the model to its predictions during training (Ranzato et al., 2015; Shen et al., 2016; Zhang et al., 2019; Wang and Sennrich, 2020); tuning directly towards BLEU (Wiseman and Rush, 2016) or using minimum Bayes risk decoding (Kumar and Byrne, 2004; Stahlberg et al., 2017). A common weakness of such methods is that they are computationally expensive.

In this paper, we adopt and experiment with two approaches inspired by previous research. We use lexical shortlisting to interpolate a statistical alignment model with NMT; on top of it, we perform n-best list re-ranking by hypothesis agreement. Our aim is to constrain the lexical choice of the decoder, to prevent hallucinations from being generated. The methods are computationally simpler, as they require no change to the model or training. We analyse the effectiveness of these methods in different scenarios of domain adaptation. We show BLEU gains on a variety of out-of-domain datasets in a low-resource English-German setting. However, the methods show no improvements once the datasets are large, or the domains are too distant.

2 Methodology

We purse and analyse two separate strategies for improving neural machine translation's performance in low-resource domain mismatched settings: lexical shortlisting and n-best list re-ranking based on inter hypothesis agreement.

2.1 Lexical shortlisting

Neural machine translation systems have a vocabulary size of tens of thousands, but for every single translation, most of the vocabulary items are improbable choices. Many researchers attempt to improve on this to speed up the computation in the output layer (Schwenk et al., 2007; Le et al., 2012; Devlin et al., 2014). This is done by preparing a list of likely word-level translations for each sentence (commonly known as lexical shortlist), by using IBM alignment models such as fast-align (Dyer et al., 2013) and limiting the output layer choices

* Equal contribution.

Proceedings of the Second Workshop on Insights from Negative Results in NLP, pages 74–80
November 10, 2021.

to it. This has been implemented in NMT frameworks for efficient systems (Junczys-Dowmunt et al., 2018b) and since widely used (Bogoychev et al., 2020, inter alia).

Recently, Li et al. (2019) showed that even in a high-resource scenario, the quality of the IBM alignments can outperform those learned by a neural model. Therefore, we find it sensible to incorporate word alignments into neural models, especially in a low-resource situation. Although shortlists have a negligible impact on the quality of strong neural systems, we can successfully limit the output layer to the likely tokens according to an IBM model trained on a particular domain, and improve out-of-domain BLEU scores in a low-resource setting. This suggests that the IBM model provides complementary information to the neural model in this scenario.

2.2 Hypothesis re-ranking

Fomicheva et al. (2020) estimate the quality of machine translation by measuring the agreement of the generated hypotheses for a given source sentence. The reason is that (higher) similarity between hypotheses reflects (higher) model confidence. In our problem, we assume that a hallucinated hypothesis will have a low agreement with the rest in the beam. Thus, we propose to re-rank the n-best list based on inter-hypothesis similarity and select the top one as the final translation.

For every source sentence, NMT generates b hypotheses where b is the beam size. For each hypothesis, we measure its similarity against others in the beam, then sort all hypotheses by their final aggregated similarity scores. The similarity score $score_i$ for a certain hypothesis hyp_i is calculated as Equation 1, where the similarity between hyp_i and every other hyp_j produced by the model is measured by an automatic metric $similarity$:

$$\text{score}_i = \sum_{j=0, i \neq j}^{b} \text{similarity}(\text{hyp}_i, \text{hyp}_j) \tag{1}$$

3 Experimental setup

For our experiments, we use OPUS English-German data (Lison and Tiedemann, 2016), with preprocessing performed as per the work of Müller et al. (2020). We follow the same data split as Wang and Sennrich (2020)'s low-resource, domain restricted setting: a model is trained on 1M sentences pairs from the *medical* domain, and is evaluated on *medical* (in-domain), *Koran*, *IT*, *subtitles* and *law* (out-of-domain). We use a joint vocabulary byte-pair encoding (BPE, Sennrich et al., 2016) trained on the *medical* domain with 32k merge operations. In this way, the vocabulary trained on the *medical* domain may be sub-optimal for the out-of-domain test sets. In reality, monolingual data from unknown domains might be available, which can reduce the bias of the BPE training towards the in-domain data. In order to simulate this scenario, we perform an analogous experiment where the BPE vocabulary is trained on all domains, except the *subtitles* corpus, as it is much larger than other domains and would dominate the vocabulary (reasons elaborated in Section 5).

For training, we used the Transformer-base preset of the Marian toolkit (Junczys-Dowmunt et al., 2018a) with transformer preprocessing normalisation as opposed to postprocessing normalisation, and additional attention and feed-forward layer dropout.

We performed ample hyperparameter search, to ensure that our neural network configuration achieves the best possible performance on this low-resource task. Decoding is always done with beam size 6 and length normalisation 0.6. On top of the baseline, we tried three different combinations of methods introduced in Section 2:

- A **shortlisting** configuration where we use a lexical shortlist generated by the *fast-align* model trained on the *medical* dataset. We try various configurations, and we settle on an optimal value of limiting the output layer to the 10 most probable unigram translations according to the IBM model.

- A **re-ranking** setup where we re-rank the n-best translation based on inter-hypothesis similarity. Like Fomicheva et al., we tested out a few different metrics to measure similarity: sentBLEU, ChrF, TER and METEOR. In an initial experiment on the *medical* domain, we found sentBLEU to have the best performance and stick to it for all experiments. We did not pick any neural metrics, as they may have a domain preference and are less interpretable.

- **Both**: shortlisting followed by re-ranking as specified above

Domain	BPE trained on *medical* only				BPE trained on all except *subtitles*			
	baseline	shortlist	re-rank	both	baseline	shortlist	re-rank	both
medical	*60.0*	*59.5*	***60.3***	*59.1*	***61.4***	*58.2*	*57.6*	*60.4*
Koran	0.9	1.0	0.7	**1.1**	0.8	0.9	0.9	**1.0**
law	19.6	**20.6**	16.6	17.8	17.8	19.3	19.8	**20.8**
IT	15.0	**16.3**	10.1	11.5	15.7	**18.0**	15.3	17.8
subtitles	2.8	**3.1**	1.4	1.9	2.6	**2.8**	2.4	**2.8**

Table 1: BLEU results on German-English systems trained on the *medical* domain, and tested on in-domain and out-domain datasets. In-domain results are in italics and the best BLEU on each domain dataset are in bold.

Domain	System	1- to 4-gram precisions				Brevity penalty	BLEU (△)	METEOR (△)
law	baseline	53.0	27.5	16.9	11.0	0.778	17.8	0.36
	shortlist	**56.1**	**29.4**	**17.9**	**11.4**	0.804	19.3 (+1.5)	**0.39 (+0.03)**
	re-rank	51.4	26.4	16.1	10.5	0.906	19.8 (+2.0)	0.31 (−0.05)
	both	53.1	27.6	16.7	10.7	**0.919**	**20.8 (+3.0)**	0.35 (−0.01)
IT	baseline	34.6	18.8	13.1	9.5	0.930	15.7	0.16
	shortlist	**43.9**	**24.7**	**17.1**	**12.1**	0.828	**18.0 (+2.3)**	**0.18 (+0.02)**
	re-rank	33.5	17.2	11.7	8.1	**1.000**	15.3 (−0.4)	0.12 (−0.04)
	both	38.0	20.1	13.6	9.7	**1.000**	17.8 (+2.1)	0.09 (−0.07)

Table 2: Breakdown of BLEU scores for "BPE on all" experiments in Table 1 for *law* and *IT* domains.

4 Results and Analysis

We present in Table 1 our models' BLEU scores on in- and out-of-domain test sets, with both BPE segmentation schemes. When applying the more restrictive BPE trained on the *medical* domain, our shortlisting mechanism always yields a slight increase in BLEU on out-of-domain sets and a small drop on the in-domain set. The *law* and *IT* domains benefit the most, whereas *subtitles* and *Koran* are largely unaffected. Re-ranking is not helpful in this BPE setting.

When using the alternative BPE segmentation trained on all datasets, we see that the baseline scores are generally lower for the out-of-domain datasets, despite a stronger in-domain BLEU. This is potentially because the rare words from out-of-domain datasets get insufficient exposure during training (on *medical* only). However, when using a lexical shortlist in this setting, we see greater improvements in terms of BLEU on the *law* and *IT* domains compared to the *medical*-only BPE scenario. Re-ranking is also much more effective, performing similarly to shortlisting. The combination of re-ranking and shortlisting delivers the best BLEU scores in nearly all out-of-domain splits.

We see that the shortlisting method is always superior to the baseline method on all out-of-domain datasets, although the results vary with the data preprocessing. This is true even more so of re-ranking, which is much better when the BPE vocabulary is learned on all domains. Combining both shortlisting and re-ranking always brings in a slight improvement over just re-ranking on the out-of-domain datasets, but its effectiveness is again preprocessing-dependent.

This clearly shows that the IBM model implemented by fast-align can learn information complementary to NMT, and interpolating them is beneficial for achieving higher BLEU scores in out-of-domain settings. The lower BLEU scores on in-domain test sets are related to the aggressive shortlist we used: by increasing the output layer limit from 10 to 50 most probable tokens, we achieve identical BLEU scores as the baseline.

4.1 BLEU breakdown

According to BLEU scores reported earlier, shortlisting and re-ranking are beneficial to NMT domain adaptation (in a relatively low-resource condition). We try to understand what contributes to the increase in BLEU scores by breaking down BLEU scores into n-gram precisions and length (brevity) penalty. In Table 2 we list the numbers for *law* and *IT* domains, under the "BPE trained on all" setting in Table 1, on which we have seen the largest leap

Domain	law	medical	subtitles†	IT	Koran
Number of sentences	695k	1M	1M	372k	529k
Avg. original sentence length	22.1	12.5	8.0	7.5	20.4
Avg. BPE sentence length	30.4	14.3	11.1	12.7	24.1
Vocab size, appearing >20 times	34k	36k	30k	15k	20k
Vocab overlap with *medical*	11.5k	36k	9.0k	5.8k	5.1k

† The *subtitles* corpus was sampled down from 20M to 1M sentence pairs.

Table 3: Corpus statistics for the different domains.

German	English
sein Pilot hat nicht die volle Kontrolle .	its p@@ il@@ ot is@@ n't in control .
und Z@@ eth@@ rid ? nur einen Strei@@ f@@ sch@@ uss .	and , Z@@ eth@@ rid , just gr@@ aze it .

Table 4: Two random German-English sentence pairs from the *subtitles* dataset after BPE.

of BLEU scores. Additionally, we include METEOR which focuses on n-gram overlap and is not influenced by the output length.

From the table, shortlisting always significantly boosts n-gram precisions, whereas re-ranking alone decreases them. On the other hand, re-ranking "rectifies" the output length, leading to a better brevity penalty (closer to 1) compared to baseline or shortlisting. When using both together, we see slight improvement on both n-gram accuracies and length penalty over baseline. This is expected: shortlisting provides extra word alignment information which aids lexical accuracy; re-ranking favours the hypothesis with an average length, since too long or too short hypotheses will receive a lower similarity score. This implies that shortlisting and re-ranking enhance BLEU from different aspects.

On the contrary, according to METEOR, re-ranking is outperformed even by the baseline, leading to a negative METEOR change. This suggests that the bump in BLEU scores by re-ranking is only due to an improved brevity penalty. While it encourages a more desirable length, re-ranking does not produce better lexical choices. Adequacy wise, shortlisting is proven to be a more constructive method.

5 Limitations

Although our methods show promising gains on the low-resource domains, we found that they have limited application when the domain mismatch is too great or there is sufficient resource available.

5.1 Large domain mismatch

In order to better interpret why our methods are much more helpful on some domains than on others (e.g. *law* versus *Koran*), we gather statistics of our test sets in different domains in Table 3, to reflect the distance between domains. We compute vocabulary overlap with the in-domain *medical* data, for each cleaned corpus prior to BPE encoding. We count only words that are seen at least 20 times, and we sample 5% of the *subtitles* corpus, since it is orders of magnitude larger than the rest. After down-sampling, it has a similar size to the *medical* corpora. We also compute the average sentence length before and after BPE to determine the extent to which BPE transforms the original sentences. Both vocabulary overlap and sentence lengths implicitly reflect the degree of domain mismatch.

For our most difficult datasets, *subtitles* and *Koran*, we see the lowest vocabulary overlap with the *medical* domain of just 22-25%. When BPE is applied to these corpora, the sentence length increases by 20-30%. In practice, extensive and uneven BPE segmentation on named entities makes it difficult for the IBM model to produce interpretable and meaningful alignments to aid a translation model, as exemplified in Table 4.

This means that lexical shortlisting is useful when we have a model trained on a relatively modest amount of data, and the out-of-domain dataset which we adapt to should share a reasonable amount of vocabulary. When the vocabulary overlap is too small, shortlisting drastically loses its effectiveness as a domain adaptation tool.

We confirm this by experimenting with another domain-distant, and extremely low-resource Burmese-English scenario. The training data consists 18k sentence pairs from *news* articles (Ding et al., 2019), and the out-of-domain test set is a *Bible* corpus (Christodouloupoulos and Steedman,

2015). The English side of the training set has 51k unique words, while the *Bible* set has 29k. The vocabulary overlap between the training and test sets is just 6k words, equivalent to 21% of the test vocabulary. After BPE, The average test sentence length increases from 25 to 38 tokens, seeing a 52% rise. We adopt the model trained by Aji et al. (2020) and add shortlisting during decoding. The results displayed in Table 5 show that out-of-domain performance does not improve with shortlisting, likely due to the high degree of vocabulary mismatch.

	baseline	shortlist
news (in-domain)	18.00	15.7
Bible	0.2	0.2

Table 5: Very low-resource Burmese-English results.

5.2 Availability of resources

Our previous German-English experiments are carried out under an artificially resource-constrained condition. We therefore verify the potential of our methods in a high-resource setting too, by applying shortlisting on a WMT19 German-English submission from Microsoft (Junczys-Dowmunt, 2019), and evaluating on the same out-of-domain datasets.

	Microsoft WMT19		low-resource
	baseline	shortlist	baseline
medical	14.4	14.4	61.4
Koran	0.0	0.0	0.8
law	8.7	8.7	17.8
IT	15.4	15.4	15.7
subtitles	1.0	1.0	2.6

Table 6: High-resource German-English results.

Results in Table 6 show that shortlisting has no impact on BLEU comparing to the baseline. We conclude that given a high-resource setting and the apparent large domain mismatch, the IBM model's alignments do not contribute additional information to the model. This finding is corroborated by Li et al. (2019): IBM model alignments are mostly better at capturing function words, not content words, compared to a neural model. Furthermore, unnatural and aggressive BPE segmentation on out-of-domain text (e.g. Table 4) could result in a lexical shortlist not capturing any meaningful alignment.

We add our low-resource baseline trained on *medical* with BPE on all data (Section 4 Table 1) to comparison, and find that it surpasses the huge WMT model on each domain. Two reasons account for this: a WMT model is heavily biased to the news domain only; and the BPE scheme learned from news data is inferior to one learned from the out-of-domain datasets, when being evaluated on these domains.

6 Conclusion

We explore computationally cheap methods to improve neural machine translation performance in out-of-domain settings. We suggest that adding a lexical shortlist trained on the same data is always beneficial. While re-ranking also improves BLEU, it targets the BLEU brevity penalty, and does not produce better word choices. Although our results are promising in a low-resource condition, they do not transfer well to a scenario with very distant domains or sufficient resources. Our analysis shows that this is due to little vocabulary overlap, and the limited contribution from the IBM model under out-of-domain BPE segmentation.

Acknowledgements

We would like to thank the anonymous reviewers, as well as the members of the AGORA research group for their valuable comments.

This work was conducted within the scope of the Connecting Europe Facility *User-Focused Marian*, which has received funding from the European Union's Horizon 2020 research and innovation programme under grant agreement No INEA/CEF/ICT/A2019/1927024. Any communication or publication related to the action, made by the beneficiaries jointly or individually in any form and using any means, shall indicate that it reflects only the author's view and that the Agency is not responsible for any use that may be made of the information it contains.

This research is based upon work supported in part by the Office of the Director of National Intelligence (ODNI), Intelligence Advanced Research Projects Activity (IARPA), via contract #FA8650-17-C-9117. The views and conclusions contained herein are those of the authors and should not be interpreted as necessarily representing the official policies, either expressed or implied, of ODNI, IARPA, or the U.S. Government. The U.S. Government is authorized to reproduce and distribute reprints for governmental purposes notwithstanding any copyright annotation therein.

References

Alham Fikri Aji, Nikolay Bogoychev, Kenneth Heafield, and Rico Sennrich. 2020. In neural machine translation, what does transfer learning transfer? In *Proceedings of the 58th Annual Meeting of the Association for Computational Linguistics*, pages 7701–7710, Online. Association for Computational Linguistics.

Dzmitry Bahdanau, Kyunghyun Cho, and Yoshua Bengio. 2015. Neural machine translation by jointly learning to align and translate. In *3rd International Conference on Learning Representations, ICLR 2015, San Diego, CA, USA, May 7-9, 2015, Conference Track Proceedings*.

Nikolay Bogoychev, Roman Grundkiewicz, Alham Fikri Aji, Maximiliana Behnke, Kenneth Heafield, Sidharth Kashyap, Emmanouil-Ioannis Farsarakis, and Mateusz Chudyk. 2020. Edinburgh's submissions to the 2020 machine translation efficiency task. In *Proceedings of the Fourth Workshop on Neural Generation and Translation*, pages 218–224, Online. Association for Computational Linguistics.

Christos Christodouloupoulos and Mark Steedman. 2015. A massively parallel corpus: The bible in 100 languages. *Lang. Resour. Eval.*, 49(2):375–395.

Jacob Devlin, Rabih Zbib, Zhongqiang Huang, Thomas Lamar, Richard Schwartz, and John Makhoul. 2014. Fast and robust neural network joint models for statistical machine translation. In *Proceedings of the 52nd Annual Meeting of the Association for Computational Linguistics (Volume 1: Long Papers)*, pages 1370–1380, Baltimore, Maryland. Association for Computational Linguistics.

Chenchen Ding, Hnin Thu Zar Aye, Win Pa Pa, Khin Thandar Nwet, Khin Mar Soe, Masao Utiyama, and Eiichiro Sumita. 2019. Towards Burmese (Myanmar) morphological analysis: Syllable-based tokenization and part-of-speech tagging. *ACM Transactions on Asian and Low-Resource Language Information Processing (TALLIP)*, 19(1):5.

Chris Dyer, Victor Chahuneau, and Noah A. Smith. 2013. A simple, fast, and effective reparameterization of IBM model 2. In *Proceedings of the 2013 Conference of the North American Chapter of the Association for Computational Linguistics: Human Language Technologies*, pages 644–648, Atlanta, Georgia. Association for Computational Linguistics.

Marina Fomicheva, Lucia Specia, and Francisco Guzmán. 2020. Multi-hypothesis machine translation evaluation. In *Proceedings of the 58th Annual Meeting of the Association for Computational Linguistics*, pages 1218–1232, Online. Association for Computational Linguistics.

Marcin Junczys-Dowmunt. 2019. Microsoft translator at wmt 2019: Towards large-scale document-level neural machine translation. In *Proceedings of the Fourth Conference on Machine Translation (Volume 2: Shared Task Papers, Day 1)*, pages 225–233, Florence, Italy. Association for Computational Linguistics.

Marcin Junczys-Dowmunt, Roman Grundkiewicz, Tomasz Dwojak, Hieu Hoang, Kenneth Heafield, Tom Neckermann, Frank Seide, Ulrich Germann, Alham Fikri Aji, Nikolay Bogoychev, André F. T. Martins, and Alexandra Birch. 2018a. Marian: Fast neural machine translation in C++. In *Proceedings of ACL 2018, System Demonstrations*, pages 116–121, Melbourne, Australia. Association for Computational Linguistics.

Marcin Junczys-Dowmunt, Kenneth Heafield, Hieu Hoang, Roman Grundkiewicz, and Anthony Aue. 2018b. Marian: Cost-effective high-quality neural machine translation in C++. In *Proceedings of the 2nd Workshop on Neural Machine Translation and Generation*, pages 129–135, Melbourne, Australia. Association for Computational Linguistics.

Philipp Koehn and Rebecca Knowles. 2017. Six challenges for neural machine translation. In *Proceedings of the First Workshop on Neural Machine Translation*, pages 28–39, Vancouver. Association for Computational Linguistics.

Shankar Kumar and William Byrne. 2004. Minimum Bayes-risk decoding for statistical machine translation. In *Proceedings of the Human Language Technology Conference of the North American Chapter of the Association for Computational Linguistics: HLT-NAACL 2004*, pages 169–176, Boston, Massachusetts, USA. Association for Computational Linguistics.

Hai Son Le, Alexandre Allauzen, and François Yvon. 2012. Continuous space translation models with neural networks. In *Proceedings of the 2012 Conference of the North American Chapter of the Association for Computational Linguistics: Human Language Technologies*, pages 39–48, Montréal, Canada. Association for Computational Linguistics.

Xintong Li, Guanlin Li, Lemao Liu, Max Meng, and Shuming Shi. 2019. On the word alignment from neural machine translation. In *Proceedings of the 57th Annual Meeting of the Association for Computational Linguistics*, pages 1293–1303, Florence, Italy. Association for Computational Linguistics.

Pierre Lison and Jörg Tiedemann. 2016. OpenSubtitles2016: Extracting large parallel corpora from movie and TV subtitles. In *Proceedings of the Tenth International Conference on Language Resources and Evaluation (LREC'16)*, pages 923–929, Portorož, Slovenia. European Language Resources Association (ELRA).

Mathias Müller, Annette Rios, and Rico Sennrich. 2020. Domain robustness in neural machine translation. In *Proceedings of the 14th Conference of the*

Association for Machine Translation in the Americas (AMTA 2020), pages 151–164, Virtual. Association for Machine Translation in the Americas.

Marc'Aurelio Ranzato, Sumit Chopra, Michael Auli, and Wojciech Zaremba. 2015. Sequence level training with recurrent neural networks.

Holger Schwenk, Marta R. Costa-jussà, and Jose A. R. Fonollosa. 2007. Smooth bilingual n-gram translation. In *Proceedings of the 2007 Joint Conference on Empirical Methods in Natural Language Processing and Computational Natural Language Learning (EMNLP-CoNLL)*, pages 430–438, Prague, Czech Republic. Association for Computational Linguistics.

Rico Sennrich, Barry Haddow, and Alexandra Birch. 2016. Neural machine translation of rare words with subword units. In *Proceedings of the 54th Annual Meeting of the Association for Computational Linguistics (Volume 1: Long Papers)*, pages 1715–1725, Berlin, Germany. Association for Computational Linguistics.

Shiqi Shen, Yong Cheng, Zhongjun He, Wei He, Hua Wu, Maosong Sun, and Yang Liu. 2016. Minimum risk training for neural machine translation. In *Proceedings of the 54th Annual Meeting of the Association for Computational Linguistics (Volume 1: Long Papers)*, pages 1683–1692, Berlin, Germany. Association for Computational Linguistics.

Felix Stahlberg, Adrià de Gispert, Eva Hasler, and Bill Byrne. 2017. Neural machine translation by minimising the Bayes-risk with respect to syntactic translation lattices. In *Proceedings of the 15th Conference of the European Chapter of the Association for Computational Linguistics: Volume 2, Short Papers*, pages 362–368, Valencia, Spain. Association for Computational Linguistics.

Ashish Vaswani, Noam Shazeer, Niki Parmar, Jakob Uszkoreit, Llion Jones, Aidan N Gomez, Łukasz Kaiser, and Illia Polosukhin. 2017. Attention is all you need. In I. Guyon, U. V. Luxburg, S. Bengio, H. Wallach, R. Fergus, S. Vishwanathan, and R. Garnett, editors, *Advances in Neural Information Processing Systems 30*, pages 5998–6008. Curran Associates, Inc.

Chaojun Wang and Rico Sennrich. 2020. On exposure bias, hallucination and domain shift in neural machine translation. In *Proceedings of the 58th Annual Meeting of the Association for Computational Linguistics*, pages 3544–3552, Online. Association for Computational Linguistics.

Sam Wiseman and Alexander M. Rush. 2016. Sequence-to-sequence learning as beam-search optimization. In *Proceedings of the 2016 Conference on Empirical Methods in Natural Language Processing*, pages 1296–1306, Austin, Texas. Association for Computational Linguistics.

Wen Zhang, Yang Feng, Fandong Meng, Di You, and Qun Liu. 2019. Bridging the gap between training and inference for neural machine translation. In *Proceedings of the 57th Annual Meeting of the Association for Computational Linguistics*, pages 4334–4343, Florence, Italy. Association for Computational Linguistics.

Backtranslation in Neural Morphological Inflection

Ling Liu and **Mans Hulden**
University of Colorado
first.last@colorado.edu

Abstract

Backtranslation is a common technique for leveraging unlabeled data in low-resource scenarios in machine translation. The method is directly applicable to morphological inflection generation if unlabeled word forms are available. This paper evaluates the potential of backtranslation for morphological inflection using data from six languages with labeled data drawn from the SIGMORPHON shared task resource and unlabeled data from different sources. Our core finding is that backtranslation can offer modest improvements in low-resource scenarios, but only if the unlabeled data is very clean and has been filtered by the same annotation standards as the labeled data.

1 Introduction

Both machine translation (MT) and morphological inflection generation are string transduction tasks: MT is typically treated as word-level (or subword-level) string transduction while morphological inflection generation can be treated as character-level string transduction. MT models and techniques can usually be naturally applied to morphological inflection, as is shown in recent work on morphological inflection (Liu, 2021; Kann and Schütze, 2016; Cotterell et al., 2016, 2017, 2018; Liu et al., 2018; McCarthy et al., 2019; Vylomova et al., 2020; Wu et al., 2020; Moeller et al., 2020, 2021).

Backtranslation (Sennrich et al., 2016) has become a common practice in machine translation in low-resource scenarios (Fadaee et al., 2017; Edunov et al., 2018; Hoang et al., 2018; Xia et al., 2019; Chen et al., 2020; Edunov et al., 2020; Marie et al., 2020; Liu et al., 2021). There has been work on data augmentation for morphological generation in low-resource scenarios (Silfverberg et al., 2017; Bergmanis et al., 2017; Anastasopoulos and Neubig, 2019; Liu and Hulden, 2021), but no previous work has applied the backtranslation technique. In this paper, we propose to apply backtranslation as a data augmentation method in morphological inflection under low-resource circumstances. Our evaluation of the method on six different languages with unlabeled data from different resources indicates that backtranslation can only improve morphological inflection in low-resource scenarios when the unlabeled data set is very clean and has been filtered by the same annotation standards as the labeled data.

(a) Labeled data

LEMMA	INFLECTED FORM	MSD TAG
enchain	enchained	V;V.PTCP;PST
bristle	bristle	V;NFIN
enforce	enforcing	V;V.PTCP;PRS
meagre	meagred	V;V.PTCP;PST
remarry	remarried	V;PST
...	...	...

(b) Morphological inflection

Input

LEMMA	MSD TAG
enchain	V;V.PTCP;PST
bristle	V;NFIN
enforce	V;V.PTCP;PRS
meagre	V;V.PTCP;PST
remarry	V;PST
...	...

Output

INFLECTED FORM
enchained
bristle
enforcing
meagred
remarried
...

(c) Morphological analysis

Input

INFLECTED FORM
enchained
bristle
enforcing
meagred
remarried
...

Output

LEMMA	MSD TAG
enchain	V;V.PTCP;PST
bristle	V;NFIN
enforce	V;V.PTCP;PRS
meagre	V;V.PTCP;PST
remarry	V;PST
...	...

Figure 1: Data example for morphological inflection and morphological analysis.

2 Method

The backtranslation method comes from machine translation. Suppose we need to translate from language A to language B, and we have a parallel text corpus. Suppose further that we have additional monolingual data for B. The idea in backtransla-

Proceedings of the Second Workshop on Insights from Negative Results in NLP, pages 81–88
November 10, 2021.

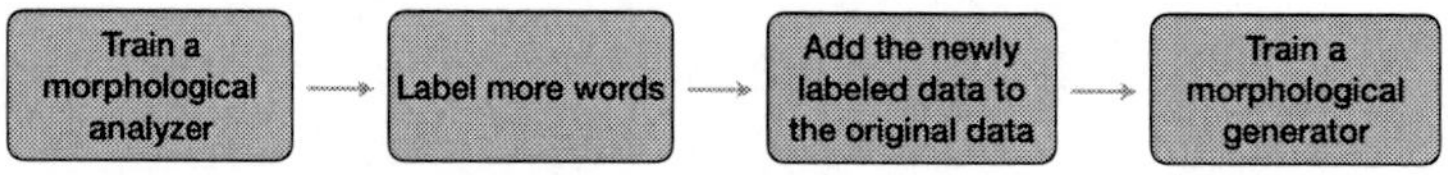

Figure 2: Pipeline for applying backtranslation to morphological inflection.

tion is to train an MT model for B-to-A translation using parallel text, use this MT model to translate our monolingual B data into A, and then add that translated data to the A-to-B parallel text corpus to (re)train an A-to-B translation model. For morphological inflection, the labeled data is usually of the type shown in Figure 1(a), where we are provided with triplets consisting of lemma, inflected form, and a morphosyntactic description (MSD) tag corresponding to the inflected form. In a morphological inflection task, the input is the lemma and the MSD, while the expected output is the inflected form, as shown in Figure 1(b). To apply the backtranslation technique to the morphological inflection task, we can follow a pipeline like the one illustrated in Figure 2: leverage the labeled data to train a morphological analyzer instead of a generator, apply the morphological analyzer to tag more unlabeled words with MSDs, and then add the newly labeled data to the original data to train models for morphological inflection. When training the morphological analyzer, the input is the inflected form and the output is the lemma and the MSD, as is illustrated in Figure 1(c).

3 Experiments and Results

We conduct several experiments to evaluate the performance of morphological inflection with the backtranslation data augmentation technique. The deep learning architecture we use is the Transformer model (Vaswani et al., 2017) as implemented in Fairseq (Ott et al., 2019). For our experiments, we use the same hyperparameter settings as the best-performing system (Liu and Hulden, 2020b,a) in the SIGMORPHON 2020 shared task on inflection (Vylomova et al., 2020). All models have been trained with a single NVIDIA Tesla P100 GPU.

Data Our experiments cover six languages: Czech, Finnish, German, Russian, Spanish and Turkish. These languages are selected to include variety in morphological inflection complexity and difficulty. Finnish and Turkish are agglutinative languages, both of which have vowel harmony and extensive agglutination. Spanish has a rich inflectional system, but is quite regular. Czech is a Slavic language that uses a Latin writing system, and is a fusional language with rich morphology. Russian is also a Slavic language with a rich fusional morphological inflection system, and is written in Cyrillic script. German has a relatively limited inflectional system, but is challenging due to a high rate of syncretism. Table 1 provides more details on the languages.

We follow two settings for our low-resource experiments: 1,000 and 500 training triplets. For the 1,000 training example setting, we use the medium-size setting data from CoNLL-SIGMORPHON 2018 shared task on type-based morphological inflection (Cotterell et al., 2018). For the 500 training triplet setting, we randomly sample 500 examples from the 1,000 setting training examples. The two training data size settings are designed with the consideration that, on the one hand, data augmentation is not necessary when abundant training data is available, and on the other that if training data is too limited, a morphological analyzer of useful quality is not trainable. The development set and test set we use are the 2018 SIGMORPHON shared task development and test sets, unchanged. Each of the development set and the test set for a language contains 1,000 triples respectively.[1]

Our initial experiments used random words from Wikipedia as unlabeled data to be backtranslated with the morphological analyzer, but these pilot experiments showed a significant decrease in the inflection performance after the backtranslated data were added. Table 3 in Appendix B shows the performance of each language with 500 original training examples after adding different amount of backtranslated Wikipedia words. We hypothesized that the reason for the decrease may be that the words available from Wikipedia often represent parts-of-speech (e.g. determiners, adverbs, etc) not found in the labeled data and thus introduce excessive noise. Therefore, we changed the source of our un-

[1]Thanks to one of the reviewers for pointing out that the amount of the development data makes the experiment not really so "low-resource". We agree that 1,000 triples for validation would be very difficult to obtain in an extremely low-resource situation.

Language	Language group	Morphological typology	Writing system
Czech	Indo-European/Balto-Slavic/Slavic/West Slavic	fusional	Latin script
Finnish	Uralic/Finnic	agglutinative	Latin script
German	Indo-European/Germanic/West Germanic	fusional	Latin script
Russian	Indo-European/Balto-Slavic/Slavic/East Slavic	fusional	Cyrillic script
Spanish	Indo-European/Italic/Romance/Western Romance	fusional	Latin script
Turkish	Turkic/Common Turkic/Oghuz	agglutinative	Latin script

Table 1: Language information.

labeled data and conducted further experiments on two sources: inflected words with labels removed in the CoNLL-SIGMORPHON 2018 shared task high-setting training set which are not included in the medium-setting training set, and words from the Universal Dependencies (UD) (version 2.6) corpus (Zeman et al., 2020) for each language, which are of the same parts-of-speech included in the shared task data. Details of the treebank data we use for each language are provided in Table 2 in Appendix A.

Transformer inflection and analyzer performance We first evaluate the base performance of the inflection model trained with only the 500 or the 1,000 triplet set. The accuracy results are presented in Figure 3.

As it has been noted that the quality of the backtranslation model (in our case, the morphological analyzer) is positively correlated to the ability of backtranslation data augmentation to yield improvements (Currey et al., 2017), we present the morphological analyzer accuracy in Figure 4. The development and test data for the morphological analyzer is created by simply reversing the input and output of the development and test set data for morphological inflection.

The reported accuracy for each morphological inflection model and each morphological analysis model are the average of five runs with different random initializations to ensure a good representation of the model performance.

Morphological inflection performance with backtranslation data augmentation We experimented with backtranslating different amounts of delabeled shared task data or UD data. For each data amount, shared task inflected word forms are randomly sampled (uniformly) to match the desired target size for backtranslation (0-9,000 words). Considering that in real low-resource situations the words we can obtain are usually frequently used

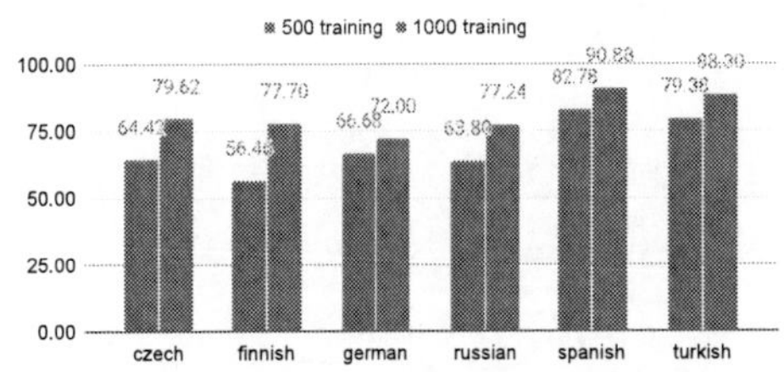

Figure 3: Basic Transformer inflection performance at different training data sizes: 500 or 1,000 training examples.

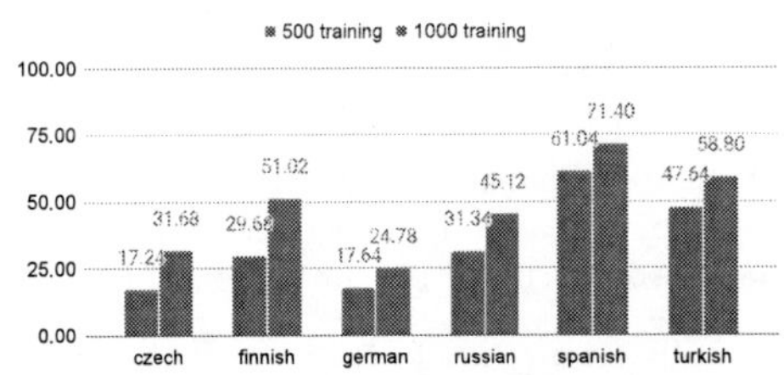

Figure 4: Transformer morphological analyzer performance at different training data sizes: 500 or 1,000 training examples.

ones, when picking from the UD data, we first rank the words from most frequent to least frequent in the corpus and pick the most frequent UD words of the respective parts-of-speech used in the given training data. We use one random morphological analyzer trained in the previous step to label the words, and add the resulting automatically labeled words to the original training data to train the augmented inflection models. Each augmented inflection model is trained with five runs using different random initializations. We use a majority vote by these five models to pick the final prediction.

The inflection performance obtained by adding different amounts of backtranslated data to the original 500 training triplets is presented in Figure 5. The legend in each plot indicates the best accuracy with the corresponding backtranslation data augmentation size for each language. Figure 5(a)

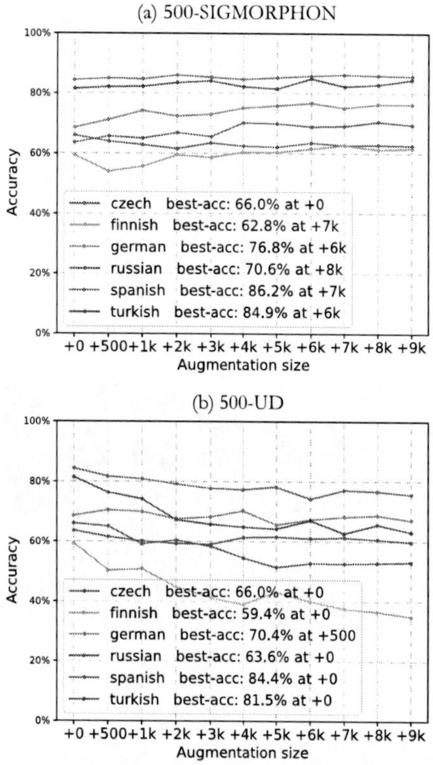

Figure 5: Performance of the Transformer inflection model trained with backtranslated SIGMORPHON shared task data or UD data on top of **500** labeled data points.

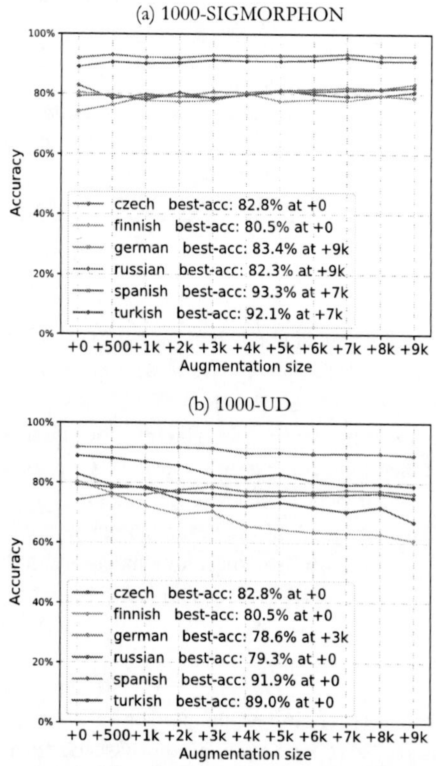

Figure 6: Performance of the Transformer inflection model trained with backtranslated SIGMORPHON shared task data or UD data on top of **1,000** labeled data points.

shows the results for adding backtranslated CoNLL-SIGMORPHON shared task data; here, we see that adding backtranslated data improves the inflection model for all languages except for Czech. However, to our surprise, the results for adding backtranslated UD words, as illustrated in Figure 5(b), show that adding backtranslated data actually hurts the inflection model.

The pattern is similar when the initial training data contains 1,000 examples, shown in Figure 6: though we see that adding backtranslated shared task words improves the inflection model, adding backtranslated UD words causes the model to deteriorate. This opposite tendency goes quite against our expectations, especially considering that the UD words were selected to ensure that they are of the same parts-of-speech covered in the original training data. In order to explain the opposite tendency and answer whether backtranslation could indeed be helpful for morphological generation, we conducted the following experiments on comparing different ways of adding backtranslated data.

Morphological inflection with tagged backtranslation Caswell et al. (2019) show that tagging backtranslated source sentences with an extra distinguishing token can improve the contribution backtranslated data can provide to machine translation. This finding is supported in later work (Marie et al., 2020). Therefore, we hypothesize that adding a special tag to the lemma and MSD tag sequence predicted by the morphological analyzer may improve the performance of the inflection model trained with the combination of the original training data and the backtranslated data.

In order to test the hypothesis, we start with experiments on the 500 training example setting. We train one morphological analyzer for each language, and use the morphological analyzer to label words from CoNLL-SIGMORPHON 2018 shared task not included in the current training set. Then we add the newly labeled data (in differing amounts as in the earlier experiment) in two different ways: (1) add the backtranslated data to the original training data without any special tag; (2) append a

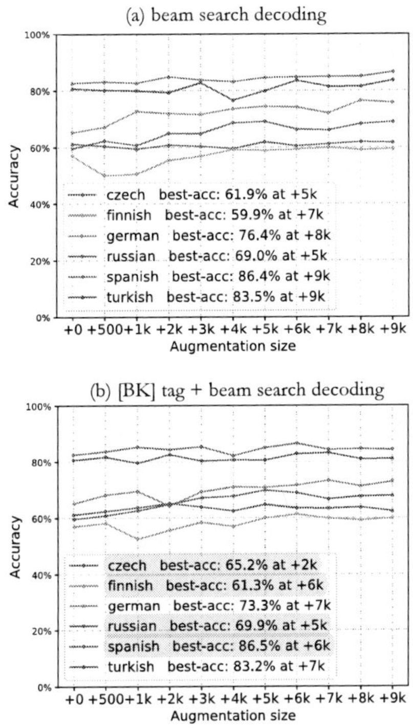

Figure 7: Performance of the Transformer inflection model trained with backtranslated SIGMORPHON shared task data on top of **500** labeled data points. The backtranslated data are added without or without a special tag *<BT>*.

special tag *<BT>* at the end of the MSD feature sequence before merging the newly automatically labeled data with the original training data. For this experiment, we report the results of one run in Figure 7. The highest accuracy for each language is presented in the legend of the each plot with the corresponding backtranslation data augmentation size. We highlight the languages which get improved accuracy with tagged backtranslation in Figure 7(b). We see that only two languages (Czech and Finnish) are significantly better with the tagged backtranslation; one language (German) is significantly worse with tagged backtranslation, and there is not a significant difference between tagging or not tagging the backtranslated data for the other three languages (Russian, Spanish and Turkish).[2]

In summary, tagged backtranslation produces similar results to backtranslation without a special tag in our experiments, and thus we would not expect any difference if the words to be analyzed are UD words with tagged backtranslation.

Result analysis In order to understand the performance difference, we examined the delabeled shared task data and UD words. We find that the following two reasons which may contribute the the differences: (1) The delabeled shared task data cover inflected forms where the lemma form is included in the development or test set, while the UD words do not. In other words, some of the delabeled shared task words are for the same lexemes as some words in the development or test set. This reveals a problem in the shared task design, as discussed in Liu and Hulden (2021). (2) There are discrepancies in the UD words and the delabeled shared task data. For example, each of the UD words we used consists of one token, while the delabeled shared task data contains words consisting of multiple tokens. However, multi-token words are common in the shared task development and test sets.

4 Discussion and Conclusion

Though backtranslation has become a common technique in machine translation for data augmentation, our experiments indicate that it is not significantly helpful—at least not by itself—for morphological inflection generation, a character-level string transduction task closely related to MT.

We find small improvements when the backtranslated data is drawn from exactly the same source as the evaluation data, i.e. the SIGMORPHON shared task data. When other sources are used, such as UD or Wikipedia text, backtranslation degrades performance across all data sizes. Though we have controlled the part-of-speech of UD words to match the original training data distribution, adding backtranslated UD words is still unhelpful. Considering that UD data set is labeled with different annotation standards and may also contain some noise, this indicates that unlabeled words used for backtranslation need to be noise-free and have been filtered with the same annotation standards as the labeled data in order to be helpful. Such a strict requirement of data correctness probably renders it unpractical to apply backtranslation to morphological inflection generation in most scenarios.

Further, we did not find any significant difference between the techniques of standard backtranslation and tagged backtranslation in our experiments for morphological inflection.

[2]We used a paired t test to measure whether the difference is statistically significant ($p < 0.05$).

References

Antonios Anastasopoulos and Graham Neubig. 2019. Pushing the limits of low-resource morphological inflection. In *Proceedings of the 2019 Conference on Empirical Methods in Natural Language Processing and the 9th International Joint Conference on Natural Language Processing (EMNLP-IJCNLP)*, pages 984–996, Hong Kong, China. Association for Computational Linguistics.

Toms Bergmanis, Katharina Kann, Hinrich Schütze, and Sharon Goldwater. 2017. Training data augmentation for low-resource morphological inflection. In *Proceedings of the CoNLL SIGMORPHON 2017 Shared Task: Universal Morphological Reinflection*, pages 31–39, Vancouver. Association for Computational Linguistics.

Isaac Caswell, Ciprian Chelba, and David Grangier. 2019. Tagged back-translation. In *Proceedings of the Fourth Conference on Machine Translation (Volume 1: Research Papers)*, pages 53–63, Florence, Italy. Association for Computational Linguistics.

Peng-Jen Chen, Ann Lee, Changhan Wang, Naman Goyal, Angela Fan, Mary Williamson, and Jiatao Gu. 2020. Facebook AI's WMT20 news translation task submission. In *Proceedings of the Fifth Conference on Machine Translation*, pages 113–125, Online. Association for Computational Linguistics.

Ryan Cotterell, Christo Kirov, John Sylak-Glassman, Géraldine Walther, Ekaterina Vylomova, Arya D. McCarthy, Katharina Kann, Sabrina J. Mielke, Garrett Nicolai, Miikka Silfverberg, David Yarowsky, Jason Eisner, and Mans Hulden. 2018. The CoNLL–SIGMORPHON 2018 shared task: Universal morphological reinflection. In *Proceedings of the CoNLL–SIGMORPHON 2018 Shared Task: Universal Morphological Reinflection*, pages 1–27, Brussels. Association for Computational Linguistics.

Ryan Cotterell, Christo Kirov, John Sylak-Glassman, Géraldine Walther, Ekaterina Vylomova, Patrick Xia, Manaal Faruqui, Sandra Kübler, David Yarowsky, Jason Eisner, and Mans Hulden. 2017. CoNLL-SIGMORPHON 2017 shared task: Universal morphological reinflection in 52 languages. In *Proceedings of the CoNLL SIGMORPHON 2017 Shared Task: Universal Morphological Reinflection*, pages 1–30, Vancouver. Association for Computational Linguistics.

Ryan Cotterell, Christo Kirov, John Sylak-Glassman, David Yarowsky, Jason Eisner, and Mans Hulden. 2016. The SIGMORPHON 2016 shared Task—Morphological reinflection. In *Proceedings of the 14th SIGMORPHON Workshop on Computational Research in Phonetics, Phonology, and Morphology*, pages 10–22, Berlin, Germany. Association for Computational Linguistics.

Anna Currey, Antonio Valerio Miceli Barone, and Kenneth Heafield. 2017. Copied monolingual data improves low-resource neural machine translation. In *Proceedings of the Second Conference on Machine Translation*, pages 148–156, Copenhagen, Denmark. Association for Computational Linguistics.

Sergey Edunov, Myle Ott, Michael Auli, and David Grangier. 2018. Understanding back-translation at scale. In *Proceedings of the 2018 Conference on Empirical Methods in Natural Language Processing*, pages 489–500, Brussels, Belgium. Association for Computational Linguistics.

Sergey Edunov, Myle Ott, Marc'Aurelio Ranzato, and Michael Auli. 2020. On the evaluation of machine translation systems trained with back-translation. In *Proceedings of the 58th Annual Meeting of the Association for Computational Linguistics*, pages 2836–2846, Online. Association for Computational Linguistics.

Marzieh Fadaee, Arianna Bisazza, and Christof Monz. 2017. Data augmentation for low-resource neural machine translation. In *Proceedings of the 55th Annual Meeting of the Association for Computational Linguistics (Volume 2: Short Papers)*, pages 567–573, Vancouver, Canada. Association for Computational Linguistics.

Vu Cong Duy Hoang, Philipp Koehn, Gholamreza Haffari, and Trevor Cohn. 2018. Iterative back-translation for neural machine translation. In *Proceedings of the 2nd Workshop on Neural Machine Translation and Generation*, pages 18–24, Melbourne, Australia. Association for Computational Linguistics.

Katharina Kann and Hinrich Schütze. 2016. MED: The LMU system for the SIGMORPHON 2016 shared task on morphological reinflection. In *Proceedings of the 14th SIGMORPHON Workshop on Computational Research in Phonetics, Phonology, and Morphology*, pages 62–70, Berlin, Germany. Association for Computational Linguistics.

Ling Liu. 2021. Computational morphology with neural network approaches. *arXiv preprint arXiv:2105.09404*.

Ling Liu and Mans Hulden. 2020a. Analogy models for neural word inflection. In *Proceedings of the 28th International Conference on Computational Linguistics*, pages 2861–2878, Barcelona, Spain (Online). International Committee on Computational Linguistics.

Ling Liu and Mans Hulden. 2020b. Leveraging principal parts for morphological inflection. In *Proceedings of the 17th SIGMORPHON Workshop on Computational Research in Phonetics, Phonology, and Morphology*, pages 153–161, Online. Association for Computational Linguistics.

Ling Liu and Mans Hulden. 2021. Can a transformer pass the wug test? tuning copying bias in neural morphological inflection models. *arXiv preprint arXiv:2104.06483*.

Ling Liu, Zach Ryan, and Mans Hulden. 2021. The usefulness of bibles in low-resource machine translation. In *Proceedings of the Workshop on Computational Methods for Endangered Languages*, volume 1, pages 44–50.

Ling Liu, Ilamvazhuthy Subbiah, Adam Wiemerslage, Jonathan Lilley, and Sarah Moeller. 2018. Morphological reinflection in context: CU boulder's submission to CoNLL–SIGMORPHON 2018 shared task. In *Proceedings of the CoNLL–SIGMORPHON 2018 Shared Task: Universal Morphological Reinflection*, pages 86–92, Brussels. Association for Computational Linguistics.

Benjamin Marie, Raphael Rubino, and Atsushi Fujita. 2020. Tagged back-translation revisited: Why does it really work? In *Proceedings of the 58th Annual Meeting of the Association for Computational Linguistics*, pages 5990–5997, Online. Association for Computational Linguistics.

Arya D. McCarthy, Ekaterina Vylomova, Shijie Wu, Chaitanya Malaviya, Lawrence Wolf-Sonkin, Garrett Nicolai, Christo Kirov, Miikka Silfverberg, Sabrina J. Mielke, Jeffrey Heinz, Ryan Cotterell, and Mans Hulden. 2019. The SIGMORPHON 2019 shared task: Morphological analysis in context and cross-lingual transfer for inflection. In *Proceedings of the 16th Workshop on Computational Research in Phonetics, Phonology, and Morphology*, pages 229–244, Florence, Italy. Association for Computational Linguistics.

Sarah Moeller, Ling Liu, and Mans Hulden. 2021. To POS tag or not to POS tag: The impact of POS tags on morphological learning in low-resource settings. In *Proceedings of the 59th Annual Meeting of the Association for Computational Linguistics and the 11th International Joint Conference on Natural Language Processing (Volume 1: Long Papers)*, pages 966–978, Online. Association for Computational Linguistics.

Sarah Moeller, Ling Liu, Changbing Yang, Katharina Kann, and Mans Hulden. 2020. IGT2P: From interlinear glossed texts to paradigms. In *Proceedings of the 2020 Conference on Empirical Methods in Natural Language Processing (EMNLP)*, pages 5251–5262, Online. Association for Computational Linguistics.

Myle Ott, Sergey Edunov, Alexei Baevski, Angela Fan, Sam Gross, Nathan Ng, David Grangier, and Michael Auli. 2019. fairseq: A fast, extensible toolkit for sequence modeling. In *Proceedings of the 2019 Conference of the North American Chapter of the Association for Computational Linguistics (Demonstrations)*, pages 48–53, Minneapolis, Minnesota. Association for Computational Linguistics.

Rico Sennrich, Barry Haddow, and Alexandra Birch. 2016. Improving neural machine translation models with monolingual data. In *Proceedings of the 54th Annual Meeting of the Association for Computational Linguistics (Volume 1: Long Papers)*, pages 86–96, Berlin, Germany. Association for Computational Linguistics.

Miikka Silfverberg, Adam Wiemerslage, Ling Liu, and Lingshuang Jack Mao. 2017. Data augmentation for morphological reinflection. In *Proceedings of the CoNLL SIGMORPHON 2017 Shared Task: Universal Morphological Reinflection*, pages 90–99, Vancouver. Association for Computational Linguistics.

Ashish Vaswani, Noam Shazeer, Niki Parmar, Jakob Uszkoreit, Llion Jones, Aidan N Gomez, Lukasz Kaiser, and Illia Polosukhin. 2017. Attention is all you need. *arXiv preprint arXiv:1706.03762*.

Ekaterina Vylomova, Jennifer White, Elizabeth Salesky, Sabrina J. Mielke, Shijie Wu, Edoardo Maria Ponti, Rowan Hall Maudslay, Ran Zmigrod, Josef Valvoda, Svetlana Toldova, Francis Tyers, Elena Klyachko, Ilya Yegorov, Natalia Krizhanovsky, Paula Czarnowska, Irene Nikkarinen, Andrew Krizhanovsky, Tiago Pimentel, Lucas Torroba Hennigen, Christo Kirov, Garrett Nicolai, Adina Williams, Antonios Anastasopoulos, Hilaria Cruz, Eleanor Chodroff, Ryan Cotterell, Miikka Silfverberg, and Mans Hulden. 2020. SIGMORPHON 2020 shared task 0: Typologically diverse morphological inflection. In *Proceedings of the 17th SIGMORPHON Workshop on Computational Research in Phonetics, Phonology, and Morphology*, pages 1–39, Online. Association for Computational Linguistics.

Shijie Wu, Ryan Cotterell, and Mans Hulden. 2020. Applying the transformer to character-level transduction. *arXiv preprint arXiv:2005.10213*.

Mengzhou Xia, Xiang Kong, Antonios Anastasopoulos, and Graham Neubig. 2019. Generalized data augmentation for low-resource translation. In *Proceedings of the 57th Annual Meeting of the Association for Computational Linguistics*, pages 5786–5796, Florence, Italy. Association for Computational Linguistics.

Daniel Zeman, Joakim Nivre, Mitchell Abrams, Elia Ackermann, Noëmi Aepli, Željko Agić, Lars Ahrenberg, Chika Kennedy Ajede, Gabrielė Aleksandravičiūtė, Lene Antonsen, et al. 2020. Universal dependencies 2.6. LINDAT/CLARIAH-CZ digital library at the Institute of Formal and Applied Linguistics (ÚFAL), Faculty of Mathematics and Physics, Charles University.

A Data details

Language	treebanks
Czech	CAC, CLTT, FicTree, PDT
Finnish	FTB, TDT
German	GSD, HDT
Russian	GSD, SynTagRus, Taiga
Spanish	AnCora, GSD
Turkish	IMST

Table 2: The UD (version 2.6) treebanks sources we use for each language's backtranslation data. We obtain the words from the training set of the treebanks.

B Pilot study results

Augmentation size	Czech	Finnish	German	Russian	Spanish	Turkish
0	66.0	59.4	68.6	63.6	84.4	81.5
500	62.3	50.5	66.9	61.8	75.2	72.4
1k	58.5	45.8	68.9	61.9	71.9	67.5
2k	57.2	41.4	66.2	58.8	68.5	62.5
3k	53.9	41.2	65.9	59.8	66.8	58.9
4k	53.9	35.8	66.2	60.3	66.8	59.3
5k	51.1	36.7	63.0	60.6	63.2	58.3
6k	51.2	36.5	63.0	59.6	61.5	55.3
7k	52.6	37.2	63.9	60.7	60.5	60.4
8k	50.1	33.7	63.8	61.4	60.3	54.0
9k	50.5	33.5	63.0	60.7	57.3	54.7

Table 3: Inflection accuracy (in %) for each language with 500 original training triples after adding different amount of backtranslated Wikipedia data.

Learning Data Augmentation Schedules for Natural Language Processing

Daphné Chopard and **Matthias S. Treder** and **Irena Spasić**
School of Computer Science and Informatics, Cardiff University
Queen's Buildings, 5 The Parade
Cardiff, CF24 3AA, United Kingdom
{ChopardDA,TrederM,SpasicI}@cardiff.ac.uk

Abstract

Despite its proven efficiency in other fields, data augmentation is less popular in the context of natural language processing (NLP) due to its complexity and limited results. A recent study (Longpre et al., 2020) showed for example that task-agnostic data augmentations fail to consistently boost the performance of pretrained transformers even in low data regimes. In this paper, we investigate whether data-driven augmentation scheduling and the integration of a wider set of transformations can lead to improved performance where fixed and limited policies were unsuccessful. Our results suggest that, while this approach can help train better models in some settings, the improvements are unsubstantial. This negative result is meant to help researchers better understand the limitations of data augmentation for NLP.

1 Introduction

In recent years, data augmentation has become an integral part of many successful deep learning systems, especially in the fields of computer vision and speech processing (Krizhevsky et al., 2012; Jaitly and Hinton, 2013; Hannun et al., 2014; Ko et al., 2015). Traditionally, data augmentation approaches take the form of label-preserving transforms that can be applied to the training datasets to expand their size and diversity. The idea of generating synthetic samples that share the same underlying distribution as the original data is often considered a pragmatic solution to the shortage of annotated data, and has been shown to reduce overfitting and improve generalisation performance (Shorten and Khoshgoftaar, 2019). However, despite a sound theoretical foundation (Dao et al., 2019), this paradigm has not yet translated to consistent and substantial improvement in natural language processing (NLP) (Longpre et al., 2020).

The inability of NLP models to consistently benefit from data augmentations can be partially attributed to the general difficulty of finding a good combination of transforms and determining their respective set of optimal hyperparameters (Ratner et al., 2017), a problem that is exacerbated in the context of text data. Indeed, since the complexity of language makes text highly sensitive to any transformations, data augmentations are often tailored to a specific task or dataset and are only shown to be successful in specific settings.

In this work, we investigate whether automatically searching for an optimal augmentation *schedule* from a wide range of transformations can alleviate some of the shortcomings encountered when applying data augmentations to NLP. This endeavour follows the recent success of automated augmentation strategies in computer vision (Cubuk et al., 2019; Ho et al., 2019; Cubuk et al., 2020). In doing so, we extend the efforts to understand the limits of data augmentation in NLP.

2 Related Work

Although there exist recent surveys (Feng et al., 2021; Shorten et al., 2021) that offer a comprehensive review of related work, they do not provide a comparative analysis of the different data augmentation approaches and of their effect on learning performance. In general, the literature lacks general comparative studies that encompass the variety of tasks and datasets in NLP. Indeed, most of the existing text data augmentation studies either focus on a single approach in a specific setting or compare a small set of techniques on a specific task and dataset (Giridhara. et al., 2019; Marivate and Sefara, 2020). In addition, many of these comparisons have been conducted before the widespread adoption of contextualized representations.

Recently, Longpre et al. (2020) showed that, despite careful calibration, data augmentation yielded little to no improvement when applied to pretrained transformers even in low data regimes. While their comparative analysis is conducted on various classification tasks, it focuses on a limited set of aug-

Proceedings of the Second Workshop on Insights from Negative Results in NLP, pages 89–102

mentation strategies that are applied independently and whose hyperparameters are optimized via a random search.

To further assess the effectiveness of data augmentation on pretrained transformers, we investigate in this work the paradigm of learning data augmentation strategies from data in the context NLP. The idea is to leverage the training data to automatically discover an optimal combination of augmentations and their hyperparameters at each epoch of the fine-tuning. First, we define a search space that consists of a variety of transformations before relying on the training data to learn an optimal schedule of probabilities and magnitudes for each augmentation. This schedule is later used to boost performance during fine-tuning.

In the following section, we present a variety of data augmentations and, for each category of transformations, we highlight a subset of augmentations that is representative of the category and that will constitute our search space.

3 Data Augmentation in NLP

In this study, we focus on *transformative* methods which apply a label-preserving transformation to existing data—rather than generative methods which create entirely new instances using generative models. Indeed their simplicity of use and their low computational cost make them good candidates for a wide deployment (Xu et al., 2016). In the last decade, we witnessed a widespread adoption of continuous vector representations of words, which can be easily fed to deep neural network architectures. As a result, transforms have been developed not only at the lexical level (i.e., words) but also at the latent semantic level (i.e., embeddings). This distinction is emphasized throughout this section.

Word Replacement A commonly used form of data augmentation in NLP is word replacement. At the lexical level, the most common approach consists in randomly replacing words with their synonyms (Zhang et al., 2015; Mueller and Thyagarajan, 2016; Vosoughi et al., 2016). Some variants include replacement based on other lexical relationships such as hypernymy (Navigli and Velardi, 2003) or simply words from the vocabulary (Wang et al., 2018; Cheng et al., 2018). Another popular approach consists in using a language model (LM) for replacement (Kolomiyets et al., 2011; Fadaee et al., 2017; Ratner et al., 2017). Because these transformations do not ensure the preservation of the sample class, Kobayashi (2018) suggested conditioning a bidirectional LM on the labels, an idea later revisited by Wu et al. (2019) who replaced the LM with a conditional BERT (Bidirectional Encoder Representations from Transformers).

At the latent semantic level, word replacement amounts to randomly replacing its embedding with some other vector. For instance, Wang and Yang (2015) choose the k-nearest-neighbour in the embedding vocabulary as a replacement for each word. Similar strategies were later adopted by Vijayaraghavan et al. (2016) and Zhang et al. (2019).

In this study, as replacement methods, we select both **synonym** and **hypernym** replacement as well as **contextual augmentation** at the word level and **nearest neighbour** at the embedding level.

Noising A simple yet effective form of augmentation that is often applied to images and audio samples is data noising. Not surprisingly, this type of data augmentation can also be found in NLP despite the discrete nature of text data.

In its simplest form, data noising when applied to text consists in inserting, swapping or deleting words at random (Wei and Zou, 2019). More generally, the process of ignoring a fraction of the input words is often referred to as *word dropout* (Iyyer et al., 2015) and can take multiple forms (Dai and Le, 2015; Zhang et al., 2016; Bowman et al., 2016; Xie et al., 2017; Li et al., 2017).

Sometimes, word replacement can also be thought of as a form of noising. For instance, replacing words at random with other words from the vocabulary introduces noise into the data (Xie et al., 2017; Cheng et al., 2018).

In contrast, at the distributed representation level, this type of augmentation often takes the form of added noise to the embeddings. Possible noising schemes include Gaussian noise (Kumar et al., 2016; Cheng et al., 2018), uniform noise (Kim et al., 2019), Bernoulli noise and adversarial noise (Zhang and Yang, 2018). Typically, noising is applied to every word embedding, but it can also be applied only to selected ones (Kim et al., 2019). Alternatively, as with word dropout, noise can be incorporated into the training by discarding, across all words, some embedding dimensions with a predefined probability (Dai and Le, 2015).

Noising strategies used in this study are based on **random deletion**, **random swap** and **random insertion** at the sentence level as well as **Gaussian noise** and **uniform noise** at the feature level.

Back-translation Back-translation provides a way for neural machine translation (NMT) systems to leverage monolingual data to increase the amount of parallel data (Sennrich et al., 2016; Edunov et al., 2018; Fadaee and Monz, 2018). Similarly, back-translation can be applied twice in a row (i.e., from English to another language and back to English) to generate new data points without the need for parallel corpora and can therefore find applications as a task-agnostic augmentation in other tasks such as text classification (Luque and Pérez, 2018; Aroyehun and Gelbukh, 2018), paraphrase generation (Mallinson et al., 2017) and question answering (Yu et al., 2018).

Here, we consider a wide range of intermediate languages to include **back-translation** into our search space

4 Automated Data Augmentation in NLP

In NLP, little effort has been put into developing strategies that can, given a task and a dataset, learn an optimal subset of data augmentation operations and their hyperparameters (Shorten et al., 2021). Yet, this idea has been very successful in computer vision (Cubuk et al., 2019; Ho et al., 2019; Cubuk et al., 2020). For instance, in the context of image classification, Cubuk et al. (2019) have proposed AutoAugment a procedure that automatically searches for optimal augmentation policies using reinforcement learning. Later, Population-Based Augmentation (PBA) (Ho et al., 2019)—an algorithm that views the data augmentation selection and calibration problem as a hyperparameter search and can thus leverage the Population-Based Training (PBT) method (Jaderberg et al., 2017) to find an optimal transformation schedule in an efficient way—was introduced as a more cost-effective yet competitive alternative to AutoAugment. Finally, Cubuk et al. (2020) introduced the RandAugment method which tackles some of the issues arising from these previous works.

In this study, we adapt the PBA framework to NLP in an attempt to learn an optimal schedule of data augmentation operations with optimized hyperparameters.

4.1 Population-Based Augmentation

Given a hyperparameter search space that consists of data augmentation operations along with their probability level (i.e., likelihood of being applied) and their magnitude level (i.e., strength with which they are applied), PBA works as follows: during a pre-defined number of epochs, k child models of identical architecture are trained in parallel for the task at hand on a given dataset. Periodically, the training is interrupted, all models are evaluated on a validation set and an "exploit-and-explore" procedure takes place. First, the worst-performing models (bottom 25%) copy the weights and hyperparameters of the best-performing models (top 25%) (**exploit**), then the hyperparameters are either slightly perturbed or uniformly resampled from all possible values (**explore**). At that point, training can continue. At the end of the training, a data augmentation policy schedule is extracted from the hyperparameters of the best performing child model. The obtained schedule can then be used to train from scratch a different model on the same task and the same dataset.

5 Experiments

Our implementation builds on the original PBA codes (Ho et al., 2019). We make the NLP adaptation of this framework publicly available[1].

5.1 Datasets

Two of the datasets suggested by Longpre et al. (2020) in their comparative analysis are used to conduct our experiments: SST-2 (Socher et al., 2013) and MNLI (Williams et al., 2018). The former is a corpus of movie reviews used for sentiment analysis (single sentence, binary classification), whereas the latter is a natural language inference corpus (two sentences, multi-class classification). Accuracy and mis-matched accuracy respectively are used for evaluation. We take $N = \{1500, 2000, 3000, 9000\}$ samples from the original train sets to constitute our train-validation sets. As test sets, we use the *full* original validation sets which—unlike the original test sets—contain publicly available ground-truths.

5.2 Hyperparameter Space

The hyperparameter space consists of 10 data augmentation operations highlighted in the previous section with associated probability and magnitude. For most replacement methods, the magnitude level can be thought of as a percentage of tokens on which the transformation is applied and, for noising transforms, it corresponds to the amount of noising. In the context of back-translation, however,

[1] https://github.com/chopardda/LDAS-NLP

	Accuracy [%]			
	$N = 1500$	2000	3000	FULL
No Augm	88.22 ±0.69	88.11 ±0.41	88.76 ±0.46	90.49 ±0.49
Schedule	**88.64** ±0.47	**88.60** ±0.68	**89.56** ±0.40	**90.91** ±0.43
Difference	*+0.42*	*+0.49*	*+0.80*	*+0.42*

(a) SST-2 test dataset.

	Mis-matched Accuracy [%]			
	$N = 1500$	2000	3000	FULL
No Augm	**65.73** ±1.12	**67.60** ±2.21	**69.67** ±0.79	**74.26** ±0.35
Schedule	64.78 ±1.20	66.21 ±0.77	68.71 ±0.49	73.95 ±0.47
Difference	*-0.95*	*-1.39*	*-0.96*	*-0.31*

(b) MNLI test dataset.

Table 1: Performance on SST-2 and MNLI. The model is trained 10 times independently either without augmentation or with the augmentation schedule yielded by the search. Since a single search is conducted per value of N, the reported standard deviation measures the robustness of the training procedure for a single schedule. (For more details about the robustness of the augmentation search, see Section 6.1.)

magnitude relates to the quality of the translation according to BLEU-3 scores (Aiken, 2019). Details concerning the implementation of these augmentations as well as how exactly magnitude is defined for each one of them can be found in Appendix A.1.

5.3 Search

The search is conducted on 48 epochs using around 20% of the N data points for training and the rest for validation. Both the child models and the final model follow the original uncased BERT base architecture suggested by Devlin et al. (2019). The learning rate is chosen so as to slow down the fine-tuning without affecting the performance. Further details are provided in Appendix A.2.

6 Results

The main results can be found in Table 1a and Table 1b. The first row corresponds to the performance on the test set when training the model on all N samples without any augmentation. The second row in the table contains the result of the evaluation on the test set of the model trained on all N samples using the discovered schedules (i.e., for each data size, the schedule of the child model with the highest validation accuracy at the end of the search is used to train the final model). The same slowed-down learning rate and the same extended number of epochs are used across all experiments to allow for a fair comparison.

Overall, the improvements yielded by the optimized data augmentation schedules are inconsistent and unsubstantial (below 0.8%). Even though the incorporation of transforms has a small positive impact on the SST-2 dataset, it has the opposite effect on MNLI (i.e., the scores plummet by as much as 1.39%). A possible reason for these poor results might be due to the difference in settings between our experiments and the ones in the PBA study. Indeed, our search is conducted on 48 epochs as opposed to the 160 to 200 epochs suggested for image classification tasks and the exploit-and-explore procedure takes place after each epoch rather than after every 3 epochs. In addition, the size of the training datasets is very different. The size of our largest experiment is roughly the same as the size of the smallest dataset in (Ho et al., 2019).

Surprisingly, our data-driven search seems unable to reproduce the performance boost reported by Longpre et al. (2020) on the MNLI dataset, even though the augmentations considered in their work are part of our search space. This might be explained by the way augmentations are applied. In our study, we transform each training sample by applying up to 2 transformations in a row with probability p and magnitude m. In contrast, Longpre et al. add $N \times \tau$ augmented samples to the training set with $\tau \in \{0.5, 1, 1.5, 2\}$, meaning that the original examples are provided along with their augmented counterparts at each iteration.

6.1 Search Robustness

Given the stochastic nature of the searching process, the discovered schedule is bound to differ from one run to another. So far, we have run a single search for each experiment setting. In this section, we investigate whether the limited effect of automatic augmentation on the model performance may be caused by the stochasticity of the search. To that end, we run 10 independent searches on the SST-2 dataset with N=1500 and use each of the 10 discovered schedules to train a separate model. All the network hyperparameters are kept the same as in the previous section. Overall, the standard deviation over 10 independent schedules is 0.55%, which indicates that the performance of the training is robust across searches. Thus, the poor results observed in the previous section cannot be explained by the variability of schedules.

However, a closer look at these 10 individual schedules reveals that the chosen augmentation hyperparameters are very different from one run to another and that the search does not seems to favour any particular set of augmentation transforms. This may indicate that, in this setting, data augmentation acts more as a regulariser rather than a way to learn invariance properties and that, as a result, any kind of augmentation transform has a similar effect on performance. In view of these findings, it would be interesting to explore whether relying on a greater number of child models during the search could potentially yield less disparate schedules and improve the overall quality of the search. For the interested reader, the various schedules are displayed in Appendix A.5.

6.2 Validation size

As mentioned earlier, the limited impact of automatic data augmentation scheduling in our settings might be due to the small number of samples available for each experiment. In particular, one of the drawbacks of PBA is that a large portion of training data (approximately 80% as suggested by Ho et al. (2019)) has to be set aside to form a validation set that is used during the search to find optimal hyperparameters. For example, at N=1500 only 250 examples are used to learn the network weights during the search while the remaining 1250 samples are used for hyperparameter selection. As a result of this discrepancy, the selected data augmentation might be relevant when only 250 data points are available for training but less effective when learning with 1500 samples as is ultimately the case. In this section, we investigate whether the poor results observed in Table 1 can be attributed to the ratio chosen to split the available data into a train and a validation set. To that end, we run the search on the SST-2 dataset using different ratios to divide the N=1500 samples at hand. The results reported in Table 2 suggest that using different proportions of train and validation examples does not affect the effectiveness of the augmentation schedule in this setting. In fact, the performance remains the same even though the model is trained with schedules that were optimized using very different split ratios. This might be explained by the fact that both the train and the validation sets are too small to find optimal augmentation hyperparameters irrespective of the chosen split ratio. Alternatively, it is possible that the chosen dataset can simply not benefit from augmentation because of its nature. To verify this hypothesis, it would be interesting to extend this analysis to a wider range of datasets, including actual low-resource datasets.

TRAIN/VAL	250/1250	750/750	1250/250
ACCURACY	**88.64** ± 0.47	**88.64** ± 0.62	**88.76** ± 0.59

Table 2: Performance on the SST-2 test set of the model trained on $N=1500$ samples with the schedule discovered using different proportions of validation and training sets. For each split ratio, the model is trained 10 times using the schedule yielded by a single search. The mean accuracy and standard deviation are reported.

7 Conclusion

The results suggest that augmentation schedules and data-driven parameter search do not provide a consistent and straightforward way to improve the performance of NLP models that use pretrained transformers. There are a few possible explanations for this phenomenon. First, the overall setup of the PBA approach (e.g., the need for large validation sets) might not be well suited for low-data regimes in NLP. A second but more likely reason is that transformers are already pre-trained on huge datasets and their representations may already be invariant to many of the transformations that are encoded into the data augmentation. A systematic investigation into the latter hypothesis is required, which, if proven, would show that data augmentation may be redundant when opting to use transformers to implement NLP solutions. A final reason might be that the search space we consider only contains transformative data augmentation techniques and omits generative ones, even though the latter have started to show some promising results.

References

Milam Aiken. 2019. An updated evaluation of google translate accuracy. Studies in linguistics and literature, 3(3):253–260.

Segun Taofeek Aroyehun and Alexander Gelbukh. 2018. Aggression detection in social media: Using deep neural networks, data augmentation, and pseudo labeling. In Proceedings of the First Workshop on Trolling, Aggression and Cyberbullying (TRAC-2018), pages 90–97.

Samuel Bowman, Luke Vilnis, Oriol Vinyals, Andrew M Dai, Rafal Jozefowicz, and Samy Bengio. 2016. Generating sentences from a continuous space. In Proceedings of the Twentieth Conference on Computational Natural Language Learning (CoNLL).

Yong Cheng, Zhaopeng Tu, Fandong Meng, Junjie Zhai, and Yang Liu. 2018. Towards robust neural machine translation. In Proceedings of the 56th Annual Meeting of the Association for Computational Linguistics (Volume 1: Long Papers), pages 1756–1766.

Ekin D Cubuk, Barret Zoph, Dandelion Mane, Vijay Vasudevan, and Quoc V Le. 2019. Autoaugment: Learning augmentation strategies from data. In Proceedings of the IEEE Conference on Computer Vision and Pattern Recognition, pages 113–123.

Ekin D Cubuk, Barret Zoph, Jonathon Shlens, and Quoc V Le. 2020. Randaugment: Practical automated data augmentation with a reduced search space. In Proceedings of the IEEE/CVF Conference on Computer Vision and Pattern Recognition Workshops, pages 702–703.

Andrew M Dai and Quoc V Le. 2015. Semi-supervised sequence learning. In C. Cortes, N. D. Lawrence, D. D. Lee, M. Sugiyama, and R. Garnett, editors, Advances in Neural Information Processing Systems 28, pages 3079–3087. Curran Associates, Inc.

David Dale. 2020. GitHub repository.

Tri Dao, Albert Gu, Alexander Ratner, Virginia Smith, Chris De Sa, and Christopher Ré. 2019. A kernel theory of modern data augmentation. In International Conference on Machine Learning, pages 1528–1537. PMLR.

Jacob Devlin, Ming-Wei Chang, Kenton Lee, and Kristina Toutanova. 2019. Bert: Pre-training of deep bidirectional transformers for language understanding. In NAACL-HLT (1).

Sergey Edunov, Myle Ott, Michael Auli, and David Grangier. 2018. Understanding back-translation at scale. In Proceedings of the 2018 Conference on Empirical Methods in Natural Language Processing, pages 489–500.

Marzieh Fadaee, Arianna Bisazza, and Christof Monz. 2017. Data augmentation for low-resource neural machine translation. In Proceedings of the 55th Annual Meeting of the Association for Computational Linguistics (Volume 2: Short Papers), pages 567–573.

Marzieh Fadaee and Christof Monz. 2018. Back-translation sampling by targeting difficult words in neural machine translation. In Proceedings of the 2018 Conference on Empirical Methods in Natural Language Processing, pages 436–446.

Steven Y Feng, Varun Gangal, Jason Wei, Sarath Chandar, Soroush Vosoughi, Teruko Mitamura, and Eduard Hovy. 2021. A survey of data augmentation approaches for NLP. Findings of ACL.

Praveen Kumar Badimala Giridhara., Chinmaya Mishra., Reddy Kumar Modam Venkataramana., Syed Saqib Bukhari., and Andreas Dengel. 2019. A study of various text augmentation techniques for relation classification in free text. In Proceedings of the 8th International Conference on Pattern Recognition Applications and Methods - Volume 1: ICPRAM,, pages 360–367. INSTICC, SciTePress.

Awni Hannun, Carl Case, Jared Casper, Bryan Catanzaro, Greg Diamos, Erich Elsen, Ryan Prenger, Sanjeev Satheesh, Shubho Sengupta, Adam Coates, et al. 2014. Deep speech: Scaling up end-to-end speech recognition. arXiv preprint arXiv:1412.5567.

Daniel Ho, Eric Liang, Xi Chen, Ion Stoica, and Pieter Abbeel. 2019. Population based augmentation: Efficient learning of augmentation policy schedules. In International Conference on Machine Learning, pages 2731–2741.

Mohit Iyyer, Varun Manjunatha, Jordan Boyd-Graber, and Hal Daumé III. 2015. Deep unordered composition rivals syntactic methods for text classification. In Proceedings of the 53rd Annual Meeting of the Association for Computational Linguistics and the 7th International Joint Conference on Natural Language Processing (Volume 1: Long Papers), volume 1, pages 1681–1691.

Max Jaderberg, Valentin Dalibard, Simon Osindero, Wojciech M Czarnecki, Jeff Donahue, Ali Razavi, Oriol Vinyals, Tim Green, Iain Dunning, Karen Simonyan, et al. 2017. Population based training of neural networks. arXiv preprint arXiv:1711.09846.

Navdeep Jaitly and Geoffrey E Hinton. 2013. Vocal tract length perturbation (vtlp) improves speech recognition. In Proc. ICML Workshop on Deep Learning for Audio, Speech and Language, volume 117.

Hwa-Yeon Kim, Yoon-Hyung Roh, and Young-Gil Kim. 2019. Data augmentation by data noising for open-vocabulary slots in spoken language understanding. In Proceedings of the 2019 Conference of the North American Chapter of the Association for Computational Linguistics: Student Research Workshop, pages 97–102.

Tom Ko, Vijayaditya Peddinti, Daniel Povey, and Sanjeev Khudanpur. 2015. Audio augmentation for speech recognition. In Sixteenth Annual Conference of the International Speech Communication Association.

Sosuke Kobayashi. 2018. Contextual augmentation: Data augmentation by words with paradigmatic relations. In Proceedings of the 2018 Conference of the North American Chapter of the Association for Computational Linguistics: Human Language Technologies, Volume 2 (Short Papers), pages 452–457.

Oleksandr Kolomiyets, Steven Bethard, and Marie-Francine Moens. 2011. Model-portability experiments for textual temporal analysis. In Proceedings of the 49th Annual Meeting of the Association for Computational Linguistics: Human Language Technologies: short papers-Volume 2, pages 271–276. Association for Computational Linguistics.

Alex Krizhevsky, Ilya Sutskever, and Geoffrey E Hinton. 2012. Imagenet classification with deep convolutional neural networks. In Advances in neural information processing systems, pages 1097–1105.

Ankit Kumar, Ozan Irsoy, Peter Ondruska, Mohit Iyyer, James Bradbury, Ishaan Gulrajani, Victor Zhong, Romain Paulus, and Richard Socher. 2016. Ask me anything: Dynamic memory networks for natural language processing. In International conference on machine learning, pages 1378–1387.

Yitong Li, Trevor Cohn, and Timothy Baldwin. 2017. Robust training under linguistic adversity. In Proceedings of the 15th Conference of the European Chapter of the Association for Computational Linguistics: Volume 2, Short Papers, pages 21–27.

Shayne Longpre, Yu Wang, and Chris DuBois. 2020. How effective is task-agnostic data augmentation for pretrained transformers? In Proceedings of the 2020 Conference on Empirical Methods in Natural Language Processing: Findings, pages 4401–4411.

Franco M Luque and Juan Manuel Pérez. 2018. Atalaya at tass 2018: Sentiment analysis with tweet embeddings and data augmentation. In TASS@ SEPLN, pages 29–35.

Jonathan Mallinson, Rico Sennrich, and Mirella Lapata. 2017. Paraphrasing revisited with neural machine translation. In Proceedings of the 15th Conference of the European Chapter of the Association for Computational Linguistics: Volume 1, Long Papers, pages 881–893.

Vukosi Marivate and Tshephisho Sefara. 2020. Improving short text classification through global augmentation methods. In International Cross-Domain Conference for Machine Learning and Knowledge Extraction, pages 385–399. Springer.

George A Miller. 1998. WordNet: An electronic lexical database. MIT press.

Jonas Mueller and Aditya Thyagarajan. 2016. Siamese recurrent architectures for learning sentence similarity. In Thirtieth AAAI Conference on Artificial Intelligence.

Roberto Navigli and Paola Velardi. 2003. An analysis of ontology-based query expansion strategies. In International Workshop & Tutorial on Adaptive Text Extraction and Mining held in conjunction with the 14th European Conference on Machine Learning and the 7th European Conference on Principles and Practice of, page 42.

Alexander J Ratner, Henry Ehrenberg, Zeshan Hussain, Jared Dunnmon, and Christopher Ré. 2017. Learning to compose domain-specific transformations for data augmentation. In Advances in neural information processing systems, pages 3236–3246.

Rico Sennrich, Barry Haddow, and Alexandra Birch. 2016. Improving neural machine translation models with monolingual data. In Proceedings of the 54th Annual Meeting of the Association for Computational Linguistics (Volume 1: Long Papers), pages 86–96.

Connor Shorten and Taghi M Khoshgoftaar. 2019. A survey on image data augmentation for deep learning. Journal of Big Data, 6(1):60.

Connor Shorten, Taghi M Khoshgoftaar, and Borko Furht. 2021. Text data augmentation for deep learning. Journal of Big Data, 8(1):1–34.

Richard Socher, Alex Perelygin, Jean Wu, Jason Chuang, Christopher D Manning, Andrew Y Ng, and Christopher Potts. 2013. Recursive deep models for semantic compositionality over a sentiment treebank. In Proceedings of the 2013 conference on empirical methods in natural language processing, pages 1631–1642.

Prashanth Vijayaraghavan, Ivan Sysoev, Soroush Vosoughi, and Deb Roy. 2016. DeepStance at SemEval-2016 task 6: Detecting stance in tweets using character and word-level CNNs. In Proceedings of the 10th International Workshop on Semantic Evaluation (SemEval-2016), pages 413–419, San Diego, California. Association for Computational Linguistics.

Soroush Vosoughi, Prashanth Vijayaraghavan, and Deb Roy. 2016. Tweet2Vec: Learning tweet embeddings using character-level CNN-LSTM encoder-decoder. In Proceedings of the 39th International ACM SIGIR conference on Research and Development in Information Retrieval, pages 1041–1044. ACM.

William Yang Wang and Diyi Yang. 2015. That's so annoying!!!: A lexical and frame-semantic embedding based data augmentation approach to automatic categorization of annoying behaviors using# petpeeve tweets. In Proceedings of the 2015 Conference on

Empirical Methods in Natural Language Processing, pages 2557–2563.

Xinyi Wang, Hieu Pham, Zihang Dai, and Graham Neubig. 2018. SwitchOut: an efficient data augmentation algorithm for neural machine translation. In Proceedings of the 2018 Conference on Empirical Methods in Natural Language Processing, pages 856–861.

Jason Wei and Kai Zou. 2019. EDA: Easy data augmentation techniques for boosting performance on text classification tasks. In Proceedings of the 2019 Conference on Empirical Methods in Natural Language Processing and the 9th International Joint Conference on Natural Language Processing (EMNLP-IJCNLP), pages 6383–6389.

Adina Williams, Nikita Nangia, and Samuel Bowman. 2018. A broad-coverage challenge corpus for sentence understanding through inference. In Proceedings of the 2018 Conference of the North American Chapter of the Association for Computational Linguistics: Human Language Technologies, Volume 1 (Long Papers), pages 1112–1122.

Xing Wu, Shangwen Lv, Liangjun Zang, Jizhong Han, and Songlin Hu. 2019. Conditional BERT contextual augmentation. In International Conference on Computational Science, pages 84–95. Springer.

Ziang Xie, Sida I. Wang, Jiwei Li, Daniel Lévy, Aiming Nie, Dan Jurafsky, and Andrew Y. Ng. 2017. Data noising as smoothing in neural network language models. In 5th International Conference on Learning Representations, ICLR 2017, Toulon, France, April 24-26, 2017, Conference Track Proceedings.

Yan Xu, Ran Jia, Lili Mou, Ge Li, Yunchuan Chen, Yangyang Lu, and Zhi Jin. 2016. Improved relation classification by deep recurrent neural networks with data augmentation. In Proceedings of COLING 2016, the 26th International Conference on Computational Linguistics: Technical Papers, pages 1461–1470.

Adams Wei Yu, David Dohan, Quoc Le, Thang Luong, Rui Zhao, and Kai Chen. 2018. Fast and accurate reading comprehension by combining self-attention and convolution. In International Conference on Learning Representations.

Dongxu Zhang, Tianyi Luo, and Dong Wang. 2016. Learning from LDA using deep neural networks. In Natural Language Understanding and Intelligent Applications, pages 657–664. Springer.

Dongxu Zhang and Zhichao Yang. 2018. Word embedding perturbation for sentence classification. arXiv preprint arXiv:1804.08166.

Jingqing Zhang, Piyawat Lertvittayakumjorn, and Yike Guo. 2019. Integrating semantic knowledge to tackle zero-shot text classification. In Proceedings of the 2019 Conference of the North American Chapter of the Association for Computational Linguistics: Human Language Technologies, Volume 1 (Long and Short Papers), pages 1031–1040.

Xiang Zhang, Junbo Zhao, and Yann LeCun. 2015. Character-level convolutional networks for text classification. In Advances in neural information processing systems, page 649–657.

A Appendix

A.1 Hyperparameter Search Space

As a reminder we consider the following 11 data augmentation methods:

- Synonym replacement
- Hypernym replacement
- Nearest neighbour
- Contextual augmentation
- Random insertion of a vocabulary word
- Random insertion of synonym
- Random deletion
- Random swap
- Gaussian noising
- Uniform noising
- Back-translation

The search space consists of augmentation operations with associated probability and magnitude. More specifically, this can be represented as a vector of 11 tuples (o_i, p_i, m_i) (i.e., one tuple for each transform). During the training, up to two data augmentation operations o_i are drawn uniformly at random for each training sample and applied with probability p_i and magnitude m_i. As suggested by Ho et al. (2019), we set the number of operations to $0, 1$ and 2 with probabilities $0.2, 0.3$ and 0.5 respectively. The operations are applied in the same order in which they are drawn. However, the two embedding-level noising operations (i.e., Gaussian noising and uniform noising) are always applied after the other augmentations since they must be applied in the middle of the graph, after the representation layers, whereas the other augmentations are applied directly on the input of the neural network.

To allow for a smooth parametrisation of the search space with large coverage, probabilities and magnitudes can take any values between 0 and 1: $p, m \in [0, 1]$. This is different from the original PBA algorithm where the parameters are limited to discrete values. The magnitude level, which represents the intensity with which each operation should be applied, is scaled down differently to fit the different operations. Maximal magnitude values are chosen so as to allow for a wide enough array of impactful values and their specific values for each augmentation are indicated in the corresponding paragraphs.

All transformation operations are detailed below, including implementation, and the ones that are applied directly on the input rather than on the embeddings are illustrated in Table 3.

Synonym Replacement The implementation follows the one suggested by the authors of the easy data augmentation (EDA) techniques (Wei and Zou, 2019) and uses the provided codes. First, the number of words that are replaced with one of their synonyms is determined as $n_i = \lfloor \hat{m}_i * |s_i| \rfloor$, with $\hat{m}$ the magnitude level scaled down between 0 and 0.25. Then stop-words are removed from the sample. While the number of words replaced is lower than n_i, one word is selected uniformly at random among the words that have not been replaced yet and is replaced with one of its synonyms. Synonyms are retrieved with WordNet (Miller, 1998). Note that since many words have multiple meanings, it is not rare that the chosen synonym carries a different meaning than the original word.

Hypernym Replacement The process for hypernym replacement is identical to that of synonym replacement in all respect except that hypernyms instead of synonyms are extracted using WordNet.

Nearest Neighbour At the beginning of each search (and at the beginning of the final training), we feed every training sample into the pretrained BERT and use the contextualized representation of each token to build a k-d tree. Note that this process is one-time only and is tailored to the train set. When applied to sample s_i, the *nearest-neighbour* operation first tokenizes the sample into WordPiece tokens using the BERT tokenizer before computing the number of tokens that will be replaced as follows: $n_i = \lfloor \hat{m}_i \cdot |s_i| \rceil$. Here, $|s_i|$ corresponds to the number of WordPiece tokens in sample s_i and $\hat{m}_i = 0.25 \cdot m_i$ is the scaled-down level of magnitude, which has a maximum value of 0.25 so that at most 25% of the tokens are replaced. Then, n_i WordPiece tokens at drawn uniformly at random. For each one of them, the 10 tokens with the nearest embeddings (in the context of sample s_i) are retrieved and one of them is selected for replacement using a geometric distribution with parameter $q = 0.5$. A geometric distribution ensures that the nearest neighbours have a higher chance to be selected as a replacement than the more distant ones. The implementation is based on the one provided by Dale (2020).

Contextual Augmentation The *contextual augmentation* transform replaces words by these pre-

	original sample ($m = 0$)	$m = 0.5$	$m = 1$
Synonym Replacement	a pretentious and ultimately empty examination of a sick and evil woman	a pretentious and ultimately empty examination of a sick and **malefic** woman	a **ostentatious** and ultimately empty **interrogatory** of a **retch** and evil woman
Hypernym Replacement	just another disjointed , fairly predictable psychological thriller	just another disjointed , fairly predictable psychological **adventure story**	just another **part** , fairly predictable psychological **heroic tale**
Nearest Neighbour	tormented by his heritage , using his storytelling ability to honor the many faceless victims	tormented by his heritage , using his storytelling ability to honor the many faceless **emotions**	tormented by his **fate** , using his **cinematic** ability to honor the many **unexplainable** victims
Contextual Augmentation	small - budget	**thin** - budget	**barely running** budget
Random Insertion (vocabulary)	actually manages to bring something new into the mix	actually manages *johns* to bring something new into the mix	*lest* actually manages to *goaltender* bring something new into the mix
Random Insertion (synonym)	is a gorgeous film - vivid with color , music and life	is a gorgeous film *brilliant* - vivid with color , music and life	*liveliness* is a gorgeous film - *medicine* vivid with color *exist* , music and life
Random Deletion	an adventurous young talent who finds his inspiration on the fringes of the american underground	an adventurous talent who finds his on the fringes of american underground	an young finds his on the of underground
Random Swap	the movie is widely seen and debated with appropriate ferocity and thoughtfulness	the movie <u>seen</u> widely <u>is</u> and debated with appropriate ferocity and thoughtfulness	<u>movie</u> <u>the</u> is widely seen <u>ferocity</u> <u>thoughtfulness</u> with appropriate <u>and</u> and <u>debated</u>
Back-translation	does n't know what it wants to be	Do not know what he wants to be	I don't know what you want to be

Table 3: Overview of the data augmentation transforms from our search space that operate directly on the input. This shows the outcome when the transformations are applied on samples from the SST-2 dataset with three different magnitude levels $m = 0, 0.5, 1$. Where relevant, tokens that have been replaced are highlighted in bold. In addition, newly inserted tokens are italicized whereas tokens that have changed places are underlined.

dicted by a language model (LM) conditioned on the labels. In this work, we use the implementation provided by Wu et al. (2019) which uses BERT as a conditional masked language model. At the beginning of the search, the model is fine-tuned on the training data on a task that applies extra label-conditional constraint to the traditional masked language objective. Once fine-tuned, the model can be used to infer masked words given a label. When applied to sample s_i, this operation replaces $n_i = \lfloor m_i \cdot |s_i| \rceil$ of the tokens with a mask, where $|s_i|$ is the number of tokens in the sample after applying the BERT tokenizer. Then, along with its label, the masked sample is fed to the fine-tuned conditional model which infers a vocabulary word for each of the masked tokens. These predictions are used as a replacement.

Random Insertion When applied to a sample s_i, the *random insertion* operation randomly adds a token to the sample. The number of tokens to insert n_i is set to a fraction of the length of s_i, namely $n_i = \lfloor \hat{m}_i \cdot |s_i| \rceil$, where $|s_i|$ is the number of tokens in s_i and $\hat{m}_i = 0.25 \cdot m_i$ is the scaled-down magnitude which ensures the number of inserted tokens does not exceed 25% of the original number of tokens and, by extension, that the new sample contains at most 20% of randomly inserted tokens. We include two independent variants: each inserted token is either a synonym of one of the tokens (selected uniformly at random) in s_i as suggested by Wei and Zou (2019) as part of their EDA techniques or is sampled uniformly at random from a subset of the BERT vocabulary. Note that we only consider words between index 1996 and 29611 of the vocabulary to exclude special and unused tokens as well as punctuation, digits and tokens with non-English characters. We also ignore tokens that start with "##" the special characters used to indicate a trailing WordPiece token. The position for the insertion of the new token in s_i is chosen uniformly at a random. The implementation uses the codes provided by Wei and Zou (2019).

Random Deletion The *random deletion* operation removes a fraction of the tokens from the sample. Each token is discarded with probability q_i, where $q_i = \hat{m}_i = 0.25 \cdot m_i$ which is the magnitude level scaled down between 0 and 0.25 to guarantee that at most half of the tokens are removed. This allows a wide range of values around the original intensity parameter of 0.1 suggested by Wei and Zou (2019) whose implementation we use.

Random Swap This augmentation swaps any two words from the sample s_i at random n_i times in a row, where $n_i = \lfloor \hat{m}_i * |s_i| \rfloor$ and $|s_i|$ is the number of tokens in sample s_i. The magnitude parameter m_i is scaled down to have a maximum value of 0.25 to ensure that at most 50% of the words are swapped. Once again, we use the implementation provided by Wei and Zou (2019).

Gaussian Noising The *Gaussian noising* operation is not applied on the input sequences but rather directly on the contextualized word representations. Let w_{ij} be the embedding of word j in sample s_i. Then, each embedding in the sample is transformed as follows:

$$\hat{w}_{ij} = w_{ij} + e_j, \quad e_{jk} \sim \mathcal{N}(0, \sigma^2) \quad , \qquad (1)$$

where $\sigma = m_i$ and e_j is a vector of the length of d (embedding dimension) with elements e_{jk} normally distributed with mean 0 and standard deviation m_i.

Uniform Noising Similarly to Gaussian noising, the *uniform noising* operation is applied directly on the contextualized embeddings. More specifically,

$$\hat{w}_{ij} = w_{ij} + e_j, \quad e_{jk} \sim \mathcal{U}(-m_i, m_i) \quad . \qquad (2)$$

Once again, e_{jk} $(0 \leq k < d)$ are the elements of noise vector e_j uniformly distributed over the half-open interval $[-m_i, m_i]$ and d is the dimension of the embeddings.

Back-translation The *back-translation* operation first translates the sample s_i to an intermediate language before translating the intermediate translation back to English. To allow us to incorporate this transform into the search space, we relate the magnitude level with the quality of the translation: when back-translation is applied with a low magnitude, the intermediate language used is one that achieves a high BLEU3 score according to Aiken (2019). Similarly, high magnitude settings back-translate samples through a language with a poor BLEU3 score. Table 4 summarizes the languages that can be chosen for each level of magnitude. To generate translations, we use the python library *Googletrans* which uses the Google Translate Ajax API to make calls.

A.2 Search

At the beginning of training, all probability and magnitude hyperparameters are set to 0. This follows suggestions by Ho et al. (2019) who postulate that little to no augmentation is needed at the beginning of the training, since the model only starts to overfit later on, and the data should increasingly become more diverse throughout the training. Because the complexity of the BERT models lies in the contextual representation layers which are already pre-trained and the task-specific layer that needs to be fine-tuned is rather simple, we keep the architecture identical both for the child models and for the final model. A key difference between applying PBA to image classification and applying PBA to NLP tasks with pre-trained BERT model is that in the former settings models are commonly trained for hundreds of epochs, whereas only two to four epochs of fine-tuning are sufficient in the latter settings. Consequently, the original strategy of running a search for 160 or 200 epochs (depending on the model and dataset) while having exploit-and-explore procedures take place after every 3 epochs is not feasible for NLP tasks with a pretrained BERT model. Hence we modify the learning rate to slow down the fine-tuning process. More specifically, we look through a small grid search for a learning rate that can replicate the performance achieved when using the original parameters (Devlin et al., 2019) but on a larger number

m_i	INTERMEDIATE LANGUAGES
1	Portuguese, Italian, French, Czech, Swedish
2	Dutch, Maltese, Polish, Romanian, Russian
3	Afrikaans, Belarusian, Slovak, Danish, Indonesian
4	German, Albanian, Bulgarian, Japanese, Spanish
5	Chinese, Croatian, Finnish, Latvian, Arabic, Malaysian
6	Greek, Korean, Norwegian, Serbian, Turkish, Welsh
7	Galician, Icelandic, Slovenian, Vietnamese
8	Catalan, Estonian, Filipino, Hungarian, Swahili
9	Irish, Thai, Hebrew, Ukrainian, Persian
10	Lithuanian, Macedonian, Yiddish, Hindi

Table 4: The intermediate translation languages for each magnitude level m_i. They are separated according to inverse BLEU3 scores.

of epochs. Thus, by reducing the learning rate, we find a way to carry out the search over a total of 48 epochs. The search is conducted on 16 child models that are trained in parallel. At the beginning of the search, approximately 80% of the training data are set aside to form the validation set, which will be used to periodically assess the performance of the child models. The remaining training data are used to optimize the networks. After each epoch (instead of 3 originally), the exploit-and-explore procedure takes place where the 4 worst performing (on the validation set) child models copy the weights and the parameters of the 4 best performing child models. At the end of the 48 epochs, the augmentation schedule of the model with the highest performance (on the validation set) is extracted.

A.3 Train

To train the final model, the train and validation data are grouped to form the final training set. Training is conducted using the same learning rate and the same number of epochs as during the search and uses the discovered schedule for augmentation. At the end of the training, the performance of the trained model is evaluated on an independent test set.

A.4 Implementation details

The implementation parameters can be found in Table 5.

A.5 Results and Discussion

Additional results, tables and figures can be found in this section.

A.5.1 Schedule Robustness Experiment

In the main text, we touched upon the fact that the schedules yielded by the same search can vary significantly from one run to another. For illustration, the schedules yielded by 10 independent searches on the SST-2 dataset with N=1500 samples are displayed in Figure 1. To reduce the number of figures, the product of the magnitude and the probability hyperparameters through the epochs is shown for each schedule. This figure shows that the optimal set of hyperparameters varies significantly from one search to another. In Figure 2 the average magnitude and probability parameters over the 10 schedules at each epoch is displayed. These plots allow us to realise that, while the parameters generally increase throughout the epochs, the magnitudes and probabilities of each transform have a similar value. Although some operations (e.g. Random Swap) have slightly higher average parameters than others, we can see that no augmentation transform clearly dominates the others. This could indicate that the role of the augmentation operations in this setting is not the one that is expected. Indeed, it seems that the data augmentation merely acts as a regulariser and do not help the network learn any kind of invariance.

	PARAMETERS [%]		
	EPOCHS	LEARNING RATE	BATCH SIZE
SST-2	48	1E-5	32
MNLI	48	5E-5	32

Table 5: Implementation details of both the child models and the final model (both with and without augmentation). The model used is the uncased BERT base model with a classification layer.

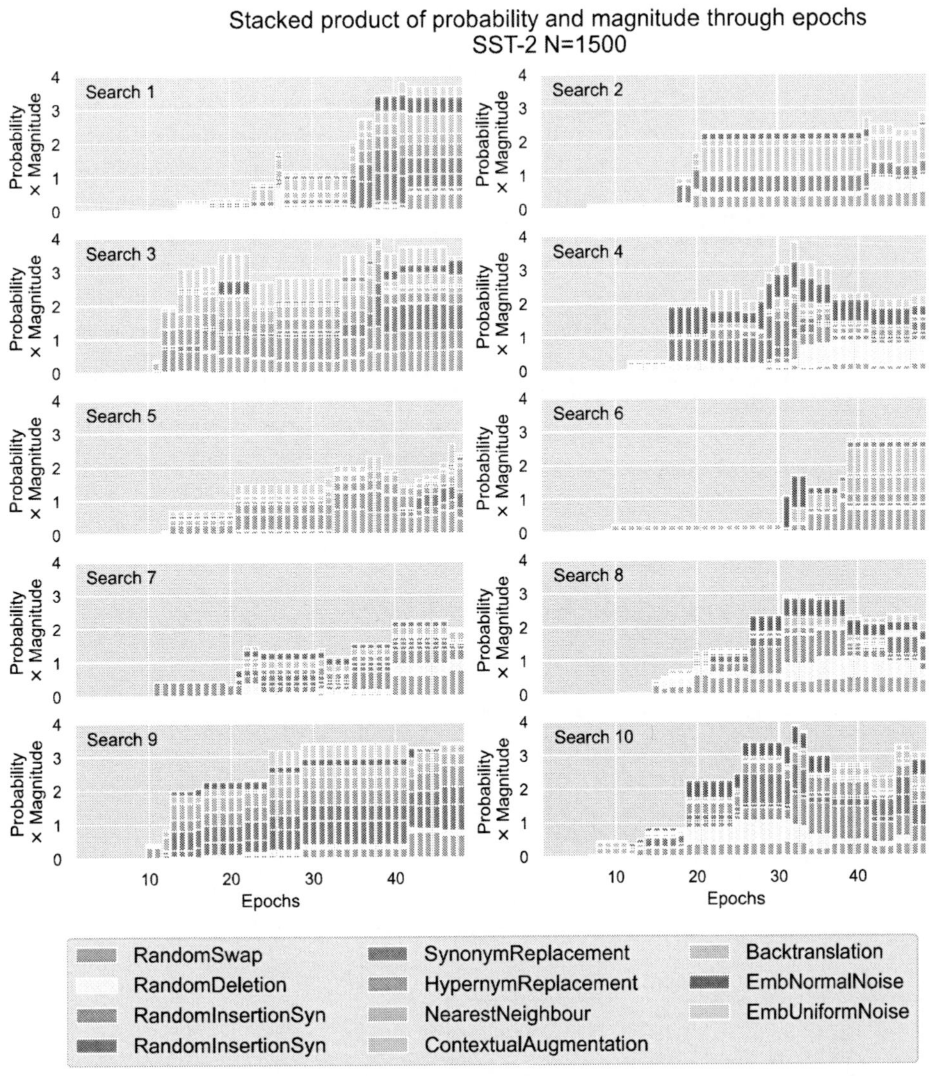

Figure 1: The schedules yielded by 10 independent searches on SST-2 with $N = 1500$ samples (using 250 for training and 1250 for validation during the search). The height of each bar corresponds to the product of the probability and the magnitude parameters at each epoch.

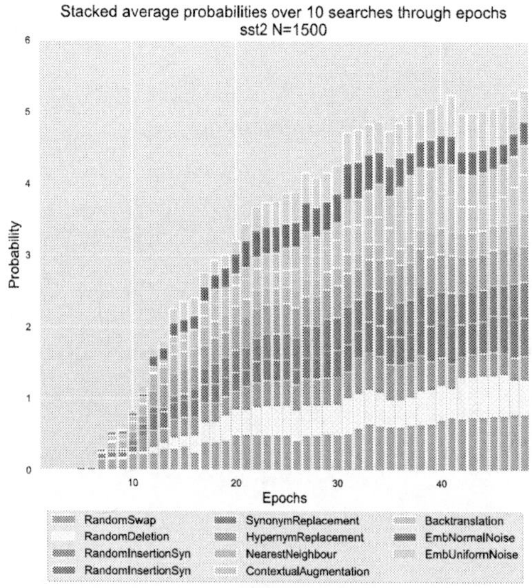

(a) Average probabilities

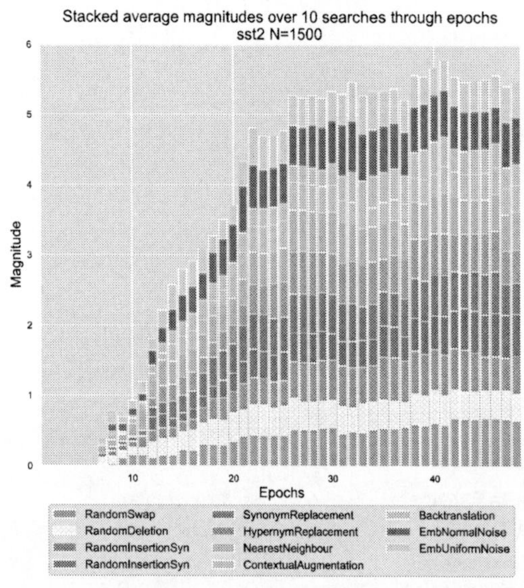

(b) Average magnitudes

Figure 2: The average probability and magnitude values for the schedules yielded by 10 independent searches on SST-2 with N=1500 samples. The height of each bar corresponds to the average probability and magnitude parameters at each epoch over the 10 schedules.

A.5.2 Validation Size Experiment

In this section, we discuss the split ratio experiment in more detail. Overall, the main idea behind using a large validation set is to choose augmentation hyperparameters that do not overfit the validation samples and thus generalize well to unseen data. However, in our case, since the total number of available samples N is small in all experiments, this implies that the size of the training set will be extremely limited. This might hinder the learning process (with too few training examples it can be difficult to learn the optimal network weights) or make the choice of augmentation hyperparameters irrelevant for larger training sets (there is no guarantee that the augmentation chosen for the small train set with will also help when ultimately training with both the training and the validation set). Thus, there exists a clear trade-off between the size of the two sets: while a large validation set can allow for better optimization of the augmentation hyperparameters, a larger training set allows for better optimization of the network weights which, in turn, has an impact on the quality of the augmentation hyperparameters evaluation.

An Investigation into the Contribution of Locally Aggregated Descriptors to Figurative Language Identification

Sina Mahdipour Saravani[♠] Ritwik Banerjee[♣] Indrakshi Ray[♠]

[♠]Department of Computer Science, Colorado State University
{sinamps, indrakshi.ray}@colostate.edu
[♣]Department of Computer Science, Stony Brook University
rbanerjee@cs.stonybrook.edu

Abstract

In natural language understanding, topics that touch upon figurative language and pragmatics are notably difficult. We probe a novel use of locally aggregated descriptors – specifically, an architecture called NeXtVLAD – motivated by its accomplishments in computer vision, achieve tremendous success in the FigLang2020 sarcasm detection task. The reported F_1 score of 93.1% is 14% higher than the next best result. We specifically investigate the extent to which the novel architecture is responsible for this boost, and find that it does not provide statistically significant benefits. Deep learning approaches are expensive, and we hope our insights highlighting the lack of benefits from introducing a resource-intensive component will aid future research to distill the effective elements from long and complex pipelines, thereby providing a boost to the wider research community.

1 Introduction

Natural language understanding often goes beyond the syntactic and semantic layers, and perhaps nowhere is this more palpable than in the use of figurative language. A better understanding of figurative language use, such as metaphors, irony, or sarcasm, can not only lead to advances in computational creativity (Veale, 2011; Kuznetsova et al., 2013), but also in understanding social media content, where users often employ such pragmatic tools as irony or sarcasm (Reyes et al., 2013; Riloff et al., 2013). This type of figurative language is difficult to identify, however, at least partly due to what the influential literary poet and critic William Empson called "ambiguities" (Empson, 1947) in the language. In particular, figurative language use with sarcasm or irony completely decouples – and even contrasts – the communicator's intent from the communicated content (Camp, 2012), rendering shallow syntactic or semantic features unsuitable. The poor fit of such features is further exacerbated in social media posts due to the ubiquity of grammatical errors, hashtags, emojis, etc.

The deeper, context-dependent inferential nature of figurative language, together with the poor fit of shallow syntactic and semantic features, makes deep neural networks a natural candidate for downstream NLP tasks like sarcasm detection (Ghosh and Veale, 2016). Unfortunately, with increasing popularity of deep learning, the reliability of findings in publications that extensively employ deep learning can be expected, in general, to decrease (Pfeiffer and Hoffmann, 2009). In light of this seminal empirical observation and the general difficulty of accurately identifying figurative language, it is reasonable to not expect outright success on a benchmark corpus simply based on the use of a deep network.

The concerns about reliability, and thus, about reproducibility, are particularly acute in deep learning. For instance, Reimers and Gurevych (2017) demonstrated that the hyperparameter settings have a significant impact on the final results obtained by a model. Crane (2018) further showed that other confounding factors such as variation of GPUs, the exact version of a framework, the randomness of a seed value provided to a learning algorithm, and the interaction between multiple such factors, can all impact the obtained results.

Beyond reproducibility, however, lies another pertinent factor: the use of increasingly complex pipelines where multiple sophisticated components are glued together for an important downstream NLP task. In such scenarios, it is not always clear *which* components within the complex system may be responsible for improved outcomes. A simple change in data preprocessing may lead to a significant difference in the final result, for example (Etaiwi and Naymat, 2017; Camacho-Collados and Pilehvar, 2018). In publications that introduce complex NLP pipelines, however, such details have sometimes been omitted.

Proceedings of the Second Workshop on Insights from Negative Results in NLP, pages 103–109
November 10, 2021.

Turn	Tweet	Label
Context-1	The [govt] just confiscated a $180 million boat shipment of cocaine from drug traffickers.	
Context-2	People think 5 tonnes is not a load of cocaine.	Sarcastic
Response	Man! I've seen more than that on a Friday night.	

Table 1: A Tweet thread in the FigLang corpus. Sarcasm being context-dependent, the entire thread serves as a single sample. The label is based on the final response in the thread.

Variable	Dataset	Mean	Median	Std
Tweet length (num. tokens)	Train	140.00	128.00	51.57
	Validation	137.00	125.00	51.17
	Test	143.00	138.00	48.56
Thread length (num. tweets)	Train	4.85	4.00	3.20
	Validation	4.93	4.00	3.29
	Test	4.16	3.00	1.95

Table 2: Overview of the FigLang corpus, showing the overall statistics for the size of individual Tweets (using the BERT tokenizer) and the size of Tweet threads.

2 Exemplar task and data

Within the limited scope of this paper, our goal is to specifically investigate the state-of-the-art sarcasm detection system presented by Lee et al. (2020) – which reported an F_1 score of 93.1%, 14% higher than the next best result reported to the FigLang 2020 workshop (Ghosh et al., 2020) for the Twitter track – and to distill a novel deep learning component used in their pipeline in order to investigate its contribution to the final result. Through a comprehensive series of experiments, we find that this novel architecture (discussed in Sections 3 and 4) does not lead to any significant improvement. The improvement may thus be attributed to components other than deep learning, such as augmenting the corpus by using additional data. Investigating the other components, however, is not in the scope of the work being presented here.

The task is to determine if the final response in a thread (*i.e.*, a sequence of Tweets where each post is in response to its previous post) is sarcastic. One such thread is shown in Table 1. All our experiments are conducted on the Twitter corpus of the FigLang 2020 sarcasm detection task (Ghosh et al., 2020), which comprises $5,000$ threads in the training set and $1,800$ in the test set. Additional properties of this corpus are shown in Table 2.

3 Background

The architecture we investigate has recently been used in downstream NLP tasks, motivated by its success in computer vision. Its origins, however, can be traced back to NLP research, when Sivic and Zisserman (2003) borrowed from the bag-of-words approach used in text retrieval. Since then, a significant body of work in computer vision has developed this approach further. The core idea being the treatment of an image as a document, and low-dimensional features[1] extracted from them forming the visual vocabulary, thus enabling a vector representation of each image, subsequently used in classification or ranking tasks.

A key advancement came in the form of Vector of Locally Aggregated Descriptors (VLAD), introduced by Jégou et al. (2010). In this work, too, low-dimensional features were extracted from images, but K clusters of the features were created, and only the difference of each feature from the cluster center was recorded. Instead of a single N-dimensional feature vector, each image would thus be represented by a $K \times N$ matrix.

The non-differentiable hard cluster assignment, however, renders it unsuitable for training a neural network. NetVLAD (Arandjelovic et al., 2016) resolves this by using the softmax function, whose parameters can be learned during training. Since the cluster assignments of a feature are not known prior to training, their approach requires K N-dimensional difference vectors to encode each feature. This increase in the number of parameters impedes model optimization, and may lead to overfitting – drawbacks discussed and subsequently addressed by NeXtVLAD (Lin et al., 2018) by introducing a step prior to the soft cluster assignments. In this step, the input is expanded to λN size by a fully-connected layer, and then decomposed into G groups of lower-dimensional vectors. Further, a sigmoid function with range $[0, 1]$ is used to assign attention scores to the groups for each vector. The process effectively provides a $\frac{G}{\lambda}$ reduction in the number of parameters, by aggregating lower-dimensional vectors. From a linear algebra perspective, this can be interpreted as representing the data using subspace projections of the original vector.

[1]The literature on image processing often uses the term "descriptor", but to stay in tune with the terminology in NLP research, we continue to use the term "feature".

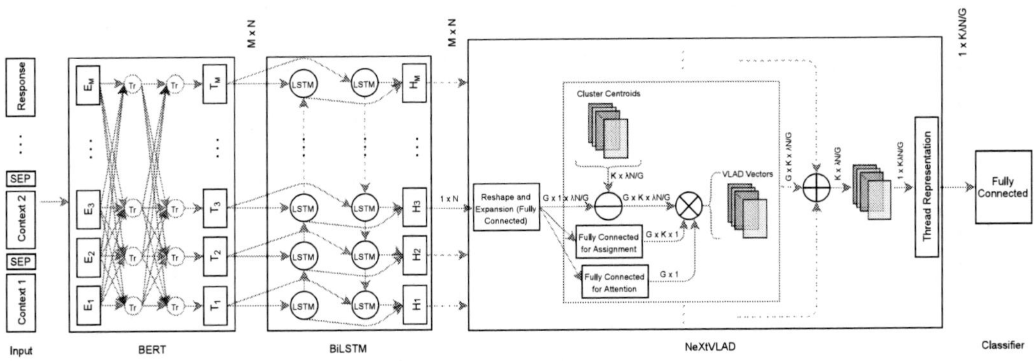

Figure 1: The architecture for sarcasm detection, where M is the number of tokens from the input text, N is the dimension of the BERT representation, and G is the number of groups into which the input is split after expansion.

4 Architecture for sarcasm detection

For an analogous use of NeXtVLAD in NLP, the token representation vectors take the place of the feature vectors used in computer vision literature. In particular, for sarcasm detection using the FigLang corpus, one entire thread needs to be represented by a $K \times N$ matrix. To achieve this, the context and response Tweets (as shown in Table 1) from a single thread are concatenated, with a special [SEP] token separating them. This token is known to BERT, and used in its next sentence prediction task. Here, the token is used to separate different posts within a thread. After concatenation, the pretrained BERT model is used to obtain a vector representation of each token. Then, it is passed through a BiLSTM layer before being fed to the NeXtVLAD component. At this point, NeXtVLAD, as a parametric intelligent pooling and aggregation layer, represents the whole Tweet thread as a $K \times N$ matrix, which is finally flattened and fed to two dense layers with a softmax function to assign the predicted label. This architecture, based on the explanation provided by Lee et al. (2020), is presented in Figure 1.

Consider M input tokens, each represented by a vector of size N produced by the language model and further tuned by the BiLSTM layer (*e.g.*, $N = 1024$ for $\text{BERT}_{\text{Large}}$). We denote these tokens by x_t, $t \in \{1, ..., M\}$. Each x_t is expanded to $\dot{x}_t$ with shape $(1, \lambda N)$ and reshaped to $\tilde{x}_t$ with shape $(G, 1, \frac{\lambda N}{G})$. Then, the (1) soft assignment of $\tilde{x}_t^g$ to the cluster k, and (2) the attention over groups, are computed as

$$\alpha_{gk}(\dot{x}_t) = \frac{e^{w_{gk}^T \dot{x}_t + b_{gk}}}{\sum_{s=1}^{K} e^{w_{gk}^T \dot{x}_t + b_{gk}}} \quad (1)$$

$$\text{and } \alpha_g(\dot{x}_t) = \sigma(w_g^T \dot{x}_t + b_g). \quad (2)$$

The locally aggregated feature vectors (*i.e.*, the VLAD vectors) are generated by computing the product of the attention, assignment, and the difference from the cluster center

$$v_{tki}^g = \alpha_g(\dot{x}_t)\alpha_{gk}(\dot{x}_t)(\tilde{x}_{ti}^g - c_{ki}).$$

Finally, the entire thread is represented by

$$r_{ki} = \sum_{t,g} v_{tki}^g.$$

In the above equations, t, g, k, and i iterate over tokens, groups, clusters, and vector elements respectively, while w and b denote the weight and bias parameters of the linear transformations in the fully-connected layers.

5 Experiments and Results

We delve into several modifications of the model, as well as various hyperparameter settings, in order to investigate how much effect the NeXtVLAD component has on the sarcasm detection task. Our experiments initially use the same training configuration as Lee et al. (2020), before exploring further.

Since Lee et al. (2020) employ additional unpublished data, an exact reproduction of the experiments is not possible. Moreover, the partition of the corpus into training and validation set is left unspecified. Thus, their results reported on the validation set are not truly comparable. Some hyperparameter settings, like the number of epochs for training, are also omitted from their report. However, the primary aim of this work is not to focus on reproduction of the results, but to determine what role the NeXtVLAD component played in the excellent final F_1 score of 93.1%.

Model	Validation set results				Test set results			
	Precision	Recall	F-1	Accuracy	Precision	Recall	F-1	Accuracy
$\text{BERT}_{\text{Large-Cased}}$	0.75	0.84	0.80	0.79	0.71	0.78	0.74	0.73
$\text{BERT}_{\text{Large-Cased}}$ + BiLSTM + NeXtVLAD	***0.74***	***0.84***	***0.79***	***0.78***	***0.71***	***0.77***	***0.74***	***0.72***
$\text{BERT}_{\text{Large-Cased}}$ + NeXtVLAD	0.71	0.82	0.76	0.74	0.69	0.77	0.73	0.71
$\text{BERT}_{\text{Large-Cased}}$ + BiLSTM	0.76	0.82	0.79	0.79	0.71	0.74	0.72	0.72
$\text{BERT}_{\text{Large-Cased}}$ + KimCNN + NeXtVLAD	0.74	0.84	0.79	0.78	0.72	0.82	0.77	0.75
$\text{BERT}_{\text{Large-Cased}}$ + OurCNN + NeXtVLAD	0.77	0.71	0.74	0.76	0.69	0.79	0.74	0.72
CTBERTv2	0.76	0.83	0.80	0.79	0.72	0.76	0.74	0.73
CTBERTv2 + BiLSTM + NeXtVLAD	0.72	0.85	0.78	0.77	0.71	0.79	0.75	0.73
$\text{BERT}_{\text{Large-Cased}}$ (DE)	0.81	0.85	0.83	0.82	0.72	0.73	0.73	0.72
$\text{BERT}_{\text{Large-Cased}}$ + BiLSTM + NeXtVLAD (DE)	0.79	0.84	0.82	0.81	0.73	0.74	0.74	0.73
$\text{BERT}_{\text{Large-Uncased}}$ (DE)	0.79	0.83	0.81	0.81	0.73	0.73	0.73	0.73
$\text{BERT}_{\text{Large-Uncased}}$ + BiLSTM + NeXtVLAD (DE)	0.79	0.87	0.82	0.82	0.73	0.79	0.76	0.75
CTBERTv2 (DE)	0.78	0.83	0.80	0.80	0.75	0.77	0.76	0.75
CTBERTv2 + BiLSTM + NeXtVLAD (DE)	0.81	0.83	0.82	0.82	0.77	0.77	0.77	0.77
$\text{BERT}_{\text{Large-Cased}}$ (DE, LA)	0.79	0.84	0.81	0.87	0.73	0.75	0.74	0.82
$\text{BERT}_{\text{Large-Cased}}$ + BiLSTM + NeXtVLAD (DE, LA)	0.67	0.60	0.63	0.77	0.63	0.52	0.57	0.74
Ensemble of 3 [CTBERTv2 + BiLSTM + NeXtVLAD] (DE)	0.62	0.61	0.61	0.62	0.60	0.54	0.57	0.59

Table 3: Sarcasm detection results. Precision, recall, and F_1 are shown for "sarcasm", while the accuracy is averaged over both classes. Experiments with dataset expansion (DE) and label augmentation (LA) are also included. The model identical to Lee et al. (2020) (minus data augmentation and modification) is shown in bold italics.

The performance of different configurations are shown in Table 3. Our results are shown for the original FigLang test set as well as the one-fifth validation set we separated from training[2]. All the models have been trained for 8 epochs with a batch size of 4. We train the models for different number of epochs ranging from 3 to 30. Lee et al. (2020) mention the use of early stopping for their number of training epochs, which aims to prevent overfitting by monitoring the model performance on a held-out set at the end of each epoch, and stopping the training when performance starts to degrade. Their work, however, leaves out two hyperparameter values required for replication: *patience*, which controls the number of consecutive times it is acceptable for a model to not improve, and *delta*, the minimum threshold for differential improvement.

Without these, we follow Fomin et al. (2020) and apply early stopping with patience and delta set to 2 and 0, respectively. With early stopping, the number of optimal epochs varied, but even while setting the random states manually to make the configuration as deterministic as possible, repeated experiments showed optimal training to always vary between 5 to 12 epochs (a subset of the more comprehensive experiments we conducted, checking from 3 to 30 epochs). In our experiments, the $\text{BERT}_{\text{large-cased}}$ + BiLSTM + NeXtVLAD model is identical to Lee et al. (2020) (without their data augmentation and modification). The hyperparameters for this model are provided in Table 4. Since this model achieves the best F_1 score on the validation set with 8 training epochs, we fix the number of training epochs to be 8 for the other models as well.

In order to replicate the ensemble model discussed by Lee et al. (2020), threads with more than one context are used to create extra samples by removing the furthest context, one at a time, until only one context remains. In the experiments using this data expansion (DE), the thread in Table 1, for instance, gives rise to one additional sample, with only context 2 and the response. Then, a separate model is trained for each context length, and majority voting assigns the final label. We also conduct a series of experiments where the response Tweet is removed from each thread, and the remaining thread is considered non-sarcastic. These are indicated in Table 3 by LA (label augmentation).

To explore further, we record the performance for all training epochs on the validation set. Table 5 shows the accuracy for epochs 2 to 8, for the model proposed by Lee et al. (2020) (the first configuration in Table 3). We compute the accuracy and F_1 score for up to 30 training epochs. A comparison of the best scores from the models that employ NeXtVLAD with the ones that do not, we find no statistically significant improvement.

We also include additional experiments that replace BiLSTM with convolution layers. We use KimCNN (Kim, 2014) as well as a custom CNN (simply called OurCNN in Table 3) with filters

[2]Our code and the choice of validation set are available at github.com/sinamps/nextvlad-for-nlp

Hyperparameter	Value
K	128
G	8
λ (expansion)	4
M	512
N	1024
Context Gating's dropout rate	0.5
BiLSTM's dropout rate	0.25
# of epochs	8
Batch size	4
Initial learning rate	10^{-6}

Table 4: The general hyperparameters for our implementation of $\text{BERT}_{\text{Large-Cased}}$ + BiLSTM + NeXtVLAD.

that always cover one response token with various number of context tokens. Appendix A provides a discussion of our custom CNN. These variations, too, however, do not outperform the baseline results obtained through BERT alone.

5.1 Discussion

In image/video processing, a large number of low-dimensional descriptors extracted from the original high-dimensional image (such as SIFT vectors of size 128) are fed to NeXtVLAD. In NLP applications, however, the token vectors have a much higher dimension. It is possible that this is why the subspace representation does not provide any advantage over the original vector representation. Another possibility is that unlike images or videos, sub-vector representations of tokens do not form meaningful units in natural language tasks, and thus, the low-dimensional split actually hurts the learner. Our experiments also show that the use of domain-specific models like CTBERT (Müller et al., 2020) offer comparable performance, but reach their best results in fewer epochs of training.

We feel that it is important to distinguish the components of a complex NLP pipeline that contribute to improvements in downstream tasks, from other components in the pipeline. While stopping short of providing explainability to a deep learning system, this type of investigation can, at the very least, provide *attribution* to specific components of NLP pipelines. In other words, it can help us identify *which* parts of a pipeline are primarily responsible for improvements in a downstream task.

Such attributions can help us build comparable systems that are significantly less resource-intensive. In our experiments, we were able to train models based on the $\text{BERT}_{\text{Large}}$ architecture with a 2-layer fully-connected classification head

Model	Accuracy for each epoch 2	3	4	5	6	7	8
w/o NeXtVLAD	0.73	0.77	0.78	0.78	0.78	0.78	0.79
w NeXtVLAD	0.51	0.49	0.49	0.76	0.77	0.77	0.78

Table 5: The validation set accuracy for training epochs 2 to 8 of the first model configuration from Table 3 (the first and second rows from Table 3).

with a batch size of 2 and sequence length of 512 on a single 12 GB GPU (NVidia GeForce GTX Titan X). But, with the addition of BiLSTM and NeXtVLAD, the same configuration was only able to fit a batch size of 1. For all the model configurations discussed in this paper, $\text{BERT}_{\text{Large-Cased}}$ + BiLSTM + NeXtVLAD required two 24 GB GPUs (Nvidia RTX 3090) to fit a batch size of 4.

6 Conclusion

We investigate the extent to which NeXtVLAD contributes to improved results in a recent sarcasm detection task, and find that it offers little in terms of additional benefits. Our conjecture at this point is, thus, that the 14% improvement achieved by Lee et al. (2020) must entirely be due to the natural language augmentation techniques used. Our work also indicates that local aggregators like NeXtVLAD are unlikely to offer significant benefits to tasks related to figurative language identification, but more empirical work is needed to confirm this hypothesis.

We hope that our insights can help future research in this direction by making it easier to channel their efforts into aspects of a pipeline that have tangible and attributable benefits to the final downstream NLP task.

Acknowledgements

This work was supported in part by funds from U.S. National Science Foundation (NSF) under award number CNS 2027750, CNS 1822118, and SES 1834597, and from NIST, Statnett, Cyber Risk Research, AMI, and ARL.

References

Relja Arandjelovic, Petr Gronat, Akihiko Torii, Tomas Pajdla, and Josef Sivic. 2016. NetVLAD: CNN architecture for weakly supervised place recognition. In *Proceedings of the IEEE Conference on Computer Vision and Pattern Recognition*, pages 5297–5307. Institute of Electrical and Electronics Engineers.

Jose Camacho-Collados and Mohammad Taher Pilehvar. 2018. On the Role of Text Preprocessing in Neural Network Architectures: An Evaluation Study on Text Categorization and Sentiment Analysis. In *Proceedings of the Workshop BlackboxNLP: Analyzing and Interpreting Neural Networks for NLP*, pages 40–46. Association for Computational Linguistics.

Elisabeth Camp. 2012. Sarcasm, Pretense, and The Semantics/Pragmatics Distinction. *Noûs*, 46(4):587–634.

Matt Crane. 2018. Questionable Answers in Question Answering Research: Reproducibility and Variability of Published Results. *Transactions of the Association for Computational Linguistics*, 6:241–252.

William Empson. 1947. *Seven Types of Ambiguity*, 2nd edition. Chatto and Windus, London.

Wael Etaiwi and Ghazi Naymat. 2017. The Impact of applying Different Preprocessing Steps on Review Spam Detection. *Procedia Computer Science*, 113:273–279.

V. Fomin, J. Anmol, S. Desroziers, J. Kriss, and A. Tejani. 2020. High-level library to help with training neural networks in PyTorch. `https://github.com/pytorch/ignite`.

Aniruddha Ghosh and Tony Veale. 2016. Fracking Sarcasm using Neural Network. In *Proceedings of the Workshop on Computational Approaches to Subjectivity, Sentiment and Social Media Analysis*, pages 161–169. Association for Computational Linguistics.

Debanjan Ghosh, Avijit Vajpayee, and Smaranda Muresan. 2020. A Report on the 2020 Sarcasm Detection Shared Task. In *Proceedings of the Workshop on Figurative Language Processing*, pages 1–11. Association for Computational Linguistics.

Hervé Jégou, Matthijs Douze, Cordelia Schmid, and Patrick Pérez. 2010. Aggregating Local Descriptors into a Compact Image Representation. In *Proceedings of the IEEE Computer Society Conference on Computer Vision and Pattern Recognition*, pages 3304–3311. Institute of Electrical and Electronics Engineers.

Yoon Kim. 2014. Convolutional Neural Networks for Sentence Classification. In *Proceedings of the Conference on Empirical Methods in Natural Language Processing*, pages 1746–1751. Association for Computational Linguistics.

Polina Kuznetsova, Jianfu Chen, and Yejin Choi. 2013. Understanding and Quantifying Creativity in Lexical Composition. In *Proceedings of the Conference on Empirical Methods in Natural Language Processing*, pages 1246–1258. Association for Computational Linguistics.

Hankyol Lee, Youngjae Yu, and Gunhee Kim. 2020. Augmenting Data for Sarcasm Detection with Unlabeled Conversation Context. In *Proceedings of the Workshop on Figurative Language Processing*, pages 12–17. Association for Computational Linguistics.

Rongcheng Lin, Jing Xiao, and Jianping Fan. 2018. NeXtVLAD: An Efficient Neural Network to Aggregate Frame-level Features for Large-scale Video Classification. In *Proceedings of the European Conference on Computer Vision Workshops*, pages 206–218. Springer.

Martin Müller, Marcel Salathé, and Per E Kummervold. 2020. COVID-Twitter-BERT: A Natural Language Processing Model to Analyse COVID-19 Content on Twitter. *arXiv preprint arXiv:2005.07503*.

Thomas Pfeiffer and Robert Hoffmann. 2009. Large-Scale Assessment of the Effect of Popularity on the Reliability of Research. *PLoS One*, 4(6):e5996.

Nils Reimers and Iryna Gurevych. 2017. Optimal Hyperparameters for Deep LSTM-Networks for Sequence Labeling Tasks. *arXiv preprint arXiv:1707.06799*.

Antonio Reyes, Paolo Rosso, and Tony Veale. 2013. A multidimensional approach for detecting irony in Twitter. In *Language Resources and Evaluation*, volume 47, pages 239–268. Springer Nature.

Ellen Riloff, Ashequl Qadir, Prafulla Surve, Lalindra De Silva, Nathan Gilbert, and Ruihong Huang. 2013. Sarcasm as Contrast between a Positive Sentiment and Negative Situation. In *Proceedings of the Conference on Empirical Methods in Natural Language Processing*, pages 704–714. Association for Computational Linguistics.

Josef Sivic and Andrew Zisserman. 2003. Video Google: A Text Retrieval Approach to Object Matching in Videos. In *Proceedings of the IEEE International Conference on Computer Vision*, volume 2, pages 1470–1477. Institute of Electrical and Electronics Engineers.

Tony Veale. 2011. Creative Language Retrieval: A Robust Hybrid of Information Retrieval and Linguistic Creativity. In *Proceedings of the Annual Meeting of the Association for Computational Linguistics: Human Language Technologies*, pages 278–287. Association for Computational Linguistics.

A Appendix

To reduce the differences in the shape (*i.e.*, dimensions) and quantity of features fed to NeXtVLAD in Computer Vision and NLP, we designed a custom Convolutional Neural Network (CNN) to transform features into probably a more suitable space. In this section, we present the details of this custom

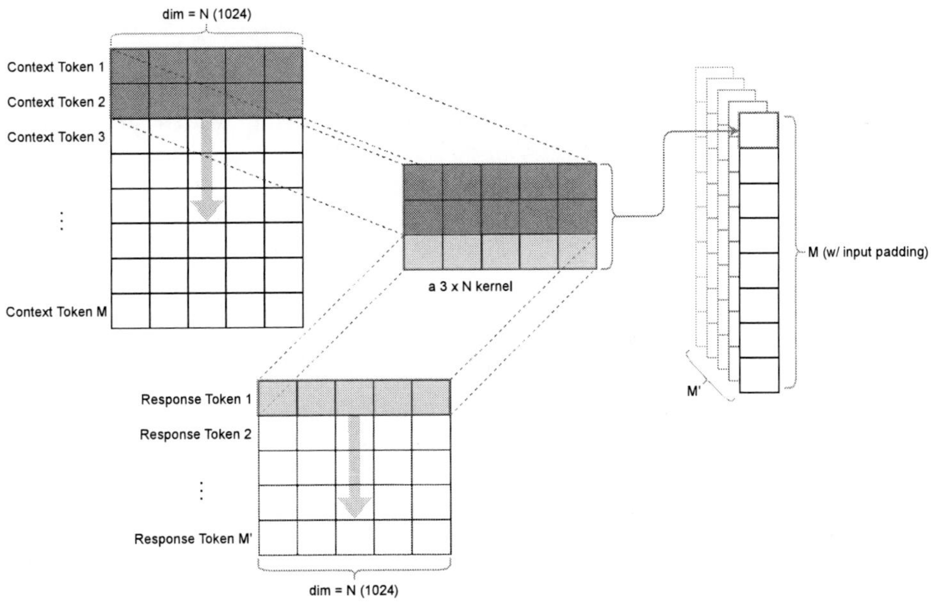

Figure 2: The custom CNN architecture for sarcasm detection in Twitter. *M* is the number of context tokens. *M'* is the number of response tokens. *N* is the token representation dimension.

CNN for extracting features for the NeXtVLAD layer. Figure 2 depicts the architecture of our CNN. First, we concatenate all the context Tweets and pass them to BERT to get the token representations and store them in a $M \times N$ matrix. The response Tweet also goes through the same process and is represented in a $M' \times N$ matrix. N is the dimension of the token representation vectors and M and M' denote the number of tokens in the contexts and response respectively. Each row in these matrices contains the vector representation of one token. Similar to KimCNN (Kim, 2014), we set the width of the kernel to the dimension of the token representation vector (N). But, distinct from KimCNN, our kernels are always applied to local areas from two distinct input matrices.

In our architecture, kernels only slide vertically to move over different tokens. To demonstrate, consider the kernel of size 3 in Figure 2. The first two rows of this kernel cover the first two tokens of the context matrix and the last row covers the first token in the response matrix. The inner product is computed and yields the first element in the first output vector. Then, the blue portion of the kernel slides downward and the computation repeats to yield the second element of the first output vector. When this sliding window reaches the end of the context matrix, the first output vector is complete. Now, the gray portion of the kernel slides downward on the response matrix and all previous steps repeat to generate the next output vector. This set of operations with F different kernels and by applying appropriate zero padding to the input, yields an output of shape (F, M', M) which is $(64, 100, 512)$ in our implementation. This output is rearranged and reshaped to shape $(M' \times M, F)$, which is much more similar to image/video features in shape and quantity. This is fed to NeXtVLAD in our sarcasm detection architecture. We use 64 kernels in our experiments with size 2, 3, 4, and 5 (16 kernels of each size; size only refers to the height of the kernel, since the width is fixed). In our implementation, the values are set as $F = 64$, $M = 512$, and $M' = 100$.

Blindness to Modality Helps Entailment Graph Mining

Liane Guillou[*†], **Sander Bijl de Vroe**[*†], **Mark Johnson**[‡], **Mark Steedman**[†]
[†]University of Edinburgh, [‡]Oracle Digital Assistant
{sbdv, liane.guillou}@ed.ac.uk
mark.mj.johnson@oracle.com, steedman@inf.ed.ac.uk

Abstract

Understanding linguistic modality is widely seen as important for downstream tasks such as Question Answering and Knowledge Graph Population. Entailment Graph learning might also be expected to benefit from attention to modality. We build Entailment Graphs using a news corpus filtered with a modality parser, and show that stripping modal modifiers from predicates in fact increases performance. This suggests that for some tasks, the pragmatics of modal modification of predicates allows them to contribute as evidence of entailment.

1 Introduction

The ability to recognise textual entailment and paraphrase is crucial in many downstream tasks, including Open Domain Question Answering from text. For example, if we pose the question "Did Joe Biden run for President?" and the text states that "Joe Biden was elected President", producing the correct answer (Yes) necessitates understanding that *being elected President* entails *running for President*[1].

Entailment Graphs, constructed via unsupervised learning techniques over large text corpora, provide a solution to this problem. They consist of nodes representing predicates and directed edges representing entailment relations between them. Given the importance of detecting uncertainty for other downstream NLP tasks such as Information Extraction (Karttunen and Zaenen, 2005; Farkas et al., 2010), Information Retrieval (Vincze, 2014), machine reading (Morante and Daelemans, 2012a), and Question Answering (Jean et al., 2016) one might expect that it would also be useful in learning Entailment Graphs. That is, they would be more reliable if learned from data in which predications are *asserted* as actually happening, rather than data with *uncertain* predications under scope of various types of modality. We investigate whether this is the case.

The Entailment Graph-learning algorithm depends on descriptions of eventualities in the news, observing directional co-occurrences of typed predicates and their arguments. For example, we expect to observe all the arguments of *being president*, such as *Biden* and *Obama*, also to be encountered in a sufficiently large multiply-sourced body of text as arguments of *running for president*, but not the other way around (*Hillary Clinton* will *run* but not *be president*). However, if all the reports of *Clinton* ***might*** *be president* are extracted as *be_president(Clinton)*, one might expect the learning signal to be confusing to the algorithm.

We use the method of Hosseini et al. (2018) combined with a modality parser (Bijl de Vroe et al., 2021) to construct typed Entailment Graphs from raw text corpora under two different settings. Modality-aware: modal predications are removed from the data entirely, and modality-unaware: the model learns from both asserted and modal predications. Our contributions are 1) a comparison of Entailment Graphs learned from modal and non-modal data, showing (counterintuitively) that ignoring modal distinctions in fact improves Entailment Graph-learning, and 2) insights as to whether this effect applies uniformly across different subdomains.

2 Background

Entailment rules specify directional inferences between linguistic predicates (Szpektor and Dagan, 2008), and can be stored in an Entailment Graph, whose global structural properties can be used to learn more accurately (Berant et al., 2011, 2015). They are defined as a directed graph $\mathcal{G} = \{N, E\}$, in which the nodes N are typed predicates and edges E represent the entailment relation. The lex-

[*]Equal contribution

[1]Assuming a democratic election. We use the typical definition of the premise *most likely* entailing the hypothesis (Dagan et al., 2006)

Proceedings of the Second Workshop on Insights from Negative Results in NLP, pages 110–116
November 10, 2021.

Category	Example
∅	Protesters attacked the police
Modal operator	Protesters **may** have attacked the police
Conditional	**If** protesters attack the police...
Counterfactual	**Had** protesters attacked the police...
Propositional attitude	Journalists **said** that protesters attacked the police

Table 1: Modality categories

ical entailment knowledge stored within them is useful for Question Answering (McKenna et al., 2021), as well as other tasks such as email categorisation (Eichler et al., 2014), relation extraction (Eichler et al., 2017) and link prediction (Hosseini et al., 2019).

A subgraph containing predicates of a type-pair (e.g. PERSON-LOCATION) can be learned in an unsupervised way from collections of multiply-sourced text. A vector of argument-pair counts for every predicate is first machine read from the corpus. Typically, relation extraction systems used for reading these corpora ignore modal modifiers, possibly introducing noise in the graph. Next, a (directed) similarity score (e.g. DIRT (Lin and Pantel, 2001), Weed's score (Weeds and Weir, 2003) or BInc (Szpektor and Dagan, 2008)) is computed between the vectors, producing a local entailment score between each predicate pair. Then a globalisation process such as the soft constraints algorithm of Hosseini et al. (2018), which transfers information both within and between type-pair subgraphs, can be used to refine these local scores. When using the graph in practice, all edges with a score above a chosen threshold can be considered an entailment.

There are various semantic phenomena a speaker can use to mark veridicality (see Table 1). *Modal operators*, e.g. *probably, might, should, need to*, allow the user to indicate their attitude beyond the propositional content of a phrase, and often don't entail that the eventuality occurs (Kratzer, 2012). The same holds for predications under scope of *conditionals* and *counterfactuals* (Dancygier, 1998; Lewis, 1973). *Propositional attitude*, indicated by verbs such as *say, imagine or want*, allows the speaker to attribute thoughts regarding some possible eventuality to a source (Nelson, 2019).

These phenomena have been investigated for various NLP tasks, including uncertainty detection (Vincze, 2014), hedge detection (Medlock and Briscoe, 2007) and modality annotation (Saurı et al., 2006). Capturing this information is valuable to tasks such as Information Extraction, Question Answering and Knowledge Base Population (Karttunen and Zaenen, 2005; Morante and Daelemans, 2012b).

Early approaches to detecting modality focused on lexicon design (Szarvas, 2008; Kilicoglu and Bergler, 2008; Baker et al., 2010), with later approaches using machine learning over annotated corpora (Morante and Daelemans, 2009; Rei and Briscoe, 2010; Jean et al., 2016; Adel and Schütze, 2017). Recently, Bijl de Vroe et al. (2021) designed a parser similar to that by Baker et al. (2010), to cover a wider range of phenomena, including conditionality and propositional attitude. While modality annotation is clearly useful for recognising entailment from a given text (Snow et al., 2006; De Marneffe et al., 2006), to our knowledge no research has been conducted on its effect on learning Entailment Graphs.

3 Methods

We extend relation extraction to pay attention to modality, so that we can distinguish modal and non-modal relations in the Entailment Graph mining algorithm. This allows us to investigate the impact of modalised predicate data on the accuracy of learned entailment edges.

We extract *binary relations* of the form arg1-predicate-arg2 using MoNTEE, an open-domain modality-aware relation extraction system (Bijl de Vroe et al., 2021). MoNTEE uses the RotatingCCG parser (Stanojević and Steedman, 2019) as the basis for extracting binary relations and a modality lexicon to identify modality triggers. A relation is tagged as modal (MOD), propositional attitude (ATT_SAY, ATT_THINK) or conditional (COND) if the CCG dependency graph contains a path between a relation node and a node matching an entry in the MoNTEE lexicon. Counterfactuals (COUNT) are tagged according to hand-crafted rules. Since we focus on uncertainty and not negation, lexical negation (LNEG) tagging is ignored.

In the modality-aware setting, we remove relations tagged by MoNTEE as any kind of modal ({MOD, ATT_SAY, ATT_THINK, COUNT, COND}). In local learning, learned entailment edges then have access only to non-modal evidence: eventualities that were asserted as actually happening. For example, the edge between *win* and *lose* should now be learned only from non-modal descriptions such as *A won today against B* or *A has been defeated by B*, leaving out modal descriptions

(*A could beat B*). The local and globalisation parts of the algorithm are otherwise unchanged.

4 Experimental Setup

Using MONTEE[2], we extract 40,669,812 binary relation triples from the NewsSpike corpus (Zhang and Weld, 2013). Of these, 14.57% are tagged; 10.04% MOD, 3.51% REP_SAY, 0.38% REP_THINK, 0.61% COND, and 0.03% COUNT. We then construct three different datasets and build an Entailment Graph with each. The modality-unaware baseline, **BaselineLarge**, is trained on the complete set of relations with modality tags removed. This corresponds to the data and model in Hosseini et al. (2018). For the modality-aware **Asserted** graph, we extract only the set of 34,744,216 asserted relations (~85% of the relations), i.e. all modal relations are excluded. To rule out effects of data size, we construct **BaselineSmall**, which is trained on a random sample of 85% relations from the total set. Comparing Asserted to BaselineLarge shows us whether it is worth filtering out modal data, and comparing Asserted to BaselineSmall shows whether asserted data or mixed data (i.e. asserted and modal) is more effective for learning entailment relations.

We follow the example of Hosseini et al. (2018) and construct typed graphs for all possible type pairs (e.g. PERSON-LOCATION). Relation arguments are typed by linking to a Named Entity Freebase identifier (Bollacker et al., 2008) using the AIDA-light linker (Nguyen et al., 2014), and mapping these identifiers to a type in the FIGER hierarchy (Ling and Weld, 2012). The typed relations become the input to the graph learning step of the Entailment Graph mining algorithm. Following previous research, we use the BInc similarity score (Szpektor and Dagan, 2008) to compute entailment scores. We first construct local typed Entailment Graphs and then globalise the scores across graphs as in Hosseini et al. (2018).

We evaluate the Entailment Graphs on two datasets. The first is the *Levy/Holt Entailment Dataset*, a set of 18,407 entailment pairs for the general domain (Levy and Dagan, 2016; Holt, 2018). As our training method is unsupervised and we do not tune hyperparameters, we evaluate on the complete Levy/Holt dataset rather than the dev/test split. We also evaluate on the *Sports Entailment Dataset* (Guillou et al., 2020), focusing on the subset of 718 examples comprising entailments and pairs of match outcome predicates (e.g. *win*, *lose*, *tie*, and their paraphrases) which are always non-entailments. This subset evaluates whether Entailment Graphs can recognise, for example, that win/lose → play but win ↛ lose (with similar patterns for other paraphrases of *win, play* and *lose*). We focus on the subgraph of ORGANISATIONs as all predicates are assumed to apply to sports teams. Both datasets use binary labels for each premise/hypothesis pair: entailment (1) and non-entailment (0).

We used the entGraph[3] code developed by Hosseini et al. (2018) to construct each of the Entailment Graphs, and the corresponding evaluation scripts[4] to evaluate performance on the Levy/Holt dataset. Performance on the Sports Entailment Dataset[5] is evaluated using scripts[6] developed for this paper. For details on hyperparameters and computational costs see Appendix A.

	Levy/Holt all	Levy/Holt directional	Sports
BaselineLarge	**0.190**	**0.163**	0.453
BaselineSmall	0.184	0.157	0.422
Asserted	0.171	0.136	**0.468**

Table 2: AUC scores

	Nodes	Edges	% Levy preds found all ex.	% Levy preds found directional
BaselineLarge	334K	72,7M	63.06	70.29
BaselineSmall	277K	58,4M	61.13	69.29
Asserted	254K	46,3M	58.51	67.92

Table 3: Graph size comparison and predicate coverage for Levy/Holt dataset (all examples) and its directional portion

	Nodes	Edges	% Sports preds found
BaselineLarge	4,514	1.65M	92.86
BaselineSmall	3,823	1.29M	90.48
Asserted	3,682	1.09M	88.10

Table 4: ORGANISATIONs subgraph size comparison and predicate coverage for the Sports Entailment Dataset

[2]https://gitlab.com/lianeg/montee

[3]https://github.com/mjhosseini/entGraph

[4]https://github.com/mjhosseini/entgraph_eval

[5]https://gitlab.com/lianeg/temporal-entailment-sports-dataset

[6]https://gitlab.com/lianeg/sports-entailment-evaluation

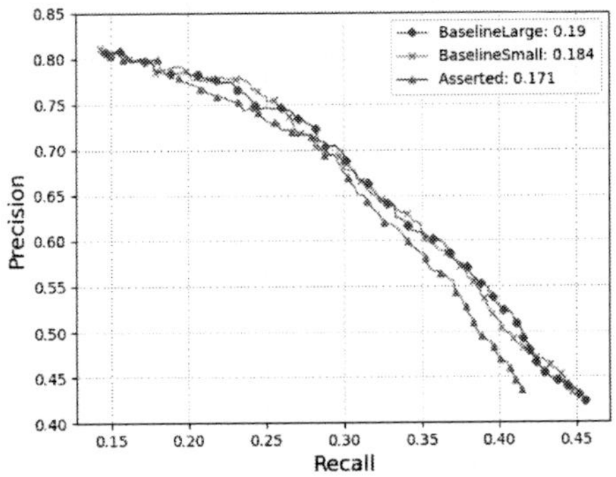

Figure 1: Precision/recall on Levy/Holt dataset

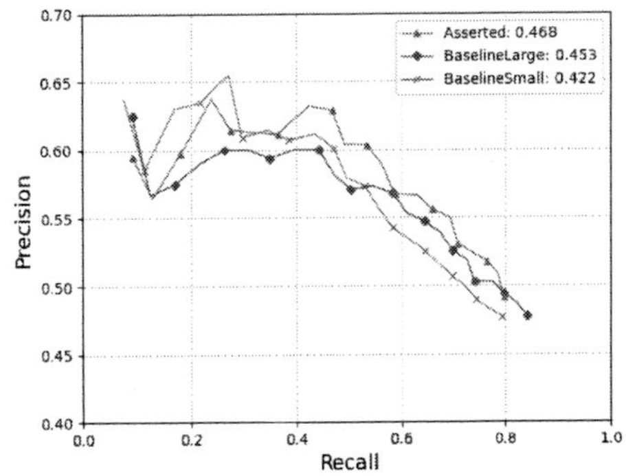

Figure 2: Precision/recall on Sports Entailment Dataset

5 Results

Table 2 contains area under the precision/recall curve (AUC) scores for Asserted, BaselineSmall, and BaselineLarge on the Levy/Holt dataset (**all** examples), the directional portion of the Levy/Holt dataset (2,414 examples), and the Sports Entailment dataset. The precision-recall curves for the Levy/Holt (all examples) and Sports Entailment datasets are displayed in Figures 1 and 2 respectively. Every point on the curve represents a different entailment score threshold (higher thresholds correspond to lower recall and vice versa). We follow the example of Hosseini et al. (2018) and compute AUC for precision in the range [0.5, 1]. All three Entailment Graphs cover this range and predictions with precision higher than random are important for downstream applications.

On the Levy/Holt dataset (all examples), BaselineLarge performs best overall. The strong performance of BaselineLarge compared to Asserted is in itself surprising, and indicates that it is usually not beneficial to distinguish modality when building Entailment Graphs. This can be understood as a data size issue: filtering out data is harmful as it introduces sparsity, and modal data is useful enough to provide a learning signal.

More counterintuitive, however, is that even BaselineSmall, which controls for training dataset size, outperforms Asserted. To understand why, we measured the size of each graph in terms of the number of nodes (predicates) and edges (entailment relations) it contained, and the percentage of predicates in the Levy/Holt dataset that were present in the graph (see Table 3). This revealed that BaselineSmall contained more of the predicates present in the Levy/Holt dataset, while also being larger in terms of both nodes and edges than Asserted. Thus, Asserted learns with more relations per predicate, while BaselineSmall has more predicate nodes overall. This may lead to the increase in recall that we see for the BaselineSmall graph.

Another explanation might be that this richer predicate coverage allows BaselineSmall to accurately correlate more of the common paraphrase examples in the Levy/Holt dataset. To this end we investigated the directional portion of the Levy/Holt dataset, which contains 2,414 examples of both the entailment pair and its reverse, where the entailment is true in one direction and false in the other. As noted by Hosseini et al. (2018) this task is much harder than that represented by the original dataset. However, the baselines both outperform the Asserted graph on the directional entailment task. We also observe a similar pattern in the percentage of predicates covered (see last column in Table 3). In general, we conclude that modal data is useful even for learning directional entailments.

Performance on the Sports Entailment dataset (Figure 2) reveals a different pattern. BaselineLarge outperforms BaselineSmall as expected, but Asserted performs best, despite lower coverage of the predicates in the Sports Entailment Dataset (see Table 4 for a size comparison of the ORGANISATIONs subgraph). This supports the suggestion by Guillou et al. (2020) that excluding modal data may help to avoid learning entailments between disjunctive outcomes, i.e. that winning entails losing, which is not measured by the Levy/Holt dataset.

6 Discussion & Future Work

Another appealing intuition for the usefulness of modal relations is that they might generally be expressed in text when the prior probability of the main predicate is already high. This would lead the distributions for the main predicates to be improved in spite of the uncertainty of the evidence. Additionally, if the probability of a premise is high enough to be worth mentioning, then in general that of its entailments will be too. However, this may not hold for the sports scenario because the outcomes are widely speculated upon despite being highly uncertain.

Indeed it is easy to find examples in the news corpus to support these intuitions. In the general domain we observe examples of eventualities initially being discussed with uncertainty, and later mentioned as asserted. An example of this is the acquisition of Dell by Michael Dell: on February 5th, 2013 we observe *"... founder and CEO Michael Dell and investment firm Silver Lake Partners will buy Dell."*, and subsequently, on February 6th, 2013 we read *"So Michael Dell and a private equity group have bought Dell and taken it private."*. We also observe the reverse scenario in the sports domain. For example, on January 10th, 2013 we observe *"The popular opinion on this game seems to be Seattle beating Atlanta because..."*, while shortly afterwards we are informed that *"Falcons come back to beat Seahawks"*. The latter is likely rather domain-specific, and we may expect to find a similar effect for other domains that share the disjunctive outcome property, for example elections, court cases and battles, where modals are used when speculating about potential and counterfactual outcomes.

We will explore ways to leverage this information and consider other sub-domains for which it is useful to retain or remove modal data. This may involve creating more domain-specific datasets. It is also worth investigating the effects of negation, which shares similar properties to modality, on learning Entailment Graphs.

Relatedly, we could retain predicates under specific modal modifiers, as these correspond to different prior probabilities of eventualities, carrying a different epistemic commitment from the writer. Eventualities that happen "undoubtedly" might be preferred over those that are "unlikely", for instance, and the modality parser can output specific categories of modality, allowing us to choose the subsets that should be kept.

Finally, we will experiment with learning Entailment Graphs with modal predicate nodes, by retaining modal relations with tags attached as input. Many of these entailments are trivial, because any entailment of a consequence can be reproduced under modal scope (if *buy* $\rightarrow$ *own*, then also *MOD_buy* $\rightarrow$ *MOD_own*). More notably, we might recover that following an entailment in the reverse direction can produce a modal entailment (e.g. if *beat* $\rightarrow$ *play*, then we know *play* $\rightarrow$ *MOD_beat*), and many preconditions will behave interestingly (e.g. *beat* $\rightarrow$ *play*, but also *MOD_beat* $\rightarrow$ *play*). To evaluate this idea, we will design a dataset of modal entailments, drawing inspiration from previous research on veridicality in entailment datasets (Staliūnaitė, 2018).

7 Conclusion

We have investigated the role of modally modified relations in Entailment Graph mining, and shown that, contrary to results from other tasks, uncertain predications actually constitute a valuable learning signal overall. Further analysis shows that there are specific predicate domains in which removing modal data is beneficial.

Acknowledgements

This work was funded by the ERC H2020 Advanced Fellowship GA 742137 SEMANTAX and a grant from The University of Edinburgh and Huawei Technologies.

The authors would like to thank Mohammad Javad Hosseini and Nick McKenna for helpful discussions, and the reviewers for their valuable feedback.

References

Heike Adel and Hinrich Schütze. 2017. Exploring different dimensions of attention for uncertainty detection. In *Proceedings of the 15th Conference of the European Chapter of the Association for Computational Linguistics: Volume 1, Long Papers*, pages 22–34, Valencia, Spain. Association for Computational Linguistics.

Kathryn Baker, Michael Bloodgood, Bonnie Dorr, Nathaniel W. Filardo, Lori Levin, and Christine Piatko. 2010. A modality lexicon and its use in automatic tagging. In *Proceedings of the Seventh International Conference on Language Resources and Evaluation (LREC'10)*, Valletta, Malta. European Language Resources Association (ELRA).

Jonathan Berant, Noga Alon, Ido Dagan, and Jacob Goldberger. 2015. Efficient global learning of entailment graphs. *Computational Linguistics*, 41(2):221–263.

Jonathan Berant, Ido Dagan, and Jacob Goldberger. 2011. Global learning of typed entailment rules. In *Proceedings of the 49th Annual Meeting of the Association for Computational Linguistics: Human Language Technologies*, pages 610–619, Portland, Oregon, USA. Association for Computational Linguistics.

Sander Bijl de Vroe, Liane Guillou, Miloš Stanojević, Nick McKenna, and Mark Steedman. 2021. Modality and negation in event extraction. In *Proceedings of the 4th Workshop on Challenges and Applications of Automated Extraction of Socio-political Events from Text (CASE 2021)*, pages 31–42, Online. Association for Computational Linguistics.

Kurt Bollacker, Colin Evans, Praveen Paritosh, Tim Sturge, and Jamie Taylor. 2008. Freebase: A collaboratively created graph database for structuring human knowledge. In *Proceedings of the 2008 ACM SIGMOD International Conference on Management of Data*, SIGMOD '08, page 1247–1250, New York, NY, USA. Association for Computing Machinery.

Ido Dagan, Oren Glickman, and Bernardo Magnini. 2006. The pascal recognising textual entailment challenge. In *Machine learning challenges. evaluating predictive uncertainty, visual object classification, and recognising textual entailment*, pages 177–190. Springer.

Barbara Dancygier. 1998. *Conditionals and Prediction: Time, Knowledge and Causation in Conditional Constructions*, volume 87 of *Cambridge Studies in Linguistics*. Cambridge University Press.

Marie-Catherine De Marneffe, Bill MacCartney, Trond Grenager, Daniel Cer, Anna Rafferty, and Christopher D Manning. 2006. Learning to distinguish valid textual entailments. In *Second Pascal RTE Challenge Workshop*, volume 62.

Kathrin Eichler, Aleksandra Gabryszak, and Günter Neumann. 2014. An analysis of textual inference in german customer emails. In *Proceedings of the Third Joint Conference on Lexical and Computational Semantics (* SEM 2014)*, pages 69–74.

Kathrin Eichler, Feiyu Xu, Hans Uszkoreit, and Sebastian Krause. 2017. Generating pattern-based entailment graphs for relation extraction. In *Proceedings of the 6th Joint Conference on Lexical and Computational Semantics (*SEM 2017)*, pages 220–229, Vancouver, Canada. Association for Computational Linguistics.

Richárd Farkas, Veronika Vincze, György Móra, János Csirik, and György Szarvas. 2010. The conll-2010 shared task: learning to detect hedges and their scope in natural language text. In *Proceedings of the fourteenth conference on computational natural language learning–Shared task*, pages 1–12.

Liane Guillou, Sander Bijl de Vroe, Mohammad Javad Hosseini, Mark Johnson, and Mark Steedman. 2020. Incorporating temporal information in entailment graph mining. In *Proceedings of the Graph-based Methods for Natural Language Processing (TextGraphs)*, pages 60–71.

Xavier Holt. 2018. Probabilistic models of relational implication. Master's thesis, Macquarie University.

Mohammad Javad Hosseini, Nathanael Chambers, Siva Reddy, Xavier R. Holt, Shay B. Cohen, Mark Johnson, and Mark Steedman. 2018. Learning typed entailment graphs with global soft constraints. *Transactions of the Association for Computational Linguistics*, 6:703–717.

Mohammad Javad Hosseini, Shay B. Cohen, Mark Johnson, and Mark Steedman. 2019. Duality of link prediction and entailment graph induction. In *Proceedings of the 57th Annual Meeting of the Association for Computational Linguistics*, pages 4736–4746, Florence, Italy. Association for Computational Linguistics.

Pierre-Antoine Jean, Sébastien Harispe, Sylvie Ranwez, Patrice Bellot, and Jacky Montmain. 2016. Uncertainty detection in natural language: A probabilistic model. In *Proceedings of the 6th International Conference on Web Intelligence, Mining and Semantics*, pages 1–10.

Lauri Karttunen and Annie Zaenen. 2005. Veridicity. In *Dagstuhl Seminar Proceedings*. Schloss Dagstuhl-Leibniz-Zentrum für Informatik.

Halil Kilicoglu and Sabine Bergler. 2008. Recognizing speculative language in biomedical research articles: a linguistically motivated perspective. *BMC bioinformatics*, 9(11):1–10.

Angelika Kratzer. 2012. *Modals and conditionals: New and revised perspectives*, volume 36. Oxford University Press.

Omer Levy and Ido Dagan. 2016. Annotating relation inference in context via question answering. In *Proceedings of the 54th Annual Meeting of the Association for Computational Linguistics (Volume 2: Short Papers)*, pages 249–255, Berlin, Germany. Association for Computational Linguistics.

David Lewis. 1973. Counterfactuals and comparative possibility. *Journal of Philosophical Logic*, pages 418–446.

Dekang Lin and Patrick Pantel. 2001. DIRT: Discovery of Inference Rules from Text. In *Proceedings of the Seventh ACM SIGKDD International Conference on Knowledge Discovery and Data Mining (KDD'01)*, pages 323–328, New York, NY, USA. ACM Press.

Xiao Ling and Daniel S. Weld. 2012. Fine-grained entity recognition. In *Proceedings of the Twenty-Sixth AAAI Conference on Artificial Intelligence*, AAAI'12, page 94–100. AAAI Press.

Nick McKenna, Liane Guillou, Mohammad Javad Hosseini, Sander Bijl de Vroe, and Mark Steedman. 2021. Multivalent entailment graphs for question answering. *arXiv preprint arXiv:2104.07846*.

Ben Medlock and Ted Briscoe. 2007. Weakly supervised learning for hedge classification in scientific literature. In *Proceedings of the 45th annual meeting of the association of computational linguistics*, pages 992–999.

Roser Morante and Walter Daelemans. 2009. Learning the scope of hedge cues in biomedical texts. In *Proceedings of the BioNLP 2009 workshop*, pages 28–36.

Roser Morante and Walter Daelemans. 2012a. Annotating modality and negation for a machine reading evaluation. In *CLEF 2012 Evaluation Labs and Workshop, Online Working Notes, Rome, Italy, September 17-20, 2012*, volume 1178 of *CEUR Workshop Proceedings*. CEUR-WS.org.

Roser Morante and Walter Daelemans. 2012b. Annotating modality and negation for a machine reading evaluation. In *CLEF (Online Working Notes/Labs/Workshop)*, pages 17–20.

Michael Nelson. 2019. Propositional Attitude Reports. In Edward N. Zalta, editor, *The Stanford Encyclopedia of Philosophy*, Spring 2019 edition. Metaphysics Research Lab, Stanford University.

Dat Ba Nguyen, Johannes Hoffart, Martin Theobald, and Gerhard Weikum. 2014. Aida-light: High-throughput named-entity disambiguation. *Workshop on Linked Data on the Web*, 1184:1–10.

Marek Rei and Ted Briscoe. 2010. Combining manual rules and supervised learning for hedge cue and scope detection. In *Proceedings of the Fourteenth Conference on Computational Natural Language Learning–Shared Task*, pages 56–63.

Roser Saurı, Marc Verhagen, and James Pustejovsky. 2006. Annotating and recognizing event modality in text. In *Proceedings of 19th International FLAIRS Conference*.

Rion Snow, Lucy Vanderwende, and Arul Menezes. 2006. Effectively using syntax for recognizing false entailment. In *Proceedings of the Main Conference on Human Language Technology Conference of the North American Chapter of the Association of Computational Linguistics*, HLT-NAACL '06, page 33–40. Association for Computational Linguistics.

Ieva R. Staliūnaitė. 2018. Learning about non-veridicality in textual entailment. Master's thesis, Utrecht University.

Miloš Stanojević and Mark Steedman. 2019. CCG parsing algorithm with incremental tree rotation. In *Proceedings of the 2019 Conference of the North American Chapter of the Association for Computational Linguistics: Human Language Technologies, Volume 1 (Long and Short Papers)*, pages 228–239, Minneapolis, Minnesota. Association for Computational Linguistics.

György Szarvas. 2008. Hedge classification in biomedical texts with a weakly supervised selection of keywords. In *Proceedings of ACL-08: HLT*, pages 281–289.

Idan Szpektor and Ido Dagan. 2008. Learning entailment rules for unary templates. In *Proceedings of the 22nd International Conference on Computational Linguistics (Coling 2008)*, pages 849–856, Manchester, UK. Coling 2008 Organizing Committee.

Veronika Vincze. 2014. *Uncertainty detection in natural language texts*. Ph.D. thesis, University of Szeged.

Julie Weeds and David Weir. 2003. A general framework for distributional similarity. In *Proceedings of the 2003 Conference on Empirical Methods in Natural Language Processing*, pages 81–88.

Congle Zhang and Daniel S Weld. 2013. Harvesting parallel news streams to generate paraphrases of event relations. In *Proceedings of the 2013 Conference on Empirical Methods in Natural Language Processing*, pages 1776–1786.

A Experimental Settings / Requirements

When using MoNTEE to extract relations we used the default settings, with the exception of disabling unary relation extraction (writeUnaryRels=False) and restricting binary relations to those that include at least one named entity (acceptGGBinary=False). When using entGraph to construct Entailment Graphs we raised the threshold values for infrequent predicates (minPredForArgPair=4) and argument pairs (minArgPairForPred=4), and used the default values for all other parameters.

All experiments were conducted on a single server with 330GB RAM, and two Intel Xeon E5-2697 v4 2.3GHz CPUs (each with 18 cores). The computational cost of training a single Entailment Graph is approximately one day for the local learning step, and eight hours for globalisation.

Investigating the Effect of Natural Language Explanations on Out-of-Distribution Generalization in Few-shot NLI

Yangqiaoyu Zhou
University of Chicago
zhouy1@uchicago.edu

Chenhao Tan
University of Chicago
chenhao@uchicago.edu

Abstract

Although neural models have shown strong performance in datasets such as SNLI, they lack the ability to generalize out-of-distribution (OOD). In this work, we formulate a few-shot learning setup and examine the effects of natural language explanations on OOD generalization. We leverage the templates in the *HANS* dataset and construct templated natural language explanations for each template. Although generated explanations show competitive BLEU scores against groundtruth explanations, they fail to improve prediction performance. We further show that generated explanations often hallucinate information and miss key elements that indicate the label.

1 Introduction

Thanks to recent advances in pre-trained language models (Vaswani et al., 2017; Devlin et al., 2018), the state-of-the-art accuracy for natural language inference (NLI) can easily exceed 90% (Pilault et al., 2020). However, these NLI models show poor out-of-distribution (OOD) generalization. For instance, McCoy et al. (2019) create a templated dataset (*HANS*) and find model performance to be about chance in this dataset.

While recent studies try to tackle this robustness problem from the perspectives of both the dataset and the model (Le Bras et al., 2020; Swayamdipta et al., 2020; Clark et al., 2019), we investigate an extra dimension of information, natural language explanations. Our work is motivated by the growing interest in explanations in the NLP community (Camburu et al., 2018; Rajani et al., 2019; Alhindi et al., 2018; Stammbach and Ash, 2020): these explanations can potentially enable models to understand the reasoning strategy beyond spurious patterns. We focus on a few-shot learning setup because it is unrealistic to expect a large number of annotated OOD examples.

To introduce an OOD setting with natural language explanations, we construct E-HANS, a dataset with natural language explanations for each template in *HANS*. By leveraging the templates in *HANS*, we avoid the challenges in crowdsourcing natural language explanations (Wiegreffe and Marasović, 2021) and manually build an explanation dataset of high-quality.

We use an EXPLAINTHENPREDICT framework to learn with explanations. An explanation generation model outputs an explanation for each input example, and the generated explanation is fed into a classifier along with the input example. While BLEU scores imply high quality of generated explanations, learning with explanations does not improve predictive performance either in-distribution or out-of-distribution. We show the generated explanations contain words in the true explanations, but they fail to reproduce important phrases and often hallucinate entities during generation.

2 Building Natural Language Explanations for *HANS*

To investigate whether natural language explanations improve the robustness of natural language inference (NLI), we build on two existing datasets: 1) *HANS*, which introduces templates to generate OOD examples for robust evaluation of NLI models; 2) E-SNLI, which provides explanations for the Stanford Natural Language Inference (SNLI) dataset. Our key contribution is to augment *HANS* by building templated natural language explanations and studying the effect of these explanations on model robustness in a few-shot learning setup. Our dataset is available at https://github.com/ChicagoHAI/hans-explanations.

2.1 Existing Datasets

We start by presenting details of existing datasets.

***HANS* (McCoy et al., 2019)** contains NLI examples designed to be challenging for models that

Proceedings of the Second Workshop on Insights from Negative Results in NLP, pages 117–124
November 10, 2021.

Premise: the psychologist by the programmers saw the essayist.
Hypothesis: the psychologist saw the essayist.
Explanation: the psychologist by the programmers is still the psychologist.

Table 1: An example from E-HANS. Average length of premise and hypothesis are 8.8 and 4.4 tokens. Average length of natural language explanation is 13.3 tokens.

tend to learn spurious patterns. It targets known heuristics for the majority of existing NLI data. For example, one heuristic assumes that a premise entails all hypotheses that are constructed using only words in the premise. There are 3 heuristics in *HANS*, each containing 10 subcases. A subcase is supported by a few templates and the dataset is constructed following these templates.

E-SNLI (Camburu et al., 2018) develops free-form self-contained explanations for the true labels in SNLI using crowdsourcing. We pretrain a model on this dataset to examine the effect of pretraining. There are three explanations collected for each example in the validation dataset, and we use the first explanation. We do not use the test set of E-SNLI.

2.2 Templated Natural Language Explanations for *HANS*

We build natural language explanations for *HANS* to examine whether explanations can help models when facing this challenging corpus. As *HANS* is constructed with templates, we develop templates for natural language explanations accordingly. They explain the reasons for the true label in human language.

Table 1 shows an example of the proposed explanations (more examples are in Appendix B). In addition to developing these templated explanations, we expand the original HANS vocabulary in terms of its nouns, verbs, adjectives, and adverbs to increase difficulty. This allows us to examine the effect of unseen words.

3 Experiments

3.1 Few-Shot Learning Set-up

To investigate whether natural language explanations improve the robustness of NLI models, we look at a few-shot learning setting. We focus on this setting since in practice one may have little or no access to OOD instances. We are interested in the following questions:

1. whether the model trained from in-distribution examples can generalize to unseen templates and words,
2. how many samples are enough for learning,
3. whether pretraining on E-SNLI improves generalization on *HANS*,
4. and most importantly, what is the effect of explanations.

We use 5-fold cross validation by splitting 118 templates randomly into 5 folds. We generate k samples for each training template using E-HANS explanation templates. We then build a corresponding development set that contains $0.2k$ samples of each training template, so that the development set is 20% the size of the training set and does not include any unseen template. This setup ensures that the size of the development set is realistic (Kann et al., 2019).

Finally, we build test instances in the following categories to evaluate the performance of the models both in-distribution and out-of-distribution:

- *IND vocab, IND template*. Both the templates and the vocabulary are matched with the training set. We expect the performance to grow steadily as k increases.
- *OOD vocab, IND template*. We use the same templates as the training set, but use unseen words to generate this test set. The challenge lies in understanding unseen words.
- *IND vocab, OOD template*. We use the unseen templates and the same vocabulary as the training set. The challenge lies in understand the logic encoded in unseen templates.
- *OOD vocab, OOD template*. Finally, we generate the test data with both the unseen templates and the unseen words.

We use the same test sets (300 examples for each template) to examine how the models' performance changes as k increases.

3.2 Models

We adapt the EXPLAINTHENPREDICT architecture introduced by Camburu et al. (2018) in our experiments. It consists of **a generation model** and **a classification model**. The generation model produces an explanation given an input premise and hypothesis pair. This generated explanation and the original input are fed into the classifier for label prediction. Our framework slightly differs from Camburu et al. (2018) in that their classifier only takes explanation as input for the classifier.

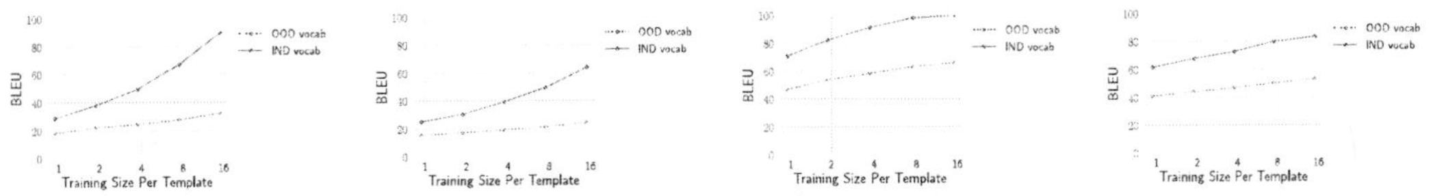

(a) IND templates with BERT (b) OOD templates with BERT (c) IND templates with ESNLI (d) OOD templates with ESNLI

Figure 1: $x-$axis shows the number of samples per template, while $y-$axis shows the BLEU score. BLEU scores are high for *IND vocab, IND template* instances. Although BLEU drops substantially for both BERT and the E-SNLI pretrained model under OOD vocab and OOD templates, it is still decent (above 40 with E-SNLI).

The explanation generation model follows an encoder-decoder framework. Both the encoder and the decoder use the BERT model, but the decoder uses a masking mechanism so that it predicts the next word considering only all the preceding words in both training and testing phases. Our generation model obtains close to SoTA performance on e-SNLI, comparing against WT5 (33.15 vs. 33.7 in BLEU) (Narang et al., 2020).

The classification model is a BERT sequence classifier, where a linear layer is applied to the pooled output of BERT encodings (i.e., embedding of the CLS token).

3.3 Experimental Setup

We used $k = 1, 2, 4, 8, 16$ to generate the training data. The explanation generator trains on groundtruth explanations. For all of our models, we saved the model with the best validation performance during training and did not tune other hyperparameters. We used a training batch size 16 and a learning rate 5e-5 for the explanation generator, and we used a training batch size 128 and learning rate 2e-5 for the classifier.

Model comparisons. To test if explanations help with learning, we compare with a baseline that only includes the classifier component with the input premise, hypothesis pair (hence "*label-only*"). We also consider a baseline that does not update with the k samples in the training set (hence "*no training*") and a majority baseline ("*majority*").

In addition, we compare the vanilla BERT model with a BERT model fine-tuned on E-SNLI during both generation and classification to investigate whether pretraining on E-SNLI helps with the *HANS* task.

4 Results

We first look at the quality of generated explanations using BLEU. Although the generated explanations match groundtruth explanations well based on BLEU, they affect downstream classification negatively in our few-shot learning set-up. We further examine the generated explanations to understand why the predictive performance drops when adding natural language explanations.

4.1 Quality of Explanations based on BLEU

Generated explanations achieve high BLEU scores based on our groundtruth templated explanations (Figure 1). IND vocab explanations can achieve BLEU scores greater than 90 on IND templates and 60 on OOD templates when $k = 16$. Even OOD vocab explanations can achieve BLEU scores close to 20. In general, the performance grows steadily as k increases for both IND and OOD.

While the BLEU scores can be quite high, OOD generalization remains a challenge. Unseen vocabulary and templates (Fig. 1b, Fig. 1d) increase the difficulty in explanation generation. That said, pretraining on E-SNLI improves generation quality for both IND and OOD cases. This improvement on OOD generalization is likely due to exposure to other data during pretraining.

We use BLEU to evaluate the quality of generated explanations with regard to groundtruth explanations because it is a commonly used metric to evaluate natural language explanations (Camburu et al., 2018; Rajani et al., 2019).

4.2 Predictive Performance

Despite the high BLEU scores, learning with the generated explanations does not help the classification task (Fig. 2). Learning with explanations consistently performs worse than the label-only baseline under both IND and OOD testing scenarios. Pretraining on E-SNLI does not change this observation either.

The only positive result we find is that pretraining helps with OOD generalization. Models pretrained on E-SNLI give better results than plain

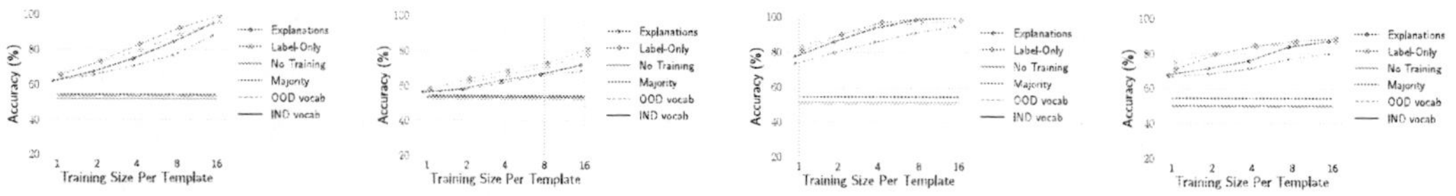

(a) IND templates with BERT (b) OOD templates with BERT (c) IND templates with ESNLI (d) OOD templates with ESNLI

Figure 2: x-axis shows the number of samples per template, while $y-$axis shows the accuracy in label prediction. Learning from explanations is always below the label-only baseline.

BERT (Fig. 2). This finding aligns with the positive effect of pretraining on explanation generation.

We also observe that testing on groundtruth explanations boosts performance drastically. This suggests that groundtruth explanations give clues for the label, but generated explanations do not capture this information.

4.3 Why Explanations Do Not Help?

To understand why explanations are not helpful, we introduce two new metrics to evaluate the effectiveness of explanation generation. We measure how often the generated explanations contain **hallucinated entities**, professions (i.e., people) and locations that do not show up in the input, and we measure how well the good label indicator word **"we do not know"** is generated. We present results on explanations generated by the BERT model and the E-SNLI-pretrained model.

An explanation contains a hallucinated entity if there is an entity that never show up in the original input. These hallucinated entities will likely hinder predictive performance when models make predictions based on generated explanations. We only count hallucinated professions and locations to avoid false positives due to synonyms used in explanations. That is, we use a conservative estimate on hallucinated keywords in generated explanations by only counting people and locations. We find that hallucinated entities are almost always generated in OOD vocab cases by the BERT model (99% of explanations consist of entities that do not exist in the premise and the hypothesis) and the hallucination rate is also high (around 60%) for the E-SNLI-pretrained model. However, the hallucination rate is much lower for IND vocab cases (Fig. 3, Fig. 4): it is close to 0 when $k = 16$ and for E-SNLI-pretrained model. But when $k = 4$, we observe a high hallucination rate ($> 50\%$) for IND vocab cases (Fig. 4a). We also notice that pretraining on E-SNLI leads to models with much lower hallucination rates for all test cases.

IND vocab, IND template ($k = 4$)
Premise: the managers who the baker addressed brought the technician.
Hypothesis: the baker addressed the managers.
Original explanations: who in who the baker addressed refers to the managers.
BERT explanations: the artisans that addressed the baker are still the managers.

IND vocab, IND template ($k = 16$)
Premise: the analysts in front of the programmers affected the scientist.
Hypothesis: the analysts affected the scientist.
Original explanations: the analysts in front of the programmers are still the analysts.
BERT explanations: the analysts in front of the programmers are still the analysts.

OOD vocab, IND template ($k = 16$)
Premise: the chaplains near the singer needed the author.
Hypothesis: the chaplains needed the author.
Original explanations: the chaplains near the singer are still the chaplains.
BERT explanations: the psychologists are in front of the musician and the strategists helped the writer, we do not know whether the illustrators helped the writer.

Table 2: Example generated explanations for IND templates cases by the BERT model trained with $k = 4, 16$. More examples are in Appendix C.

"We do not know" is a predictive phrase because it is only present in non-entailment examples. We find that when generated explanations contain "we do not know", so do the corresponding groundtruth explanations (in other words, precision is 100%). However, when "we do not know" is in the groundtruth explanations, it is not necessarily always generated, so the recall is not perfect (Fig. 3c). In fact, recall decreases as we switch to harder test cases. OOD templates also has greater negative impact than OOD vocab on recall.

Finally, we look closely at some of the generated explanations (Table 2). We observe that models struggle to learn the templates even for the IND templates case. In the easiest case (*IND vocab, IND template*), although the explanation uses the right template when $k = 16$, it uses a wrong template when $k = 4$. Once we switch from *IND vocab,*

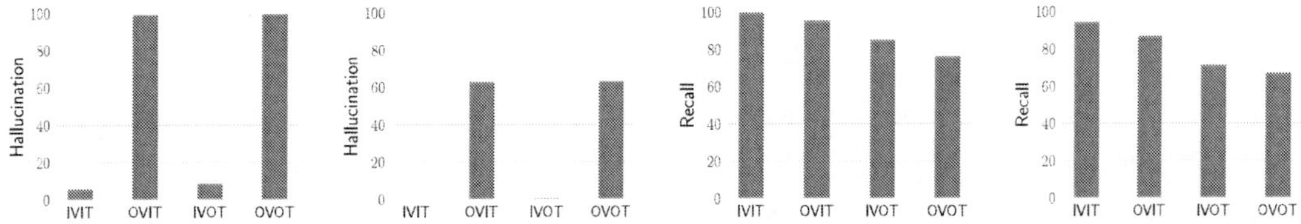

(a) % of explanations with hallucinated entities. (BERT)

(b) % of explanations with hallucinated entities. (E-SNLI)

(c) Recall of generating "we do not know". (BERT)

(d) Recall of generating "we do not know". (E-SNLI)

Figure 3: Fig. 3a and Fig. 3b show that the BERT model and the E-SNLI-pretrained model (trained with $k = 16$) hallucinate for OOD vocab. Fig. 3c and Fig. 3d suggest that the explanations fail to include "we do not know" for instances with the non-entailment label for OOD vocab and OOD templates (with $k = 16$).

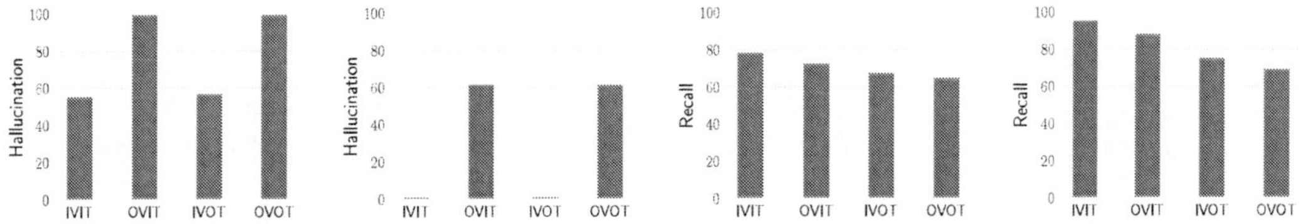

(a) % of explanations with hallucinated entities. (BERT)

(b) % of explanations with hallucinated entities. (E-SNLI)

(c) Recall of generating "we do not know". (BERT)

(d) Recall of generating "we do not know". (E-SNLI)

Figure 4: Fig. 4a and Fig. 4b show that both the BERT model and E-SNLI-pretrained model (trained with $k = 4$) hallucinate for OOD vocab, and the hallucination rate is slightly worse for OOD templates. Similarly, Fig. 4c and Fig. 4d suggest that the explanations fail to include "we do not know" for instances with the non-entailment label for OOD vocab and OOD templates (with $k = 4$).

IND template to *OOD vocab, IND template*, even the $k = 16$ models fail to learn which template should be used to generate explanations.

5 Conclusion

We construct a HANS-based dataset with explanations. On this dataset, we find natural language explanations do not help few-shot NLI to generate out-of-domain under an EXPLAINTHENPREDICT framework. While the genearted explanations obtain high BLEU scores, they do not learn information crucial for downstream classification. Our generation model is close to the SoTA model, yet it still generates nonsensical explanations. Better metrics for explanation evaluation and explanation generation models are key to success for learning with natural language explanations to be effective.

Acknowledgments

We thank anonymous reviewers for their valuable feedbacks. We thank members of the Chicago Human+AI Lab for their insightful suggestions. We thank Tom Mccoy, one author for the HANS paper, for a detailed explanation on their data when we reached out. We thank techstaff members at the University of Chicago CS department for their technical support. This work is supported in part by research awards from Amazon, IBM, Salesforce, and NSF IIS-2126602.

References

Tariq Alhindi, Savvas Petridis, and Smaranda Muresan. 2018. Where is your evidence: Improving fact-checking by justification modeling. In *Proceedings of the First Workshop on Fact Extraction and VERification (FEVER)*, pages 85–90.

Oana-Maria Camburu, Tim Rocktäschel, Thomas Lukasiewicz, and Phil Blunsom. 2018. e-snli: Natural language inference with natural language explanations. In *Advances in Neural Information Processing Systems*, pages 9539–9549.

Christopher Clark, Mark Yatskar, and Luke Zettlemoyer. 2019. Don't take the easy way out: Ensemble based methods for avoiding known dataset biases. *arXiv preprint arXiv:1909.03683*.

Jacob Devlin, Ming-Wei Chang, Kenton Lee, and Kristina Toutanova. 2018. Bert: Pre-training of deep bidirectional transformers for language understanding. *arXiv preprint arXiv:1810.04805*.

Katharina Kann, Kyunghyun Cho, and Samuel R Bowman. 2019. Towards realistic practices in low-resource natural language processing: the development set. In *EMNLP*.

Ronan Le Bras, Swabha Swayamdipta, Chandra Bhagavatula, Rowan Zellers, Matthew Peters, Ashish Sabharwal, and Yejin Choi. 2020. Adversarial filters of dataset biases. In *International Conference on Machine Learning*, pages 1078–1088. PMLR.

R Thomas McCoy, Ellie Pavlick, and Tal Linzen. 2019. Right for the wrong reasons: Diagnosing syntactic heuristics in natural language inference. *arXiv preprint arXiv:1902.01007*.

Sharan Narang, Colin Raffel, Katherine Lee, Adam Roberts, Noah Fiedel, and Karishma Malkan. 2020. Wt5?! training text-to-text models to explain their predictions. *arXiv preprint arXiv:2004.14546*.

Jonathan Pilault, Amine Elhattami, and Christopher Pal. 2020. Conditionally adaptive multi-task learning: Improving transfer learning in nlp using fewer parameters & less data. *arXiv preprint arXiv:2009.09139*.

Nazneen Fatema Rajani, Bryan McCann, Caiming Xiong, and Richard Socher. 2019. Explain yourself! leveraging language models for commonsense reasoning. *arXiv preprint arXiv:1906.02361*.

Dominik Stammbach and Elliott Ash. 2020. e-fever: Explanations and summaries for automated fact checking. In *Proceedings of the 2020 Truth and Trust Online Conference (TTO 2020)*, page 32. Hacks Hackers.

Swabha Swayamdipta, Roy Schwartz, Nicholas Lourie, Yizhong Wang, Hannaneh Hajishirzi, Noah A Smith, and Yejin Choi. 2020. Dataset cartography: Mapping and diagnosing datasets with training dynamics. *arXiv preprint arXiv:2009.10795*.

Ashish Vaswani, Noam Shazeer, Niki Parmar, Jakob Uszkoreit, Llion Jones, Aidan N Gomez, Łukasz Kaiser, and Illia Polosukhin. 2017. Attention is all you need. In *Advances in neural information processing systems*, pages 5998–6008.

Sarah Wiegreffe and Ana Marasović. 2021. Teach me to explain: A review of datasets for explainable nlp. ArXiv:2102.12060.

A Replicability Details

We pretrain the BERT model on E-SNLI for 5 epochs and evaluate at every epoch. The model with best dev performance is saved as the final E-SNLI model that we use as the initial model in few-shot learning.

On the E-HANS dataset, we run 2000 steps to train the generation model and evaluate every 200 steps. We choose this number because the best dev performance is usually achieved within 2000 steps. As for the explain-then-predict classifier, we run 200 training steps and evaluate every 4 steps because the model quickly reaches best dev performance as training starts. On the other hand, label-only classifier takes more steps in learning. We train for 1000 steps and evaluate every 50 steps.

It takes around 30 minutes to train a generation model and 10 minutes to train a classification model on our machine (with 4 gpus).

B Samples from E-HANS

Premise: the scientists that talked thanked the psychotherapists. **Hypothesis**: the scientists thanked the psychotherapists. **Explanation**: the scientists that talked are still the scientists.
Premise: if the psychologists ran, the programmers existed. **Hypothesis**: the psychologists ran. **Explanation**: the programmers existed if the psychologists ran, we do not know whether the psychologists ran.
Premise: though the president voted, the musician existed. **Hypothesis**: the president voted. **Explanation**: though suggests the president voted happened.
Premise: the scientist was addressed by the psychotherapist. **Hypothesis**: the psychotherapist addressed the scientist. **Explanation**: addressed is the active form of was addressed by, so we swap the scientist and the psychotherapist.
Premise: if the directors addressed the illustrators, the president listened. **Hypothesis**: the directors addressed the illustrators. **Explanation**: the president listened if the directors addressed the illustrators, we do not know whether the directors addressed the illustrators.

Table 3: Examples from E-HANS.

C Example Generated Explanations

Examples of generated explanations on different test types.

IND vocab, IND template **Premise**: the musician by the psychiatrists offended the strategists. **Hypothesis**: the musician offended the strategists. **Original explanations**: the musician by the psychiatrists is still the musician. **BERT explanations**: the strategists offended the musician and the strategists are by the musician, we do not know whether the strategists offended the musician.
OOD vocab, IND template **Premise**: the administrators near the penciller supported the lyricist. **Hypothesis**: the administrators supported the lyricist. **Original explanations**: the administrators near the penciller are still the administrators. **BERT explanations**: the musician is the subject of the relative clause that addressed the illustrators and the programmers encouraged the programmer, we do not know whether the planners encouraged the illustrators.
IND vocab, OOD template **Premise**: the scientists who affected the colorists helped the psychotherapists. **Hypothesis**: the scientists helped the psychotherapists. **Original explanations**: the scientists who affected the colorists are still the scientists. **BERT explanations**: the scientists are the subject of the relative clause who addressed the psychotherapists and the scientists helped the colorists, we do not know whether the scientists helped the psychotherapists.
OOD vocab, OOD template **Premise**: the professor who deceived the athletes called the doctors. **Hypothesis**: the professor called the doctors. **Original explanations**: the professor who deceived the athletes is still the professor. **BERT explanations**: the psychiatrists who the president offended is still the psychiatrist.

Table 4: Example explanations for all test case generated by the BERT model trained with $k = 4$.

IND vocab, IND template **Premise**: the directors in front of the analysts avoided the designer. **Hypothesis**: the directors avoided the designer. **Original explanations**: the directors in front of the analysts are still the directors. **BERT explanations**: the directors in front of the analysts are still the directors.
OOD vocab, IND template **Premise**: the chaplains near the singer needed the author. **Hypothesis**: the chaplains needed the author. **Original explanations**: the chaplains near the singer are still the chaplains. **BERT explanations**: the psychologists are in front of the musician and the strategists helped the writer, we do not know whether the illustrators helped the writer.
IND vocab, OOD template **Premise**: the technician that thanked the planners encouraged the worker. **Hypothesis**: the technician encouraged the worker. **Original explanations**: the technician that thanked the planners is still the technician. **BERT explanations**: the technician that encouraged the worker is still the technician, so the technician encouraged the worker and we do not know whether the technician encouraged the worker.
OOD vocab, OOD template **Premise**: the senators that recognized the nurses recommended the chaplains. **Hypothesis**: the senators recommended the chaplains. **Original explanations**: the senators that recognized the nurses are still the senators. **BERT explanations**: the presidents are the subject of the relative clause that offended the psychiatrists and the presidents advised the stylists, we do not know whether the officers advised the bakers.

Table 5: Example explanations for all test case generated by the BERT model trained with $k = 16$.

Generalization in NLI: Ways (Not) To Go Beyond Simple Heuristics

Prajjwal Bhargava[1], Aleksandr Drozd[2,3], Anna Rogers[3,4]
[1] The University of Texas at Dallas
[2] RIKEN Center for Computational Science
[3] Tokyo Institute of Technology
[4] Center for Social Data Science, University of Copenhagen
[1]`prajjwalin@protonmail.com`, [2]`alex@blackbird.pw`, [3]arogers@sodas.ku.dk

Abstract

Much of recent progress in NLU was shown to be due to models' learning dataset-specific heuristics. We conduct a case study of generalization in NLI (from MNLI to the adversarially constructed HANS dataset) in a range of BERT-based architectures (adapters, Siamese Transformers, HEX debiasing), as well as with subsampling the data and increasing the model size. We report 2 successful and 3 unsuccessful strategies, all providing insights into how Transformer-based models learn to generalize.

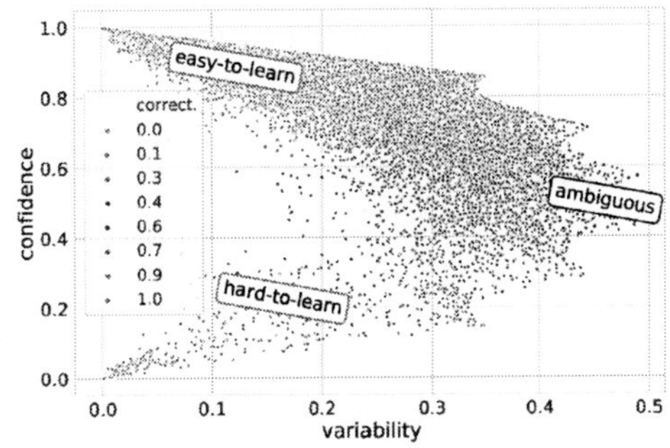

Figure 1: MNLI data map (with RoBERTa-large)

1 Introduction

Many popular NLP datasets contain spurious patterns, which get learned instead of the actual task (Gururangan et al., 2018; Belinkov et al., 2019; Rogers et al., 2020a; Gardner et al., 2021). This raises the issue of learning methods that would avoid that problem. We present a case study of generalization to adversarial data in Natural Language Inference (NLI), reporting both positive and negative results for a range of BERT-based approaches.

2 Methodology

Data. NLI is a 3-class classification task: does the premise entails, contradicts, or is neutral with respect to the hypothesis? MNLI (Williams et al., 2018) is one of the most popular resources for this task, but it has been shown to suffer from both annotation artifacts (Gururangan et al., 2018; Poliak et al., 2018) and annotator bias (Geva et al., 2019). A cartography (Swayamdipta et al., 2020) map of MNLI (fig. 1) suggests that most of its examples are easy to learn, which explains why vanilla fine-tuning with modern models is sufficient to achieve high accuracy on MNLI benchmark.

We measure generalization of models fine-tuned on MNLI with HANS (McCoy et al., 2019b), a synthetic dataset targeting *lexical overlap, subsequence* and *constituent* heuristics. According to McCoy et al. (2019b), a model trained on MNLI is likely to learn these heuristics and thus predict the "entailment" label for most HANS examples. E.g. it would incorrectly predict that "*The doctor was paid by the actor*" entails "*The doctor paid the actor*", simply because these sentences contain the same words. See Appendix A for more examples.

Methodology. We experiment with variants[1] of BERT (Devlin et al., 2019), RoBERTa (Liu et al., 2019), and ALBERT (Lan et al., 2020). Our implementation[2] is based on Transformers (Wolf et al., 2019) and Pytorch (Paszke et al., 2019), and for two experiments we also report results with a custom Pytorch-Lightning trainer[3]. HANS has 30K examples used only for testing, where we report the accuracy[4]. MNLI test set is not public, and we report accuracy on the "matched" dev set (20K examples, 393K for training).

[1]Most models we used were provided by HuggingFace Transformers library. In scope of this project we ported the smaller BERT versions by Turc et al. (2019) for that library.

[2]`https://github.com/prajjwal1/generalize_lm_nli`

[3]`https://github.com/vecto-ai/langmo`

[4]Since HANS contains only two labels (entailment, non-entailment), and a model trained on MNLI would have three (entailment, contradiction, neutral), a completely random model would be biased towards the "non-entailment". For direct comparison with MNLI we report the average accuracy for the two HANS labels, unless specified otherwise.

Proceedings of the Second Workshop on Insights from Negative Results in NLP, pages 125–135
November 10, 2021.

3 Experiments

There are two main directions for solving the generalization challenge: modifying the training distribution and the model itself. For the former we experimented with subsampling (§3.1), and for the latter – with bottlenecking with Siamese Transformers (§3.2) and adapters (§3.3), explicit debiasing (§3.4), and increasing model size (§3.5). This section presents the motivation and setup for all experiments, and all the results are shown in §4.

§3.1 Subsampling the training data with cartography. Data cartography (Swayamdipta et al., 2020) characterizes training data points via the model's confidence in the true class, and the variability of this confidence across epochs. Figure 1 shows that MNLI examples form a spectrum: some are consistently "easy" (high-confidence) and "hard" (low-confidence) across epochs. "Ambiguous" samples have midrange confidence and high variability. If much of MNLI is "easy", presumably these samples are less informative.

Experiments. We partition MNLI based on the training dynamics of RoBERTa-large and BERT-base, and train the respective models on varying amounts of "hard" and "ambiguous" examples (preceded by 25% of "easy" samples for 2 epochs). See appendix B for more details.

§3.2 Siamese Networks. In this architecture predictions are based on a pair of inputs (Chopra et al., 2005; Koch et al., 2015). It was successful on NLI (Chen et al., 2017) and in conjunction with BERT encoders (Reimers and Gurevych, 2019). One of their properties is forcing the model to consider the relation between two sequences in a more holistic way than with cross-attention between concatenated premise+hypothesis (as in standard BERT fine-tuning). Intuitively, encoding premise and hypothesis separately could bottleneck[5] their interaction and encourage learning more abstract patterns, which is what we need here: ideally, an NLI model would learn logical rules rather than numerous lexical or syntactic patterns.

Experiments. Our Siamese Transformer consists of a MLP and two BERT encoders which receive hypotheses and premises in a segregated manner. We used mean-pooled outputs of last transformer layer (CLS embedding yielded similar results) combined as $[U, V, U - V, U * V]$ as inputs to MLP classifier. We experiment with base and large BERTs, with both frozen and trainable encoders.

§3.3 Adapter Networks. Intuitively, standard fine-tuning of BERT changes the amount of task-independent linguistic knowledge that the model can store, and may corrupt it (if the supervised task has significant artifacts). Therefore, by adding separate task-specific components rather than changing the language model weights, we could expect to increase the amount of non-task-specific knowledge in the model. This could be done with adapters (Houlsby et al., 2019; Pfeiffer et al., 2020): trainable MLPs inserted within each sub-layer of encoder. Concretely, in a transformer layer l, additional adapter parameters ϕ_l are introduced to learn task specific parameters while keeping pre-trained parameters intact. Having smaller trainable components should also bottleneck the model and encourage it to learn higher-level patterns.

Experiments. We add adapters in each sub-layer as proposed in Houlsby et al. (2019) to BERT and RoBERTa with the configuration defined in Pfeiffer et al. (2020). The adapter consists of two linear layers (up and down) with a bottleneck of reduction factor of 16 and the ReLU non-linearity.

§3.4 Explicit De-biasing. If MNLI 'teaches' to rely on superficial features, we could try to avoid them. Following Zhou and Bansal (2020), we use HEX projection (Wang et al., 2019). The system includes the main Transformer encoder and a 'naive' model learning superficial features. HEX orthogonally projects the Transformer representation into the affine space the most different from the 'naive' representation, hopefully removing the bias.

Experiments. We extract pooled representations from our main model (BERT-base). The 'naive' model is a CBOW model with a self-attention layer (Vaswani et al., 2017) to capture co-occurrence information from the sequence with input and token embeddings. See Wang et al. (2019) for more details on the method, and Appendix C for implementation and hyperparameter details. During inference, we use logits from BERT only.

§3.5 Increasing Model Size. Scaling language models to massive amounts of data has been a reliable source of success on NLP leaderboards, and yielded some interesting emergent properties (Brown et al., 2020; Raffel et al., 2020). If pre-

[5]The information bottleneck idea (Tishby et al., 2000; Alemi et al., 2016) has recently been successfully adapted for BERT fine-tuning to avoid overfitting in a low-resource setting by Mahabadi et al. (2020), who propose a regularization term suppressing the learning of irrelevant information.

Architecture	Encoder	HF trainer MNLI/std	HF trainer HANS/std	HF trainer runs	Custom Trainer MNLI/std	Custom Trainer HANS/std	Custom Trainer runs
Siamese networks / frozen encoder	BERT-base	51.43	50.74	1	57.2 / 0.2	51.3 / 0.1	3
	BERT-large	51.72	51.12	1	61.4 / 0.1	51.6 / 0.1	5
Siamese networks / trainable encoder	BERT-base	58.9	52.79	1	76.5 / 0.03	51.3 / 0.03	3
	BERT-large	59.9	51.21	1	78.7	52.5	1
Adapter networks	BERT-base	82.6	50.97	1			
	BERT-large	84.75	57.17	1			
	RoBERTa-base	86.33	57.21	1			
	RoBERTa-large	90.4	75.93	1			
HEX debiasing	BERT-base	56.25	50.58	1			
Vanilla finetuning: increased model size	BERT-tiny (4.4M)	64.48/0.24	50/0	3	67.4 / 0.2	50 / 0.02	5
	BERT-mini (11.3M)	72.3/0.29	50.97/0.04	3	76.3 / 1	52.3 / 0.3	10
	BERT-small (29.1M)	76.48/0.12	50.39/0.14	3	78.4 / 0.5	51.1 / 0.3	5
	BERT-medium (41.7M)	79.64/0.14	51.02/0.26	3	80 / 0.3	52 / 0.4	5
	BERT-base (110M)	83.74/0.04	53.98/0.78	3	84 / 0.2	69 / 4	16
	BERT-large (340M)	85.9/0.02	72.04/1.97	3	86.5 / 0.1	77.8 / 2.4	3
	RoBERTa-base (125M)	87.46/0.1	73.11/1.13	3	87.5 / 0.3	77.7 / 1.7	10
	RoBERTa-large (355M)	90.3/0.07	79.95/0.56	3	90 / 0.4	82.05 / 1	3
	ALBERT-base-v2 (11M)	83.06/0.13	66.6/0.78	3	84.2 / 0.6	69.2 / 2.2	4
	ALBERT-large-v2 (17M)	85.08/0.3	70.64/2.91	3	85.5 / 0.9	70.5 / 1.6	4

Table 1: Generalization from MNLI to HANS in selected approaches.

training "teaches" transferable linguistic knowledge, the models absorbing more data could be expected to generalize better.

Experiments. We perform standard fine-tuning on MNLI with variants of BERT: tiny, mini, small, medium by Turc et al. (2019), base and large by Devlin et al. (2019), as well as RoBERTa (Liu et al., 2019) and ALBERT (Lan et al., 2020). In this and the Siamese network experiment we report not only the results obtained with the HuggingFace Trainer, but also with our custom implementation based on Pytorch Lightning (also with the AdamW optimizer and with similar learning rates).

4 Results and Discussion

4.1 Negative Results

Table 1 shows that **Siamese networks and HEX debiasing perform at chance level on HANS. Adapters work better, but do not match vanilla fine-tuning of their base models**. While it is impossible to prove the negative, our experience suggests that, given a reasonable amount of effort, these approaches are not the most promising for the generalization problem we considered. The paper is accompanied by code for our implementations.

Our Siamese model would be expected to fail if high performance of vanilla BERT was largely due to cross-attention across [premise + hypothesis], enabling it to learn many specific patterns (such as negation in the hypothesis). Our bottleneck MLP would not have the capacity to do that, and it clearly also fails to find a more abstract pattern in the representations it receives. Further experiments are needed to verify this hypothesis. Whether or not overall we would like our NLI models to be able to operate with independent representations of premise and hypothesis rather than cross-attention within one representation, is an open question.

For HEX, Zhou and Bansal (2020) suggest that the problem might be that it has access only to the final output of BERT, which could contain more information about the predicted NLI labels than the input sequence as such. Then there would be little to debias. Our results support this hypothesis, but more qualitative research is needed to verify it.

The RoBERTa-large MNLI results of our adapter implementation is on par with the recent state-of-the-art Compacter adapters on T5 (Mahabadi et al., 2021), but generalization in both BERT and RoBERTa is overall worse than with vanilla fine-tuning. Following on the recent report of adapter efficacy in low-resource setting (He et al., 2021), we conducted an additional experiment with adapters and RoBERTa-large, where the model had to learn from a small, more informative subsample. At 1024 training examples adapters performed better when the MNLI subsample was diverse (selected with K-means-based clustering, see appendix D) rather than randomly selected: 80.7% vs 85%. But the generalization to HANS was still not very impressive: 67.8% vs 57.5%, respectively. This strategy does seem to select more informative examples for MNLI distribution, but not for HANS.

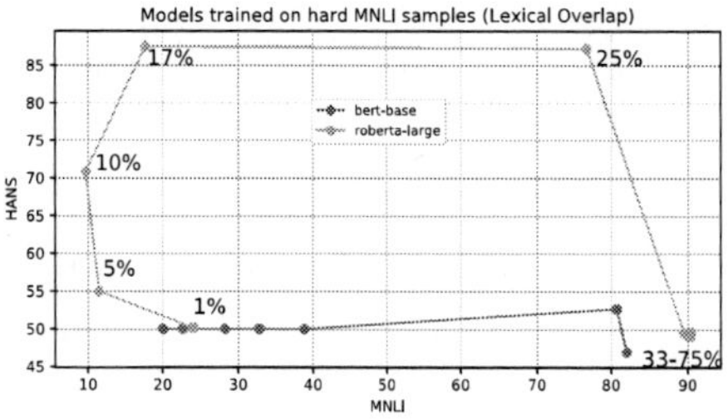

Figure 2: Generalization to HANS at varying stages of training on "hard" MNLI samples. Graph labels indicate % of MNLI training data used.

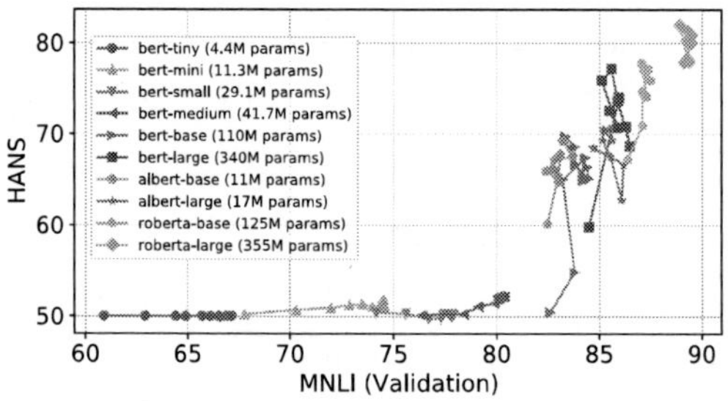

Figure 3: Generalization from MNLI to HANS: model size effect (custom Pytorch Lightning implementation). The dots on the line for each model indicate performance after training epochs 1-4.

4.2 (Cautiously) Positive Results

Figure 2 shows that when trained on the "hard" samples, **for RoBERTa-large there does exist a MNLI subsample (at about 25% training data) yielding good performance on both HANS and MNLI**. Further 13% addition of biased MNLI data makes the model lose its performance on HANS. But we could not find such a sample for BERT-base, although the cartography samples were model-specific. This also does not happen for either model when training on the "ambiguous" subsamples: RoBERTa initially "learns" HANS at 5% of training data, but "loses" it before reaching even 60% accuracy on MNLI (see fig. 4 in the Appendix).

The most encouraging results come from the increased model size with our custom trainer, as shown in fig. 3. **For BERT, RoBERTa and ALBERT, the "large" versions generalize consistently better than the "base" versions**. Concurrent work (Anonymous, 2021) focusing specifically on the effect of model size on the learning of lexical overlap heuristic came to a similar conclusion.

However, "larger is better" is not the whole story. The improvement occurs only past a certain threshold: going from BERT-tiny to BERT-medium does not help generalization. At the same time, both ALBERTs have fewer parameters than BERT-small, but they do generalize, which suggests that their parameter sharing is truly effective. Also RoBERTa-base learns to generalize more consistently than BERT-large, which may be either due to some inherent superiority of RoBERTa, or because this instance of RoBERTa happens to be better than this instance of BERT. One point that is clear is that **better generalization also requires longer fine-tuning**, which interestingly barely affects the core MNLI performance on the larger models, but makes a lot of difference for the smaller BERTs.

5 Related work

Several studies have reported successful generalization from MNLI to HANS. Among data-based strategies, it has been achieved via augmenting MNLI data with predicate-argument structures (Moosavi et al., 2020) and syntactic transformations (Min et al., 2020). Although there are many reports of syntactic knowledge in pre-trained BERT (Rogers et al., 2020b), Min et al. (2020) suggest that pre-training does not yield a strong inductive bias to *use* syntax in downstream tasks, and augmentation "nudges" the model towards that.

Theoretically, subsampling that reduces the saliency of spurious patterns should have a similar effect, but our cartography-based subsampling did not work consistently, possibly because MNLI has little counter-evidence to spurious patterns, and the right subsample is hard to find reliably. We have additional negative results for subsampling with K-means clustering (see Appendix D for details).

The idea of using shallow models to identify biases *before* training and "teach" the model to treat them differently has been successfully explored by Utama et al. (2020), Clark et al. (2020), and Sanh et al. (2021). Our negative results with HEX debiasing *after* training complements these reports.

Our results corroborate that generalization is improved by larger models (Anonymous, 2021) and longer fine-tuning (Tu et al., 2020). The latter work shows that this happens thanks to the few HANS-like samples in MNLI: they take longer to learn, and without them longer fine-tuning does not help.

A general challenge for DL-based NLP research is variability due to extraneous factors. Generalization from MNLI to HANS may be much improved simply with a lucky fine-tuning initialization (Mc-

Coy et al., 2019a). For QA Crane (2018) show that there are many other external factors (down to linear algebra library version) that also play a role, and for Transformers overall implementations make a big difference (Narang et al., 2021). Our work provides an illustration of that phenomenon in NLI. The reported HANS performance of vanilla fine-tuned BERT-base varies in the published studies from 50.0% to 62.5%. Our Pytorch-Lightning implementation at 4 epochs achieves 69% (avg. of 16 runs), not due to any architectural differences. Overall it also has higher variability between runs, possibly due to batch size differences.

6 Analysis: Bias Under Low Confidence

Our overall ratio of positive to negative results illustrates the difficulty of the spurious patterns problem. Once the model learns that some pattern is a strong signal for a label, it will over-rely on it. But how much heuristic-matching evidence does it need?

In this experiment we fine-tune the base versions of BERT and RoBERTa for 4 epochs. We use the dataset cartography to identify the "hard" training samples for both models. As shown in Figure 1, the classifier has overall low confidence for the "hard" samples. We corrupt these "hard " samples by inserting extra characters randomly in 30% content words in the sequence. For example:

Premise: do it now, $\overbrace{\text{think'}}^{\text{ythink}}$ $\overbrace{\text{bout}}^{\text{ubout}}$ it later

Hypothesis: $\overbrace{\text{think}}^{\text{zthink}}$ about it now, do it $\overbrace{\text{later}}^{\text{late (r}}$

The corrupted sequences remain relatively readable for humans, but this reduces the signal from direct lexical matches seen by the model (even with BERT tokenization). Note that the model has already seen these samples 4 times before corruption. We repeated this experiment with substituting, deleting and swapping characters.

Since the classifier confidence for the "hard" examples is low, and the perturbations are random, they could be expected to just flip the predictions in random directions, equally across MNLI labels. Instead, with all corruption strategies and for both models we see the pattern shown in Table 2: the accuracy drops significantly for contradiction (by 10-20 points), and improves significantly for entailment (by 10-30 points). For the neutral class the change is not as large (mostly gaining 5-13 points).

These results suggest that **in low-confidence context even *decreased* lexical overlap still nudges the model towards entailment** rather than contradiction. This runs contrary to the overall strategy shown by HANS, and it is not due to the majority class bias (as MNLI train set is balanced between entailment and contradiction). One possible explanation is that if it is non-entailment that the generalizing models slowly learn from the little supporting evidence in MNLI (Tu et al., 2020), then corruption would make that already-difficult job even harder for the model, decreasing the accuracy on non-entailment. On the other hand, even corrupted MNLI examples still have some lexical overlap, and so the model, unable to recognize any subtler patterns, might default to that.

Corruption	Labels	BERT	RoBERTa
Character insert	Entailment	+18.2	+11.9
	Neural	+13.78	+0.8
	Contradiction	−28.89	−8.4
Character substitute	Entailment	+35.5	+20.4
	Neural	+1.6	+5.9
	Contradiction	−23.9	−17.6
Character swap	Entailment	+23.8	+18.1
	Neural	−1.6	+3.3
	Contradiction	−15.5	−13.9
Character delete	Entailment	+31.73	+18.4
	Neural	−11.2	+5.8
	Contradiction	−10.3	−16.3

Table 2: "Hard" samples: changes in prediction accuracy for MNLI classes by BERT-base and RoBERTa-base after random character corruption.

This finding has implications for high-cost-of-error applications where false positives are preferable to false negatives. If the data has spurious patterns, the model may score well on a generalization benchmark, but be still biased towards a certain label when its confidence is low. Consider e.g. most of COVID detection models are "at high risk of bias" due to noisy data (Wynants et al., 2020).

7 Conclusion

Most supervised datasets are biased in one way or the other, and task-independent techniques to improve NLP model generalization are crucial for further advances. We experimented with 5 strategies to improve generalization of BERT-class models for NLI task: explicit debiasing, bottlenecking the model, adapters, data subsampling, and increasing model size. We find the latter strategy the most promising, but we also report all the negative results, which contribute to the overall knowledge about generalization in BERT-based models.

Acknowledgments

This work was partially supported by JST CREST Grant Number JPMJCR19F5, Japan. We thank the anonymous reviewers for their insightful comments, T. McCoy and T. Linzen for the help with HANS data, and E. Vatai for the help with langmo implementation.

References

Alexander A. Alemi, Ian Fischer, Joshua V. Dillon, and Kevin Murphy. 2016. Deep Variational Information Bottleneck.

Anonymous. 2021. Largely, right for better reasons:lexical generalization improves with model size. *(Under review)*.

Yonatan Belinkov, Adam Poliak, Stuart Shieber, Benjamin Van Durme, and Alexander Rush. 2019. Don't take the premise for granted: Mitigating artifacts in natural language inference. In *Proceedings of the 57th Annual Meeting of the Association for Computational Linguistics*, pages 877–891, Florence, Italy. Association for Computational Linguistics.

Tom Brown, Benjamin Mann, Nick Ryder, Melanie Subbiah, Jared D Kaplan, Prafulla Dhariwal, Arvind Neelakantan, Pranav Shyam, Girish Sastry, Amanda Askell, Sandhini Agarwal, Ariel Herbert-Voss, Gretchen Krueger, Tom Henighan, Rewon Child, Aditya Ramesh, Daniel Ziegler, Jeffrey Wu, Clemens Winter, Chris Hesse, Mark Chen, Eric Sigler, Mateusz Litwin, Scott Gray, Benjamin Chess, Jack Clark, Christopher Berner, Sam McCandlish, Alec Radford, Ilya Sutskever, and Dario Amodei. 2020. Language Models are Few-Shot Learners. 33:1877–1901.

Qian Chen, Xiaodan Zhu, Zhen-Hua Ling, Si Wei, Hui Jiang, and Diana Inkpen. 2017. Enhanced LSTM for natural language inference. In *Proceedings of the 55th Annual Meeting of the Association for Computational Linguistics (Volume 1: Long Papers)*, pages 1657–1668, Vancouver, Canada. Association for Computational Linguistics.

Sumit Chopra, Raia Hadsell, and Yann LeCun. 2005. Learning a similarity metric discriminatively, with application to face verification. In *Proceedings of the 2005 IEEE Computer Society Conference on Computer Vision and Pattern Recognition (CVPR'05) - Volume 1 - Volume 01*, CVPR '05, page 539–546, USA. IEEE Computer Society.

Christopher Clark, Mark Yatskar, and Luke Zettlemoyer. 2020. Learning to Model and Ignore Dataset Bias with Mixed Capacity Ensembles. In *Findings of the Association for Computational Linguistics: EMNLP 2020*, pages 3031–3045, Online. Association for Computational Linguistics.

Matt Crane. 2018. Questionable Answers in Question Answering Research: Reproducibility and Variability of Published Results. *Transactions of the Association for Computational Linguistics*, 6:241–252.

Jacob Devlin, Ming-Wei Chang, Kenton Lee, and Kristina Toutanova. 2019. BERT: Pre-training of deep bidirectional transformers for language understanding. In *Proceedings of the 2019 Conference of the North American Chapter of the Association for Computational Linguistics: Human Language Technologies, Volume 1 (Long and Short Papers)*, pages 4171–4186, Minneapolis, Minnesota. Association for Computational Linguistics.

Matt Gardner, William Merrill, Jesse Dodge, Matthew E. Peters, Alexis Ross, Sameer Singh, and Noah Smith. 2021. Competency Problems: On Finding and Removing Artifacts in Language Data. *arXiv:2104.08646 [cs]*.

Mor Geva, Yoav Goldberg, and Jonathan Berant. 2019. Are We Modeling the Task or the Annotator? An Investigation of Annotator Bias in Natural Language Understanding Datasets. In *Proceedings of the 2019 Conference on Empirical Methods in Natural Language Processing and the 9th International Joint Conference on Natural Language Processing (EMNLP-IJCNLP)*, pages 1161–1166, Hong Kong, China. Association for Computational Linguistics.

Suchin Gururangan, Swabha Swayamdipta, Omer Levy, Roy Schwartz, Samuel Bowman, and Noah A. Smith. 2018. Annotation artifacts in natural language inference data. In *Proceedings of the 2018 Conference of the North American Chapter of the Association for Computational Linguistics: Human Language Technologies, Volume 2 (Short Papers)*, pages 107–112, New Orleans, Louisiana. Association for Computational Linguistics.

Ruidan He, Linlin Liu, Hai Ye, Qingyu Tan, Bosheng Ding, Liying Cheng, Jiawei Low, Lidong Bing, and Luo Si. 2021. On the Effectiveness of Adapter-based Tuning for Pretrained Language Model Adaptation. In *Proceedings of the 59th Annual Meeting of the Association for Computational Linguistics and the 11th International Joint Conference on Natural Language Processing (Volume 1: Long Papers)*, pages 2208–2222, Online. Association for Computational Linguistics.

Neil Houlsby, Andrei Giurgiu, Stanislaw Jastrzebski, Bruna Morrone, Quentin De Laroussilhe, Andrea Gesmundo, Mona Attariyan, and Sylvain Gelly. 2019. Parameter-efficient transfer learning for NLP. In *Proceedings of the 36th International Conference on Machine Learning*, volume 97 of *Proceedings of Machine Learning Research*, pages 2790–2799, Long Beach, California, USA. PMLR.

Angelos Katharopoulos and François Fleuret. 2018. Not all samples are created equal: Deep learning with importance sampling. In *Proceedings of the 35th International Conference on Machine Learning,*

ICML 2018, Stockholmsmässan, Stockholm, Sweden, July 10-15, 2018, volume 80 of *Proceedings of Machine Learning Research*, pages 2530–2539. PMLR.

Gregory Koch, Richard Zemel, and Ruslan Salakhutdinov. 2015. Siamese neural networks for one-shot image recognition. In *ICML deep learning workshop*, volume 2. Lille.

Zhenzhong Lan, Mingda Chen, Sebastian Goodman, Kevin Gimpel, Piyush Sharma, and Radu Soricut. 2020. Albert: A lite bert for self-supervised learning of language representations. In *International Conference on Learning Representations*.

Yinhan Liu, Myle Ott, Naman Goyal, Jingfei Du, Mandar Joshi, Danqi Chen, Omer Levy, Mike Lewis, Luke Zettlemoyer, and Veselin Stoyanov. 2019. Roberta: A robustly optimized BERT pretraining approach. *CoRR*, abs/1907.11692.

Rabeeh Karimi Mahabadi, Yonatan Belinkov, and James Henderson. 2020. Variational Information Bottleneck for Effective Low-Resource Fine-Tuning. In *International Conference on Learning Representations*.

Rabeeh Karimi Mahabadi, James Henderson, and Sebastian Ruder. 2021. Compacter: Efficient low-rank hypercomplex adapter layers.

R. Thomas McCoy, Junghyun Min, and Tal Linzen. 2019a. BERTs of a feather do not generalize together: Large variability in generalization across models with similar test set performance. *arXiv:1911.02969 [cs]*.

Tom McCoy, Ellie Pavlick, and Tal Linzen. 2019b. Right for the wrong reasons: Diagnosing syntactic heuristics in natural language inference. In *Proceedings of the 57th Annual Meeting of the Association for Computational Linguistics*, pages 3428–3448, Florence, Italy. Association for Computational Linguistics.

Junghyun Min, R. Thomas McCoy, Dipanjan Das, Emily Pitler, and Tal Linzen. 2020. Syntactic data augmentation increases robustness to inference heuristics. In *Proceedings of the 58th Annual Meeting of the Association for Computational Linguistics*, pages 2339–2352, Online. Association for Computational Linguistics.

Nafise Sadat Moosavi, Marcel de Boer, Prasetya Ajie Utama, and Iryna Gurevych. 2020. Improving Robustness by Augmenting Training Sentences with Predicate-Argument Structures. *arXiv:2010.12510 [cs]*.

Sharan Narang, Hyung Won Chung, Yi Tay, William Fedus, Thibault Fevry, Michael Matena, Karishma Malkan, Noah Fiedel, Noam Shazeer, Zhenzhong Lan, Yanqi Zhou, Wei Li, Nan Ding, Jake Marcus, Adam Roberts, and Colin Raffel. 2021. Do Transformer Modifications Transfer Across Implementations and Applications? *arXiv:2102.11972 [cs]*.

Adam Paszke, Sam Gross, Francisco Massa, Adam Lerer, James Bradbury, Gregory Chanan, Trevor Killeen, Zeming Lin, Natalia Gimelshein, Luca Antiga, Alban Desmaison, Andreas Kopf, Edward Yang, Zachary DeVito, Martin Raison, Alykhan Tejani, Sasank Chilamkurthy, Benoit Steiner, Lu Fang, Junjie Bai, and Soumith Chintala. 2019. Pytorch: An imperative style, high-performance deep learning library. In H. Wallach, H. Larochelle, A. Beygelzimer, F. d'Alché Buc, E. Fox, and R. Garnett, editors, *Advances in Neural Information Processing Systems 32*, pages 8024–8035. Curran Associates, Inc.

Jonas Pfeiffer, Aishwarya Kamath, Andreas Rücklé, Kyunghyun Cho, and Iryna Gurevych. 2020. Adapterfusion: Non-destructive task composition for transfer learning.

Adam Poliak, Jason Naradowsky, Aparajita Haldar, Rachel Rudinger, and Benjamin Van Durme. 2018. Hypothesis only baselines in natural language inference. In *Proceedings of the Seventh Joint Conference on Lexical and Computational Semantics*, pages 180–191, New Orleans, Louisiana. Association for Computational Linguistics.

Colin Raffel, Noam Shazeer, Adam Roberts, Katherine Lee, Sharan Narang, Michael Matena, Yanqi Zhou, Wei Li, and Peter J. Liu. 2020. Exploring the limits of transfer learning with a unified text-to-text transformer. *Journal of Machine Learning Research*, 21(140):1–67.

Nils Reimers and Iryna Gurevych. 2019. Sentence-BERT: Sentence embeddings using Siamese BERT-networks. In *Proceedings of the 2019 Conference on Empirical Methods in Natural Language Processing and the 9th International Joint Conference on Natural Language Processing (EMNLP-IJCNLP)*, pages 3982–3992, Hong Kong, China. Association for Computational Linguistics.

Anna Rogers, Olga Kovaleva, Matthew Downey, and Anna Rumshisky. 2020a. Getting Closer to AI Complete Question Answering: A Set of Prerequisite Real Tasks. In *Proceedings of the AAAI Conference on Artificial Intelligence*, pages 8722–8731.

Anna Rogers, Olga Kovaleva, and Anna Rumshisky. 2020b. A Primer in BERTology: What We Know About How BERT Works. *Transactions of the Association for Computational Linguistics*, 8:842–866.

Victor Sanh, Thomas Wolf, Yonatan Belinkov, and Alexander M. Rush. 2021. Learning from others' mistakes: Avoiding dataset biases without modeling them. In *International Conference on Learning Representations*.

Swabha Swayamdipta, Roy Schwartz, Nicholas Lourie, Yizhong Wang, Hannaneh Hajishirzi, Noah A. Smith, and Yejin Choi. 2020. Dataset cartography: Mapping and diagnosing datasets with training dynamics. In *Proceedings of the 2020 Conference on*

Empirical Methods in Natural Language Processing (EMNLP), pages 9275–9293, Online. Association for Computational Linguistics.

Naftali Tishby, Fernando C. Pereira, and William Bialek. 2000. The information bottleneck method. *arXiv:physics/0004057*.

Lifu Tu, Garima Lalwani, Spandana Gella, and He He. 2020. An Empirical Study on Robustness to Spurious Correlations using Pre-trained Language Models. *Transactions of the Association for Computational Linguistics*, 8:621–633.

Iulia Turc, Ming-Wei Chang, Kenton Lee, and Kristina Toutanova. 2019. Well-read students learn better: On the importance of pre-training compact models.

Prasetya Ajie Utama, Nafise Sadat Moosavi, and Iryna Gurevych. 2020. Towards debiasing NLU models from unknown biases. In *Proceedings of the 2020 Conference on Empirical Methods in Natural Language Processing (EMNLP)*, pages 7597–7610, Online. Association for Computational Linguistics.

Ashish Vaswani, Noam Shazeer, Niki Parmar, Jakob Uszkoreit, Llion Jones, Aidan N Gomez, Ł ukasz Kaiser, and Illia Polosukhin. 2017. Attention is all you need. In I. Guyon, U. V. Luxburg, S. Bengio, H. Wallach, R. Fergus, S. Vishwanathan, and R. Garnett, editors, *Advances in Neural Information Processing Systems 30*, pages 5998–6008. Curran Associates, Inc.

Haohan Wang, Zexue He, Zachary L. Lipton, and Eric P. Xing. 2019. Learning robust representations by projecting superficial statistics out. In *International Conference on Learning Representations*.

Adina Williams, Nikita Nangia, and Samuel Bowman. 2018. A broad-coverage challenge corpus for sentence understanding through inference. In *Proceedings of the 2018 Conference of the North American Chapter of the Association for Computational Linguistics: Human Language Technologies, Volume 1 (Long Papers)*, pages 1112–1122. Association for Computational Linguistics.

Thomas Wolf, Lysandre Debut, Victor Sanh, Julien Chaumond, Clement Delangue, Anthony Moi, Pierric Cistac, Tim Rault, R'emi Louf, Morgan Funtowicz, and Jamie Brew. 2019. Huggingface's transformers: State-of-the-art natural language processing. *ArXiv*, abs/1910.03771.

Laure Wynants, Ben Van Calster, Gary S. Collins, Richard D. Riley, Georg Heinze, Ewoud Schuit, Marc M. J. Bonten, Darren L. Dahly, Johanna A. Damen, Thomas P. A. Debray, Valentijn M. T. de Jong, Maarten De Vos, Paula Dhiman, Maria C. Haller, Michael O. Harhay, Liesbet Henckaerts, Pauline Heus, Michael Kammer, Nina Kreuzberger, Anna Lohmann, Kim Luijken, Jie Ma, Glen P. Martin, David J. McLernon, Constanza L. Andaur Navarro, Johannes B. Reitsma, Jamie C. Sergeant, Chunhu Shi, Nicole Skoetz, Luc J. M. Smits, Kym I. E. Snell, Matthew Sperrin, René Spijker, Ewout W. Steyerberg, Toshihiko Takada, Ioanna Tzoulaki, Sander M. J. van Kuijk, Bas C. T. van Bussel, Iwan C. C. van der Horst, Florien S. van Royen, Jan Y. Verbakel, Christine Wallisch, Jack Wilkinson, Robert Wolff, Lotty Hooft, Karel G. M. Moons, and Maarten van Smeden. 2020. Prediction models for diagnosis and prognosis of covid-19: Systematic review and critical appraisal. 369:m1328.

Xiang Zhou and Mohit Bansal. 2020. Towards robustifying NLI models against lexical dataset biases. In *Proceedings of the 58th Annual Meeting of the Association for Computational Linguistics*, pages 8759–8771, Online. Association for Computational Linguistics.

A Additional details and samples from the used datasets

We use MNLI to perform training of LMs and evaluate their generalization capabilities on HANS. See Table 3 for some sample sentences from MNLI and HANS. MNLI has three classes ("entailment", "contradiction" and "neutral"), while HANS only has "entailment" and "non-entailment". HANS targets the three heuristics ("lexical overlap", "subsequence" and "constituent") which are usually adopted by pre-trained LMs such as BERT.

MNLI contains 393K and 20K examples in the train and dev sets respectively (the test set is not publicly available). HANS contains 30K examples split across 10K across each heuristic, which were used entirely for testing.

Label	Premise	Hypothesis
Entailment	A member of my team will - execute your orders with immense precision. This information belongs to them.	One of our number will carry out - your instructions minutely. How do you know? - All this is their information again.
Neutral	Product and geography are - what make cream skimming work The speaker doesn't know who it is.	Conceptually cream skimming has two - basic dimensions - product and geography. Who could there be ?
Contradiction	I ignored Ben. He only muttered something about - splitting the sky.	Hello, Ben. He distinctly said - you were to repair the sky.

(a) Examples of sentences from MNLI (Williams et al., 2018)

Heuristic	Premise	Hypothesis	Label
Lexical overlap	The banker near the judge saw the actor. The judge by the actor stopped the banker.	The banker saw the actor. The banker stopped the actor.	E N
Subsequence	The artist and the student called the judge. The senator near the lawyer danced.	The student called the judge. The lawyer danced.	E N
Constituent	Before the actor slept, the senator ran. If the actor slept, the judge saw the artist.	The actor slept. The actor slept.	E N

(b) Examples of sentences from HANS (McCoy et al., 2019b).
The *label* column shows the correct label for the sentence pair; *E* stands for *entailment* and *N* stands for *non-entailment*. A model relying on the heuristics would label all examples as *entailment* (incorrectly for those marked as N)

Table 3: The NLI data used in this study

B Cartography

Cartography is a recent method for characterizing the difficulty of training samples. It describes data points as "easy", "ambiguous" and "hard" through analyzing predictions of the model during training on those samples (training dynamics).

Sampling. In our experiments, we sample the datasets in the ranked order. For example, the easiest example is at the top, so it is first in the sampled batch of dataset. Our implementation of obtaining ranked ordering is based on the original implementation by the authors of the method[6].

Role of "easy" examples. During vanilla finetuning on randomly subsampled data, the model encounters all three kinds of examples some of which may provide meaningful signals to learn and some may aid in out-of-domain generalization. In our experiments, we find that training solely on "ambiguous" and "hard" examples do not aid the network in improving the performance. This finding is consistent with the observation from (Swayamdipta et al., 2020) wherein they showed that "easy" examples aid in optimization of the network during initial stages and are crucial for training. Therefore, in our experiments the models were trained first on 25% "easy" examples, and then on subsets of "hard" examples containing the top 1%, 5%, 10%, 17%, 25%, 33%, 50% and 75% of the "hard" data (for consistency with the experiment by Swayamdipta et al. (2020), see sec. 4). The results of this experiment are shown in fig. 2. The same experiment was repeated with the "ambiguous" samples, shown in fig. 4.

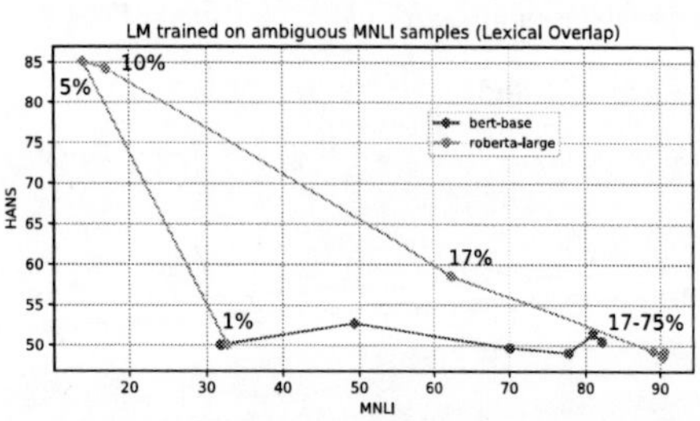

Figure 4: Evaluating generalization at varying stages of training on "ambiguous" samples. Percentages on marker represents percentage of MNLI train data used as training progresses.

[6] https://github.com/allenai/cartography

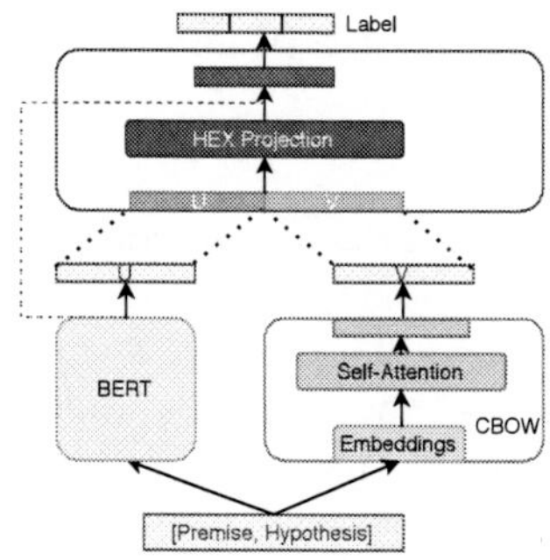

Figure 5: Orthogonal debiasing with HEX projection

C Stabilizing HEX

Here we provide more details about how HEX is being used. The self-attention output from BERT is pooled and passed through two MLP layers to get an individual representation of each input sequence, as shown in fig. 5. We feed the pooled representation of BERT and the intermediate representation of CBOW into two MLPs to obtain vectors U and V. We use f to represent classification layer parameterized by ξ. The output vectors $F_A = f([U, V]; \xi)$ and $F_G = f([0, V]; \xi)$ are concatenated along the non-batch dimension.

$$\begin{aligned} F_A &= f([U, V]; \xi), \\ F_G &= f([0, V]; \xi) \end{aligned} \tag{1}$$

where F_A, F_G denotes both concatenated representations and zero matrix prepended with network B's representation $[,]$ denotes concatenation operation along the non-batch dimension.

Following Vaswani et al. (2017), we project F_A:

$$F_L = (I - F_G(F_G^T F_G + \lambda I)^{-1} F_G^T) F_A \tag{2}$$

Table 4 shows hyperparameter search for λ. During inference, we use logits obtained through BERT only.

We follow a slight variation of Equation 2 to smoothen the process of optimization. The addition of λ hyper-parameter has been done to ensure that inverse is carried out on a non-singular matrix. The value of λ plays a significant role in determining how these representations are being learned. In our experiments, $1e-4$ worked well and was used for initializing it after which it was set as a model's parameter. We observe that pseudo-inverse of $F_G^T F_G$ is unstable and can make optimization

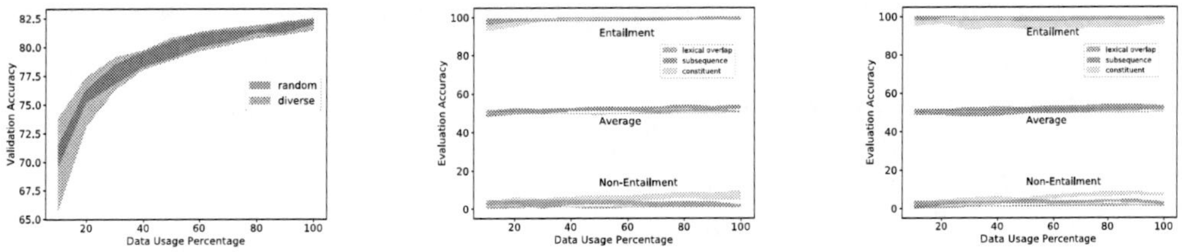

(a) Diverse vs Random sampling: MNLI (b) Random sampling: HANS (c) Diverse sampling: HANS

Figure 6: Fine-tuning BERT-base on varied amounts of MNLI data: in-domain and generalization performance

λ	**MNLI**	**HANS** (Average) L S C
1e-4	55.2	49.50 / 52.62 / 52.52
2e-4	56.54	49.81 / 50.90 / 50.83
3e-4	57.02	50.03 / 50.11 / 49.93
4e-4	57.72	49.49 / 52.39 / 51.42
5e-4	57.09	49.93 / 50.16 / 50.03
6e-4	55.26	49.66 / 51.59 / 52.68
7e-4	57.25	49.60 / 51.09 / 49.63
8e-4	57.78	49.60 / 51.20 / 51.37
9e-4	48.58	50.00 / 50.00 / 49.98
1e-5	53.45	49.80 / 50.69 / 50.68
2e-5	53.77	50.00 / 50.00 / 50.00
3e-5	56.46	49.19 / 52.84 / 54.41
4e-5	47.30	49.61 / 50.90 / 49.28
5e-5	50.80	49.69 / 51.07 / 50.41

Table 4: Performance on MNLI and HANS with HEX (BERT-base) with different values of λ. L, S, C denote lexical overlap, subsequence and constituent heuristic

process hard, so we make U and V square matrices to obtain inverse instead. Additionally, during inference time, we directly feed outputs from the main network to the MLP layer to obtain logit vectors instead of using F_L. It has been reported (Wang et al., 2019) that this doesn't have any profound impact on the logit vector and makes inference faster. We also applied L1 and L2 normalization on U and V to account for differences in scale but did not see any noticeable improvement. We found that values of λ greater than 0.0001 do not aid the network in learning.

D Subsampling the Training Data with K-means clustering

Motivation. Fundamentally, the problem is the mismatch between MNLI and HANS distributions. For a biased dataset, one solution could be to find such a subsample that would enable the model to perform well on both distributions.

Experiments. We encode MNLI examples as BERT [CLS] embeddings and cluster them in 512 clusters using K-means. We then fine-tune BERT-base on varying amounts of MNLI data, progressively increasing the amount of training examples by 10%. The data in the sub-sample is selected (a) randomly (as a control), (b) so as to maximize the diversity of examples within the sample (Katharopoulos and Fleuret, 2018). At the smallest subsample size we sample the data from all clusters. As data size increases, smaller clusters are exhausted while the larger ones remain, so the smallest subsamples are the most diverse, and the diversity decreases as the sample size increases. The experiment is repeated with 5 random seeds.

Results. Figure 6 shows that on MNLI, diverse sampling yields much more variation with small amounts of data than random sampling, but as the subsample approaches the full dataset the performance also becomes the same. Neither subsampling strategy improves generalization: the model still predicts "entailment" for most HANS examples. Thus overall the result for this strategy is negative.

Challenging the Semi-Supervised VAE Framework for Text Classification

Ghazi Felhi, Joseph Le Roux
LIPN
Université Sorbonne Paris Nord - CNRS UMR 7030
F-93430, Villetaneuse, France
{felhi, leroux}@lipn.fr

Djamé Seddah
INRIA Paris
Paris, France
djame.seddah@inria.fr

Abstract

Semi-Supervised Variational Autoencoders (SSVAEs) are widely used models for data efficient learning. In this paper, we question the adequacy of the standard design of sequence SSVAEs for the task of text classification as we exhibit two sources of overcomplexity for which we provide simplifications.

These simplifications to SSVAEs preserve their theoretical soundness while providing a number of practical advantages in the semi-supervised setup where the result of training is a text classifier. These simplifications are the removal of *(i)* the Kullback-Liebler divergence from its objective and *(ii)* the fully unobserved latent variable from its probabilistic model. These changes relieve users from choosing a prior for their latent variables, make the model smaller and faster, and allow for a better flow of information into the latent variables.

We compare the simplified versions to standard SSVAEs on 4 text classification tasks. On top of the above-mentioned simplification, experiments show a speed-up of 26%, while keeping equivalent classification scores. The code to reproduce our experiments is public[1].

1 Introduction

Obtaining labeled data to train NLP systems is a process that has often proven to be costly and time-consuming, and this is still largely the case (Martínez Alonso et al., 2016; Seddah et al., 2020). Consequently, semi-supervised approaches are appealing to improve performance while alleviating dependence on annotations. To that end, Variational Autoencoders (VAEs) (Kingma and Welling, 2014) have been adapted to semi-supervised learning (Kingma et al., 2014), and subsequently applied to several NLP tasks (Chen et al., 2018a; Corro and Titov, 2019; Gururangan et al., 2020).

A notable difference between the generative model case from where VAEs originate, and the semi-supervised case is that only the decoder (generator) of the VAE is kept after training in the first case, while in the second, it is the encoder (classifier) that we keep. This difference, as well as the autoregressive nature of text generators has not sufficiently been taken into account in the adaptation of VAEs to semi-supervised text classification. In this work, we show that some components can be ablated from the long used semi-supervised VAEs (SSVAEs) when only aiming for text classification. These ablations simplify SSVAEs and offer several practical advantages while preserving their performance and theoretical soundness.

The usage of unlabeled data through SSVAEs is often described as a *regularization* on representations (Chen et al., 2018a; Wolf-Sonkin et al., 2018; Yacoby et al., 2020). More specifically, SSVAEs add to the supervised learning signal, a conditional generation learning signal that is used to train on unlabeled samples. From this observation, we study two changes to the standard SSVAE framework. The first simplification we study is the removal of a term from the objective of SSVAEs: the Kullback-Leibler term. This encourages the flow of information into latent variables, frees the users from choosing priors for their latent variables, and is harmless to the theoretical soundness of the semi-supervised framework. The second simplification we study is made to account for the autoregressive nature of text generators. In the general case, input samples in SSVAEs are described with two latent variables: a partially-observed latent variable, which is also used to infer the label for the supervised learning task, and an unobserved latent variable, which describes the rest of the variability in the data. However, autoregressive text generators are powerful enough to converge without the need for latent variables. Therefore, removing the unobserved latent variable is the second change we study in SSVAEs. The above modifications can be found in some rare works throughout the literature,

[1] https://github.com/ghazi-f/Challenging-SSVAEs

Proceedings of the Second Workshop on Insights from Negative Results in NLP, pages 136–143
November 10, 2021.

e.g. (Corro and Titov, 2019). We, however, aim to provide justification for these changes beyond the empirical gains that they exhibit for some tasks.

Our experiments on four text classification datasets show no harm to the empirical classification performance of SSVAE in applying the simplifications above. Additionally, we show that removing the unobserved latent variable leads to a significant speed-up.

To summarize our contribution, we justify two simplifications to the standard SSVAE framework, explain the practical advantage of applying these modifications, and provide empirical results showing that they speed up the training process while causing no harm to the classification performance.

2 Background

2.1 Variational Autoencoders

Variational Autoencoders (Kingma and Welling, 2019) are a class of generative models that combine Variational Inference with Deep Learning modules to train a generative model. For a latent variable z, and an observed variable x, the generative model p_θ consists of a prior $p_\theta(z)$ and a decoder $p_\theta(x|z)$. VAEs also include an approximate posterior (also called the encoder) $q_\phi(z|x)$. Both are used during training to maximize an objective called the Evidence Lower Bound (ELBo), a lower-bound of the log-likelihood:

$$\log p_\theta(x) \geq \mathbb{E}_{z\sim q_\phi(z|x)}\left[\log p_\theta(x|z)\right] - \mathrm{KL}\left[q_\phi(z|x); p_\theta(z)\right] = \mathrm{ELBo}(x; z) \quad (1)$$

Throughout the paper, we will continue to use this ELBo(.;.) operator, with the observed variable(s) as a first argument, and the latent variable(s) as a second argument. In the original VAE framework, after training, the encoder q_ϕ is discarded and only the generative model (the prior and the decoder) are kept.

2.2 Semi-Supervised VAEs

The idea of using the VAE encoder as a classifier for semi-supervised learning has first been explored in (Kingma et al., 2014). Besides the usual unobserved latent variable z, the semi-supervised VAE framework also uses a partially-observed latent variable y. The encoder $q_\phi(y|x)$ serves both as the inference module for the supervised task, and as an approximate posterior (and encoder) for the y variable in the VAE framework.

Consider a set of labeled examples $L = \{(x_1, y_1), ..., (x_{|L|}, y_{|L|})\}$, and a set of unlabeled examples $U = \{x'_1, ..., x'_{|U|}\}$. For the set L, $q_\phi(y|x)$ is trained *i)* with the usual supervised objective (typically, a cross-entropy objective for a classification task) *ii)* with an ELBo that considers x and y to be *observed*, and z to be a *latent* variable. A weight α is used on the supervised objective to control its balance with ELBo. For the set U, $q_\phi(y|x)$ is only trained as part of the VAE model with an ELBO where y is used, this time, as a *latent* variable like z. Formally, the training objective $\mathcal{J}^\alpha$ of a SSVAE is as follows:

$$\mathcal{J}^\alpha = \sum_{(x,y)\in L}\Big(\mathrm{ELBo}((x,y); z) + \alpha\,\log q_\phi(y|x)\Big) + \sum_{x\in U}\mathrm{ELBo}(x; (y,z)) \quad (2)$$

3 Simplifying SSVAEs for Text Classification

The simplifications we propose stem from the analysis of an alternative form under which ELBO can be written (Eq. 2.8 in Kingma and Welling, 2019). Although it is valid for any arguments of ELBo(.;.), we display it here for an observed variable x, and the couple of latent variables (y, z):

$$\mathrm{ELBo}(x; (y,z)) = \log p_\theta(x) - \mathrm{KL}[q_\phi(y,z|x)||p_\theta(y,z|x)] \quad (3)$$

For the case of SSVAEs, this form provides a clear reading of the additional effect of ELBo on the learning process: *i)* maximizing the log-likelihood of the generative model $p_\theta(x)$, *ii)* bringing the parameters of the inference model $q_\phi(y,z|x)$ closer to the posterior of the generative model $p_\theta(y,z|x)$. Since $p_\theta(y,z|x)$ is the distribution of the latent variables expected by the generative model p_θ for it to be able to generate x, we can conclude that ELBo trains *both* latent variables for conditional generation on the unsupervised dataset U.

3.1 Dropping the Unobserved Latent Variable

Building on observations from equation 3, we question the usefulness of training both latent variables for conditional generation when semi-supervised learning only aims for an improvement on the inference of the partially-observed latent variable y.

For the case of language generation, the sequence of discrete symbols in each sample is often modeled by an autoregressive distribution $p_\theta(x|y,z) = \prod_i p_\theta(x_i|y,z,x_{<i})$ where x_i is the ith symbol in the sequence, and $x_{<i}$ are the symbols preceding x_i. Such a distribution is able to generate realistic samples when trained on a target text corpus, so much that text VAEs are plagued with a problem known as *posterior collapse* (Bowman et al., 2016) where the latent variable is ignored by the generative model. We therefore propose to keep only y and to drop z from the model avoiding its presence in the Kullback-Leibler divergence in Equation 3 and saving some parameters.[2]

3.2 Dropping the Kullback-Leibler Term

Previous work on VAE-based language models showed that the KL divergence in Eq. 1 sometimes discourages the model from using latent variables and makes them useless in practice (Bowman et al., 2016; Zhao et al., 2017; Chen et al., 2018b).

An interesting result from Zhao et al. (2017) is that ELBo without KL divergence (*KL-free*) is still a theoretically sound objective for generative modeling with VAEs. The difference between the generative model resulting from a regular ELBo and a KL-free ELBo is the prior of the model. A KL-free ELBo results in a generative model that uses as a prior $q_\phi(z) = \int_z q_\phi(z|x)p_{data}(x)dx$. This prior is intractable which makes the resulting model impractical for generation, but causes no problem for semi-supervised VAEs. We therefore propose, as a second change to the standard SSVAE framework, the removal of the KL-divergence in Eq. 1.

Note that in this case, the network formulates its own prior instead of requiring the user to choose it. That is a significant advantage since the choice of a good prior is difficult: it must model adequately the *default* behavior of the latent variables, and requires a closed form for the KL-divergence in Eq. 1 to stabilize training.

3.3 Resulting Objective

Applying both of the previous simplifications to the semi-supervised objective in Eq. 2 leads to the following objective:

$$\sum_{(x,y)\in L} \Big(\log p_\theta(x|y) + \alpha \, \log q_\phi(y|x) \Big) + \sum_{x\in U} \mathbb{E}_{y\sim q_\phi(y|x)} \left[\log p_\theta(x|y)\right]) \quad (4)$$

As can be seen, the first ELBo in Eq. 2 turns into a supervised conditional generation objective, while the second ELBo turns into a reconstruction term that relies only on y. Nevertheless, we stress that the second term is still an ELBo, and the whole objective is still a VAE-based semi-supervised learning objective. It should also be noted that, without z, the latent variables cannot provide the decoder with the full information about a sentence and, therefore, cannot reach a state where each sample is *reconstructed*. To avoid confusion, instead of *reconstructing* from y, the role of the reconstruction term is better read in our case as *raising the probability* of the sample at hand under the associated label y.

4 Experiments

In this section, we display comparisons between instances of standard SSVAEs and the same SSVAEs after applying the changes we propose.

4.1 Setup

Datasets We consider 4 Datasets for our study: the IMDB (Maas et al., 2011) and Yelp review (Li et al., 2018) binary sentiment analysis datasets, and the AG News and DBPedia (Zhang et al., 2015) topic classification datasets. The Datasets have been chosen to represent a range over different tasks (Sentiment Analysis and Topic Classification), different numbers of classes, and different sentence lengths. A summary of dataset statistics is in Table 1.

dataset	Labels	Av. Sample length	N° Classes
AG News	Topic	37.85±10.09	4
DBPedia	Topic	46.13±22.46	14
IMDB	Sentiment	233.79±173.72	2
Yelp	Sentiment	8.88±3.64	2

Table 1: Dataset properties.

As was done in Chen et al. (2020), we measure performance on the different datasets with equal numbers of samples. Accordingly, for each dataset, we randomly subsample 10K samples from the

[2]In this case, one may be tempted to drop the VAE framework entirely and resort to other learning algorithms such as EM or direct likelihood maximization. Although possible in theory, this would disconnect q_ϕ from the generator's training, and thus discard the benefit from using unlabeled data.

Objective	AGNEWS	DBPedia	IMDB	Yelp
Supervised	86.98(0.74)	96.97(0.28)	81.02(0.64)	92.47(0.48)
SSVAE	87.89(0.54)	**97.75**(0.11)	83.34(0.91)	92.85(0.78)
SSVAE-{KL}	**87.95**(0.19)	97.58(0.13)	83.87(0.47)	92.90(0.54)
SSVAE-{z}	87.94(0.33)	97.40(0.14)	81.90(5.17)	93.60(0.74)
SSVAE-{KL, z}	87.85(0.29)	97.58(0.19)	**84.79**(1.34)	**93.77**(0.61)

Table 2: Accuracies On AGNEWS, DBPedia, IMDB, and Yelp. The values are averages over 5 runs with standard deviations between parentheses. The best score for each dataset and each amount of labeled data is given in bold.

original training set as *unlabeled* data. We also use 4K labeled samples a training set and 1K as development set. We use the original test sets from each dataset. All the samples are tokenized using a simple whitespace tokenizer.

Network Architecture The size of z is set to 32. For experiments without z, we simply drop all the components associated to it from the network.

The encoder consists of a pre-trained 300-dimensional fastText (Bojanowski et al., 2017) embedding layer, and 2 Bidirectional LSTM networks with 100 hidden states each, one for each of the latent variables y and z. The logits of y are then obtained by passing the last state of its Bidirectional LSTM through a linear layer. Similarly the last state of the Bidirectional LSTM for z is passed through a linear layer to obtain its mean parameter, and a linear layer with a softplus activation to obtain its standard deviation parameter.

As for the decoding step, to allow backpropagation, z is sampled using the reparameterization trick (Kingma and Welling, 2014), and y is sampled using the Gumbel-Softmax trick (Jang et al., 2017). Xu et al. (2017) have shown that latent variables are best exploited in SSVAEs when concatenated with the previous word at each generation step to obtain the next word. We design our decoder accordingly and use a 1-layered LSTM with size 200. The only hyper-parameter we tune on the development set is α, the coefficient weighting the supervised learning objective in Eq. 2, which is selected in the set $\{10^0, 10^{-1}, 10^{-2}, 10^{-3}\}$. Further implementation details are provided in Appendix A.

4.2 Results

Classification performance In Table 2, we compare the performance of a standard SSVAE, to a SSVAE where we remove the KL-divergence (SSVAE-{KL}) another where z is removed (SSVAE-{z}) and a third version where both the KL-divergence and z are removed (SSVAE-{KL, z}). We measure performance on all datasets using *accuracy*. As a baseline, we also include the results of an objective that does not use unlabeled data. The architecture we use for this objective is simply the LSTM encoder that we use to obtain y for the SSVAE objectives. This baseline is referred to as *Supervised.*

The aim of our experiment is to see whether we observe that there is a harm to the performance of SSVAEs when applying the proposed simplifications. In Table 2, we see that applying both changes compares favorably to the standard SSVAE 2 times out of 4. The removal of z yields the same comparison, while removing the KL term causes improvement 3 times out of 4. For more extensive testing, we ran experiments for varying amounts of labeled data (from 1% to 100%; *cf.* Appendix C), and only found 4 statistically significant differences between SSVAE and its variants: 3 in favor of one of our Simplified SSVAEs, and 1 in favor of the standard SSVAE.

We performed additional experiments in an out-of-domain setting (*c.f* Appendix B.) using our sentiment analysis datasets, and also observed improvements with our simplifications.

Speeding Up the Learning Process By removing the KL-divergence and the components associated with z, an improvement on the speed of the learning process is to be expected. This improvement is highly dependent on the model and on the implementation at hand. As an example, we measure the average speed of an optimization iteration for each dataset, and each version of SSVAE. In Table 3, the speed of each objective is displayed proportionally to the speed of standard SSVAEs. The calculations associated with the KL-divergence do not seem to slow down the iterations. However, removing z and its associated components consistently cuts out a considerable proportion of the duration of optimization steps. This proportion ranges from 14% (DBPedia) to 26%(AGNEWS).

Dataset	SSVAE-{KL}	SSVAE-{z}	SSVAE-{KL, z}
AGNEWS	0.911(0.73)	**0.742**(0.65)	**0.742**(0.81)
DBPedia	1.03(0.56)	**0.861**(0.61)	0.867(0.56)
IMDB	1.018(0.25)	0.822(0.25)	**0.816**(0.25)
Yelp	0.986(1.52)	**0.819**(1.39)	**0.819**(1.52)

Table 3: Training durations for each objective relative to standard SSVAE, averaged over 200 iterations. Standard deviations are given between parentheses. Lowest duration for each dataset is given in bold.

5 Related Works

After the pioneering work of Kingma et al. (2014), SSVAEs were extended to tasks such as morphological inflections (Wolf-Sonkin et al., 2018), controllable speech synthesis (Habib et al., 2019), parsing (Corro and Titov, 2019), sequential labeling (Chen et al., 2018a) among many others. VAE internals have also been *tweaked* in various manners to improve the learning performance. For instance, Gururangan et al. (2020) introduce a low resource pretraining scheme to improve transfer with VAEs, while Zhang et al. (2019) propose to use the deterministic ancestor of a latent variable to perform classification, and constrain it with an adversarial term to have it abide by the values of the random latent variable.

While our work is a focused contribution dedicated to the theoretical soundness and the practical advantages of two simplifications to the SSVAE framework for text classifications, it could be extendend to other tasks involving text generation as the unsupervised VAE objective. For instance, the work of Corro and Titov (2019) shows that semi-supervised dependency parsing scores higher with both the changes we study.

6 Conclusion

Starting from the observation that SSVAEs can be viewed as the combination of a supervised learning signal with an unsupervised conditional generation learning signal, we show that this framework needs neither to include a KL-divergence nor an unobserved latent variable (z) when dealing with text classification. We subsequently perform experimental comparisons between standard SSVAEs and simplified SSVAEs that indicate that they are globally equivalent in performance.

Our changes provide a number of practical advantages. First, removing the KL-divergence frees practitioners from choosing priors for the variables they use, and allows information to flow freely into these variables. Second, removing the latent variable z from the computational graph speeds up computation and shrinks the size of the network. Despite their popularity, VAEs are often tedious to train for NLP tasks. In that regard, our simplifications should facilite their usage in future works.

Acknowledgments

This work is supported by the PARSITI project grant (ANR-16-CE33-0021) given by the French National Research Agency (ANR), the *Laboratoire d'excellence "Empirical Foundations of Linguistics"* (ANR-10-LABX-0083), as well as the ONTORULE project. It was also granted access to the HPC resources of IDRIS under the allocation 20XX-AD011012112 made by GENCI.

References

Piotr Bojanowski, Edouard Grave, Armand Joulin, and Tomas Mikolov. 2017. Enriching Word Vectors with Subword Information. *Transactions of the Association for Computational Linguistics*, 5:135–146.

Samuel R Bowman, Luke Vilnis, Oriol Vinyals, Andrew M Dai, Rafal Jozefowicz, and Samy Bengio. 2016. Generating sentences from a continuous space. *CoNLL 2016 - 20th SIGNLL Conference on Computational Natural Language Learning, Proceedings*, pages 10–21.

Jiaao Chen, Zichao Yang, and Diyi Yang. 2020. MixText: Linguistically-Informed Interpolation of Hidden Space for Semi-Supervised Text Classification. In *Proceedings of the 58th Annual Meeting of the Association for Computational Linguistics*, pages 2147–2157.

Mingda Chen, Qingming Tang, Karen Livescu, and Kevin Gimpel. 2018a. Variational sequential labelers for semi-supervised learning. *Proceedings of the 2018 Conference on Empirical Methods in Natural Language Processing, EMNLP 2018*, pages 215–226.

Tian Qi Chen, Xuechen Li, Roger Grosse, and David Duvenaud. 2018b. Isolating sources of disentanglement in variational autoencoders. In *6th International Conference on Learning Representations, ICLR 2018 - Workshop Track Proceedings*.

Caio Corro and Ivan Titov. 2019. Differentiable perturb-and-parse: Semi-supervised parsing with a structured variational autoencoder. *7th International Conference on Learning Representations, ICLR 2019*, pages 1–24.

Suchin Gururangan, Tam Dang, Dallas Card, and Noah A Smith. 2020. Variational pretraining for semi-supervised text classification. *ACL 2019 - 57th*

Annual Meeting of the Association for Computational Linguistics, Proceedings of the Conference, pages 5880–5894.

Raza Habib, Soroosh Mariooryad, Matt Shannon, Eric Battenberg, R J Skerry-Ryan, Daisy Stanton, David Kao, and Tom Bagby. 2019. Semi-Supervised Generative Modeling for Controllable Speech Synthesis. In *International Conference on Learning Representations*, pages 1–13.

Eric Jang, Shixiang Gu, and Ben Poole. 2017. Categorical reparameterization with gumbel-softmax. *5th International Conference on Learning Representations, ICLR 2017 - Conference Track Proceedings*, pages 1–13.

Diederik P Kingma and Jimmy Ba. 2015. Adam: A Method for Stochastic Optimization. In *3rd International Conference on Learning Representations, ICLR 2015, San Diego, CA, USA, May 7-9, 2015, Conference Track Proceedings San Diego, CA, USA, May 7-9, 2015, Conference Track Proceedings*.

Diederik P Kingma, Danilo J Rezende, Shakir Mohamed, and Max Welling. 2014. Semi-Supervised Learning with Deep Generative Models. *Advances in Neural Information Processing Systems*, 4(January):3581–3589.

Diederik P. Kingma and Max Welling. 2014. Auto-encoding variational bayes. In *2nd International Conference on Learning Representations, ICLR 2014 - Conference Track Proceedings*, Ml, pages 1–14.

Diederik P Kingma and Max Welling. 2019. An introduction to variational autoencoders. *Foundations and Trends in Machine Learning*, 12(4):307–392.

Bohan Li, Junxian He, Graham Neubig, Taylor Berg-Kirkpatrick, and Yiming Yang. 2020. A surprisingly effective fix for deep latent variable modeling of text. In *EMNLP-IJCNLP 2019 - 2019 Conference on Empirical Methods in Natural Language Processing and 9th International Joint Conference on Natural Language Processing, Proceedings of the Conference*, pages 3603–3614.

Juncen Li, Robin Jia, He He, and Percy Liang. 2018. Delete, retrieve, generate: a simple approach to sentiment and style transfer. In *Proceedings of the 2018 Conference of the North American Chapter of the Association for Computational Linguistics: Human Language Technologies, Volume 1 (Long Papers)*, pages 1865–1874, New Orleans, Louisiana. Association for Computational Linguistics.

Andrew L Maas, Raymond E Daly, Peter T Pham, Dan Huang, Andrew Y Ng, and Christopher Potts. 2011. Learning word vectors for sentiment analysis. *ACL-HLT 2011 - Proceedings of the 49th Annual Meeting of the Association for Computational Linguistics: Human Language Technologies*, 1:142–150.

Héctor Martínez Alonso, Djamé Seddah, and Benoît Sagot. 2016. From noisy questions to Minecraft texts: Annotation challenges in extreme syntax scenario. In *Proceedings of the 2nd Workshop on Noisy User-generated Text (WNUT)*, pages 13–23, Osaka, Japan. The COLING 2016 Organizing Committee.

Geoffrey Roeder, Yuhuai Wu, and David Duvenaud. 2017. Sticking the landing: Simple, lower-variance gradient estimators for variational inference. *Advances in Neural Information Processing Systems*, 2017-Decem:6926–6935.

Djamé Seddah, Farah Essaidi, Amal Fethi, Matthieu Futeral, Benjamin Muller, Pedro Javier Ortiz Suárez, Benoît Sagot, and Abhishek Srivastava. 2020. Building a User-Generated Content North-African Arabizi Treebank: Tackling Hell. In *Proceedings of the 58th Annual Meeting of the Association for Computational Linguistics*, pages 1139–1150. Association for Computational Linguistics.

Lawrence Wolf-Sonkin, Jason Naradowsky, Sebastian J Mielke, and Ryan Cotterell. 2018. A structured variational autoencoder for contextual morphological inflection. *ACL 2018 - 56th Annual Meeting of the Association for Computational Linguistics, Proceedings of the Conference (Long Papers)*, 1:2631–2641.

Weidi Xu, Haoze Sun, Chao Deng, and Ying Tan. 2017. Variational autoencoder for semi-supervised text classification. *31st AAAI Conference on Artificial Intelligence, AAAI 2017*, pages 3358–3364.

Yaniv Yacoby, Weiwei Pan, and Finale Doshi-Velez. 2020. Failure Modes of Variational Autoencoders and Their Effects on Downstream Tasks. In *ICML Workshop on Uncertainty {\&} Robustness in Deep Learning (UDL)*.

Cheng Zhang, Judith Butepage, Hedvig Kjellstrom, and Stephan Mandt. 2019. Advances in Variational Inference. *IEEE Transactions on Pattern Analysis and Machine Intelligence*, 41(8):2008–2026.

Xiang Zhang, Junbo Zhao, and Yann LeCun. 2015. Character-level convolutional networks for text classification. *Advances in neural information processing systems*, 28:649–657.

Shengjia Zhao, Jiaming Song, and Stefano Ermon. 2017. Towards deeper understanding of variational autoencoding models. *CoRR*, abs/1702.08658.

Dataset	Supervised	SSVAE	SSVAE-{KL}	SSVAE-{z}	SSVAE-{KL, z}
IMDB⟶Yelp	59.07(1.19)	61.78(6.03)	68.67$^+$(4.85)	**71.30**$^+$(7.67)	64.69$^+$(3.84)
Yelp⟶IMDB	66.17(2.62)	**69.54**(2.49)	66.67(3.26)	65.15(2.31)	66.13(3.82)

Table 4: Out-of-domain Accuracies between IMDB and Yelp for the different objectives. The best objective for each out-of-domain inference direction is given in bold. The scores displaying statistically significant improvement compared to the score of the supervised objective are marked with $^+$

A Implementation Details

Training and validation data splits We sample 5 *labeled* data splits of size 1K. Each of these 5 splits will, in turn, play the role of validation set for one experiment, while the other 4 splits are used for training. Looping over these splits yields 5 runs for each experiment. The results we display are the average (and standard deviation) of the results for each of these runs. The validation score serves selecting hyper-parameters (in our case only α from Eq. 2). The final test scores are measured on the original test set of each dataset.

Probabilistic Graphical Model For models that use both z and y, we consider the latent variables to be conditionally independent in the inference model (*i.e.* $q_\phi(y, z|x) = q_\phi(y|x)q_\phi(z|x)$)) and independent in the generation model (*i.e* $p_\theta(y, z) = p(y)p(z)$).

Training Procedure We use the STL estimator (Roeder et al., 2017) which is a low-variance unbiased gradient estimator for ELBo.

The network is optimized using ADAM (Kingma and Ba, 2015), with a learning rate of 4e-3 and a dropout rate of 0.5. If the accuracy on the validation set doesn't increase for 4 epochs, the learning rate is divided by 4. If it doesn't increase for 8 epochs, the training is stopped. For objectives that include a KL-divergence, we scale it with a coefficient that is null for 3K steps then linearly increased to 1 for the following 3K steps to avoid posterior collapse (Li et al., 2020).

B Out-of-domain experiments

The sentiment analysis tasks we use for these experiments take place in different domains (Restaurant reviews for Yelp, and Movie reviews for IMDB). Using models trained for each domain (with %100 of the data), we measure performance on the other domain to see whether the changes we study have an effect on out-of-domain generalization. In Table 4, we compare the out-of-domain performances of each of the objectives to that of the baseline that doesn't use unlabeled data (*Supervised*).

The table shows no statistically significant gains from using unlabeled Yelp training data for inference on IMDB. This is to be expected as reviews from Yelp are drastically shorter than those from IMDB (*cf.* Table 1). However, for out-of-domain inference in the opposite direction, all the semi-supervised objectives except the standard SSVAE show statistically significant gains. Removing the KL-divergence to accumulate more information in y, and removing z to have conditional generation exclusively rely on y seem to be effective to help generalization beyond the original domain of the task.

C Results Over Varying Amounts of Data

We display results with varying amounts of data in Table 5.

Dataset	Objective	1%	3%	10%	30%	100%
IMDB	Supervised	54.62(3.30)	56.47(1.02)	62.01(2.75)	69.65(2.02)	81.02(0.64)
	SSVAE	53.92(2.34)	56.03(4.20)	62.15(5.03)	75.39(0.49)	83.34(0.91)
	SSVAE-{KL}	52.70(1.72)	54.95(0.77)	62.37(4.45)	74.18(1.97)	83.87(0.47)
	SSVAE-{z}	**54.15**(2.46)	**56.86**(1.77)	62.15(2.87)	75.42(1.80)	81.90(5.17)
	SSVAE-{KL, z}	53.51(1.99)	56.58(2.22)	**63.24**(4.15)	**75.87**(1.30)	**84.79**(1.34)
AGNEWS	Supervised	68.60(4.88)	75.92(1.74)	81.96(0.83)	84.59(0.67)	86.98(0.74)
	SSVAE	65.79(5.02)	75.95(1.27)	82.47(0.43)	85.50(0.30)	87.89(0.54)
	SSVAE-{KL}	**68.56**(1.89)	76.25(2.21)	82.76(0.45)	85.73(0.80)	**87.95**(0.19)
	SSVAE-{z}	67.13(6.55)	**77.28**(1.81)	**83.48***(0.75)	**85.75**(0.74)	87.94(0.33)
	SSVAE-{KL, z}	66.96(3.42)	76.47(1.24)	82.58(0.97)	85.51(0.57)	87.85(0.29)
Yelp	Supervised	70.32(1.84)	76.32(2.07)	83.41(1.75)	87.85(0.58)	92.47(0.48)
	SSVAE	**71.34**(1.93)	76.96(1.64)	82.96(0.69)	89.35(0.39)	92.85(0.78)
	SSVAE-{KL}	69.85(2.86)	76.82(1.31)	82.90(2.23)	88.33(0.99)	92.90(0.54)
	SSVAE-{z}	68.74(2.95)	**78.26**(1.70)	84.11(1.25)	**90.27***(0.28)	93.60(0.74)
	SSVAE-{KL, z}	69.21(1.10)	77.30(2.57)	**85.02***(1.24)	89.74(1.31)	**93.77**(0.61)
DBPedia	Supervised	63.67(1.74)	81.49(2.25)	90.56(1.21)	94.63(0.32)	96.97(0.28)
	SSVAE	64.42(1.83)	83.16(1.49)	92.95(0.82)	96.26(0.25)	**97.75**(0.11)
	SSVAE-{KL}	**66.09**(3.05)	81.97(1.54)	**93.64**(0.76)	96.32(0.28)	97.58(0.13)
	SSVAE-{z}	62.56(5.60)	**83.40**(2.42)	93.37(1.00)	**96.39**(0.21)	97.40†(0.14)
	SSVAE-{KL, z}	62.15(1.68)	82.67(2.16)	93.40(1.10)	96.31(0.24)	97.58(0.19)

Table 5: Accuracies on IMDB, AGNEWS, Yelp and DBPedia with varying amount of **labeled** data. The values are averages over 5 runs with standard deviations between parentheses. The best score for each dataset and each amount of labeled data is given in bold. Each semi-supervised objective that scores above (resp. below) SSVAE with p-value<0.05 is marked with * (resp. †)

Active Learning for Argument Strength Estimation

Nataliia Kees and **Michael Fromm** and **Evgeniy Faerman** and **Thomas Seidl**
LMU Munich, Germany
kees.nataliia@gmail.com, fromm@dbs.ifi.lmu.de

Abstract

High-quality arguments are an essential part of decision-making. Automatically predicting the quality of an argument is a complex task that recently got much attention in argument mining. However, the annotation effort for this task is exceptionally high. Therefore, we test uncertainty-based active learning (AL) methods on two popular argument-strength data sets to estimate whether sample-efficient learning can be enabled. Our extensive empirical evaluation shows that uncertainty-based acquisition functions can not surpass the accuracy reached with the random acquisition on these data sets.

1 Introduction

Argumentative quality plays a significant role in different domains of social activity where information and idea exchange are essential, such as the public domain and the scientific world. Theoretical discussions about what constitutes a good argument can be traced back to the ancient Greeks (Smith, 2020). Researchers nowadays continue exploring this topic, trying out approaches that employ empirical machine learning estimation techniques (Simpson and Gurevych, 2018).

One of the most expensive and time-consuming tasks for machine learning-driven argument strength prediction is data labeling. Here, the result is highly dependent on the quality of labels, while the annotation task demands cognitive and reasoning abilities. One way to guarantee good annotations is to perform labeling with schooled experts, raising project costs extensively. For this reason, a common approach involves employing crowd workers. As argument strength detection is a highly subjective task, crowd workers' labeling results are often identified by low reliability and prompt researchers to counter-check the results with more crowd workers and as specifically developed agreement-based techniques. Sometimes a threshold for agreement cannot be reached at all, which might lead to data loss (see e.g. (Habernal and Gurevych, 2016a; Toledo et al., 2019).

This motivates us to investigate the applicability of some existing methods for reducing the amount of training data for automatic argument strength prediction. To this end, we look closely at the technique of active learning (AL). In this paper, we evaluate standard uncertainty-based acquisition functions for the argument strength prediction. We perform several experiments for the task of binary argument-pair classification (see Table 1) with several uncertainty-based data selection rounds. Our findings show that uncertainty-based AL techniques do not provide any advantages compared to random selection strategies. The cold-start problem and unreliable nature of annotations concerning argument strength might constitute the reasons for the failure of these techniques.

Argument 1	**Argument 2**
School uniforms are a BAD idea. I'm to lazy to explain it but trust me, I wore them 4 years.	School uniform cant save person out of cold or heat like special clothes. It is not comfortable when you sit for an hours in a classroom.

Table 1: Example of an argument pair both arguing against school uniforms (Habernal and Gurevych, 2016b)

2 Related Work

2.1 Argument Quality Estimation

In general, there is no agreement on how to operationalize argumentation quality (Toledo et al., 2019; Wachsmuth et al., 2017; Simpson and Gurevych, 2018; Persing and Ng, 2015; Lauscher et al., 2020). In some studies, argument strength is regarded in

Proceedings of the Second Workshop on Insights from Negative Results in NLP, pages 144–150
November 10, 2021.

its persuasiveness and quantified as the proportion of people persuaded by the given argument (Habernal and Gurevych, 2016b; Persing and Ng, 2015; Toledo et al., 2019). Persuasiveness makes argument strength easy to operationalize and serves as a way of dealing with the unclear nature of the concept by approximating its meaning through relying on the majority's wisdom. This approach lies at the center of the crowd-sourcing data labeling efforts and is the most common approach undertaken in existing data sets. This limits the reliability of the labels attained in such a manner, though, due to the highly subjective nature of such labels.

2.2 Active Learning

Active learning is defined as a machine learning technique designed to assist in annotating unlabelled data sets by automatically selecting the most informative examples, which are subsequently labeled by human experts (the so-called *oracles*) (Hu, 2011; Cohn et al., 1996). A popular approach to estimating the informativeness of single data points involves quantifying model uncertainty from a sample of stochastic forward passes for a given data point. Common techniques such as entropy, mutual information, or variation ratios (see Appendix A.1 for more details) reportedly help reach good results on a range of tasks on high-dimensional data, e.g., in Computer Vision or Natural Language Processing (Gal et al., 2017; Siddhant and Lipton, 2018; Hu, 2011). The assumption behind this is that in this way, data points which are closest to the decision boundary can be selected, helping to fine-tune the line dividing the classes most efficiently.

So far, AL in argument mining has received little attention. In the work of (Ein-Dor et al., 2020), the authors propose an Iterative Retrospective Learning (IRL) variant for the argument mining task. Their approach, however, is focused on solving the class imbalance problem between arguments and non-arguments and is *precision-* rather than *accuracy-oriented* as AL is. Another approach is suggested by (Simpson and Gurevych, 2018). They apply the Gaussian process preference learning (GPPL) method for performing AL for estimating argument convincingness, which the authors expect to be helpful against the cold-start problem.

3 Data Set

For our analysis, we use two publicly available data sets suitable for the task of pairwise argument strength prediction:

- *UKPConvArg1Strict*, published by (Habernal and Gurevych, 2016b), consists of 11,650 argument pairs distributed over 16 topics.
- *IBM-9.1kPairs*, presented by (Toledo et al., 2019) consists of 9,125 argument pairs distributed over 11 topics.

Because supporting and opposing arguments often share the same vocabulary and semantics, we do not treat each stance within a given topic as a separate topic, contrary to the authors of the two data sets. Instead, we combine the "for" and "against" arguments within the same topic under the same topic index and, thus, avoid leakage of semantic information between train and test data split. This preprocessing makes the performance of our models not directly comparable with the performance from the original papers. However, reproducibility of the original papers' results is beyond the scope of this work, as our focus lies on testing AL acquisition functions instead of reaching higher performance with our models.

Due to the high computational costs of the AL process, we decide to select the three most representative topics from each data set. One way to reach high representativeness would be to select topics that are average in difficulty. Since we try to approximate a real-world setting where the labels are unknown, it is not clear at the beginning which topics are more challenging to learn than the others. For this reason, we decide to select our test topics according to their size. Thus, we cross-validate our models on each data set's smallest topic, the largest one, and the median-sized one. Thus, the topics we select according to this procedure are topics 10 ("Is the school uniform a good or bad idea?"), 13 ("TV is better than books") and 14 ("Personal pursuit or advancing the common good?") in *UKPConvArg1Strict* and topics 3 ("Does social media bring more harm than good?"), 4 ("Should we adopt cryptocurrency?") and 7 ("Should we ban fossil fuels?") in *IBM-9.1kPairs* data.

4 Experimental Setting

4.1 Research Design

This study aims to test the hypothesis that *uncertainty-based data acquisition strategies can help to achieve a better model performance than a mere random selection of the data for argument strength estimation*. We test this by comparing different data selection strategies against random data selection, serving as a baseline.

We test our acquisition strategies on a task of pairwise (relative) argument strength comparison, constructed as a binary classification task, for which we use the *UKPConvArg1Strict* (Habernal and Gurevych, 2016b) and *IBM-9.1kPairs* (Toledo et al., 2019) data sets. The code to our experiments is publicly available.[1]

In order to employ uncertainty-based acquisition functions, we need to measure model uncertainty at prediction time. This is possible either by using Bayesian methods or by approximating their effect via obtaining distributions for output predictions by some other means. Based on the ground work layed out by (Gal and Ghahramani, 2016), who show that dropout training in deep neural networks help approximate Bayesian inference in deep Gaussian processes, we design our experiments as MC dropout. With this, we simulate several stochastic forward passes through the model at prediction time and sample repeatedly from softmax outputs to obtain prediction distributions.

4.2 Method and Procedure

Similar to the procedure stipulated by (Toledo et al., 2019), we fine-tune the pre-trained BERT-Base Uncased English (Devlin et al., 2018) for the task of binary argument-pair classification by adding a single classification layer on top. The BERT architecture includes dropout layers with a probability of 0.1 (Devlin et al., 2018). We keep it this way, which allows us to approximate model uncertainty as described above and test the uncertainty-based acquisition functions on the fine-tuned BERT-based. To do that, we enable dropout at inference time.

In order to estimate topic difficulty and validate our topic selection procedure described above, we train and test the models on all available labels of both data sets separately with the method of k-fold cross-validation, where k stands for the respective number of topics in a given data set. We separate every topic and use it as test data, with model training performed on the rest of the data, which helps to isolate the topics and measure their respective difficulty.

Our active learning experiments are conducted in a setting of a 3-fold cross-validation, with 3 indicating the number of most representative topics selected by us from the given data sets, as mentioned in Section 3. Thus, in each fold in our experiments, we test on one of the three selected topics for each data set (holdout data) and train on the rest of the compete data set (train-dev).

The train-dev data in each fold consists of random splits into train (85%) and validation (15%) data, whereas the validation, or development, data are used for measuring the goodness of fit of the model trained on the training data. Having separated and fixed the validation data, a batch of 130 argument pairs is selected randomly from the train split. These data are used as initial training data on which bert-base-uncased is fine-tuned according to our classification task.

Model evaluation is performed via accuracy measurement. Training on each of the three folds per data set is conducted ten times for improved reliability of the results. Thus, for each fold, we produce ten validation splits and ten initial training data batches to add some randomness into the experiments but in a controlled manner. They are kept fixed for every training fold to control for the effect of random initial data selection and enable a reliable comparison between the acquisition functions.

We add another 130 argument pairs in each learning round and re-train the fine-tuned model. Within this setting, the whole data set would be selected within approx. 55 iterations for *IBM-9.1kPairs* data and approx. 72 iterations for *UKPConvArg1Strict* data (when calculated with the median-sized test split size). In an attempt to minimize the burden associated with heavy training, we decide to limit each active learning process to (less than) a half iterations, stopping at the 27th iteration.

Further details on the hyperparameters and the computing and software infrastructure can be found in Appendix sections A.2 and A.4.

4.3 Acquisition Functions

We perform AL on three uncertainty-based acquisition functions one by one. In particular, we compare the performance of variation ratios, entropy, and BALD (Houlsby et al., 2011; Gal et al., 2017) against a random acquisition baseline. For each of the learning rounds, we acquire data based on the heuristics calculated over a sample of 20 stochastic forward pass outputs. Our expectation is that other measures will outperform the random acquisition.

[1]https://github.com/nkees/active-learning-argument-strength

5 Results

For the estimation of the performance of the models trained on the whole data with k-fold cross-validation, we reach a comparable performance of our BERT-based binary classification technique on both of the data sets (average accuracy on *UKPConvArg1Strict*: 0.76, on *IBM-9.1kPairs*: 0.77). This is a slightly worse performance than (Toledo et al., 2019) achieves with the same architecture; the reason could be attributed to a different topic attribution strategy, as well as to some differences in the used hardware or hyperparameters, such as batch size or the number of epochs.

We find that the topics selected by us from the *UKPConvArg1Strict* stand rather on the low end of difficulty, with model accuracy tending towards the upper end of the scale when validated on these topics: all of them are higher than the mean performance of 0.76 (see Appendix A.3 for more details). However, from the distribution point of view, two of the topics, namely 10 and 13, yield median model performance, making them, in our opinion, suitable representatives of the whole data.

As for the *IBM-9.1kPairs* data set, our selected topics produce on average comparable performance with the model performance on the whole topic set (accuracy of 0.776 vs. 0.77 respectively). They also represent the most difficult topic, the easiest topic, and one closely neighboring the median topic (accuracy of 0.78 being slightly higher than the median performance of 0.77). In this case, the selected topics provide a better representation of the whole data set and grant strong validity when it comes to generalizing the results of our experiments.

The series of experiments we conducted in order to test whether our proposed heuristics for AL data acquisition provide us with any significant improvement surprisingly do not reveal any heuristic which would perform better than in the case of a random acquisition. This is true both for *UKPConvArg1Strict* and *IBM-9.1kPairs* data; a detailed overview is presented in Tables 2 and 3. Statistical significance of the results has been tested with a Wilcoxon signed-rank test, which provides a non-parametric alternative to the paired T-test and is more suitable due to the non-Gaussian distribution of the differences in the results.

All heuristics result in performance that is lower than that of the random baseline. All of our results are statistically significant with p-values ≤ 0.0001.

Despite the fact that random acquisition turns out to be the best one in terms of performance, with our results being consistent through both data sets and the difference being statistically significant, it is still noticeable that the differences in each case are rather small (see Figures 1 and 2 for graphic visualization of the model performance during active learning rounds comparing the acquisition functions).

Heuristic	Mean	Variat.	Avg.Diff.
random (b.)	0.747	0.0881	-
entropy	0.7388	0.0925	-0.0082
variation ratios	0.7368	0.0922	-0.0103
bald	0.7377	0.0928	-0.0093

Table 2: Results of active learning experiments on *UKPConvArg1Strict*. Abbreviations: *b.* stands for *baseline*, *variat.* stands for *variation*, *avg.diff.* stands for *average difference*. Negative average difference means that the challenger heuristic has not outperformed the baseline.

Heuristic	Mean	Variat.	Avg.Diff.
random (b.)	0.7491	0.0855	-
entropy	0.7414	0.0878	-0.0077
variation ratios	0.7377	0.0923	-0.0114
bald	0.7412	0.0882	-0.0079

Table 3: Results of active learning experiments on *IBM-9.1kPairs*. Abbreviations: *b.* stands for *baseline*, *variat.* stands for *variation*, *avg.diff.* stands for *average difference*. Negative average difference means that the challenger heuristic has not outperformed the baseline.

6 Discussion

The results of our experiments do not point to any acquisition functions which outperform random acquisition. This finding does not exclude the possible existence of some other suitable acquisition functions, even from the same class (such as uncertainty-based). This remains an open question and should be considered in further research on the topic. For the time being, the random acquisition should be considered the approach of choice when selecting data for labeling for the task of pairwise argument strength prediction. This is sensible both from an accuracy standpoint as well as due to the computational cheapness of a random process.

As the literature suggests, a possible reason why uncertainty-based methods perform so unimpressively is their proneness to picking outliers – a disadvantage that some other methods, such

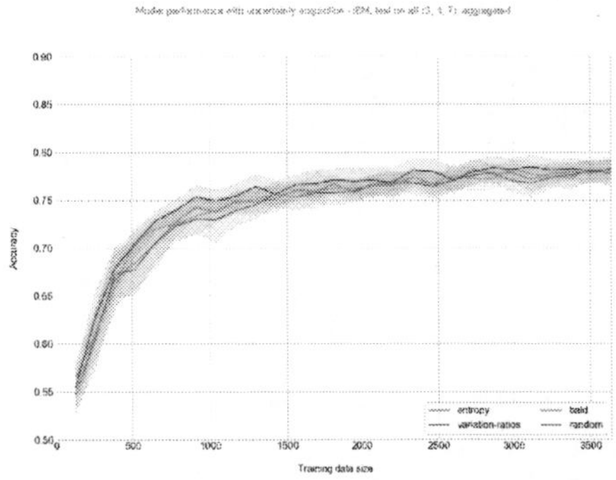

Figure 1: Overview of the training results on the *UKP-ConvArg1Strict* dataset based on different uncertainty-based acquisation methods

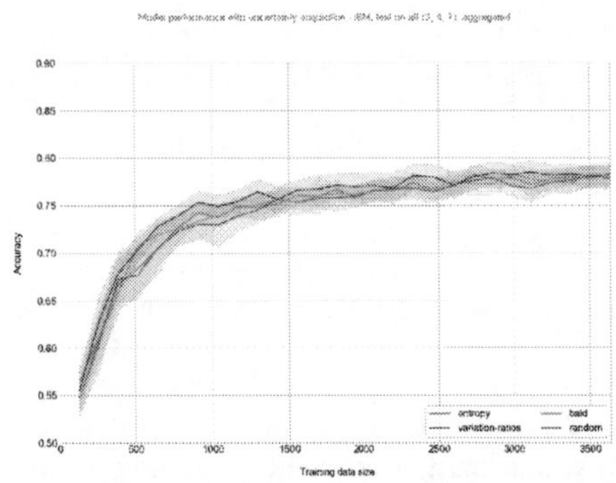

Figure 2: Overview of the training results on the *IBM-9.1kPairs* dataset based on different uncertainty-based acquisition methods

as diversity-based acquisition (e.g., (Sener and Savarese, 2018), do not have. This might be especially critical in the realm of argument strength prediction, as outliers might represent the arguments where relative argument strength difference is marginal, the data are noisy, or where the provided labeling is too subjective. Another critical factor is the cold-start problem, i.e., overfitting on the small initial data set of data, for which no initial informativeness estimation could be performed. This poses a drawback for the uncertainty-based methods, relying on the initial data sample for subsequent data acquisition.

7 Conclusion

This paper evaluates the effect of uncertainty-based acquisition functions, such as variation ratios, entropy, and BALD, on the model performance in the realm of argument strength prediction. As no acquisition function tested helps improve model performance in comparison to the random acquisition, we have not found any justification for using uncertainty-based active learning for pairwise argument strength estimation.

8 Acknowledgments

This work has been funded by the German Federal Ministry of Education and Research (BMBF) under Grant No. 01IS18036A and by the Deutsche Forschungsgemeinschaft (DFG) within the project Relational Machine Learning for Argument Validation (ReMLAV), Grant Number SE 1039/10-1, as part of the Priority Program "Robust Argumentation Machines (RATIO)" (SPP-1999). The authors of this work take full responsibility for its content.

References

David A. Cohn, Zoubin Ghahramani, and Michael I. Jordan. 1996. Active learning with statistical models. *CoRR*, cs.AI/9603104.

Jacob Devlin, Ming-Wei Chang, Kenton Lee, and Kristina Toutanova. 2018. BERT: pre-training of deep bidirectional transformers for language understanding. *CoRR*, abs/1810.04805.

Liat Ein-Dor, Eyal Shnarch, Lena Dankin, Alon Halfon, Benjamin Sznajder, Ariel Gera, Carlos Alzate, Martin Gleize, Leshem Choshen, Yufang Hou, Yonatan Bilu, Ranit Aharonov, and Noam Slonim. 2020. Corpus wide argument mining—a working solution. *Proceedings of the AAAI Conference on Artificial Intelligence*, 34(05):7683–7691.

Yarin Gal. 2016. *Uncertainty in Deep Learning*. Ph.D. thesis, University of Cambridge.

Yarin Gal and Zoubin Ghahramani. 2016. Dropout as a bayesian approximation: Representing model uncertainty in deep learning. In *Proceedings of The 33rd International Conference on Machine Learning*, volume 48 of *Proceedings of Machine Learning Research*, pages 1050–1059, New York, New York, USA. PMLR.

Yarin Gal, Riashat Islam, and Zoubin Ghahramani. 2017. Deep bayesian active learning with image data. *CoRR*, abs/1703.02910.

Ivan Habernal and Iryna Gurevych. 2016a. What makes a convincing argument? empirical analysis and detecting attributes of convincingness in web argumentation. In *Proceedings of the 2016 Conference on Empirical Methods in Natural Language Processing*, pages 1214–1223, Austin, Texas. Association for Computational Linguistics.

Ivan Habernal and Iryna Gurevych. 2016b. Which argument is more convincing? analyzing and predicting convincingness of web arguments using bidirectional LSTM. In *Proceedings of the 54th Annual Meeting of the Association for Computational Linguistics (Volume 1: Long Papers)*, pages 1589–1599, Berlin, Germany. Association for Computational Linguistics.

Neil Houlsby, Ferenc Huszár, Zoubin Ghahramani, and Máté Lengyel. 2011. Bayesian active learning for classification and preference learning.

Rong Hu. 2011. *Active Learning for Text Classification*. Doctoral Thesis, Technological University Dublin.

Anne Lauscher, Lily Ng, Courtney Napoles, and Joel Tetreault. 2020. Rhetoric, logic, and dialectic: Advancing theory-based argument quality assessment in natural language processing.

Isaac Persing and Vincent Ng. 2015. Modeling argument strength in student essays. In *Proceedings of the 53rd Annual Meeting of the Association for Computational Linguistics and the 7th International Joint Conference on Natural Language Processing (Volume 1: Long Papers)*, pages 543–552.

Ozan Sener and Silvio Savarese. 2018. Active learning for convolutional neural networks: A core-set approach. In *International Conference on Learning Representations*.

Aditya Siddhant and Zachary C. Lipton. 2018. Deep bayesian active learning for natural language processing: Results of a large-scale empirical study. *CoRR*, abs/1808.05697.

Edwin Simpson and Iryna Gurevych. 2018. Finding convincing arguments using scalable Bayesian preference learning. *Transactions of the Association for Computational Linguistics*, 6:357–371.

Robin Smith. 2020. Aristotle's Logic. In Edward N. Zalta, editor, *The Stanford Encyclopedia of Philosophy*, Fall 2020 edition. Metaphysics Research Lab, Stanford University.

Assaf Toledo, Shai Gretz, Edo Cohen-Karlik, Roni Friedman, Elad Venezian, Dan Lahav, Michal Jacovi, Ranit Aharonov, and Noam Slonim. 2019. Automatic argument quality assessment – new datasets and methods.

Henning Wachsmuth, Nona Naderi, Yufang Hou, Yonatan Bilu, Vinodkumar Prabhakaran, Tim Alberdingk Thijm, Graeme Hirst, and Benno Stein. 2017. Computational argumentation quality assessment in natural language. In *Proceedings of the 15th Conference of the European Chapter of the Association for Computational Linguistics: Volume 1, Long Papers*, pages 176–187, Valencia, Spain. Association for Computational Linguistics.

A Appendix

A.1 Uncertainty-based Acquisition Functions

In our work, we refer in particular to the following uncertainty-based acquisition functions (Gal et al., 2017):

- **variation ratios**: given a set of labels y_T from T stochastic forward passes, variation ratio for a given input point is calculated as:

$$varrat(x) = 1 - \frac{f_x}{T} \tag{1}$$

  with f_x denoting the number of times the most commonly occurring category (mode of the distribution) has been sampled. This serves as an indication of how concentrated the predictions are, with 0.5 being the highest dispersion, i.e. uncertainty, and 0 being the highest concentration (certainty) in the case of binary classification.

- **predictive entropy**: stems from information theory and is calculated by averaging the softmax values for each class :

$$\begin{aligned} predentr(x) = -\sum_c p(y = c|\mathbf{x}, D_{train}) \\ \times \log_2(p(y = c|\mathbf{x}, D_{train})), \end{aligned} \tag{2}$$

  where $p(y = c|\mathbf{x}, D_{train})$ stands for average probability of a data point adhering to a specific class given the outputs of the stochastic forward passes and the training data. c denotes the label class, i.e. we sum the values over all the classes to receive a measure of entropy for a given data point.

- **Bayesian Active Learning by Disagreement (BALD)** (Houlsby et al., 2011), also called **mutual information** (Gal, 2016), is a function of predictive entropy as described above and averaged predictive entropies that have been calculated separately for each output:

$$\begin{aligned} bald(x) = -[\sum_c p(y = c|\mathbf{x}, D_{train}) \\ \times \log(p(y = c|\mathbf{x}, D_{train}))] \\ + E_{p(\omega|D_{train})}[\sum_c p(y = c|\mathbf{w}, \omega) \\ \times \log(p(y = c|\mathbf{x}, \omega))]. \end{aligned} \tag{3}$$

A.2 Computing & Software Infrastructure

The experiments were conducted on a Ubuntu 18.04 system with an AMD Ryzen Processor with 16 CPU-Cores, 126 GB memory, and a single NVIDIA RTX 2080 GPU with 11 GB memory. We further used Python 3.7, PyTorch 1.4 and the Huggingface-Transformer library (2.11.0).

A.3 Topic Size and Difficulty

No.	Topic	Size	Acc.
0	Ban Plastic Water Bottles?	688	0.86
1	Christianity or Atheism	588	0.81
2	Evolution vs. Creation	782	0.78
3	Firefox vs. Internet Explorer	748	0.81
4	Gay marriage - right or wrong?	851	0.8
5	Should parents use spanking?	706	0.76
6	If your spouse committed murder, would you turn them in?	687	0.67
7	India has the potential to lead the world	822	0.81
8	Is it better to have a lousy father or to be fatherless?	616	0.64
9	Is porn wrong?	571	0.79
10	*Is the school uniform a good or bad idea?*	*878*	*0.78*
11	Pro choice vs. Pro life	845	0.61
12	Should physical edu. be mandatory?	568	0.74
13	*TV is better than books*	*747*	*0.79*
14	*Personal pursuit or common good?*	*733*	*0.84*
15	Farquhar as the founder of Singapore	820	0.7
	Total Size/Average Acc.	**11 650**	**0.76**

Table 4: Topic sizes in *UKPConvArg1Strict*. Topics are provided with their corresponding numbers and size within the data set, as well as our model's performance at test time. The topics selected for testing the acquisition functions have been highlighted in italics.

No.	Topic	Size	Acc.
0	Should flu vaccinations be mandatory?	731	0.75
1	Should gambling be banned?	503	0.8
2	Does online shopping bring more harm than good?	278	0.79
3	*Does social media bring more harm than good?*	*2587*	*0.78*
4	*Should we adopt cryptocurrency?*	*719*	*0.82*
5	Should we adopt vegetarianism?	1073	0.77
6	Should we sale violent video games to minors?	484	0.74
7	*Should we ban fossil fuels?*	*263*	*0.73*
8	Should we legalize doping in sport?	737	0.77
9	Should we limit autonomous cars?	1217	0.79
10	Should we support information privacy laws?	533	0.77
	Total Size/Average Acc.	**9 125**	**0.77**

Table 5: Topic sizes in *IBM-9.1kPairs*. Topics are provided with their corresponding numbers and size within the data set, as well as our model's performance at test time. The topics selected for testing the acquisition functions have been highlighted in italics.

A.4 Hyperparameters

For the evaluation we initialized all methods for **ten** runs with different seeds and reported the **mean accuracy score**. We used early stopping with a patience of three on a pre-selected validation set for regularization. As loss function we used weighted binary-cross-entropy for the (relative) Argument Strength task.

We train our models on top of the pre-trained BERT-Base uncased with a dropout probability of 0.1. Learning rate is 2^{-5} (same as in (Toledo et al., 2019)). The batch size per GPU is 64 and the model is validated after every half epoch.

Association for Computational Linguistics
209 N. Eighth Street
Stroudsburg, Pennsylvania 18360

ISBN 978-1-7138-9182-6

CURRAN ASSOCIATES INC.
proceedings.com